# Integrating Standards in Early Childhood Settings: Language and Literacy

Jeanne M. Machado

CENGAGE
Learning·

Australia • Brazil • Japan • Korea • Mexico • Singapore • Spain • United Kingdom • United States

**Integrating Standards in Early Childhood Settings: Language and Literacy**

Early Childhood Experiences in Language Arts: Early Literacy, 10th Edition
Jeanne M. Machado

© 2013, 2008 Wadsworth, Cengage Learning

Library of Congress Control Number: 2011937458

Senior Project Development Manager:
  Linda deStefano

Market Development Manager:
  Heather Kramer

Senior Production/Manufacturing Manager:
  Donna M. Brown

Production Editorial Manager:
  Kim Fry

Sr. Rights Acquisition Account Manager:
  Todd Osborne

For product information and technology assistance, contact us at
**Cengage Learning Customer & Sales Support, 1-800-354-9706**

For permission to use material from this text or product,
submit all requests online at **cengage.com/permissions**
Further permissions questions can be emailed to
**permissionrequest@cengage.com**

This book contains select works from existing Cengage Learning resources and was produced by Cengage Learning Custom Solutions for collegiate use. As such, those adopting and/or contributing to this work are responsible for editorial content accuracy, continuity and completeness.

**Compilation © 2013 Cengage Learning**
ISBN-13: 978-1-285-54950-7

ISBN-10: 1-285-54950-3

**Cengage Learning**
5191 Natorp Boulevard
Mason, Ohio 45040
USA

Cengage Learning is a leading provider of customized learning solutions with office locations around the globe, including Singapore, the United Kingdom, Australia, Mexico, Brazil, and Japan. Locate your local office at:
**international.cengage.com/region.**
Cengage Learning products are represented in Canada by Nelson Education, Ltd.
For your lifelong learning solutions, visit **www.cengage.com/custom.**
Visit our corporate website at **www.cengage.com.**

Printed in the United States of America

# Brief Contents

SECTION 1

**Language Development: Emerging Literacy in the Young Child**

**1** Beginnings of Communication 1

**2** The Tasks of the Toddler 41

**3** Preschool Years 73

**4** Growth Systems Affecting Early Language Ability 95

SECTION 2

**Language and Literacy Programs: Recognizing Diverse Needs and Goals**

**5** Understanding Differences 117

**6** Achieving Language and Literacy Goals through Program Planning 152

**7** Promoting Language and Literacy 193

**8** Developing Listening Skills 222

SECTION 6

**School and Home: Environments, Family, and Partnerships**

**18** Developing a Literacy Environment 525

**19** The Parent-Center Partnership 542

CHAPTER

1

# Beginnings of Communication

## A New Sign

*Noah, 10 months, had a new sign for "cracker" that he had used a few times during the day at the infant center. He was very pleased when his "sign" resulted in someone bringing him a cracker. At pick-up time, one of the staff believed it important to talk to Noah's dad. Mr. Soares did not really understand what the teacher, Miss Washington, was talking about when she said "signing." Miss Washington gave Mr. Soares a quick explanation. He smiled proudly and then said, "That's great. I'll talk to his mom and let her know."*

## Questions to Ponder

1. Miss Washington had a new language-related topic for the next staff meeting. What would you suspect it was?

2. Did this episode tell you something about the language-developing quality of the infant center?

3. What do you know about male infants and their signing ability compared with that of female infants? Could you describe infant signing behavior?

*(If you are hesitating, this chapter supplies answers.)*

## OBJECTIVES

After reading this chapter, you should be able to:

- Compare two theories of human language emergence.
- Identify major factors that influence language development.
- Discuss the reciprocal behaviors of infants, parents, and caregivers.
- Create or demonstrate three child-adult play activities for infants 1 to 6 months or infants 6 to 12 months.
- Explain the significance of infant signaling.

## KEY TERMS

| | |
|---|---|
| affective sphere | moderation level |
| articulation | neurolinguistics |
| attachment | parentese |
| auditory | perception |
| acuity | phonation |
| babbling | resonation |
| cognition | responsive |
| communication | mothers |
| cooing | rhythm |
| cues | sensory-motor |
| dual coding | development |
| echolalia | signing |
| equilibrium | spatial-temporal |
| gaze coupling | reasoning |
| holophrases | synapses |
| language | |

In this chapter the reader is acquainted with those elements in an infant's life that facilitate optimal growth in communication and language development. Socioemotional, physical, cognitive, and environmental factors that influence, promote, or deter growth are noted. Recommended interaction techniques and strategies are supported by research and reflect accepted appropriate practices and standards. As foundational aspects of infant communication are presented, *boxed* descriptions of the attuned and reciprocal behaviors caregivers make with infants are provided. Caregivers establish a relationship with each infant in their care, and the quality of that relationship serves to motivate each infant to engage in learning (McMullen & Dixon, 2006). Higher levels of warmth are connected to positive caregiver sensitivity. Gerber, Whitebook, & Weinstein (2007) note that the quality of caregiver practices has been linked to children's brain development and cognitive functioning.

For you to become the kind of educator children deserve, one who enhances language growth, you should begin by believing that most infants are able and natural communicators from birth onward unless some life circumstance has modified their natural potential. Infant care

facilities with well-planned, positive, and growth-producing environments that are staffed with skilled, knowledgeable, and well-trained adults who offer developmentally appropriate activities provide a place where infants can and do thrive.

Each infant is a unique combination of inherited traits and environmental influences. Structural, hormonal, and chemical influences present before birth may have affected the growth and development of the fetus (Gould, 2002).

Researchers confirm that newborns seem to assimilate information immediately and are interested in their surroundings. Some suggest an infant possesses "the greatest mind" in existence and is the most powerful learning machine in the universe. During the third trimester of pregnancy, most mothers notice that their babies kick and move in response to music or loud noises. The sound of speech may draw a less spirited reaction, but there is little question that fetuses hear and react to a wide variety of sounds.

Technology can now monitor the slightest physical changes in breathing, heartbeat, eye movement, and sucking rhythm and rates. Researchers suggest that babies begin learning how to carry on conversations quickly and sucking patterns produce a **rhythm** that mimics that of give-and-take dialogues. Infants respond to very specific maternal signals, including tone of voice, facial changes, and head movements.

Greenspan (1999) suggests what may happen when interacting with a 1- or 2-month-old baby at a relaxed time after a nap or feeding:

> . . . when you hold him at arm's length and look directly into his eyes with a broad smile on your face, watch his lips part as if he's trying to imitate your smile. (p. 31)

Babies gesture and make sounds and seem to hold up their ends of conversations, but at times, they appear to suppress output and channel their energy into seeing and hearing. Their eye contact with their caregivers, called **gaze coupling**, is

---

**rhythm** — uniform or patterned recurrence of a beat, accent, or melody in speech.
**gaze coupling** — infant-mother extended eye contact.

believed to be one of their first steps in establishing communication. Infants can shut off background noises and pay attention to slight changes in adult voice sounds.

An attuned adult is responsive. Petersen and Wittmer (2008) define a responsive caregiver by how sensitively and accurately an adult responds and understands an infant's (child's) cues.

### *An attuned adult would:*

○ *notice infant actions, including gestures, body positioning, noisemaking, eye gazing, and any shift from listening to watching.*

○ *make face-to-face contact frequently.*

○ *display admiration, affection, and pleasure and smile frequently.*

○ *provide verbal and nonverbal communication.*

○ *seek to maintain and prolong eye contact.*

## GENETIC INHERITANCE AND EMERGING BEHAVIORS

The qualities an infant inherits from parents and the events that occur in the child's life help shape the child's language development. Gender, temperament, and a timetable for the emergence of intellectual, emotional, and physical capabilities are all genetic givens. In the short 4 to 5 years after birth, the child's speech becomes purposeful and similar to adult speech. This growing language skill is a useful tool for satisfying needs and exchanging thoughts, hopes, and dreams with others. As ability grows, the child understands and uses more of the resources of oral and recorded human knowledge and is well on the way to becoming a literate being.

The natural capacity to categorize, to invent, and remember information aids the child's language acquisition. Although unique among the species because of the ability to speak, human beings are not the only ones who can communicate. Birds and animals also imitate sounds and signals and are believed to communicate. For instance, chimpanzees exposed to experimental language techniques (American Sign Language, specially equipped machines, and plastic tokens) have surprised researchers with their language abilities. Some have learned to use symbols and follow linguistic rules with a sophistication that rivals that of some 2-year-olds. Researchers

continue to probe the limits of their capabilities. However, a basic difference between human beings and other species exists.

It is the development of the cerebral cortex that sets humans apart from less intelligent animals. Our advanced mental capabilities, such as thought, memory, language, mathematics, and complex problem solving, are unique to human beings.

Humans have the unique species-specific ability to test hypotheses about the structure of language. They can also develop rules for a particular language and remember and use them to generate appropriate language. Within a few days after birth, human babies recognize familiar faces, voices, and even smells and prefer them to unfamiliar ones.

Infant research has advanced by leaps and bounds to reveal amazing newborn abilities. Long before they can talk, for example, babies remember events and solve problems. They can recognize faces, see colors, hear voices, discriminate speech sounds, and distinguish basic tastes. When you combine the psychological and neurological evidence, it is hard not to conclude that babies are just plain smarter than adults. This is especially true when it comes to learning something new.

Begley (2009) urges teachers to be aware that a child's genes (inherited DNA) in themselves do not determine intelligence or any other complex human trait. An infant or child's appearance and temperament may elicit particular parent and teacher behaviors. These can include the adult's responsiveness, ability to pay attention to, interact with, speak with, and provide intellect-building interaction.

## INFANT ACTIONS PROMPT CAREGIVER BEHAVIORS

The human face becomes the most significantly important communication factor for the infant, and the facial expressions, which are varied and complex, eventually will influence infant body reactions (interior and exterior). Caregivers strive to understand the infant's state of well-being by interpreting the infant's face and postures, as infants also search faces in the world around them.

Figure 1–1 identifies a number of signals infants use and their probable meanings. Response

| INFANT ACTS | PROBABLE MEANING |
|---|---|
| turning head and opening mouth | feeling hungry |
| quivering lips | adjusting to stimuli |
| sucking on hand, fist, thumb | calming self, feeling overstimulated |
| averting eyes | tuning out for a while |
| turning away | needing to calm down |
| yawning | feeling tired/stressed |
| looking wide-eyed | feeling happy |
| cooing | feeling happy |
| appearing dull with unfocused eyes | feeling overloaded, needing rest |
| waving hands | feeling excited |
| moving tongue in and out | feeling upset/imitating |

FIGURE 1–1  Born communicators.

and intentional behavior become apparent as infants age and gain experience. Infants initially respond with various preprogrammed gestures such as smiling, intent and interested looking, crying, satisfied sucking, and snuggling. Soon these behaviors are followed by active demanding and attention-seeking patterns in which attempts to attract and solicit caregiver attention rapidly become unmistakable and intentional.

Researchers are studying the roles of facial expressions, gestures, and body movements in human social communication (Figure 1–2).

FIGURE 1–2  "Wow, that is interesting!"

Early expressions that look like smiling may occur minutes after birth and are apparent in the faces of sleeping babies, whose facial expressions seem to constantly change. Researchers studying infant smiling during an infant's first week of life, such as Dondi et al. (2007), suggest that infants smile in various behavioral states, including during brief alertness, drowsiness, active sleep, and quiet sleep, but they also confirm what many parents have noticed—smiling most often occurs in deep sleep.

Caregivers observe that infants search for the source of the human voice and face. An infant may become wide-eyed and crane his neck and lift his chin toward the source. His body tension increases as he becomes more focused and somewhat inactive. Most caregivers respond to these signals by picking up the infant and cuddling him.

### An attuned adult would:

○ be aware of opportunities to soothe and touch and engage in some way with an infant.

○ pick up and hold an infant gently while providing firm support.

○ note an infant's well-being and comfort.

○ attempt to interpret an infant's facial and body signals.

## DEFINITIONS

**Language,** as used in this text, refers to a system of intentional communication and self-expression through sounds, signs (gestures), or symbols that are understandable to others. The language-development process includes both sending and receiving information. Input (receiving) comes before output (sending); input is organized mentally by an individual long before there is decipherable output.

**Communication** is a broader term, defined as giving and receiving information, signals, or messages. A person can communicate with or receive communications from animals, infants, or foreign speakers in a variety of ways. Even a whistling teakettle sends a message that someone

---

**language** — the systematic, conventional use of sounds, signs, or written symbols in a human society for communication and self-expression. It conveys meaning that is mutually understood.
**communication** — the giving (sending) and receiving of information, signals, or messages.

can understand. Infants appear to be "in tune," focused on the human voice, hours after birth.

Speech is much more complex than simple parroting or primitive social functioning. The power of language enables humans to dominate other life forms. The ability to use language secured our survival by giving us a vehicle to both understand and transmit language and to work cooperatively with others. Language facilitates peaceful solutions between people.

## INFLUENCES ON DEVELOPMENT

A child's ability to communicate involves an integration of body parts and systems allowing hearing, understanding, organizing thoughts, learning, and using language. Most children accomplish the task quickly and easily, but many factors influence the learning of language.

Research suggests that babies instinctively turn their heads to face the source of sound and can remember sounds heard before birth. This has prompted mothers to talk to, sing to, and read classic literature and poetry to the unborn. Research has yet to document evidence of the benefits of these activities.

Of all sounds, nothing attracts and holds the attention of infants as well as the human voice—especially the higher-pitched female voice. "Motherese," a distinct caregiver speech, is discussed later in this chapter. Dietrich, Swingley, and Werker (2007) note:

> Infants begin to acquire their language by learning phonetic categories. At birth infants seem to distinguish most of the phonetic contrasts used by the world's languages. However, over the first year, this "universal" capacity shifts to a language-specific pattern in which infants retain or improve categorization of native-language sounds but fail to discriminate many non-native sounds. (p. 16030)

Rhythmic sounds and continuous, steady tones soothe some infants. A number of commercial sound-making products that attempt to soothe can be attached to cribs or are imbedded in plush stuffed animals. Most emit a type of static or heartbeat sound or a combination of the two. Too much sound in the infant's environment, especially loud, excessive, or high-volume sounds, may have the opposite effect. Excessive household noise can come from televisions or other sources. Many have described sensory-overload situations when infants try to turn off sensory input by turning away and somehow blocking that which is at the moment overwhelming, whether the stimulus is mechanical or human. This blocking includes falling asleep.

Although hearing ability is not fully developed at birth, newborns can hear moderately loud sounds and can distinguish different pitches. Newborns' auditory systems are better developed than their sight systems, so the importance of language and voices to children's development is evident from the start (Galinsky, 2010). Scientists believe that during the last weeks of pregnancy a child's auditory system becomes ready to receive and remember sounds (p. 101).

**Auditory acuity** develops swiftly. Infants inhibit motor activity in response to strong auditory stimuli or when listening to the human voice and attempt to turn toward it. Some researchers see this as an indication that infants are geared to orient their entire bodies toward any signal that arouses interest (Figure 1–3). Infants' body responses to human verbalizations are a rudimentary form of speech development (Figure 1–4).

**Sensory-motor development**, which involves the use of sense organs and the coordination of motor systems (body muscles and parts), is vital to language acquisition. Sense organs gather information through seeing, hearing, smelling, tasting, and touching. These sense-organ impressions of people, objects, and life encounters are sent to the brain, and each **perception** (impression received through the senses) is recorded and stored, serving as a base for future oral and written language.

Newborns and infants are no longer viewed as passive, unresponsive "mini-humans."

---

**auditory** — relating to or experienced through hearing.
**acuity** — how well or clearly one uses the senses; the degree of perceptual sharpness.
**sensory-motor development** — the control and use of sense organs and the body's muscle structure.
**perception** — mental awareness of objects and other data gathered through the five senses.

FIGURE 1–3 Sound-making toys attract attention.

| AGE | APPROPRIATE HEARING BEHAVIORS |
|---|---|
| birth | awakens to loud sounds |
| | startles, cries, or reacts to noise |
| | makes sounds |
| | looks toward then looks away from environmental sounds |
| 0–3 months | turns head to hear parent's or others' speech |
| | reacts to speech by smiling |
| | opens mouth as if to imitate adult's speech |
| | coos and goos |
| | seems to recognize a familiar voice |
| | calms down when adult's voice is soothing |
| | repeats own vocalizations |
| | seems to listen to and focus on familiar adults' voices |
| 4–6 months | looks toward environmental noise (e.g., barking, vacuum, doorbell, radio, TV) |
| | attracted to noise-making toys |
| | babbles consonant-like sounds |
| | makes wants known with voice |
| | seems to understand "no" |
| | reacts to speaker's change of tone of voice |
| 7–12 months | responds to own name |
| | may say one or more understandable but not clearly articulated words |
| | babbles repeated syllables or consonant- and vowel-like sounds |
| | responds to simple requests |
| | enjoys playful word games like Peak-a-boo, Pat-a-cake, etc. |
| | imitates speech sounds frequently |
| | uses sound making to gain others' attention |

FIGURE 1–4 Auditory perception in infancy.

Instead, infants are seen as dynamic individuals, preprogrammed to learn, with functioning sensory capacities, motor abilities, and a wondrous built-in curiosity. Families and caregivers can be described as guides who provide opportunity and act *with* newborns rather than *on* them.

## Beginning Socialization

A child's social and emotional environments play a leading role in both the quality and the quantity of beginning language. Many researchers describe communicative neonatal behaviors that evoke tender feelings in adults. Human children have the longest infancy among animals. Our social dependency is crucial to our individual survival and growth. Much learning occurs through contact and interaction with others in family and social settings. Basic attitudes toward life, self, and other people form early, as life's pleasures and pains are experienced. The young child depends on parents and other caregivers to provide what is needed for growth and **equilibrium** (a balance achieved when consistent care is given and needs are satisfied). This side of a child's

---

**equilibrium** — a balance attained with consistent care and satisfaction of needs that leads to a sense of security and lessens anxiety.

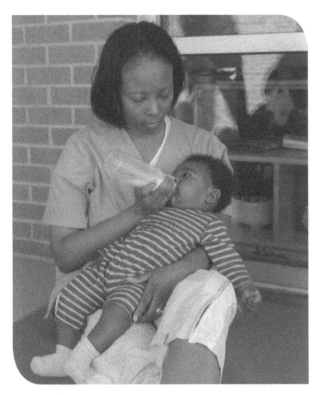

FIGURE 1–5 Care and attention in the early years influence language development.

FIGURE 1–6 An infant who feels comfortable and whose needs are satisfied is alert to the world.

development has been called the **affective sphere**, referring to the affectionate feelings—or lack of them—shaped through experience with others (Figure 1–5). Most experts believe that each time an infant takes in information through the senses, the experience is double-coded as both a physical/cognitive reaction and as an emotional reaction to those sensations.

Textbooks often speak indirectly about the infant's need to feel loved consistently, using words like *nurturance, closeness, caring,* and *commitment.* The primary goal of parents and caregivers should be handling the infant and satisfying the child's physical needs in a way that leads to mutual love and a bond of trust (Figure 1–6). This bond, often called **attachment**, is an event of utmost importance to the infant's progress. A developmental milestone is reached when a baby responds with an emotional reaction of his own by indicating obvious pleasure or joy in the company of a parent or caregiver. Attachment is formed through mutual gratification of needs

and reciprocal communication influenced by the infant's growing cognitive ability. The two-way nature of the attachment process is also referred to as bonding. The infant develops a beginning mental picture of the way people in his life interact with one another in systematic and loving relationships. Bardige (2009) describes early bonding in this way:

> Call it chemistry, natural attraction, or falling in love—babies lure adults from the start, and adults who tune in are easily lured. Bonding begins when parent and baby see each other for the first time— and it's a two-way street. With their large eyes and sweet expressions, babies are as cute as they are helpless. Adults naturally soften in their presence, and soon baby and parent are gazing into each other's eyes and forging a connection. (p. 20)

The special feelings an infant develops for a main caregiver later spreads to include a group of

---

**affective sphere** — the affectionate feelings (or lack of them) shaped through experience with others.
**attachment** — a two-way process formed through mutual gratification of needs and reciprocal communication influenced by the infant's growing cognitive abilities. It is sometimes referred to as bonding or a "love affair" relationship.

beloved family members. If an attachment bond is evident and consistent care continues, the child thrives. Social interaction with an empathic and attuned caregiver plays the major role in the growth and regulation of the child's nervous system, and it helps the infant develop the strength needed to become socially competent (Gould, 2002).

Newborns seem to have an individual preferred level of arousal, a **moderation level**, neither too excited nor too bored. They seek change and stimulation and seem to search out newness. Each human may possess an optimal level of arousal—a state when learning is enhanced and pleasure peaks. Mothers and experienced caregivers try to keep infants at moderate levels of arousal, neither too high nor too low. One can perceive three states during an older infant's waking hours: (1) a state in which everything is all right and life is interesting; (2) a reactive state to something familiar or unfamiliar, when an observer can see an alert "what's that?" or "who's that?" response; and (3) a crying or agitated state. One can observe a switch from feeling safe or happy to feeling unsafe or unhappy in a matter of seconds (Figure 1–7). Loud noises can startle the infant and elicit distressed crying. Infants control input and turn away or turn off by moving their eyes and head or body and by becoming fussy or falling asleep.

Greenspan (1999) urges parents and caregivers of infants to improve their observational skills.

FIGURE 1–7 With tears still wet, this infant has moved on to observing another feature of his environment.

As you sharpen your observational skills and pay attention to the times when your baby seems to have more trouble becoming calm and sharing attention with you, you'll begin to assemble a truly revealing developmental profile of your child. You'll start recognizing whether an unpleasant smell, an unexpected hug or cuddle, or a piercing noise overwhelms your child. Don't forget, though, that even a crying, finicky baby is capable of a lot of looking and listening. You may receive some very expressive looks from your three-month-old when he's got a gas bubble in his stomach! If you rub his back while murmuring sympathetically, he may be encouraged to keep his looking and listening skills even when he's not feeling so good. He may be able to use your soothing sounds and touches to calm him. Practicing under slightly stressful conditions will make him into a stronger looker and listener later on. (p. 201)

### *An attuned adult would:*

○ *observe closely.*

○ *assess infants' needs and work to satisfy them.*

○ *notice reactions to room sounds—sound intensity or rhythm or other features.*

○ *calm infants when necessary by trying a variety of strategies.*

○ *use an attention-getting voice, voice variety, and/or high-pitched tones.*

## Parent and Caregiver Attitudes and Expectations

As was mentioned earlier, research indicates that parent and caregiver attitudes and expectations about infants' awareness and sensory abilities may be predictive of developmental growth.

Certainly there are many possible explanations for developmental differences. But the fact remains: The earlier a mother thought her baby would be aware of the world, the more competent

---

**moderation level** — an individual preferred state of arousal between bored and excited when learning and pleasure peak.

her baby grew to be. Why was this so? It is because the mothers treated the babies according to their expectations. In home visits, researchers observed that mothers who knew more about their infants' abilities were more emotionally and verbally responsive to their babies. They talked to them more. They provided them with more appropriate play materials and initiated more stimulating experiences. And they were more likely to allow their babies to actively explore the world around them. (Acredolo & Goodwyn, 2000, p. 102)

How we perceive children (infants) shapes how we treat them and therefore what experiences we give them (2009, Begley). Eliot, a neuroscientist and author of *Pink Brain, Blue Brain* (2009), believes there is little solid evidence that sex differences exist in young children's brains. She maintains the sex differences in adult brains are the result of parent actions and expectancies and life experiences in infancy and childhood.

Eliot points out baby boys are often more irritable than girls making parents less likely to interact with their thought-to-be nonsocial sons. She notes that, at four months, infant boys and girls differ in amount of eye contact, sociability, emotional expressivity, and verbal ability they exhibit. This, she feels, is not an innate trait but a self-fulfilling prophecy arising from an expectation that males are nonverbal and emotionally distant. Eliot entreats educators to not act in ways that make these perceived characteristics come true.

### Growing Intellect

Other important factors related to the child's mental maturity or ability to think are ages, stages, and sequences of increased mental capacity that are closely related to language development. Language skill and intellect seem to be growing independently, at times, with one or the other developing at a faster rate. The relationship of intelligence and language has been a subject of debate for a long time. Most scholars, however, agree that these two areas are closely associated. Researchers suspect the mind's most important faculties are rooted in emotional experiences from very early in life.

The natural curiosity of humans requires discussion here. Curiosity can be defined as a compulsion (drive) to make sense of life's happenings. Over time, exploring, searching, groping, and probing by infants shift from random to controlled movements. At approximately 8 months of age, infants begin to possess insatiable appetites for new things—touching, manipulating, and trying to become familiar with everything that attracts them. Increasing motor skill allows greater possibilities for exploration. Skilled caregivers of infants are kept busy trying to provide novelty, variety, and companionship while monitoring safety. The curiosity of infants  seems to wane only when they are tired, hungry, or ill, but even then they are learning. Galinsky (2010) notes:

> Some people think babies aren't learning about talking until they start to babble or say actual words, but that couldn't be farther from the truth. (p. 112)

**Cultural Ideas Concerning Infant Communication.** Cultural and social forces affect language acquisition. They influence young lives through contact with group attitudes, values, and beliefs. Some cultures expect children to look downward when adults speak, showing respect by this action. Other cultures make extensive use of gestures and signaling. Still others seem to have limited vocabularies or believe that engaging in conversations with infants is inappropriate.

## THEORIES OF LANGUAGE EMERGENCE

Many scholars, philosophers, linguists, and researchers have tried to pinpoint exactly how language is learned. People in major fields of study—human development, linguistics, sociology, psychology, anthropology, speech-language pathology, and animal study (zoology)—have contributed to current theory. The following are major theoretical positions.

### Behaviorist/Environmentalist (or Stimulus-Response) Theory

As parents and main caregivers reward, correct, ignore, or punish the young child's communication, they exert considerable influence over both the quantity and quality of language usage and the child's attitudes toward communicating. Under this theory, the reactions of the people in a child's environment have an important effect on a child's language development. In other words, positive, neutral, and negative

**FIGURE 1–8** Enjoyable conversational interactions occur early in life.

reinforcement play a key role in the emergence of communicational behaviors.

The child's sounds and sound combinations are thought to be uttered partly as imitation and partly at random or on impulse, without pattern or meaning. The child's utterances may grow, seem to stand still, or become stifled, depending on feedback from others (Figure 1–8). This theory is attributed to the work of B. F. Skinner, a pioneer researcher in the field of learning theory.

## Maturational (Normative) Theory

The writings of Arnold Gesell and his colleagues represent the position that children are primarily a product of genetic inheritance and that environmental influences are secondary. Children are seen as moving from one predictable stage to another, with "readiness" the precursor of actual learning. This position was widely accepted in the 1960s, when linguists studied children in less-than-desirable circumstances and discovered consistent patterns of language development. Using this theory as a basis for planning instruction for young children includes (1) identifying predictable stages of growth in language abilities and (2) offering appropriate readiness activities to aid children's graduation to the next higher level.

## Predetermined/Innatist Theory

Under this theory, language acquisition is considered innate (a predetermined human capacity). Each new being is believed to possess a mental ability that enables that being to master any language

to which he has been exposed from infancy. Chomsky (1968), a linguistic researcher, theorizes that each person has an individual language acquisition device (LAD). Chomsky also theorizes that this device (capacity) has several sets of language system rules (grammar) common to all known languages. As the child lives within a favorable family climate, his perceptions spark a natural and unconscious device, and the child learns the "mother tongue." Imitation and reinforcement are not ruled out as additional influences.

Chomsky notes that 2- and 3-year-olds can utter understandable, complicated sentences that they have never heard. More current theory also suggests that young children are equipped with an implicit set of internal rules that allows them to transform the sequences of sounds they hear into sequences of ideas—a remarkable thinking skill. Theorists who support this position note the infant's ability to babble sounds and noises used in languages the child has never heard.

## Cognitive-Transactional and Interactionist Theory

Under a fourth theory, language acquisition develops from basic social and emotional drives. Children are naturally active, curious, and adaptive and are shaped by transactions with the people in their environment. Language is learned as a means of relating to people. Others provide social and psychological supports that enable the child to be an effective communicator. L. S. Vygotsky's major work, *Thought and Language* (1986), suggests that children's meaningful social exchanges prepare them for uniting thought and speech into "verbal thought." This inner speech development, he theorizes, promotes oral communication and is the basis for written language. Drives stem from a need for love and care, and the need prompts language acquisition.

Children are described as reactors to the human social contact that is so crucial to their survival and well-being. They are natural explorers and investigators. The adult's role is to prepare, create, and provide environments and events. Children's views of the world consist of their mental impressions, which are built as new life events are fit into existing ones or as categories are created for new events. Language is an integral part of living; consequently, children seek to fit language into some pattern that allows understanding. With enough exposure and with functioning sensory receiving systems, children slowly crack the "code" and eventually become fluent speakers. The works of Jean Piaget, Jerome Bruner, and J. McVicker Hunt have promoted a wide acceptance of this theory by early childhood professionals.

Vygotsky (1980) argues that language learning is, in part, biological but that children need instruction in the zone between their independent language level and the level at which they can operate with adult guidance. Bodrova and Leong (1996) list four basic principles underlying the Vygotskian framework:

1. Children construct knowledge.

2. Development cannot be separated from its social context.

3. Learning can lead development.

4. Language plays a central role in mental development.

The early childhood practitioner adopting Vygotsky's ideas would believe both the teacher's behaviors and the child's active physical manipulation of the environment influence and mediate what and how a young child learns or "constructs" mentally.

In other words, without the teacher's social interaction, a child does not learn which characteristics are most important or what to notice and act upon. The teacher's role is to find out through thoughtful conversation, observation, and collaboration what concept a child holds during a jointly experienced happening and to aid the child to further mental construction(s). Consequently, under Vygotskian theory, teachers can affect young children's cognitive processes—the way they think and use language. Other individual and societal features that affect children's thinking are family, other children and people in their lives, and society at large, including language, numerical systems, and technology. Children learn or acquire a mental process by sharing or using it in circumstances with others, and then move forward in an independent manner.

## Constructivist Theory

Proponents of constructivist theory propose that children acquire knowledge by constructing it mentally in interaction with the environment. Children are believed to construct theories (hypothesize) about what they experience and then put happenings into relationships. Later, with more life experiences, revisions occur and more adequate explanations are possible. Constructivists point to young children's speech errors in grammar. Internal rules have been constructed and used for a period of time, but with more exposure to adult speech, these rules change and speech becomes closer to adult forms. The rules young children used previously were their own construct and never modeled by adult speakers.

Planning for language development and early literacy using a constructivist perspective would entail offering wide and varied activities while emphasizing their interrelatedness. Teachers and parents are viewed as being involved jointly with children in literacy activities from birth onward. The overall objective of a constructivist's approach is to promote children's involvement with interesting ideas, problems, and questions. Teachers would also help children put their findings and discoveries into words, notice relationships, and contemplate similarities and differences. Children's hands-on activity is believed to be paired with mental action. A secure, unstressed environment encourages the development of children's ability to cooperate, respect one another, exercise curiosity, gain confidence in themselves, and figure things out on their own. They become autonomous learners.

## Other Theories

There is no all-inclusive theory of language acquisition substantiated by research. Many relationships and mysteries are still under study. Current teaching practices involve many different styles and approaches to language arts activities. Some teachers may prefer using techniques in accord with one particular theory. One goal common among educators is to provide instruction that encourages social and emotional development while also offering activities and opportunities in a warm, language-rich, supportive classroom, center, or home. Educators believe children should be included in talk and treated as competent language partners.

This text promotes many challenging activities that go beyond simple rote memorization or passive participation. It offers an enriched program of literary experience that encourages children to think and use their abilities to relate and share their thoughts.

The text is based on the premise that children's innate curiosity, their desire to understand

and give meaning to their world, and their predisposition equip them to learn language. Language growth occurs simultaneously in different yet connected language arts areas and all other curriculum offerings. Children continually form, modify, rearrange, and revise internal knowledge as experiences, activities, opportunities, and social interactions are encountered. Children's unconscious mental structuring of experience proceeds in growth spurts and seeming regressions, with development in one area influencing development in another.

## RESEARCH ON INFANTS' BRAIN GROWTH   **IRA**

Rich early experience and time with caring and loving families or early childhood educators has become even more important as researchers of **neurolinguistics** make new discoveries about infants' and young children's brain growth. Although awed by the brain's exceptional malleability, flexibility, and plasticity during early years and its ability to "explode" with new **synapses** (connections), scientists also warn of the effects of abuse or neglect on the child's future brain function.

It is estimated that at birth, each neuron in the cerebral cortex has approximately 2,500 synapses, and the number of synapses reaches its peak at 2 to 3 years of age, when there are about 15,000 synapses per neuron.

A discipline called cognitive science has appeared, uniting psychology, philosophy, linguistics, computer science, and neuroscience. New technology gives researchers additional tools to study brain energy, volume, blood flow, oxygenation, and cross-sectional images. Neuroscientists have found that through-out the entire process of development, beginning even before birth, the brain is affected by environmental conditions, including the kind of nourishment, care, surroundings, and stimulation an individual receives. The brain is profoundly flexible, sensitive, and plastic and is deeply influenced by events in the outside world. The new developmental

research suggests that humans' unique evolutionary trick, their central adaptation, their greatest weapon in the struggle for survival, is precisely their dazzling ability to learn while they are babies and to teach when grown-ups (Gopnik et al., 1999).

Early experience has gained additional importance and attention. New scientific research does not direct families to provide special "enriching" experiences to children over and above what they experience in everyday life. It does suggest, however, that a radically deprived environment could cause damage. Gould (2002) reports that various types of unpredictable, traumatic, chaotic, or neglectful environments can physically change the infant's brain by over activating and/or stressing the brain's neural pathways. According to Gould, these changes may include a change in the child's muscle tone, profound sleep difficulties, an increased startle response, and significant anxiety. Life experiences are now believed to control both how the infant's brain is "architecturally formed" and how intricate brain circuitry is wired. Infant sight and hearing acuity need to be assessed as early as possible given this new information. If a newborn's hearing disability is diagnosed and treated within 6 months, the child usually develops normal speech and language on schedule (Spivak, 2000).

With new technology, hearing tests are far more accurate and can pinpoint the level of hearing loss in babies who are only a few hours old. The American Academy of Pediatrics recommends that all infants be examined by 6 months of age and have regular checkups after age 3.

Researchers, such as Wingert and Brant (2005), provide a description of what is believed to be happening in infants without neural limitations:

Science is now giving us a much different picture of what goes on inside their [babies] hearts and heads. Long before they form their first words or attempt the feat of sitting up, they are already

---

**neurolinguistics** — a branch of linguistics that studies the structure and function of the brain in relation to language acquisition, learning, and use.
**synapses** — gap-like structures over which the axon of one neuron beams a signal to the dendrites of another, forming a connection in the human brain. They affect memory and learning.

mastering complex emotions—jealousy, empathy, frustration—that were once thought to be learned much later in toddlerhood.

Infants are also far more sophisticated intellectually than we once believed. Babies, as young as 4 months, have advanced powers of deduction and an ability to decipher intricate patterns. They have a strikingly nuanced visual palette, which enables them to notice small differences, especially in faces. This is an ability that adults or older children lose. Until a baby is 3 months old, he can recognize a scrambled photograph of his mother just as quickly as a photograph in which everything is in the right place.

Older debates about nature (genetic givens) versus nurture (care, experiential stimulations, parental teaching, and so on) are outdated (Figure 1–9). Nature and nurture are inseparably intertwined, Genetics lay out our neurological blueprint, but parents and life experiences wire infant's brains (Raftery, 2009).

Many scientists believe that in the first few years of childhood there are a number of critical or sensitive periods, or "windows," when the brain demands certain types of input. If a child's brain is not stimulated during a specific window of time, consequences occur. For example, researchers posit vision will not be normal if by approximately 6 months an infant is not seeing things in the world around him. In neurobiological literature, these special periods are described as "critical periods" or "plastic periods," and they are believed to be one of nature's provisions for humankind to be able to use environmental exposure to change the anatomy of the brain and make it more efficient.

Kantrowitz (1997) points out:

Every lullaby, every giggle and peek-a-boo, triggers a crackling along his neural pathways, laying the groundwork for what could someday be a love of art or a talent for soccer or a gift for making and keeping friends. (p. 152)

Other scientists are skeptical and observe clear evidence of differential abilities to learn language during certain time periods is not easily forthcoming. They suggest that critical periods may seem to exist only because brain structures have already developed through early experiences, affecting the way in which one perceives and interprets the world. These neuroscientists note that the subject of critical periods is hotly debated. One thing is clear—children who learn a second language between 3 and 7 years of age perform like native speakers on various tests, whereas children who learn a second language after puberty speak it with an accent.

| OLD THINKING . . . | NEW THINKING . . . |
|---|---|
| How a brain develops depends on the genes you are born with. | How a brain develops hinges on a complex interplay between the genes you are born with and the experiences you have. |
| The experiences you have before age three have a limited architecture impact on later development. | Early experiences have a decisive impact on the architecture of the brain and on the nature and extent of adult capacities. |
| A secure relationship with a primary caregiver creates a directly favorable context for early development and learning. | Early interactions do not just create a context; they affect the way the brain is "wired." |
| Brain development is linear: the brain's capacity to learn and change grows steadily as an infant progresses toward adulthood. | Brain development is nonlinear: there are prime times for acquiring different kinds of knowledge and skills. |
| A toddler's brain is much less active than the brain of a college student. | By the time children reach age three, their brains are twice as active as those of adults. Activity levels drop during adolescence. |

**FIGURE 1–9** Rethinking the brain. (From Shore, R. [1997]. *Rethinking the brain.* New York: Families and Work Institute. Reprinted with permission.)

Wardle (2003) believes brain research also supports early second language learning, for it suggests that young children have the brain capacity and neural flexibility to undertake the challenging task. She observes that second language learning creates new neural networks that increase the brain's capacity for all sorts of future learning, not just language learning.

What specific courses of action do brain researchers recommend?

- Providing excellent child care for working parents
- Talking to babies frequently
- Cuddling babies and using hands-on parenting
- Using **parentese**, the high-pitched, vowel-rich, singsong speech. The way we typically talk to infants—speaking more slowly, enunciating words, pausing between sounds, and varying the pitch of our voice—makes learning language much easier (Galinsky 2010),
- Giving babies freedom to explore within safe limits
- Providing safe objects to explore and manipulate
- Giving babies regular eye examinations and interesting visual opportunities
- Providing loving, stress-reduced care for the child's emotional development
- Believing an infant's brain is actively seeking meaning in speech sounds and is trying to understand the actions, intentions, and behaviors of others.

Experts describe possible infant learning difficulties related to brain function.

- 0–3 months: Infant does not turn head toward a speaker or try to make vocal sounds.
- 4–6 months: Infant does not respond to *no* or note changes in others tone of voice. Does not search for sources of sounds or babble and make consonant-like sounds.
- 7–12 months: Infant does not react to his name; imitate speech sounds, or use actions or sounds to gain attention (Figure 1–10).

Educators and families agree that infant care should be provided by knowledgeable adults

**FIGURE 1–10** Knowledgeable teachers respond with attention and warmth.

who realize that early experiences and opportunities may have long-term developmental consequences. Caregivers should also provide rich, language-filled experiences and opportunities and recognize delayed development.

Many educators worry that "excessive pressure" for inappropriate skills at early ages may cause later problems. Adults' enthusiasm for creating "super babies" may motivate untrained caregivers to offer meaningless age-inappropriate activities.

Greenspan's (1999) observations make it clear that certain kinds of emotional nurturing propel infants and young children to intellectual and emotional health and that affective experience helps them master a variety of cognitive tasks. He states:

As a baby's experience grows, sensory impressions become increasingly tied to

---

**parentese** — a high-pitched, rhythmic, singsong, crooning style of speech. It is also known as motherese or baby talk.

feelings. It is the **dual coding** of experience that is the key to understanding how emotions organize intellectual capacities and indeed create the sense of self. (p. 78)

Coles (2004), a reviewer of brain research, also points out that growing evidence suggests that thinking is an inseparable interaction of both **cognition** and emotion (feelings, desires, enthusiasms, antipathies, etc.). Interactive emotional exchanges with caregivers and their reciprocal quality are increasingly viewed as being critical to human infants' growth and development, including language development. Early childhood caregivers realize:

> . . . the adult a baby will someday become is the end result of the thousands of times a parent or caregiver comforted her when she cried, helped her to play well with others in the sandbox and sang just one more lullaby before she finally closed her eyes for the night. Each of these seemingly simple acts gently shapes a child's growing sense of self. (Kantrowitz, 2000, p. 6)

The importance of environmental feedback is considerable. Feedback by caregivers includes giving words of praise and providing caregiver attention, and it promotes the emotional satisfaction an infant feels when he is successful in doing something he set out to do.

Some developers of infant materials, equipment, books, and services suggest they can speed brain development. Families may feel they need to find ways to accelerate early childhood experiences and believe that it is up to them to find products and services. Most educators believe this is unnecessary and suggest spending time with infants and providing natural parenting, such as playing, engaging in reciprocal talk, and simply putting plastic mixing bowls on the floor. Honig (2007) concurs and points out that when an infant shakes a bell or pulls a toy on a string to make it move, he is delightedly learning he can get a specific effect. She notes scientists use these same strategies in their laboratories every day.

## ADDITIONAL COMMUNICATIVE ABILITIES IN INFANCY

Newborns quickly make their needs known. They cry, and their parents or caregivers respond. Adults feed, hold, and keep infants warm and dry. The sounds of footsteps or voices or a caring touch often stops infants' crying. Babies learn to anticipate. The sense perceptions they receive begin to be connected to stored impressions of the past.

Infants are very powerful in shaping relationships with significant caregivers. They are a wonderful combination of development, potential development, and cognitive flexibility. An infant can perceive from caregivers' behavior a willingness to learn from the infant and respond to his patterns of behavior and rhythms of hunger. This is accomplished by a caregiver's close observation of the infant's vocal and body clues, which indicate the child's state of being. At some point, the caregiver notices that a pattern of mutual gazing is established. Then a type of proto-conversation begins with caregiver vocalizations followed by infant response and noisemaking. Two important developmental tasks that confront infants are learning to regulate and calm themselves and learning to interact and "play" with caregivers. The first may be difficult for some infants, but the second seems to come naturally.

The infant is a noisemaker from birth. The child's repertoire includes sucking noises, lip smacking, sneezes, coughs, hiccups, and, of course, different types of cries. As an infant grows, he makes vocal noises, such as **cooing** after feeding. During feeding, slurping and guzzling sounds indicate eagerness and pleasure. Cooing seems to be related to a child's comfort and satisfaction. Cooing consists of relaxed, low-pitched vowel sounds that are made in an open-mouthed way; for example, *e* (as in see), *e* (get), *a* (at), *ah*, and *o*, *oo*, *ooo*. The infant appears to be in control of this sound making. Discomfort, by comparison, produces consonant sounds, made in a tense manner with the lips partly closed and the tongue and the ridge of the upper or lower jaw constricting airflow.

---

**dual coding** — the belief that infants' experiences and emotions influence cognition.
**cognition** — the process that creates mental images, concepts, and operations.
**cooing** — an early stage during the prelinguistic period in which vowel sounds are repeated, particularly the *u-u-u* sound.

Families who attend to infant crying promptly and who believe that crying stems from legitimate needs rather than attempts to control tend to produce contented, trusting infants. Advice for families of colicky babies consists of holding and carrying the infant more frequently in an effort to soothe.

Infants differ in numerous ways from the moment of birth. In speaking to parents about the unique differences in infants, Greenspan (1999) notes the following:

> For most babies, swaddling (gently but firmly bundling the baby's arms and legs in a receiving blanket wrapped around their bodies) is soothing. Other babies enjoy a body massage in which their limbs are gently flexed and extended.
>
> Up until recently, scientists assumed that all human beings experienced sensations in similar ways. We now know that individuals perceive the same stimulus very differently. Your feathery touch could feel tickly and irritating on your newborn's skin, while another baby might take delight in the same caress. (p. 91)

The individual pace of development varies. Whether an infant reaches developmental milestones on the early or late side of normal seems to bear little relation to either cognitive skills or future proficiency (Raymond, 2000). However, in most cases, milestones in language development are reached at about the same age and in a recognizable sequence (Figures 1–11 and 1–12).

Babies learn quickly that communicating is worthwhile because it results in action on the part of another. Greenspan (1999) warns that unless a child masters the level we call two-way intentional communication, normally achieved by an 8-month-old infant, the child's language, cognitive, and social patterns ultimately develop in an idiosyncratic, piecemeal, disorganized manner. There is a high degree of relationship between a caregiver's responsiveness and a child's language competence. By 9 to 18 months of age, the more responsive mothers promoted greater language facility and growth.

Infants quickly recognize subtle differences in sounds. This helps infants calm down and

| AGE | NONWORD VOCALIZATIONS |
|---|---|
| newborn | cries |
| 1–3 months | makes cooing sounds in response to speech (*oo*, *goo*) |
| | laughs |
| | cries in different ways when hungry, angry, or hurt |
| | makes more speechlike sounds in response to speech |
| 4–6 months | plays with some sounds, usually single syllables (e.g., *ba*, *ga*) |
| 6–8 months | babbles with duplicated sounds (e.g., *bababa*) |
| | attempts to imitate some sounds |
| 8–12 months | babbles with consonant or vowel changes (e.g., *badaga*, *babu*) |
| | babbles with sentencelike intonation (expressive jargon/ conversational babble) |
| | produces protowords |

**FIGURE 1–11** Examples of the typical order of emergence of types of nonword vocalizations in the first year, with approximate.

**FIGURE 1–12** Infants often babble to toys especially ones that make noise.

pay attention—in other words, listen.  Infants move their arms and legs in synchrony to the rhythms of human speech. Random noises, tapping sounds, and disconnected vowel sounds do not produce this behavior.

There is a difference between people in an infant's life. Some talk and touch. Others show delight. Some pause after speaking and seem to wait for a response. The child either "locks on" to the conversationalist, focusing totally, or breaks eye contact and looks away. It is almost as though the infant controls what he wants to receive. Of course, hunger, tiredness, and other factors also influence this behavior and may stop the child's interest in being social.

The special people in the infant's life adopt observable behaviors when "speaking" to them, just as the infant seems to react in special ways to their attention. Talking to babies differs from other adult speech in that the lyric or musical quality of speech seems more important than words. Infants listening to these long, drawn-out vowels experience an increase in heart rate. At the same time, it speeds up the brain's ability to recognize connections between words and objects. Educators believe "baby-talk" speech modifications can vary among cultures. The attention-holding ability of this type of adult speech may help the infant become aware of the linguistic function of vocalizations (Sachs, 1997). Mothers sometimes raise their voice pitch to a falsetto, shorten sentences, simplify their syntax and vocabulary, use nonsense sounds, use a slower tempo, and use longer pauses than in adult conversations. They maintain prolonged eye contact during playful interchanges. Most infants are attracted to high-pitched voices, but a few infants seem to overreact and prefer lower speech sounds. Infants can pick up higher-pitched sounds better than lower-frequency ones, which may be why they are entranced by the high-pitched coos and singsong nature of parent talk. Parents' voices when talking to their infants can be described as playful, animated, warm, and perhaps giddy. Falk (2004) proposes that parent talk forms a scaffold for infants' language acquisition, and caregivers often use vocal means to placate and reassure. They attempt to control their infant's state of well-being. Falk notes that vowels are lingered over, phrases are repeated, and questions carry exaggerated inflections.

### ▶❚❚ VIDEO ACTIVITY

Go to the Education CourseMate website to watch the TeachSource Video, *0-2 Years: Observation Module for Infants and Toddlers*, and then answer the following questions:

1. The caregiver interacted with the infant with words and touching and also talking to and touching at the same time. Could you tell which was the most effective by watching the infant's reaction?

2. What strategies were used to calm the first infant who was crying?

A mutual readiness to respond to each other appears built-in to warm relationships. The infant learns that eye contact can hold and maintain attention and that looking away usually terminates both verbal and nonverbal episodes. They learn a great deal about language before they ever say a word. Most of what they learn at a very early age involves the sound system of language.

## Crying

Crying is one of the infant's primary methods of communication. Cries can be weak or hardy, and they provide clues to the infant's general health. Crying may be the only way an infant can affect his situation of need or discomfort. Infants begin early in life to control the emotional content of their cries. Many parents believe they can recognize different types of crying, such as sleepy, frightened, hungry, and so on, especially if infant body actions are observed concurrently. Researchers have discovered that parents do indeed accurately infer the intensity of an infant's emotional state from the sound of the cry itself, even if the baby is not visually observed. Even adults inexperienced with infants seem to possess this ability.

Child development specialists advise adult alertness and responsiveness to minimize crying. Crying will take place in the best of circumstances, and research has indicated that there are some positive aspects of crying, including stress reduction, elimination of toxin in tears, and reestablishment of physical and emotional balance. However, although crying may have its benefits, it is not recommended that infants be left to cry, but rather that adults continue to attempt to soothe and satisfy infant's needs.

A baby's crying may cause strong feelings in some adults, including anger, frustration, irritation, guilt, and rejection. Successful attempts at soothing the infant and stopping the crying give both the infant and the caregiver satisfaction, feelings of competence, and a possible sense of pleasure. When out-of-sorts infants cease crying, alertness, attentiveness, and visual scanning usually happen and/or the infants fall asleep (Figure 1–13). Infant-caregiver interaction has been described as a rhythmic drama, a reciprocal dance, and a family melody. All of these touch on the beauty and coordination of sound-filled moments between the adult and child.

Emotions are expressed frequently in crying as the infant nears his first birthday. Fear, frustration, uneasiness with novelty or newness, separation from loved ones, and other strong emotions can provoke crying through childhood and beyond.

Infant care providers in group programs engage in frank staff discussions concerning infant crying. Normal and natural staff feelings concerning crying need open discussion so that strategies can be devised in the best interests of both the infants and staff members. Many techniques exist to minimize crying and also to monitor the crying levels of individual infants so that health or developmental problems can be spotted quickly.

## Smiling and Laughing

True smiling can occur before 6 months of age and is usually associated with a caretaker's facial, auditory, or motor stimuli. Laughter may occur as early as 4 months of age and is believed to be a good predictor of cognitive growth. Some developmental experts suggest that the earlier the baby laughs, the higher the baby's developmental level is. In the second half of the first year, infants smile at more complex social and visual items. Laughter at this age may be full of squeals, howls, hoots, giggles, and grins. Incongruity may be noticed by the infant, and laughter follows. If an infant laughs when he sees the family dog in the driver's seat with its paws on the wheel, the child may be showing recognition of incongruity—the child has learned something about car drivers.

Responsive caregivers promote infant smiling. Ainsworth and Bell (1972) concluded that **responsive mothers**, those who are alert in caring for the infant's needs, had babies who cried less frequently and had a wider range of different modes of communication (Figure 1–14). These

**FIGURE 1–13** A child may fall asleep while being soothed.

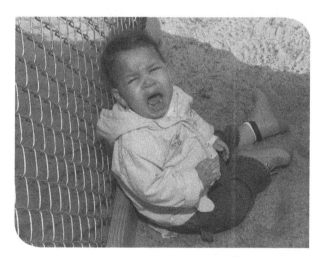

**FIGURE 1–14** A quick parental response to crying is appropriate and recommended.

---

**responsive mothers** — mothers who are alert and timely in responding to and giving attention to infants' needs and communications.

responsive mothers created a balance between showing attention and affording the infant autonomy (offering a choice of action within safe bounds) when the infant became mobile. They also provided body contact and involved themselves playfully at times.

Gonzalez-Mena (2007) notes there may be times when infant's needs are met and the infant still cries. She recommends:

> If you've done all you can to meet the needs and the baby's still crying, it is not a reflection on you, your caring, or your skills—it's about allowing emotions to be expressed instead of repressed. When babies understand that what they feel is okay with the people around them, they have a better chance of learning to calm themselves—or in technical terms, learn self-regulation, a problem solving skill. (p. 23)

Gonzalez-Mena (2007) states she does not mean for the adult to exit completely and let the infant "cry it out"; instead one should make periodic contact and continue to reassure the infant. Naturally, most caregivers will try checking for possible discomfort and use calming strategies that have been successful in the past.

### An attuned adult:

○ *notices infant reactions to auditory stimuli.*

○ *is aware of infant preferences.*

○ *notices if an infant has an attachment to a caregiver and/or expresses pleasure in another's company.*

○ *seeks to help the infant maintain a state of balance and a comfort level.*

○ *is attentive and consistent in recognizing and satisfying a child's needs.*

○ *has sufficient energy and seeks to engage frequently with an infant.*

○ *monitors an infant's health and safety and observes closely.*

○ *provides a variety of experience and sensory materials for exploration.*

○ *uses words to accompany child and adult actions.*

○ *records milestones in development and uses them to guide caregiver interactions.*

○ *is playful, gives attention, and provides feedback to an infant's efforts.*

## Infant Imitation

Acredolo and Goodwyn (2000) suggest that infants as young as 1 or 2 days old may imitate parent head movements and facial behaviors; they explain:

> This inborn push to mimic others gets babies into a problem-solving mode from the very beginning. And as we mentioned earlier, babies thrive on problem solving. The payoff is such a pleasant one—Dad sticks around to interact some more, and baby is amused. Imitation is such an important developmental component that Mother Nature has not left it up to chance. She has made sure that each of us begins life's journey with a necessary tool in hand. (p. 185)

## Babbling

Early random sound making is often called **babbling**. Infants the world over babble sounds they have not heard and that they will not use in their native language. This has been taken to mean that each infant has the potential to master any world language. Close inspection shows repetitive sounds and "practice sessions" present. Babbling starts at about the fourth to sixth month and continues in some children through the toddler period. However, a peak in babbling is usually reached between 9 and 12 months. Periods before the first words are spoken are marked by a type of babbling that repeats syllables, as in *dadadada*. This is called **echolalia**. Infants seem to echo themselves and others. Babbling behavior overlaps the stages of making one and two or more words, and may end for some children at about 18 months of age.

---

**babbling** — an early language stage in sound production in which an infant engages in vocal play with vowel and consonant sounds, including some sounds not found in his or her language environment.

**echolalia** — a characteristic of the babbling period. The child repeats (echoes) the same sounds over and over.

Infants who are deaf also babble. In play sessions, they will babble for longer periods without hearing either adult sound or their own sounds, as long as they can see the adult responding. However, these children stop babbling at an earlier age than do hearing children. It is not clearly understood why babbling occurs, either in hearing or hearing-impaired children, but it is thought that babbling gives the child the opportunity to use and control the mouth, throat, and lung muscles. Researchers trying to explain babbling suggest that infants are not just exercising or playing with their vocal apparatus. Instead, they may be trying out and attempting to control their lips, tongues, mouths, and jaws to produce certain sounds. A child's babbling amuses and motivates the child, acting as a stimulus that adds variety to the child's existence.

In time, the child increasingly articulates clear, distinct vowel-like, consonant-like, and syllabic sounds. *Ba* and *da* are acquired early because they are easy to produce, whereas *el* and *ar* are acquired late because they require a sophisticated ability to articulate sounds. Although babbling includes a wide range of sounds, as children grow older, they narrow the range and begin to focus on the familiar language of the family. Other sounds are gradually discarded. Almost any feature of environment may promote verbal attempts.

Physical contact continues to be important. Touching, holding, rocking, and engaging in other types of physical contact bring a sense of security and a chance to respond through sound making. The cooing and babbling sounds infants make may also draw caregivers into "conversations." Babies learn to wait for the adult's response after they have vocalized, and both infants and adults are constantly influencing one another in establishing conversation-like vocal interactions (Figure 1–15).

Bardige (2008) points out babies need to hear everyday language during their babbling period. She suggests adults talk about what the baby and they themselves are doing and continue to make language part of their daily care as they bathe, change, feed, play, and soothe the infant.

The active receiving of perceptions is encouraged by warm, loving parents who share a close relationship. Secure children respond more readily to the world around them. Children who lack social and physical contact or those who live in insecure home environments fall behind

**FIGURE 1–15** Infants' vocal and playful interactions with caregivers are the precursors of conversations.

in both the number and range of sounds made; differences start showing at about 6 months of age. Sound imitation eventually becomes syllable imitation, and short words are spoken near the end of the child's first year.

## Stages of Vocalization

Stoel-Gammon (1997) outlines stages in infants' production of sounds and notes that vocalization types typically overlap from one stage to another.

> Stage 1 (birth to 2 months): Reflexive vocalization. Characterized by crying, fussing, vegetative sounds like coughing, burping, sneezing, and some vowel-like sounds.
>
> Stage 2 (2–4 months): Cooing and laughter. Characterized by comfort-state vocalizations and chuckles.
>
> Stage 3 (4–6 months): Vocal play. Characterized by very loud and very soft sounds, yells and whispers, very high and low sounds—squeals and growls, raspberries (bilabial trills), and sustained vowels.
>
> Stage 4 (6 months and older): Canonical babbling. The appearance of sequences of consonant-vowel syllables with 'similar-to–adult' timing, 'near-to-a–word' utterances, reduplicated babbles (babababa), and variegated babbles (bagidabu). The infant's ability to hear his and others' vocalization takes on increased importance. The vocalization of babies with deafness decreases.

Stage 5 (10 months and older): Jargon stage. Babbling overlaps the early period of meaningful speech and is characterized by strings of sounds and syllables uttered with a rich variety of stress and intonation. Sound play, containing recurring favorite sequences, or even words, may occur. (p. 21)*

### A Shared Joint Attention Milestone

By the last half of the first year, children begin to take part in a new type of interaction with their caretakers. They share attention given to objects with another person by following that individual's gaze or pointing, responding to the individual's emotional reaction to an event, and imitating that person's object-directed actions (Nelson & Shaw, 2002). This gives adults who notice this behavior a chance to pair words with objects. First words or sounds are usually simple associates of objects or situations. The infant simply voices a shared reference. Nelson and Shaw note that the leap from shared reference associations to meaningful language requires the child to integrate skills with communicative patterns and conceptual knowledge. The child is then standing on a first communicative step.

## INFANT SIGNALING/ SIGNING

During the latter part of the first year, alert caregivers notice hand and body positions that suggest the child is attempting to communicate (Figure 1–16). Researchers suggest that parents pair words with easy-to-do gestures. At the age of 1 year, children cannot gain enough mastery over their tongues to form many words. Gesturing with their fingers and hands is simpler. For example, infants as young as 7 months may bang on a window to get a family cat's attention or reach out, motion, or crawl toward something or someone they want. The use of signs continues until the child's ability to talk takes off. Some educators believe **signing** may spark other critical thinking

*From Berko Gleason, J. (1997). *The development of language* (4th ed.). Boston: Allyn and Bacon. Copyright © 1997 by Pearson Education. Reprinted by permission of the publisher.

| GESTURE | POSSIBLE MEANING |
|---|---|
| allows food to run out of mouth | satisfied or not hungry |
| pouts | displeased |
| pushes nipple from mouth with tongue | satisfied or not hungry |
| pushes object away | does not want it |
| reaches out for object | wants to have it handed to him |
| reaches out to person | wants to be picked up |
| smacks lips or ejects tongue | hungry |
| smiles and holds out arms | wants to be picked up |
| sneezes excessively | wet and cold |
| squirms and trembles | cold |
| squirms, wiggles, and cries during dressing or bathing | resents restriction on activities |
| turns head from nipple | satisfied or not hungry |

**FIGURE 1–16** Some common gestures of babyhood. (From Hurlock, E. B. [2009]. *Child development* [5th ed.]. New York: McGraw-Hill. Copyright © 2009. Reproduced by permission of The McGraw-Hill Companies, Inc.)

skills and lead to better intelligence quotient (IQ) scores when testing begins.

Toward the end of the child's first year, pointing becomes goal-oriented—the infant will point to a desired object. As time progresses, more and more infant body signaling takes place. Signals are used over and over, and a type of sign language communication emerges. It can be a "signal and sound system" understood by caregivers. When caregivers respond appropriately, the infant easily progresses to word use and verbal aptitude. Signing by infants and young toddlers is believed to stimulate brain development, particularly brain areas involved in language, memory, and concept development.

Some studies of communication gestures note that infants with more advanced gestures have larger vocabularies and that girls seem slightly more advanced in gesturing than do boys. (This paragraph offered an answer to one of the questions in this chapter's beginning vignette. The next paragraph answers another.)

---

**signing** — a body positioning, sound, action, gesture, or combination of these undertaken by an infant in an effort to communicate a need, desire, or message.

Well-meaning parents or caregivers may choose not to respond to infant gestures and signals, thinking this will accelerate or force the use of words. The opposite is thought to be true. Alert parents who try to read and receive signals give their infant the message that communication leads to fulfillment of wishes. Successful signaling becomes a form of language—a precursor of verbal signals (words). Some experts believe baby signers by age 2 are better at both expressing themselves and understanding others' speech and, on average, have slightly larger vocabularies than their peers who do not sign. Sitting down at the child's level at times when the infant is crawling from one piece of furniture to another may facilitate the adult's ability to pick up on signaling. Watching the infant's eyes and the direction the infant's head turns gives clues. Infants about 8 months old seem fascinated with the adult's sound-making ability. They often turn to look at the adult's lips or want to touch the adult's mouth.

Early childhood educators employed by infant-toddler centers need to know their center's position regarding expected educator behaviors. Most centers expect educators to actively pair words with adult or child signs, encourage child use of signs, and learn and respond to each child's individual sign language.

## UNDERSTANDING

Most babies get some idea of the meaning of a few words at about 6 to 9 months. At about 10 months of age, some infants start to respond to spoken word clues. Somewhere between 8 and 13 months, the child's communication, whether vocal or a type of gesture, becomes intentional. The child makes a connection between his behavior, and the parent's or early childhood educator's response (Figure 1–17). A game such as Pat-a-cake may start the baby clapping, and "bye-bye" or Peek-a-boo brings about other imitations of earlier play activities with the parents. The child's language is called passive at this stage, for he primarily receives (or is receptive). Speaking attempts will soon become active (or expressive). Vocabulary provides a small portal through which adults can gauge a little of what the child knows. There is a point at which children expand nonverbal signals to true language.

**FIGURE 1–17** This infant has learned to respond to the adult's pointing gestures.

Older infants still communicate with their caregivers through many nonverbal actions; one common way is by holding up their arms, which most often means, "I want to be picked up." Other actions include facial expression, voice tone, voice volume, posture, and gestures such as "locking in" by pointing fingers and toes at attention-getting people and events.

Although infants at this stage can respond to words and changes in caregivers' facial expressions, voice tone, and voice volume, actions and gestures also carry feelings and messages important to infants' well-being. Understanding the tone of caregivers' speech comes before understanding the words used.

Gopnik et al. (1999) describe what happens when infants are about 1 year old.

> One-year-old babies know that they will see something by looking where other people point; they know what they should do to something by watching what other people do; they know how they should feel about something by seeing how other people feel. (p. 243)

Research suggests infants at 20 months have what Galinsky (2010) calls *language sense*. This means they can detect statistical patterns in which speech sounds go together in their native language (or languages) to determine the beginnings and endings of words (p. 2). She also suggests new research theorizes another infant sense, *people sense*, exists in infancy as infants focus on people's intentions rather than seeing what people do as random movements.

## FIRST WORDS

Before an understandable, close approximation of a word is uttered, the child's physical organs need to function in a delicate unison and the child must reach a certain level of mental maturity. Close to 12 months of age, the speech centers of the brain have developed the capacity to enable the infant to produce his first word— a great accomplishment and milestone. The child's respiratory system supplies the necessary energy. As the breath is exhaled, sounds and speech are formed with the upward movement of air. The larynx's vibrating folds produce voice (called **phonation**). The larynx, mouth, and nose influence the child's voice quality (termed **resonation**). A last modification of the breath stream is **articulation**—a final formation done through molding, shaping, stopping, and releasing voiced and other-than-voiced sounds that reflect language heard in the child's environment.

Repetition of syllables such as *ma*, *da*, and *ba* in a child's babbling occurs toward the end of the first year. If *mama* or *dada* or a close copy is said, parents and caregivers show attention and joy. Language, especially in the area of speech development, is a two-way process; reaction is an important feedback to action.

The term *protoword* is often used for the invented words a child may use during the transition from prespeech to speech. During this transition, a child has acquired the difficult concept that sounds have meaning and is unclear only about the fact that one is supposed to find out what words exist instead of making them up.

Generally, first words are nouns or proper names of foods, animals, or toys; vocabulary may also include *gone*, *there*, *uh-oh*, *more*, and *dat* ("what's that?"). Greetings, farewells, or other social phrases, such as *peek-a-boo*, are also among the first recognizable words.

Monolingual (one-language) children utter their first words at approximately 11 months of age; the range is from about 9 months to about 16 months. At about a year and a half the child learns approximately one new word every 3 days. Most experts believe that talking alone shows no link to mental development at age 2, but a child's comprehension of words is paramount. Experts conclude that there is little scientific evidence to suggest that late talkers will become less fluent than early talkers. Some children acquire large numbers of object names in their first 50 to 100 words. The first spoken words usually contain *p*, *b*, *t*, *d*, *m*, and *n* (front of the mouth consonants), which require the

---

**phonation** — exhaled air passes the larynx's vibrating folds and produces "voice."
**resonation** — amplification of laryngeal sounds using cavities of the mouth, nose, sinuses, and pharynx.
**articulation** — the adjustments and movements of the muscles of the mouth and jaw involved in producing clear oral communication.

least use of the tongue and air control. They are shortened versions, such as *da* for "daddy," *beh* for "bed," and *up* for "cup." When two-syllable words are attempted, they are often strung together using the same syllable sound, as in *dada* or *beebee*. If the second syllable is voiced, the child's reproduction of the sound may come out as *dodee* for "doggy" or *papee* for "potty."

At this stage, words tend to be segments of wider happenings in the child's life. A child's word *ba* may represent a favorite, often-used toy (such as a ball). As the child grows in experience, any round object seen in the grocery store, for instance, will also be recognized and called *ba*. This phenomenon has been termed *overextension*. The child has embraced "everything round," which is a much broader meaning for ball than the adult definition of the word.

Following is a list of words frequently understood between 8 and 12 months of age: *mommy, daddy, bye-bye, baby, shoe, ball, cookie, juice, bottle, no-no*, and the child's own name and names of family members.

A child finds that words can open many doors. They help the child get things and cause caregivers to act in many ways. Vocabulary quickly grows from the names of objects to words that refer to actions. This slowly decreases the child's dependence on context (a specific location and situation) for communication and gradually increases the child's reliance on words—the tools of abstract thought. Children learn very quickly that words not only name things and elicit action on another's part but also convey comments and express individual attitudes and feelings.

---

### An attuned adult:

○ *nurtures infant curiosity.*

○ *uses words and gestures in communication.*

○ *builds a sign language relationship with infants.*

○ *tries to judge the intensity of infants' emotions.*

○ *offers a choice of child actions and explorations within safe limits.*

○ *responds to and promotes reciprocal communication.*

○ *pairs words with actions and objects.*

○ *observes the direction of infants' gazes for clues to infants' moment to moment interests.*

○ *continues to be at eye level when possible.*

○ *expects and recognizes invented words.*

○ *encourages first word use by repeating word back to child and connecting the child's word to objects or actions as appropriate.*

○ *guesses frequently about a child's meaning in communication.*

○ *works toward a child's success at using words to fulfill his desires, needs, and interests.*

## TODDLER SPEECH

Toddlerhood begins, and the child eagerly names things and seeks names for others. The child echoes and repeats to the best of his ability. At times, the words are not recognizable as the same words the caregiver offered. When interacting with young speakers, an adult must listen closely, watch for nonverbal signs, scan the situation, and use a good deal of guessing to understand the child and respond appropriately. The child's single words accompanied by gestures, motions, and intonations are called **holophrases**. They usually represent a whole idea or sentence.

While the child is learning to walk, speech may briefly take a backseat to developing motor skill. At this time, the child may listen more intently to what others are saying.

The slow-paced learning of new words (Figure 1–18) is followed by a period of rapid growth. The child pauses briefly, listening, digesting, and gathering forces to embark on the great adventure of becoming a fluent speaker.

## IMPLICATIONS FOR INFANT CENTER STAFF MEMBERS

The importance of understanding the responsive, reciprocal nature of optimal care giving in group infant centers cannot be overestimated. The soothing, calming, swaddling, rocking,

---

**holophrases** — the expression of a whole idea in a single word. They are often found in the speech of children at about 12 to 18 months of age.

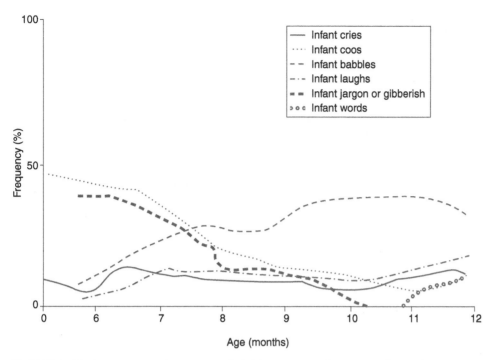

**FIGURE 1–18** Approximate frequency of child utterances from 6 to 12 months.

sympathizing, and responding behaviors of infant care specialists help infants maintain a sense of security and a relaxed state, calmness, and equilibrium.

The emotional well-being of infants has been given increased attention as research on infant development uncovers its importance. Physician Chet Johnson (2005) points out:

> The research shows how powerful emotional well-being is to a child's future health. A baby who fails to meet certain key "emotional milestones" may have trouble learning to speak, read, and later, do well in school. By reading emotional responses, doctors have begun to discover ways to tell if a baby as young as 3 months is showing early signs of possible psychological disorders, including depression, anxiety, learning disabilities and perhaps autism. Instead of just asking if they're crawling or sitting we're asking more questions about how they share their world with their caregivers. (p. 35)

See Figure 1–19 for infants' emotional milestones.

At about 4 months, babies begin to gaze in the direction in which caregivers are looking. Caregivers are able to follow the line of vision of babies as well. Well-trained caregivers will naturally comment and offer language labels and a running commentary. This process is known as *joint attentional focus*. When adults know that the infant does not yet understand language, most adults behave as if the child's response is a turn in the conversation. Adult caregivers need to read both nonverbal and vocalized cues and react appropriately (Figure 1–20). They need to be attentive and loving. Learning to read each other's signals is basic to the quality of the relationship. Liberal amounts of touching; holding, smiling, and looking promote language and the child's overall sense that the world around him is both safe and fascinating. Recognizing the child's individuality, reading nonverbal behaviors, and reacting with purposeful actions are all expected of professional infant specialists, as is noticing activity level, moods, distress threshold, rhythms of the body, intensity, sense of adventure, distractibility, adaptability, and attention span.

There are many skills that well-trained caregivers possess, beginning with holding the infant firmly yet gently and making soft, gentle

| AGE | EMOTIONAL/SOCIAL CHARACTERISTICS |
|---|---|
| Birth to around 3–4 months | At birth, the infant is able to feel fear and contentment and is self-absorbed. During first 3–4 months, infant becomes aware of the environment around him and is attentive and interested. Seems able to calm self at times. Develops deliberate responses. Focuses on the faces of people and smiles at them. Eyes may widen in anticipation. May react to strong scents or odors. Has a developing sense of security. Holding and touching may reduce stress, and rhythmic motion may soothe. May enjoy swaddling. Pays attention and reacts to sounds. Some infants are oversensitive to some types of sounds. Reacts to visual cues, especially from care provider's face. |
| Around 5–6 or more months | Displays emotions such as surprise, joy, and frustration. Falls in love with care provider. Beams with delight at times. Able to see the pattern formed by features on care provider's face. Smiles in recognition. May display sorrow and annoyance. Builds a stronger relationship with primary care provider. Begins to realize he can make things happen. Is comforted by physical closeness. Develops feelings of being loved, valued, and esteemed by others. Easy to tell when infant is happy. Sense of self is a reflection of care provider's emotional interactions with infant. May experience jealousy. |
| Around 10 or more months | Initiates two-way communication. Notices where care provider looks and often follows by also looking. Tries to catch care provider's eye and gives physical cues to others to obtain a desired action, such as being held. May use signs and signals to make things happen. May respond to rhythm with rhythmic movements. Expects his action will prompt a reaction. May mimic gestures. May express fear, anger, anticipation, caution, and surprise with strangers. Responds to name, words, and sounds, and attempts to imitate them. Is curious and perhaps assertive and negative at times. May experience a sense of loss at something removed. May show fear if care provider looks angry, frowns, or stares (not recommended). Seeks pleasure and enjoys stimulating self (for example, touching toes and participating in adult-infant games that involve moving or touching body parts, such as "This Little Piggy." |
| | Note: This is not intended to be a complete inventory of emotional milestones; research in identifying infant emotional development and capacity is still in its infancy. Notice social skill and emotional response is intertwined and dependent on environmental and human experience. |

**FIGURE 1–19** Emotional milestones and social skill characteristics.

sounds while moving smoothly and holding the infant close. Others are identified in the following list.

### An attuned adult:

○ talks in a pleasant, soothing voice; uses simple language; and makes frequent eye contact.

○ emphasizes and expects two-way "conversation"; hesitates; and pauses for an infant response.

○ makes a game out of the infant's smiles, sounds, and movements when the infant is responsive.

○ speaks clearly.

○ explains what is happening and what will happen next.

○ is consistently attentive.

○ does not interrupt the infant's vocal play, jargon, or self-communication.

○ engages in word play, rhyme, chants, and fun-to-say short expressions.

○ is an animated speaker and a responsive companion.

○ may, with an older infant, attempt to offer simple finger plays.

○ plans real and concrete participatory activities with textures, sights, and sounds.

FIGURE 1–20 *"You can do it. Just take one small step."*

- ○ *encourages sound making and provides noisemaking and musical toys.*
- ○ *labels objects, happenings, actions, and emotions.*
- ○ *uses highly intonated speech that may be high pitched at times with very young infants.*
- ○ *speaks distinctly with clear enunciation to help children identify phonemes.*
- ○ *emphasizes, at times, one word in a sentence.*
- ○ *uses repetition but avoids overdoing it.*
- ○ *gives feedback by responding with both words and actions.*
- ○ *creates and pursues game-like strategies and techniques.*
- ○ *serves as a co-explorer.*

Being playful and initiating singing conversations with infants can be enjoyable and may lay the foundation for later music activities. Both recorded and live musical sounds are part of an auditory-rich environment for infants. For identified early childhood goals and additional caregiver activities, see Figure 1–21.

Williams (2008) urges caregivers to explore the world outside the classroom or home with older infants and toddlers. Children are born with a desire to understand the environment around them, and they possess incessant curiosity that compels them to explore it (Medina, 2008). Their discoveries can bring joy. Like an addictive drug, Medina believes, exploration creates the need for even more discovery.

Think about watching or feeling raindrops, experiencing mud, touching a caterpillar, smelling flowers, or hearing birds. The reality and beauty of natural landscapes surrounds us, and there are multiple ways to experience it safely.

Remember that infants are alike yet uniquely different. Some sensitive infants may appear overwhelmed and require little stimuli to maintain equilibrium. Others will thrive in an environment that provides a multitude of people, sights, sounds, and new activities. Each infant

| AGE | ADULT GOALS | ADULT ACTIVITY |
|---|---|---|
| birth to 2 months | 1. to create a trusting, intimate relationship<br>2. to take pleasure in the reciprocal infant-adult interactions<br>3. to help infant calm and regulate himself<br>4. to verbally communicate and promote a two-way pattern of responses<br>5. to maintain eye contact and spend time face to face<br>6. to seek to create an appropriate environmental moderation level | 1. anticipate and satisfy infant needs<br>2. show interest and provide positive reactions and joy in the infant's presence and communicative attempts<br>3. provide sights, sounds, touches, and playful companionship<br>4. talk, croon, whisper, sing, and mimic infant gesture<br>5. repeat infant sounds<br>6. provide a comfortable environment that satisfies the child's needs |
| 2–6 months | 1. to keep alert to infant attempts to communicate distress or needs<br>2. to strengthen growing bond of enjoyment in adult-infant "together time" and explorations<br>3. to recognize child individuality, moods, likes and dislikes, uniqueness<br>4. to encourage "you talk" and "I talk" behaviors<br>5. to see infant gestures as possibly purposeful<br>6. to hold child's eye contact when speaking and gain child's attention with animated speech<br>7. to use clear and simple speech | 1. provide adult-infant play time and joint new experiences<br>2. provide infant exploring of sights, sounds, music, and play materials and indoor and outdoor environments<br>3. offer "talking" opportunities with others<br>4. name child's actions, toys, happenings while changing, bathing, and feeding<br>5. play baby games such as Pat-a-cake<br>6. use talk and touch as a reward for the child's communication attempts<br>7. repeat child sounds and gestures |
| 6–12 months | 1. to pursue infant interests, tailoring your talk to child focus<br>2. to promote the idea that language is used for naming and describing<br>3. to play with rhythm and rhyme in adult-infant communications<br>4. to speak clearly, emphasizing new words when appropriate<br>5. to show delight in child's verbal and physical accomplishments<br>6. to pair your words with actions, happenings, and objects<br>7. to recognize and respond appropriately to child signaling and words<br>8. to make sure sound level and noise is appropriate<br>9. to listen for intent, not perfection<br>10. to provide safe environment conducive to child exploring and action | 1. expand the child's world with neighborhood trips, people, playthings, and experiences<br>2. name and describe happenings, emotions, actions, and environments as things take place<br>3. introduce and read board books to the child, letting child explore them himself<br>4. sing songs, perform finger plays, play word games with visual and touching actions<br>5. listen and pause for infant response<br>6. name body parts, colors, and objects<br>7. tell simple stories<br>8. delight in the world and its joyful pursuits with the child |

**FIGURE 1–21** Adult goals and activities for language development during infancy.

provides a challenge one must "puzzle out" to decide best courses of action—what works, what does not work, and what is best. Bardige (2009) suggests adult-infant connection may not always go smoothly.

> Some babies are fussy and hard to soothe, some are so sensitive that they have to be approached carefully and given lots of support before they can engage, and some are challenged in one modality (e.g., hearing or sight) but hyper-acute in another. Some babies are flexible by nature, but others are fearful or feisty. Babies also differ in their natural activity levels and in their rates of development. Some babies give clear signals when they need food or play or comfort or rest; others are much harder to read. (p. 23)

Because infants' first sensory experiences are part of emotional relationships with caregivers, caregivers' efforts to provide developmental care go hand in hand with providing positive emotional support in daily reciprocal exchanges between the child and adult. The terms *child-centered* and *child-focused* need to be coupled with reactive, observant, playful, and nurturing adult behaviors. This type of infant care is nearly impossible when adult-infant ratios are inadequate.

Generally, the types of adults who promote language are those who are alert to the child's achievements, notice them, and enjoy interacting, as well as adults who can offer novelty, assistance, and enthusiasm in addition to focusing on the child's interests Mangione (2010) believes the emotional security infants derive from positive caring relationships with primary and secondary care providers, provides infants with a buffer for the negative stresses he might encounter in daily experiences.

## BABY GAMES AND EXPLORATIONS

Almost daily, infants seem to increase the ways they can explore and enjoy verbal-physical games. Birchmayer, Kennedy, and Stonehouse

(2008) urge caregivers to explore creative ways to communicate with infants to sustain their interest.

> For very young children, spoken language can be extended through face and body games and rhymes. Though infants still will not understand many or even most words used, they will nevertheless enjoy the sound, rhythm, and tone of the language and other creative elements of the experience. (p. 31)

Most adults know that holding an infant and singing or dancing with him are good ways to comfort the fussy child or to foster interest in place of boredom.

Infant educators create their own games and activities that are enjoyable to both infants and caregivers. They become aware of their infants' focus and reactions. Games that deal with child anticipation often elicit smiles or giggles. Playing classics such as Peek-a-boo or Johnny Jump Up or hiding an object under a cloth has delighted generations of children. More newly devised activities include tying a soft tinkling bell to the wrist or leg of an infant or connecting a soft ribbon from an infant's ankle to an overhead mobile (under adult supervision).

Experts recommend that, from a baby's earliest days, caregivers begin with simple imitation games during face-to-face interaction, making sure to pause long enough for the infant to take in the information and mount a response. The best distance for these games is 8 to 12 inches away from the child's face. Imitation of the baby's movement or vocal efforts is also suggested, as is rewarding the baby's effort with attention or smiles.

The following classic language and body action play has brought delight to generations of infants. The most enjoyed play activities include tickling, bouncing, and lifting with accompanying words and rhymes.

### This Little Piggy

(Each line is recited while holding a toe, moving toward the pinkie.)

*This little pig went to market. This little pig stayed home. This little pig had roast beef. This little pig had none. This little piggy cried, "Wee, wee, wee, wee!" all the way home.*

(First published in 1728.)

### Pat-a-Cake

(Recited while helping the child with hand clapping.)

*Pat-a-cake, pat-a-cake, baker's man.*
*Bake me a cake as fast as you can.*
*Pat it and prick it and mark it with a "B."*
*And put it in the oven for baby and me.*

### So Big

*Say, "Look at you—so big!" Slowly raise both of the infant's arms up, extending them over the child's head while saying, "[child's name] is so-o-oh big" and then slowly bring the arms down.*

*Repeat.*

*Say the child's name slowly as you raise the infant close to your face at eye level. Then say, "So-o-oh big." Then gently say, "Wow, wow, wow—what a baby. A so-o-oh big baby!" with a big smile.*

Other play games are found in the Activities section.

## MUSICAL PLAY

Music, singing, and musical expression appear to be a central part of the crucial interaction that occurs between caregivers and infants as infants develop over the first year of life. Two types of musical or singing interaction take place: (1) a soothing go-to-sleep lullaby-style interaction and (2) a playful, upbeat adult behavior that might be described as rhythmic and joyful. The first style is seen as caregivers attempt to regulate or promote a particular infant state (such as relaxation, contentment, or sleep), and the second style, the communication of emotional information (such as mutual enjoyment and love of music).

Experts believe babies as young as 3 months can distinguish between certain melodies. Musical infant babbling has been described as tonal and rhythmic babble (Gordon, 1986). Tonal babble is babbling in a single pitch, the babble sounding like a monotone singer. In rhythmic babble the child's body or voice displays a rhythmic beat or quality.

Nursery, cultural, and folk tunes can be introduced in intimate and pleasant settings. Simple, safe musical instruments are enjoyed, and moving to music is natural to young children. Wolf (2000) suggests that educators start with songs they love, ones sung to them as children. Others suggest using children's music recorded by well-known performers. Names like Raffi, Ella Jenkins, Hap Palmer, Tom Hunter, and others are familiar to most early childhood educators. Some educators recommend Bach preludes and Vivaldi's *Springtime* Symphony along with other classical pieces. Two benefits of musical activities for some older preschoolers and primary children are believed to be enhanced abstract reasoning and **spatial-temporal reasoning**.

Scientists are finding that the human brain may be "prewired" for music. They suspect that some forms of intelligence are heightened by music. Although controversial at present, some researchers believe learning musical skills in childhood can help children do better at mathematics.

Schmid (2010) confirms the beliefs of many educators.

Words and music are such natural partners that it seems obvious they go together. Now science is confirming that those abilities are linked in the brain, a finding that might even lead to better stroke treatment. (p. A6)

Only more studies with more children will prove whether music produces lasting benefits in cognition.

---

**spatial-temporal reasoning** — the mental arrangement of ideas and/or images in a graphic pattern indicating their relationships over time.

See Additional Resources at the end of this chapter for favorite musical and movement activities and song books.

## READING TO INFANTS

Some parents read books aloud during a mother's later stages of pregnancy, believing the practice will produce some positive results. Research findings suggest that infants remember and give greater attention to stories read to them before their birth. Conclusive research evidence is yet to verify this. Zambo and Hansen (2007) suggest that from birth to 3 months, read-alouds are purely an emotional connection between the infant and caregiver.

> Being held, feeling good, and having a familiar, conforming voice are more important than the kind of book or the content of the story. Lullabies, singsong stories, and other repetitive, rhythmic experiences bring joy and comfort to infants and establish a special time together for child and caregiver. (p. 34)

Between 6 and 12 months, some infants will sit and look at a picture book with an adult. It is the sound of the reader's voice that gets the young child's attention, even before the child's focus shifts to the pictures. The warmth and security of being held and the reader's voice make for a very pleasurable combination.

The child may want to grab pages and test the book in his mouth or try to turn pages. His head may swivel to look at the adult's mouth. If the child has brought a book to the adult, he will usually want to sit on the adult's lap as both go through the book. Children get ever more adept at turning pages as their first birthday nears (Figure 1–22). Familiar objects in colorful illustrations set on white or plain backgrounds and large faces seem to be particularly fascinating. Infants seem to respond well to and enjoy the rhyme they hear.

Adult reading to infants younger than 12 months of age is increasingly recommended, for researchers believe the infant is learning about the sound patterns in words and how words are formed. Book-reading techniques include reading something the adult enjoys with average volume and expression, using gesturing or pointing when called for, promoting child

FIGURE 1–22 Ryan is trying to turn a page.

imitation, letting the child turn sturdy pages, and making animal or sound noises. A good rule of thumb is to stop before the child's interest wanes. Adults may find that many infants enjoy repeated reading of the same book. Some parents are very adept at sharing picture books. These parents find **cues** in book features, such as familiar objects, events depicted, sounds, colors, and so on, that give the infant pleasure, as may be evidenced by the adult saying, "It's a dog like our Bowser!" Skilled early childhood educators realize it is the colorful illustrations that attract, so they name and point to features and when possible relate word to like objects found in the classroom. They also attempt to make illustrations relevant to the child's past experience.

Colorful books with sturdy or plastic-coated pages or cardboard books are plentiful. Books of cotton fabric and ones with flaps to lift and peek under, soft furry patches to feel, rough sandpaper to touch, and holes to look through or stick a finger through are books that include enjoyable sensory exploration. Homemade collections of family photographs have delighted many young children. Picture books with simple, large illustrations or photos that are set against a contrasting background and books that are constructed to stand on their own when opened are also popular.

There are a number of literary classics (although not all experts agree to the same titles) that most children in our culture experience. Many of these involve rhyme and rhythm. They have, over time, become polished gems passed onto succeeding generations. Some of these are songs that have been published as books, and include:

Here We Go Round the Mulberry Bush

One, Two, Buckle My Shoe

Hush-a-Bye Baby

Twinkle, Twinkle, Little Star

Rock-a-Bye Baby

Ba Ba Blacksheep

## RECORDINGS

Growing numbers of CDs, tapes, and videos are being produced for infants. Infants listen and sometimes move their bodies rhythmically. Research is yet to confirm the educational or language-developing benefits claimed by manufacturers of infant recordings whether audio or visual. In *The Journal of Pediatrics*, Interlandi (2007) reports a new study that included a group of 1,000 families and reviewed the use of infant DVDs; this report suggests that babies who watch recordings fared worst with DVDs than with several other types of programming in terms of educational or language-developing benefits.

> Exposure to educational shows, like "Sesame Street," and non-educational ones, like "SpongeBob SquarePants," had no net effect on language, researchers said—but for every hour that infants 8 to 16 months spent watching the baby DVDs, they understood six to eight fewer words, out of a set of 90, than infants who didn't watch. (p. 14)

## EARLY EXPERIENCE WITH WRITING TOOLS

As early as 10 to 12 months, infants will watch intently as someone makes marks on a surface or paper. They will reach and attempt to do the marking themselves. Large chalk, thick crayons, or large crayon "chunks" are recommended for exploring, but caregivers are reminded to supervise closely because of infants' tendency to put small objects in their mouths. Large-sized paper (for example, torn flat grocery brown bags) taped at the edges to surfaces and chalkboards work well. The child may not realize the writing tool is making marks but may imitate and gleefully move the whole arm. Many believe it is simply not worth the effort to supervise very young children during this activity and save this activity until the children are older.

---

**cues** — prompts or hints that aid recognition, such as a parent pointing to and/or saying "teddy bear" when sharing a picture book illustration. This is done because the infant is familiar with his own teddy bear.

## MONITORING INFANT DEVELOPMENT

Stark, Chazen-Cohen, and Jerald (2002) point out that normal paths of development within various domains serve as reference points to assess infant competence. Infant assessments undertaken by educators try to identify strengths and developmental areas where the infant and/or family may need supportive assistance to promote optimal infant growth. Maternal health histories sometimes provide clues, as do home visits and daily or periodic educator-family interactions. An examination of whether the school's schedules, activities, staff, and curriculum need to change or adapt takes place frequently so that each child's individual needs have every chance of being met.

Infants should be observed daily with an eye toward assessing developmental milestones and mental and physical health, and educators must be knowledgeable of ages and stages. In a busy center, making dated notes is suggested as new, questionable, or important behaviors are observed. A notepad in a handy pocket is recommended. Frequent staff meetings should discuss individual infant language behaviors and development. This is followed by planning sessions that create individual learning plans and family consultation when necessary.

Eiserman and associates (2007) note that hearing loss may be an "invisible" condition. Dramatic improvements in hearing screening technology and growth in the number of hospitals that do at-birth screenings have occurred in the past 10 years. Educators realize hearing loss can occur at anytime, either swiftly or gradually. The American Speech-Language-Hearing Association (2001, 2004) estimates approximately 35 percent of preschoolers (including infants) will have repeated episodes of ear infection that nearly always cause a temporary loss that can significantly disrupt language acquisition.

## IMPLICATIONS FOR FAMILIES

Family attitudes about their infant's communicating abilities may influence the infant's progress, in part by affecting how the family responds to the infant. These attitudes are the early roots of the critical partnership between adult and child and the child's sense of feeling lovable and powerful. Consequently, they influence the child's assessment of self.

Men Fox, bestselling author of children's books, and *Reading Magic: Why Reading Aloud to Our Children Will Change Their Lives Forever* (2001) offers the following information to parents and families with infants.

Recent brain research has revealed that the early years of life are more critical to a child's development than we ever realized. Children's brains are only 25 percent developed at birth. From that moment, whenever a baby is fed, cuddled, played with, talked to, sung to or read to, the other 75 percent of its brain begins to develop. And the more stimulation the baby has through its senses of touch, taste, smell, sight, and hearing, the more rapidly that development will occur. It's as if the brain were an excited acrobat learning fantastic tricks with every new piece of information, with every scrap of new stimulation. Amazing though it may seem, the crucial connections that determine how clever, creative, and imaginative a child will be are already laid down by the time that child turns one. (p. 13–14)

Special infant projects to promote later school success have provided information in this area. Positive home factors mentioned include the following:

- a lot of attention by socially responsive caregivers
- little or no disruption of bonding attachment between the infant and his primary caregiver during the first year
- availability of space and objects to explore
- good nutrition
- active and interactive exchanges and play time
- parent knowledge of developmental milestones and the child's emerging skills
- parent confidence in infant handling

● maintenance of the child's physical robustness

● positive attention and touching in play exchange

Parent (or family) stress and less-than-desirable quality in child-parent interactions seem to hinder children's language development. Because most families face stress, a family's reaction to stress, rather than stress itself, is the determining factor. In today's busy families, time spent interacting and talking to infants and young children needs to remain a family priority.

Good advice for families includes not worrying about teaching as much as creating a rich and emotionally supportive home atmosphere. A rich atmosphere is one that offers opportunity and companionship rather than expensive toys and surroundings. Current research indicates that families who spontaneously speak about what the child is interested in and who zoom in and out of the child's play as they go about their daily work are responsive and effective families. Also, families should know early and late "talkers" usually show little difference in speaking ability by age 3. The variation between children with respect to the onset and accomplishment of most human characteristics covers a wide range when considering what is normal and expected.

Munir and Rose (2008) describe healthy social behavior in infancy as well as infants who display possible early autistic behaviors.

Healthy infants as young as 6 or 8 months do communicate and respond nonverbally to social cues. Most look up or turn at the sound of their name. By 12 months, they typically babble and point at objects. By 16 months, they say single words; by 24 months, two-word phrases. In contrast, children with autism seldom make meaningful eye contact or respond to familiar voices. They may never speak. Their play is often repetitive and characterized by limited imagination. Others may simply flap their hands in excitement or disappointment.

On their own, none of these signs means a child has autism or another development disorder. Nevertheless, if a child has any of these signs, he or she merits evaluation. (p. 64)

Regardless of the setting, the experts agree the primary need of infants and toddlers is emotional connection (Lloyd-Jones, 2002). Human relationships are the key, and emotional development is critical for growth. Children of the poor, who are considered to be at-risk, may escape at-risk status if they share the following commonalities. They live in large, extended families that provide supportive language stimulation and encouragement, and they have no other social or biological risks present. Their families manage to safeguard their infants' and older children's health. Intervention and social service programs may also have been accessible. It is the isolated poor families with multiple risk factors, including abusive home environments, whose children are the most negatively affected.

## SUMMARY

Each child grows in language ability in a unique way. The process starts before birth with the development of sensory organs. Caregivers play an important role in a child's growth and mastery of language.

Perceptions gained through life experiences serve as the base for future learning of words and speech. Babbling, sound making, and imitation occur, and first words appear.

A number of environmental factors, including poverty, may influence a child's language acquisition. Adults' attitudes concerning infants' intellectual and communication abilities are important also. Most children progress through a series of language ability stages and milestones at about the same ages (Figure 1–23) and become adult-like speakers during the preschool period. The way children learn language is not clearly understood, hence the numerous differing theories of language acquisition.

Technology has permitted neuroscientists to research infant abilities in greater depth than ever before. Research has enlightened educators who are awed by discoveries concerning infant's learning capacities and abilities

| INFANT'S AGE | STAGES OF LANGUAGE DEVELOPMENT |
|---|---|
| before birth | Listens to sounds. Reacts to loud sounds. |
| at birth | Birth cry is primal, yet individual—vowel-like. Cries to express desires (for food, attention, and so on) or displeasure (pain or discomfort). Makes eating, sucking, and small throaty sounds. Hiccups. Crying becomes more rhythmic and resonant during first days. Shows changes in posture—tense, active, or relaxed. |
| first days | Half cries become vigorous; whole cries begin to take on depth and range. Coughs and sneezes. |
| 1 month | Three to four vowel sounds apparent. Seems to quiet movements and attend to mother's voice. Eating sounds mirror eagerness. Sighs and gasps. Smiles in sleep. |
| 2–3 months | Coos and makes pleasurable noises (babbling) and blowing and smacking sounds. Most vowel sounds are present. Open vowel-like babbles may begin. Consonant sounds begin, usually the following—*b, d, g, h, l, m, n, p, t.* Markedly less crying. Smiles and squeals and may coo for half a minute. Peers into faces. Adults may recognize distinct variations in cries (i.e., cries that signal fear, tiredness, hunger, pain, and so on). Focuses on mother's face and turns head to her voice. May be frightened by loud or unfamiliar noise. May blow bubbles and move tongue in and out. |
| 4–5 months | Sound play is frequent. Social smiling more pronounced. Can whine to signal boredom. May laugh. Reacts to tone of voice. Seems to listen and enjoy music. Likes adult vocal play and mimicking. Favorite people seem to induce verbalness. Babbles several sounds in one breath. Body gestures signal state of comfort or discomfort. Attracted to sounds. Approaching 6 months of age, may start to show understanding of words often used in household. Turns head and looks at speaking family members. Consonant sounds more pronounced and frequent. |
| 6–8 months | Increased babbling and sound making; repeats syllables; imitates motions and gestures; uses nonverbal signals; vocalizes all vowel sounds; reduplication of utterances; more distinct intonation. Increases understanding of simple words. Enjoys making noise with toys and household objects. Repeats actions to hear sounds again. May blow toy horn. Delights in rhythmic vocal play interchange, especially those that combine touching and speaking. Twists and protrudes tongue, smacks, and watches mother's mouth and lips intently. May look at picture books for short period or watch children's television programs. |
| 9–10 months | May make kiss sounds. Increasing understanding of words like *no-no, mommy, daddy, ball, hat,* and *shoe.* May play Pat-a-cake and wave bye-bye. May hand books to adults for sharing. Uses many body signals and gestures. May start jargonlike strings of sounds, grunts, gurgles, and whines. Listens intently to new sounds. Imitates. |
| 11–14 months | Reacts to an increasing number of words. Speaks first word(s) (usually words with one syllable or repeated syllable). Points to named objects or looks toward named word. Makes sounds and noises with whatever is available. Imitates breathing noises, animal noises (like dog's bark or cat's meow), or environmental noises (like "boom" or train toot). Uses many body signals, especially "pick me up" with arms outstretched and reaching for another's hand, meaning "come with me." May understand as many as 40 to 50 words. At close to 15 months, one word has multiple meanings. Jargonlike strings of verbalness continue. The child's direction of looking gives clues to what the child understands, and the child may have a speaking vocabulary of 10 or more words. Uses first pretend play gestures such as combing hair with a spoon-shaped object, drinking from a pretend cup, pretending to eat an object, and pretending to talk with another on a toy telephone. |

**FIGURE 1–23** Milestones in developing language behavior.

to sort and categorize human speech sounds. Deprivation, abuse, and neglect can affect infants' brain function, as can sight and hearing acuity.

Early in life, infants and parents form a reciprocal relationship, reacting in special ways to each other. The quality and quantity of caregiver attention becomes an important factor in language development.

The child progresses from receiving to sending language, which is accompanied by gestures and nonverbal communication. From infancy, the child is an active participant, moving closer to the two-way process required in language usage and verbal communication.

Staff members in infant care programs can possess interaction skills that offer infants optimal opportunities for speech development. Constant monitoring of each child's progress in reaching milestones is undertaken to ensure that each child's needs are evaluated. Recognized needs can then receive staff attention and program particulars can be adjusted.

## ADDITIONAL RESOURCES

### Readings

Acredolo, L., & Goodwyn, S. (2000). *Baby minds: Brain-building games your baby will love to play.* New York: Bantam Books.

Anderson, N. A. (2007). *What should I read aloud? A guide to 200 best-selling picture books.* Newark, DE: International Reading Association.

Jahromi, L. B., & Shifter, C. A. (2007). Individual differences in the contribution of maternal soothing to infant stress reduction. *Infancy, 11*(3), 1061–1099.

Karp, H. (2002). *The happiest baby on the block.* New York: Bantam Dell.

Lewis, T., Amini, F., & Lannon, R. (2000). *A general theory of love.* New York: Random House.

Murray, C. G. (2007). *Simple signing with young children: A guide for infant, toddler, and preschool teachers.* Beltsville, MD: Gryphon House.

### Infant Books

Alborough, J. (2000). *Hugs.* Cambridge, MA: Candlewick Press.

Aston, D. H. (2006). *Mamma outside, mama inside.* New York: Henry Holt.

Bauer, M. D. (2003). *Toes, ear, and nose.* New York: Little Simon.

Boyton, S. (2004). *Moo baa, la la la!* New York: Simon & Schuster.

DK Publishing Inc. (1998). *Touch and feel farm* [sensory board book]. New York: Author.

Hindley, J. (2006). *Baby talk: A book of first words and phrases.* New York: Candlewick Press.

Katz, K. (2000). *Where is baby's belly button?* New York: Little Simon.

Miller, M. (1998). *Baby faces.* New York: Little Simon.

Oxenbury, H. (1981). *Dressing.* New York: Little Simon.

Oxenbury, H. (1995). *I hear.* New York: Candlewick Press.

Saltzberg, B. (2004). *Noisy kisses.* San Diego: Red Wagon.

Shott, S. (1996). *Baby's world.* New York: Dutton.

### Infant Play Games

Lansky, V. (2001). *Games babies play: From birth to twelve months.* New York: Book Peddlers.

Rowley, B. (2000). *Baby days: Activities, ideas, and games.* New York: Hyperion.

Silberg, S. (2001). *Games to play with babies.* Beltsville, MD: Gryphon House

Wilner, I. (2000). *Baby's game book.* New York: Greenwillow.

### Infant Music, Movement Activities, and Song Books

Beaton, C. (2008). *Playtime rhymes for little people.* Cambridge, MA: Barefoot Books (CD and book)

Beall, P. C., & Nipp, S. (1996). *Wee sing for baby.* New York: G. P. Putnam Publishing.

Burton, M. (1989). *Tail, toes, eyes, ears, nose.* New York: Harper and Row.

Charmer, K., Murphy, M., & Clark, C. (2006). *The encyclopedia of infant and toddler activities.* Beltsville MD: Gryphon House.

Flom, R., Gentile, D. A., & Pick, A. D. (2008). Infants' discrimination of happy and sad music, Infant *Behavior and Development* 31(4)716-28.

Long, S. (2002). *Hush little baby.* San Francisco: Chronicle Books.

Manning, J. (1998). *My first songs.* New York: Harper-Collins.

Nursery songs. (1997). New York: McClanahan Book Co.

Shore, R. (1998). *Bach and baby bedtime* [cassette or CD]. Huntington Beach, CA: Youngheart Music.

### Helpful Websites

Beginning with Books
http://www.clpgh.org/clp/bwb/bestbaby.html
Useful for infant book selection.

National Federation of Families for Children's Mental Health
http://www.ffcmh.org

Contains information on government policy and research. Spanish publications available.

National Parent Information Network
http://npin.org
Contains readings and parenting resources.

Sensory Awareness Foundation
http://www.sensoryawareness.org
Lists available infant experiences.

Go to www.cengagebrain.com to access this text's Education Course-Mate website where you'll find helpful resource such as video activities, glossary flashcards, interactive exercises, quiz questions, and more!

# Review It and Use It

A. Write your own theory of language acquisition. (A child learns language . . .) Compare and contrast your theory with those in this chapter.

B. Finish the following: Early childhood educators working in group infant care programs who wish to give infants opportunities to acquire language should carefully monitor their ability to . . . (list specific techniques).

C. Write definitions for the following: articulation, bonding, echolalia, moderation level, infant signing phonation, critical brain growth periods, larynx, and joint attention milestone.

D. Explain the difference between cooing and babbling.

E. Finish the following passage: Language is a kind of game infants learn—a game played with precise recognizable rules. To learn the game, it is best to have adults in your life who . . .

F. Select the best answer.

1. Environmental factors that can affect future language development start
   a. at birth.
   b. before birth.
   c. during infancy.
   d. during toddlerhood.

2. The tone of a parent's voice is
   a. understood when a child learns to speak in sentences.
   b. less important than the parent's words.
   c. understood before actual words are understood.
   d. less important than the parent's actions.

3. In acquiring language, the child
   a. learns only through imitation.
   b. is one participant in a two-part process.
   c. learns best when parents ignore the child's unclear sounds.
   d. does not learn by imitating.

4. Select the true statement about babbling.
   a. Why babbling occurs is not clearly understood.
   b. Babbling is unimportant.
   c. Babbling predicts how early a child will start talking.
   d. Babbling rarely lasts beyond 1 year of age.

5. How a child acquires language is
   a. clearly understood.
   b. not important.
   c. only partly understood.
   d. rarely a subject for study.

G. With a partner, create a parent billboard drawing or other pictorial artwork and relate it to infant language development. Write a clever caption (slogan). Share with the group. [Example: Picture of an infant and father. Caption: "Hey big daddy, that sweet talk and hug are just what I needed." (Not very clever? You can do better.)]

H. What is the significance for early childhood educators of current discoveries concerning young children's brain growth?

## STUDENT ACTIVITIES

1. What parental expectations of infants might interfere with the infant's ability to develop the idea he is an effective communicator? List three or four. Give examples from your own experience if possible. Compare your list with that of a classmate.

2. Observe two infants (birth to 12 months). Note situations in which the infants make sounds and how adults (parents or teachers) react to the sound making.

3. Sit with a young infant facing you. Have a notepad handy. Remain speechless and motionless. Try to determine what moment-to-moment needs the child has, and try to fulfill each need you recognize. Try not to add anything new; just respond to what you think the child needs. Write a description of the needs observed and your feelings.

4. Try sharing a colorful, simple book with an 8- to 12-month-old. What behaviors did you observe?

5. Create a new game, rhyme, or movement word play, and test it on an infant 6 to 12 months of age.

6. Locate three books you think would be appropriate for older infants, and share them with the class.

7. Observe three children younger than 1 year of age each interacting with an adult for one 10- to 30-minute period. Try parks, family homes, or doctors' waiting rooms. Take notes concerning their verbal ability and conversational interactions. What language-developing techniques were present? Which child would you choose to be if you could change places with one of the observed children? List your reasons why.

8. Read and then pair up with a classmate to discuss and react to the following. Keep notes.

What research actually shows is that infant-directed speech which is high-pitched, sing-song, repetitive and drawn out is the type of speech that infants in their first year of life not only hear better but also the language to which they are most responsive. In the first year speaking to infants in a way that gets a response is far more important than using "proper" adult grammar and words. It's not so much what parents say as that they say anything at all. Using "baby talk" beyond one year is probably not the best idea. (Ciccarelli, 2006, p. 3E)

What are presented here are classic games that have pleased many infants over the years. You are urged to try your hand at creating others. Pleasurable features to add to your creations are sound variety, rhymes, noises, emphasized words, and touching and encouraging infant movements.

### What Have We Here?

*Here's two little eyes big and round*
*And two little ears to hear all sounds,*
*One little nose smells a flower sweet,*
*One little mouth likes food to eat.*
*Here are ten little fingers to grasp and wiggle,*
*Tickle ten toes and there's a giggle.*
*Here's a button on a tiny tummy*
*Around and around—that feels funny!*

### Round And Round

(This is a frequently used tickling verse of English mothers.)

*Round and round the garden (Said slowly while circling the baby's palm)*
*One step, two steps (Walking fingers toward a tickling spot at neck, stomach, or underarms, and said a little faster)*
*Tickle you there! (Said very fast)*

### Two Little Eyes

*Two little eyes that open and close.*
*Two little ears and one little nose.*
*Two little cheeks and one little chin.*
*Two little lips that open and grin.*

### Baby Rides

*This is the way baby rides, (Bounce infant on knees; with each new verse, bounce a little faster)*
*The baby rides, the baby rides.*
*This is the way baby rides, so early in the morning.*
*This is the way the farmer rides . . .*
*This is the way the jockey rides . . .*

### Little Mouse

*Hurry, scurry little mouse*
*There he is down at your toes. (Touch child's toes)*
*Hurry, scurry little mouse*
*Past your knees up he goes. (Touch child's knees)*
*Hurry, scurry little mouse*
*Up to where your tummy is. (Touch child's tummy)*
*Hurry, scurry little mouse*
*He wants to give you a mousy kiss. (Give child a loud kiss)*

### Here We Go

*Here we go up, up, up (Lift child's legs up)*
*Here we go down, down, down (Lower child's legs down)*
*Here we go backward and forward (Sway child backward and forward)*
*And here we go round and round (Move child's legs in air)*

### What Have We Here?

*These are baby's fingers, (Touch child's fingers)*
*These are baby's toes, (Touch child's toes)*
*This is baby's belly button, (Touch child's tummy)*
*Round and round it goes! (Tickle child's tummy button)*

### Whoa Horse

*Giddy-up, giddy-up, giddy-up horsey (Bounce child on knees—last line, let child slip over knees while sliding lower on adult's extended legs)*
*Giddy-up, giddy-up, go, go, go. Giddy-up, giddy-up, Whoa!*

## OBJECTIVES

After reading this chapter, you should be able to:

- Discuss phonology, grammar, and semantics.
- List three characteristics of toddler language.
- Identify adult attitudes and behaviors that aid toddlers' speech development.

## KEY TERMS

| | |
|---|---|
| concept | phoneme |
| grammar | phonetics |
| inflections | phonology |
| inner speech | pragmatics |
| joint attention | prosodic speech |
| modifiers | semantics |
| morpheme | symbols |
| morphology | syntax |
| over-regularization | telegraphic speech |

## The Toddler Teacher

*Kelsa (26 months) and her grandfather entered the classroom. He drew me aside after his granddaughter had run off to the housekeeping area. With a smile he shared what Kelsa had done and said to him. "We were watching TV, and I commented on something," he said. "She got up and stood right in front of me. Next, she cupped my cheeks with her hands and said, 'Look at me when you say words.'" He laughed. I explained, "Sometimes with toddlers we can understand their words only if they speak right into our face."*

## Questions to Ponder

1. Is this a teacher strategy that helps toddlers?
2. Was the teacher's explanation to Kelsa's grandfather sufficient, or would a longer explanation have been better?
3. Is Kelsa's language acquisition advanced or about average for her age?

If you were amazed at the infant's and the 1-year-old's ability, wait until you meet the toddler! Toddlerhood marks the beginning of a critical language-growth period. Never again will words enter the vocabulary at the same rate; abilities emerge in giant spurts almost daily. When children stop and focus on things, from specks on the floor to something very large, concentration is total—every sense organ seems to probe for data.

Toddlerhood begins with the onset of toddling (walking), a little before or after the child's first birthday. The toddler is perched at the gateway of a great adventure, eager to proceed, investigating as she goes, and attempting to communicate what she discovers and experiences (Figure 2–1). "The bags are packed" with what has been learned in infancy. The child will both monologue and dialogue as she ages, always knowing much more than can be verbally expressed. During toddlerhood she uses words whose meanings have been rooted in social acts and may have significance.

**FIGURE 2–1** Exploring a small slide is a toddler adventure.

Toddlers are action-oriented. They simultaneously act on and perceive the environment around them. Toddlers' thoughts become a sensorimotor activity. As they age higher-level thinking happens, and toddlers begin to think first and then act.

By the age of 2, toddlers' brains are as active as those of adults. The metabolic rate keeps rising, and by the age of 3, toddlers' brains are two and a half times more active than the brains of adults—and they stay that way throughout the first decade of life (Shore, 1997). Quindlen (2001) compares the working rate of a toddler's mind to an adult's mind as that of a race car to a lawn tractor.

An important milestone during the toddler period occurs when the toddler uses symbolic (speech) communication rather than communicating primarily through body actions and gestures. This is made possible by the child's growing mental capability and the richness of the child's affective and life experiences. Many experts believe that a warm, close relationship with a caregiver promotes the child's communication ability and provides satisfaction in itself. Experts agree that the primary need of toddlers (and infants) is emotional connection.

From a few spoken words, the toddler will move to purposeful speech that gains what is desired, controls others, allows personal comments, and accompanies play. It becomes evident that the toddler recognizes the give and take of true conversation. She also realizes the difference between being the speaker and being the one who listens and reacts—the one who persuades or is persuaded, the one who questions or is questioned. Toddlers become aware that everything has a name and that playfully trying out new sounds is an enjoyable pursuit. The child's meanings for the few words she uses at the start of the toddler period may or may not be the same as common usage. As children age, they will continually and gradually modify their private meanings of the words in their speaking vocabulary to conform to public meanings.

Cambourne (1988) describes the enormous complexity of learning to talk:

> When one has learned to control the oral version of one's language, one has learned literally countless thousands of conventions. Each language spoken

on the Earth today (some three or four thousand) comprises a unique, arbitrary set of signs, and rules for combining those signs to create meaning. These conventions have no inherent "rightness" or "logic" to them, just as driving on the right or left side of the road has no intrinsic rightness or logic to it. Yet each language is an amazingly complex, cultural artifact, comprising incredibly complex sets of sounds, words, and rules for combining them, with equally numerous and complex systems for using them for different social, personal, and cognitive purposes. (p. 252)*

Even though toddlers have an innate predisposition for learning to communicate, they face four major tasks in learning the rule systems of language: (1) understanding phonology (the sound system of a language); (2) learning syntax (a system of rules governing word order and combinations that give sense to short utterances and sentences, often referred to as *grammar*); (3) learning semantics (word meanings); and (4) learning pragmatics (varying speech patterns depending on social circumstances and the context of situations). The understanding of these rule systems takes place concurrently—one area complementing and promoting the other. Rule systems form without direct instruction as toddlers grope to understand the speech of others, to express themselves, and to influence others both verbally and nonverbally. We can think of the toddler as one who tests many hypotheses—the kind of thinker who over time can unconsciously discover and formulate the rules of language.

Language emergence is but one of the toddler's achievements. Intellectually, toddlers' process, test, and remember language input. They develop their own rules, which change as they recognize what are and are not permissible structures in their native language. Other important developmental achievements intersect during late toddlerhood as children increasingly shift

to symbolic thinking and language use. Gains in social, emotional, and physical development are apparent, as are issues of power and autonomy.

## PHONOLOGY

Toddlers learn the **phonology** of their native language—its phonetic units and its particular and sometimes peculiar sounds. This is no easy job! The young language learner must sort sounds into identifiable groups and categories while she is possibly experiencing the speech of a variety of people in various settings. Because spoken language is characterized by a continuous flow of word sounds, this makes the task even more difficult.

After the child learns sounds, she learns sound combinations. It is prudent to point out here that not every sound in one language exists in another. Consequently, English language learners may be unfamiliar with new sounds in English.

A **phoneme** is the smallest unit of sound that distinguishes one utterance from another—implying a difference in meaning. English has 46 to 50 phonemes, depending on which expert is consulted. Language from a phonetic perspective might be conceived as a continuous sequence of sounds produced when air is pushed through the throat and mouth, and then received and recognized by sensitive ear structures.

Languages are divided into vowels and consonants. When pronouncing vowels, the breath stream flows freely from the vocal cords; when pronouncing consonants, the breath stream is blocked and molded in the mouth and throat area by soft tissue, muscle tissue, and bone, with the tongue and jaw often working together. The child focuses on those sounds heard most often. The toddler's speech is full of repetitions and rhythmic speech play. Toddler babbling of this type continues and remains pleasurable during early toddlerhood. Sounds that are combinations of vowels and consonants increase. Vowels are acquired early, and most studies suggest that vowel production is reasonably accurate by age 3 (Donegan, 2002). Low, unrounded vowels (that is, *i, o, u*) are favored during infancy. Consonant sounds that are difficult to form will continue to be spoken without

*From Brian Cambourne, *The Whole Story*. Copyright ©1988.

---

**phonology** — the sound system of a language and how it is represented with an alphabetic code.
**phoneme** — the smallest unit of speech that distinguishes one utterance from another.

Learned by
    Age 1 to 3 = h, m, n, p, w.
    Age 2 to 4 = b, d, g, k.
    Age 2-1/2 to 4 = f, y.
    Age 2 to 6 = t, ng.
    Age 3 to 6 = r, l.
    Age 3 to 8 = s, z.
    Age 3-1/2 to 7 = ch, sh.
    Age 4 to 7 = j.
    Age 4 to 8 = v.
    Age 4-1/2 to 7 = th (unvoiced)
    Age 5 to 8 = th (voiced)
    Age 6 to 8 = zh.

**FIGURE 2–2** Average age of consonant sound production.

being close approximations of adult sounds until the child reaches 5 or 6 years of age or is even slightly older (Figure 2–2). Early childhood teachers realize that, in many instances, they will have to listen closely and watch for nonverbal clues to understand child speech.

It is a difficult task for the child to make recognizable sounds with mouth, throat, and breath control working in unison. Perfecting the motor control of speech-producing muscles is a sophisticated skill that comes ahead of many other physical skills. It requires precise and swift movements of the tongue and lips. This is all but fully developed when most other mechanical skills are far below levels of their future accomplishment.

Much of early speech has been described as unintelligible or gibberish. The toddler seems to realize that conversations come in long strings of sound. Rising to the occasion, the child imitates the rhythm of the sound but utters only a few understandable words.

Toddlers hear a word as an adult hears it. Sometimes, they know the proper pronunciation but are unable to reproduce it. The child may say "pway" for *play*. If the parent says "pway," the child objects, showing confusion and perhaps frustration. Toddler talk represents the child's best imitation, given present ability. Parents and teachers are urged to look at toddlers' speech mistakes as evidence that children are learning in an intelligent way.

Adult-to-child talk can be defined as "child-directed speech," that is, a set of speech modifications commonly found in the language adults use to address young children. Most speech researchers divide adult-child language into five main categories: pedagogy, control, affection, social exchange, and information.

The pedagogy mode is characterized by slow adult speech that is over enunciated or overemphasizes one or two words. This type of adult speech is "tailor-made" for 1- or 2-year-olds trying to segment the speech stream into comprehensible units.

Many adults tend to label happenings and objects with easy-to-learn, catchy variations, such as *choo-choo*, *bow-wow*, and so forth. Additional parental language techniques include the following:

1. Labeling themselves as "Mommy" or "Daddy," instead of "I" or "me" in speech.
2. Limiting topics in sentences.
3. Using short and simple sentences.
4. Using repetition.
5. Expanding or recasting children's one-word or unfinished utterances. If the toddler says "kitty," the parent offers "Kitty's name is Fluff."
6. Using a wide range of voice frequencies to gain the child's attention and initiate a communication exchange.
7. Carrying both sides of an adult-child conversation. The adult asks questions, and then answers them too. This technique is most often used with infants but is also common during the toddler period. The adult is modeling a social exchange.
8. Echoing a child's invented word. Many toddlers adopt a special word for a certain object (Figure 2–3). The whole family may use the child's word in conversational exchanges also.

When adults feel infants and toddlers are able communicators, it is reflected in their actions and speech. This can, and usually does, increase children's communicative abilities and opportunities.

Early childhood educators believe caregivers should treat toddlers as communicating children, and avoid childlike or cutesy

**FIGURE 2–3** The teacher's comments concentrate on the hat when the hat is the object of children's attention.

expressions. They offer simple forms of speech and easy-to-pronounce words whenever possible, especially when they introduce new words.

Views on adult use of baby talk after the infancy period stress the idea that the practice may limit more mature word forms and emphasize dependency. On the other hand, adults may offer simplified, easily pronounced forms, such as *bow-wow* for a barking poodle. They later quickly switch to harder-to-pronounce forms when the child seems ready. In the beginning, though, most adults automatically modify their speech when speaking with toddlers by using short sentences and stressing key words.

Children progress with language at their individual rates and with varying degrees of clarity. Some children speak relatively clearly from their first tries. Other children, who are also progressing normally, take a longer time before their speech is easily understood. All basic sounds (50 including diphthongs) are perfected by most children by age 7 or 8.

## Morphology

A **morpheme** is the smallest unit of language standing by itself with recognized meaning. It can be a word or part of a word. Many prefixes (*un-*, *ill-*) and suffixes (*-s*, *-ness*, *-ed*, *-ing*) are morphemes with their own distinct meanings. The study of morphemes is called **morphology**. There are wide individual differences in the rates toddlers' utter morphemes. It is unfortunate if early childhood teachers or families attempt to compare the emerging speech of toddlers or equate greater speech usage with higher ability, thus giving the quiet toddler(s) perhaps less of their time.

Between the ages of 2 and 4 years, children gradually include a variety of different morphemes in their spontaneous utterances. There seems to be a common sequence in their appearance.

## SYNTAX

Languages have word orders and rules, and young children speak in word order and follow the rules of their native tongue. Children typically acquire the rules of grammar in their native language, with little difficulty, from normal communicative interactions with adults.

The rules for ordering words in sentences do not operate on specific words, but on classes of words such as nouns, verbs, and adjectives, and a relatively small number of syntactical rules can account for the production of a very large number of sentences. In some languages, the subject of a sentence follows the verb; in other languages, it precedes the verb.

**Modifiers** (descriptive words) in some languages have gender (male and female forms), but in others they do not. Plurals and possessive forms are unique to each language. Young speakers will make mistakes, but adults marvel at the grammar the child does use correctly, having learned the rules without direct instruction. One can compare children's mastery of **phonetics** to their mastery of **syntax**. The child's mastery of phonology is gradual, but the child's use of correct syntax is almost completely mastered from early beginning attempts.

**morpheme** — the smallest unit in a language that by itself has a recognizable meaning.
**morphology** — the study of the units of meaning in a language.
**modifiers** — words that give a special characteristic to a noun (for example, a large ball).
**phonetics** — pertaining to representing the sounds of speech with a set of distinct symbols, each denoting a single sound.
**syntax** — the arrangement of words as elements in a sentence to show their relationship.

By age 2, and sometimes as early as 18 months, children begin to string together two or more holophrases and have thereby arrived at the telegraphic stage. All telegraphic speech consists of acceptable grammatical sequences that are the precursors of the sentence.

From all the perceptions she has received and the words spoken to and about her, the child has noted regularities and has unconsciously formed rules, which are continually revised. Chukovsky (1963) describes this task:

> It is frightening to think what an enormous number of grammatical forms are poured over the poor head of the young child. And he, as if it were nothing at all, adjusts to all the chaos, constantly sorting out in rubrics the disorderly elements of words he hears, without noticing as he does this, his gigantic effort. If an adult had to master so many grammatical rules within so short a time, his head would surely burst. (p. 31)

**Grammar** involves the way sounds are organized to communicate meaning. With grammatical knowledge the young child can produce and understand a wide range of new, novel, grammatically correct, and meaningful sentences. As the child learns to talk during preschool years, she may construct many ungrammatical sentences and use words in unusual ways. The errors of the 2-year-old disappear as the child gains more control over language, but new kinds of errors appear in 3-year-olds, who are trying new forms of expression. An understanding of the general rules of grammar develops before an understanding of the exceptions to the rules. Correct grammar forms may change to incorrect forms as the child learns new rules. Slobin

(1971) gives an interesting example of this phenomenon:

> In all of the cases which have been studied . . . the first past tenses used are the correct forms of irregular verbs—came, broke, went, and so on. Apparently these irregular verbs in the past tense—which are the most frequent past tense forms in adult speech—are learned as separate vocabulary items at a very early age.
>
> Then, as soon as the child learns only one or two regular past tense forms—like helped and walked—he immediately replaces the correct irregular past tense forms with their incorrect overgeneralizations from the regular forms. Thus children say "it came off," "it broke," and "he did it" before they say "it comed off," "it breaked," and "he doed it." Even though the correct forms may have been practiced for several months, they are driven out of the child's speech by the **over-regularization**, and may not return for years. (p. 103)

In later years, during elementary school, the child will formally learn the grammar rules of the English language. What the child has accomplished before that time, however, is monumental. The amount of speech that already conforms to the particular syntactical and grammatical rules of language is amazing. The child has done this through careful listening and by mentally reorganizing the common elements in language that have been perceived.

The toddler's growing use of intonation and **inflections** (changes in loudness of voice) adds clarity, as do nonverbal gestures. The child is often insistent that adults listen.

The toddler's system of nonverbal signals, body postures, and motions that were used in

---

**grammar** — the rules of a specific language that include both written and spoken utterances and describe how that specific language works and the forms of speech that conform to the rules that well-schooled speakers and writers observe in any given language.

**over-regularization** — the tendency on the part of children to make the language regular, such as using past tenses like -ed on verb endings.

**inflections** — the grammatical "markers" such as plurals. Also, a change in pitch or loudness of the voice.

FIGURE 2–4 Teachers try to identify each child's individual communication style.

late infancy continues and expands, becoming part of the toddler's communication style (Figure 2–4). Many signals translated by mothers or care providers to strangers leave strangers bewildered as to how the mother or another adult could possibly know what the child wants. It may seem impossible based on what the stranger observed and heard.

English sentences follow a subject-verb-object sequence. The three fundamental properties of sentences are verb-object, subject-predicate, and modification, and most all human languages have rules for these basic sentential structures.

Learning grammar rules helps the toddler express ideas, and her understanding of syntax helps the child to be understood.

Our knowledge of the rules of combination determines how we construct and understand an infinite number of sentences from a finite vocabulary. Syntax gives language its power.

A person who listens closely to the older toddler will sometimes hear the child self-correct speech errors. Toddlers talk to themselves and to their toys often. It seems to aid the storage of words and memory. The toddler understands adult sentences because the child has internalized a set of finite rules or combinations of words.

## SEMANTICS

**Semantics** is the study of meanings and acquisition of vocabulary. It probes how the sounds of language are related to the real world and life experiences. The toddler absorbs meanings from both verbal and nonverbal communication sent and received. The nonverbal refers to expressive associations of words, such as rhythm, stress, pitch, gesture, body position, facial change, and so on. Adults perform important functions in the child's labeling and concept formation by giving words meaning in conversations.

The toddler who comes from a home that places little emphasis on expressing ideas in language may be exposed to a relatively restricted range of words for expressing conceptual distinctions. Every early childhood center should offer opportunities for children to learn a rich and varied vocabulary to refer to various experiences and to express ideas (Figure 2–5).

FIGURE 2–5 Toddlers begin to engage in social interactions with others.

---

**semantics** — the study of meanings associated with words and the acquisition of vocabulary.

In toddler classrooms, teachers have many opportunities to name objects and happenings as the day unfolds. Using teacher gesturing along with words (or pointing to illustrations and photographs in simple picture books or classroom signs) helps the toddler form a connection between what is seen and heard. Repeating words with voice stress can be done in a natural way while monitoring whether the child is still interested.

Word meanings are best learned in active, hands-on experiences rather than "repeat-after-me" situations. Meanings of words are acquired through their connotations, not their denotations, that is, in situations that consist of feelings and verbal and nonverbal messages with physical involvement. The word *cold*, for instance, means little until physically experienced. Toddlers assume that labels (words) refer to wholes instead of parts (the creature, not the tail) and to classes instead of items (all horses, not one horse) (Cowley, 2000).

When an older infant is first learning to talk, the same sound often serves for several words; for instance, *bah* can mean "bottle," "book," "bath," and "bye." And sometimes infants use one sound to name an object and also to express a more complicated thought; for example, a child may point to a ball and name it, but later may say the same word and mean, "I want to play with the ball. Roll it to me."

The child's **concept** building is an outgrowth and result of a natural human tendency to try to make sense of the surroundings. Attending to and pondering about the relationships, similarities, and differences in events and happenings, and mentally storing, remembering, and retrieving those ideas and impressions are important aspects of concept development. With young children's innate curiosity, drive, and desire to explore and experience, concepts are continually being formed, reformed, and modified.

Examples of toddler behavior demonstrate that conceptual conclusions happen daily in group and home care settings. When a child blows a whistle-shaped toy, licks and bites a plastic fruit, tightly clings to an adult when a dog barks, or says "hot" when pointing to a water faucet, one can see past experiences are basic to the child's concept development.

To understand how concept development is individual and based on life experiences, ask yourself what makes a cup a cup. How many distinguishing features can you list? Ask another adult to do the same. You will both probably list some of the following characteristics:

- has a handle
- holds liquids and substances
- is often round on top, tapering to a smaller round base or can be cylindrical
- is used as a standard measurement in cooking (8 ounces)
- is made from clay, plastic, glass, metal, or other solid substances
- can be used to drink liquids

Adults speaking about cups understand one another because they usually recognize the same distinguishing characteristic(s). If asked to get the cup on the shelf, they won't get a glass. A toddler using the word cup often means his personal drinking cup.

A toddler may overuse concepts in new situations. Perhaps a bandage on the tip of a brother's finger will be called a thimble. For a short time, all men are daddies, a cow may be called a big dog, and all people in white are feared. As mental maturity and life experiences increase, concepts change; small details and exceptions are noticed. Toddlers may use a word to refer to a smaller category than would adults. An example of this phenomenon is the toddler's use of the word *dog* only in reference to the child's pet rather than all dogs encountered.

Concepts, often paired mentally with words, aid categorizing. Concept words may have full, partial, or little depth of meaning. The toddler's level of thought is reflected in speech. When counting to three, the toddler may or may not know what "three" represents. Words are **symbols**.

---

**concept** — a commonly recognized element (or elements) that identifies groups or classes; usually has a given name.
**symbols** — things that stand for or suggest (such as pictures, models, word symbols, and so forth).

Pan and Gleason (1997) explain how young children acquire word meaning and also the symbolic nature of words:

First, it is important to note that the meaning of a word resides in speakers of a common language, not in the world of objects. The word is a sign that signifies a referent, but the referent is not the meaning of the word.

Let us assume that a child learns that the word *kitty* refers to her cat; in this case, the actual cat is the referent of the word kitty.

There is nothing intrinsic to cats that makes one or another name more appropriate or fitting—the relationship between the name and the thing is thus arbitrary, and it is by social convention in a particular language that speakers agree to call the animal by a particular word. This arbitrary relationship between the referent (the cat) and the sign for it (the word *cat*) is symbolic.

In a few words the relationship between a word and a referent is not arbitrary; an example of this is the word *hiss*. In this case the word resembles the sound; other words, such as *tick-tock*, *tinkle*, and *woof*, also fall in this category.

A toddler's firsthand sensory experiences are very important. Stored mental perceptions are attached to words. Words are only as rich as the experiences and depth of understanding behind them.

The activities and experiences found in subsequent chapters will help the early childhood teacher enrich the child's concepts by providing deeper meanings in a wide range of language arts. Every activity for young children—a total school program—gives them a language arts background full of opportunities to explore by handling, tasting, using their bodies, smelling, and touching, as well as by seeing and listening.

## PRAGMATICS

The subtleties of our language are multifaceted. **Pragmatics** is the study of how language is used effectively in a social context, or the practical aspect of oral communication. It is the study of who can say what, in what way, where and when, by what means, and to whom (Figure 2–6). Language is a tool in questioning, ordering, soothing, ridiculing, and engaging in other social actions. One can request quiet in the form of a question such as, "Can't anyone get a peaceful moment around here?" or talk longingly about the candy in a store for the purpose of obtaining it without making a direct request—as in, "Oh, they have my favorite kind of chocolate bar!".

The language that young children use to express desires, wishes, concerns, and interests becomes a reflection of their social selves. When a toddler communicates effectively, the toddler receives feedback from others. Many times, a sense of well-being elicited by positive events helps the child shape a feeling of competency and self-esteem. Not yet socially subtle in speech, the toddler has not learned the pragmatically useful or appropriate behaviors of older

### PRAGMATIC SKILLS

1. taking turns in a conversation with another
2. knowing you are supposed to answer when a question is asked
3. noticing nonverbal body cues, signals, gestures, and signs and then responding
4. introducing a topic in a conversation for the listener to understand
5. having the ability to stay on the subject of a conversation
6. maintaining the right amount of eye contact; not staring or turning away too frequently
7. using different communicative styles that suit different communicative partners
8. learning that in certain situations talking is inappropriate

**FIGURE 2–6** Pragmatic skills.

**pragmatics** — the study of how language is used effectively in a social context; varying speech patterns depending on social circumstances and the context of situations.

children. Toddlers seem to have just one goal: to get messages across by gaining adult attention regardless of who is present and in what situation. The world, from the toddler's perspective, revolves around the toddler and her need to communicate.

## ATTACHMENT AND DEVELOPMENT OF LANGUAGE SKILLS

Attachment problems can slow communicative development. Observers describe infants and toddlers in less-than-adequate care situations as fearful, apathetic, disorganized, and distraught. If responsive social interaction and adult feedback exchanges are minimal, limited, frightening, or confusing, the infant or toddler may display a marked lack of interest in holding or obtaining adult attention. During toddlerhood these children can fall behind in speech development. Lally (1997) describes the importance of toddler social interaction:

> Infants and toddlers develop their sense of who they are from the adults who care for them. They learn from their caregivers what to fear, what behaviors are appropriate, and how their communications are received and acted upon. They learn how successful they are at getting their needs met by others, what emotions and intensity levels of emotions to safely display, and how interesting others find them. (p. 288)

Toddlers are sometimes shy with newcomers, so caregivers cast their eyes to the side rather than searching a toddler's face at first meeting. They bend or squat to toddler eye level. When more comfortable conversing takes place, teachers comment on toddler movements while watching for child wariness and/or acceptance. They react and respond to all of toddlers' verbal overtures including babble, gestures, miscellaneous sound making, hand or body signs, or words. Teachers are enthusiastic and joyful companions celebrating toddler accomplishments with attentive and appreciative feedback. They explain what is happening between themselves and the toddler and also what is occurring in the environment around them.

## FIRST WORDS

Any time between 10 and about 22 months is considered within the normal range for first words. A vocabulary growth spurt happens around 18 to 22 months (Strickland & Schickedanz, 2004). First words are "building blocks" and "content words" (nouns, verbs) that carry a lot of meaning. They usually consist of names of important people or objects the toddler encounters daily and include functional words such as *up*, *out*, *night-night*, and *bye-bye* used in social contexts (Figure 2–7). Easy-to-pronounce words are more likely to be included in toddlers' early expressive vocabularies.

Single words can frequently go further than naming by representing a meaningful idea

---

**Sound effects**
baa baa, meow, moo, ouch, uh-oh, woof, yum-yum

**Food and drink**
apple, banana, cookie, cheese, cracker, juice, milk, water

**Animals**
bear, bird, bunny, dog, cat, cow, duck, fish, kitty, horse, pig, puppy

**Body parts and clothing**
diaper, ear, eye, foot, hair, hand, hat, mouth, nose, toe, tooth, shoe

**House and outdoors**
blanket, chair, cup, door, flower, keys, outside, spoon, tree, TV

**People**
baby, daddy, gramma, grampa, mommy, [child's own name]

**Toys and vehicles**
ball, balloon, bike, boat, book, bubbles, plane, truck, toy

**Actions**
down, eat, go, sit, up

**Games and routines**
bath, bye, hi, night-night, no, peek-a-boo, please, shhh, thank you, yes

**Adjectives and descriptives**
allgone, cold, dirty, hot

**FIGURE 2–7** Children's earliest words: examples from the vocabularies of children younger than 20 months. (From Berko Gleason, J. [1997]. *The development of language* [4th ed.]. Boston: Allyn and Bacon. Copyright © 1997 by Pearson Education. Reprinted by permission of the publisher.)

(a holophrase). The task of the adult includes both being responsive and guessing the child's complete thought. This may sound simple, but many times it is difficult and frustrating. Many factors influence the degree of adult responsiveness and talkativeness, particularly in child center settings—room arrangements, adult-child ratios, level of staff training, and other emotional and environmental factors. The greatest inhibitor of adults' speaking and responding to children seems to be adults' talking to one another instead of the children. Professionals save chatting for breaks and after school meetings. The nature of the work in a group care program can easily be described as emotion packed and demanding, in addition to rewarding and challenging. On the surface, the general public may not see or understand skilled verbal interactions taking place between toddlers and caregivers. What seems to be random, natural playfulness and verbal responsiveness can be really very skilled and professionally intentional behavior. The same, of course, is true regarding family behavior.

Adults sometimes question the practice of responding to toddlers' grunts and "uhs"; instead they respond only to toddlers' spoken words. Many toddlers seem to understand everything said to them and around them but get by and satisfy most of their needs with sounds and gestures. The points for adults to consider are that the child is performing and learning a difficult task and that speech will soon follow. The message that responsive adults relay to children when rewarding their early attempts with attention is that children can be successful communicators and that further attempts at speech will get results.

## FROM EGOCENTRIC SPEECH TO INNER SPEECH

During the toddler period, observers notice that words or short phrases spoken by adults are remembered and spoken out loud. The toddler's "hot," "no," "kitty," or similar words accompany the child's actions or a simple viewing of objects at hand. Vygotsky (1986) has called this "egocentric" speech, which is ultimately and usefully tied to the toddler's thinking.

As the child matures, this type of speech slowly becomes **inner speech**; part of the child's thinking process. Egocentric speech is regulatory, that is, useful in helping the child regulate (manage) her own behavior. As adults, we see examples of this regulatory function when we talk ourselves through particular perplexing situations. For example, "First the key goes in the lock, then turn the handle, and the bar moves to the left."

## SYMBOLIC GESTURING

It is old-fashioned to believe that real communication does not exist before a child's first words (Figure 2–8). Researchers have helped us understand that gestures and signs (signals) occur in tandem with early vocalizing. Young toddlers can possess a rich repertoire of signals, and female infants tend to rely on or produce them with slightly greater frequency than male infants. Signs have been defined as nonverbal gestures symbolically representing objects, events, desires, and conditions that are used by toddlers to communicate with those around them. They literally can double a young toddler's vocabulary.

Toddlers' interest in learning hand signals (signing) varies greatly. Conducting an infant-toddler program in which signing is a regular part of the curriculum has become popular.

**FIGURE 2–8** Gestures often indicate a child's desire or need.

---

**inner speech** — mentioned in Vygotsky's theory as private speech that becomes internalized and is useful in organizing ideas.

Some toddlers may use 20 or more signs for various objects, feelings, and needs; other toddlers mixed only a few gestures with their beginning words. Both would be displaying normal development.

The use of words and symbols to influence other people in predictable ways requires the child to represent mentally the relationship between the symbol (word or gesture), the meaning for which it stands, and the intended effect on the other person. A symbol—a word, a picture, a dance—exists because of human intention to infuse some tangible form—a sound, a mark, a movement—with meaning and thereby to comment on or take action in the social world.

Various researchers have studied a child whose parents felt that their child was capable of learning nonverbal as well as verbal labels. The parents informally concocted signs on the spot for new events without any reference to a formal sign language system. Figure 2–9, from a study by Acredolo and Goodwyn (1985), describes the signs and gives the age the signs appeared in the child's communicative behaviors and the age

| SIGNS | DESCRIPTION | AGE OF SIGN ACQUISITION (MONTHS) | AGE OF WORD ACQUISITION (MONTHS) |
|---|---|---|---|
| flower | sniff, sniff | 12.5 | 20.0 |
| big | arms raised | 13.0 | 17.25 |
| elephant | finger to nose, lifted | 13.5 | 19.75 |
| anteater | tongue in and out | 14.0 | 24.0 |
| bunny | torso up and down | 14.0 | 19.75 |
| Cookie Monster | palm to mouth plus smack | 14.0 | 20.75 |
| monkey | hands in armpits, up-down | 14.25 | 19.75 |
| skunk | wrinkled nose plus sniff | 14.5 | 24.00 |
| fish | blow through mouth | 14.5 | 20.0 |
| slide | hand waved downward | 14.5 | 17.5 |
| swing | torso back and forth | 14.5 | 18.25 |
| ball | both hands waved | 14.5 | 15.75 |
| alligator | palms together, open-shut | 14.75 | 24.0 |
| bee | finger plus thumb waved | 14.75 | 20.00 |
| butterfly | hands crossed, fingers waved | 14.75 | 24.0 |
| I dunno | shrugs shoulders, hands up | 15.0 | 17.25 |
| hot | waves hand at midline | 15.0 | 19.0 |
| hippo | head back, mouth wide | 15.0 | 24.0 |
| spider | index fingers rubbed | 15.0 | 20.0 |
| bird | arms out, hands flapping | 15.0 | 18.5 |
| turtle | hand around wrist, fist in-out | 15.0 | 20.0 |
| fire | waving of hand | 15.0 | 23.0 |
| night-night | head down on shoulder | 15.0 | 20.0 |
| X-mas tree | fists open-closed | 16.0 | 26.0 |
| mistletoe | kisses | 16.0 | 27.0 |
| scissors | two fingers open-closed | 16.0 | 20.0 |
| berry | "raspberry" motion | 16.5 | 20.0 |
| kiss | kiss (at a distance) | 16.5 | 21.0 |
| caterpillar | index finger wiggled | 17.5 | 23.0 |

**FIGURE 2–9** Symbolic signs, in order of acquisition, produced by case study subject. (From Acredolo, L. P. & Goodwyn, S. W. [1985]. Symbolic gesturing in language development. *Human Development*, 28, 53–58. Reproduced with permission from S. Karger A. G.)

the child said the word represented by the sign. The list of signs includes the signs the child learned with and without direct parent teaching.

Gestures are integral companions of toddler verbalizations. Adults may have modeled the gestures in their adult-child interactions. A family's signals are "read" by toddlers, and a hand held palm up is usually read as "give it to me." Toddlers show their understanding by behaviors. Toddlers can and do invent new gestures; consequently, signing is not simple, imitative behavior. Pointing is probably the most commonly used gesture of toddlers. Eventually, words are preferred and gesturing remains as an accompaniment of speech. We have all slipped back into a gesturing mode as we search for words in conversation, and hand gestures are used automatically to convey the word(s) that we cannot quite express.

Early childhood educators employed by infant-toddler centers need to know their centers' position regarding expected language-developing behaviors. Most centers expect educators to pair words with adult hand signs, to encourage toddler use of signs, and to learn and respond to each child's individual sign language. To do this, teachers must be alert to children's cues, in particular noticing what in the environment attracts them so that words can be supplied and the children's intentions "read." Teachers' behaviors should reflect their awareness, intentional efforts, and attention to toddlers' efforts to communicate. Their continual goal is to establish a warm, emotionally fulfilling connection to each child in their care.

Toddlers are very interested in exploring. Teachers should "hang back" when toddlers interact with other toddlers and try not to interrupt play. Becoming social with peers is given priority and promoted.

Teachers of toddlers do a lot of "word modeling." They attempt to be both calm and fun companions. Most will tell you that after a full day with toddlers they look forward to conversing with adults.

## FIRST SENTENCES

The shift from one word to a two-word (or more) stage at approximately 18 months is a milestone. At that time, the toddler has a speaking vocabulary of about 50 words; by 36 months, upward of 1,000 words. It is crucial in talking about vocabulary to acknowledge that children not only acquire new words as they get older but also expand their understanding of old words.

If one looks closely at two-word utterances, two classes of words become apparent. The smallest group of words is made up of what are called "pivot words." Examples of toddlers' two-word sentences, with pivot words underlined, are shown in Figure 2–10. Pivot words are used more often than other words, and seem to enter the vocabulary more slowly, perhaps because they are stable and fixed in meaning. In analyzing two-word toddler comments, one finds they are both subject-predicate and topic-comment in nature. Frequently stressed syllables in words and word endings are what toddlers' first master, filling in other syllables later. At times, toddlers use *-um* or *-ah* as placeholders for syllables and words. They replace these with correct syllables and words as they age.

Understanding of grammar rules at this two-word stage is displayed even though many words are missing. Toddlers frequently use a simple form and, almost in the same breath, clarify by expansion (by adding another word). The invention of words by toddlers is common. One 18-month-old had her own private word for "sleep," consistently calling it "ooma." Families trying to understand their toddlers get good at filling in the blanks. They then can confirm the child's statement and can add meaning at a time when the child's interest is focused.

| TWO-WORD SENTENCES | MEANINGS |
|---|---|
| Dat* car | nomination |
| Daddy dare | location |
| See kitty | identification |
| More cookie | repetition, recurrence |
| Milk allgone | nonexistence |
| Sit chair | action—location |
| No car, no want dat | negation |
| Todd shoe, mine toy | possession, possessor |
| Big cup | attribute description |
| Jin walk, truck go | agent—action |
| Kiss you, fix car | action—direct object |
| Where ball? | question |
| *Underlined words are pivots. | |

**FIGURE 2–10** Pivot words in toddlers' two-word sentences.

**VIDEO ACTIVITY**

Go to the Education CourseMate website to watch the TeachSource Video, *0–2: Language Development in Infants and Toddlers.*

1. What examples of telegraphic speech or pivot words can you cite from the children's speech in this video clip?

2. Describe the amount and kind of touching caregivers provided.

3. How responsive was the child in the video segment that saw his own reflection in the mirror? How did he react to his own image?

## TODDLER-ADULT CONVERSATIONS

Toddlers control attending or turning away when interacting with others, as do infants. At about 1 year, they understand many words and begin to display turn-taking in conversation, with "you talk, I answer" behaviors. **Joint attention** starts around 10 months of age. At this time infants develop intentional communication and willingly share emotions, intentions, and interest in the outside world. To do this, the child has to be sure that both she (the speaker) and her intended receiver is focused on the same thing. She does this by capturing another's attention, establishing the topic of conversation, and maintaining attention on the topic by looking back and forth.

Her communication usually consists of one or more of the following: looking, pointing, gesturing, showing, giving, making sounds, and changing her facial expression.

Toddlers learn that speech deserves attention and that speech is great for getting adults to notice them. They seem to revel in the joint-endeavor aspect of conversations.

Toddlers are skillful communicators. They converse and correct adult interpretations, gaining pleasure and satisfaction from language exchanges. The following incident shows more than toddler persistence:

A first-time visitor to the home of a 20-month-old toddler is approached by the toddler. The visitor eventually rises out of his chair, accompanies the toddler to the kitchen, gets a glass of water, and hands it to the child. The toddler takes a tiny drink, and returns, satisfied, to the living room. Parents were not involved. Thirst, itself, was unimportant. The pleasure gained by the child seemed to motivate her actions.

For the child to accomplish her ends, the following actions occurred. The visitor:

1. focuses attention on child.
2. realizes a "talking" situation is occurring.
3. listens and maintains a receiver attitude.
4. corrects his own behavior, guesses at the child's meaning, and tries new actions.
5. realizes the conversation is over.

While the toddler:

1. stands in front of visitor; searches face to catch eye; makes loud vocalization, dropping volume when eye contact is made; observes visitor behavior.
2. repeats first sound (parents understand, visitor does not) and observes visitor reaction.
3. grabs visitor's hand, vocalizes loudly, and looks in visitor's eyes.
4. tugs at hand, uses insistent voice tone, and gestures toward the kitchen.
5. pulls visitor to sink and uses new word (visitor does not understand); corrects through gestures when visitor reaches for the cookie jar.
6. corrects visitor's guess (milk), gestures toward water, and holds out hand.
7. drinks a small sip and hands back the glass, smiles, and walks away.

This type of behavior has been called *instrumental expression* because vocalization and nonverbal behaviors were used to obtain a certain goal.

The toddler seeks out people willing to listen and learns from each encounter. Adults modify and adapt their speech based on the abilities they observe in the child. This is done intuitively by use of shorter and less complex comments, and it changes when adults notice increased capacity (Figure 2–11).

Many experienced caregivers describe a time when some toddlers in their care remain very close. During this time, the toddler's behavior is

---

**joint attention** — child's awareness that he or she must gain and hold another's focus during communicational exchanges to get his or her message understood.

**FIGURE 2–11** Children seek out people willing to show interest in what they are doing.

characterized by clinging to a primary caregiver, watching adult lips intently, showing decreased interest in toys or playing independently, frequently bringing objects to the caregiver, and attempting to say words. The duration and appearance of these behaviors is unique to each toddler, and some do not display them at all. Families can worry about spoiling the toddler, if these behaviors persist, and educators urge families to satisfy children's needs for increased attention and language input. Usually the child will emerge with a longer attention span and branch out to explore a wider world.

## CHARACTERISTICS OF TODDLER LANGUAGE

The speech of young children speaking in two-word, or longer, sentences is termed **telegraphic** and **prosodic**. It is telegraphic because many words are omitted because of the child's limited ability to express and remember large segments of information; the most important parts of the sentence are usually present. Prosodic refers to the child's use of voice modulation and word stress with a particular word or words to give special emphasis and meaning. Telegraphic speech can be defined as utterances that are devoid of function words and resemble messages sent by telegraph, for instance, "Jimmy truck"

could represent "That truck belongs to Jimmy" or "Give me my truck." Meanings often depend upon context and intonation of the utterance.

For additional toddler language characteristics that may appear before the child's third birthday, see Figure 2–12.

### TODDLER LANGUAGE CHARACTERISTICS

- Uses two- to five-word sentences.
  "Baby down."
  "Baby boom boom."
  "No like."
  "No like kitty."
  "Me dink all gone."
  "See me dink all gone."
- Uses verbs.
  "Dolly cry."
  "Me going."
  "Wanna cookie."
- Uses prepositions.
  "In car."
  "Up me go."
- Adds plurals.
  "Birdies sing."
  "Gotta big doggies."
  "Bears in dat."
- Uses pronouns.
  "Me big boy."
  "He bad."
- Uses articles.
  "The ball gone."
  "Gimme a candy."
- Uses conjunctions.
  "Me and gamma."
- Uses negatives.
  "Don't wanna."
  "He no go."
- Runs words together.
  "Allgone," "gotta," "gimme," "lookee."
- Asks questions.
  "Wa dat?"
  "Why she sleep?"
- Does not use letter sounds or mispronounces spoken words.
  "Iceam," "choo" (for shoe), "member" (for remember), "canny" (for candy).
- Sings songs.
- Tells simple stories.
- Repeats words and phrases.
- Enjoys word and movement activities.

**FIGURE 2–12** Toddler language characteristics.

---

**telegraphic speech** — a characteristic of young children's sentences in which everything but the crucial word(s) is omitted, as if for a telegram.
**prosodic speech** — the child's use of voice modulation and word stress to give special emphasis and meaning.

## Negatives

No discussion of older toddlers' language would be complete without mentioning the use of "no." There seems to be an exasperating time when children say "no" to everything—seemingly testing whether there is a choice. Young children first use "no" to indicate nonexistence. Later it is used to indicate rejection and denial. Even when the child can speak in sentences longer than three words, the "no" often remains the first in a sequence of words. A typical example is "No want go bed." Soon, children insert negatives properly between the subject and the verb into longer utterances, as sentence length increases. Of all speech characteristics adults remember, toddlers' use of negatives and their avid energetic demands to be "listened to" stick in the memories of their caregivers.

## AIDS TO TODDLER SPEECH DEVELOPMENT

The swift rate of new words entering toddlers' vocabularies indicates that educators caring for them should begin to become increasingly specific with descriptive terms in their speech. If a truck is blue, a comment like "The blue truck rolled in the mud" is appropriate. If an object is on the bottom shelf, in the top drawer, or under the table, those words can be stressed. A color, number, or special quality, like fast or slow, big or little, or many other adjectives and adverbs, can be inserted in simple comments.

Playing detective to understand toddlers will always be part of adults' conversational style. Teachers may request that toddlers look directly at them when they communicate so that teachers can better hear each word and determine intent.

Many experts offer adults advice for providing an optimal toddler environment for language stimulation. The following are some specific tips.

- Expose the child to language with speech neither too simple nor too complex, but just slightly above the child's current level.
- Stay in tune with the child's actual abilities.
- Omit unreasonable speech demands, yet encourage attempts.
- Remember that positive reinforcement is a more effective tool than negative feedback.

- Accept the child's own formulation of a language concept.
- Provide a correct model.
- Make a point of being responsive.
- Follow the child's interest by naming and simple discussion.

Other suggested pointers follow.

- Explain what you are doing as you work.
- Describe what is happening.
- Display excitement for the child's accomplishments (Figure 2–13).
- Talk about what the child is doing, wanting, or needing.
- Pause and listen with ears and eyes after you have spoken.
- Encourage toddler imitation of gestures and sounds.
- Imitate the child's sounds playfully at times.

Language and self-help skills blossom when 2-year-olds have opportunities to participate in "real" activities such as cutting bananas (using

FIGURE 2–13 "I see you found a green block!"

a plastic knife), emptying baskets, sponging off the table, and helping sweep the floor.

The following adult behaviors are included in appropriate practices identified by the National Association for the Education of Young Children (NAEYC) (Bredekamp & Copple, 1997):

> Adults engage in many one-to-one, faces-to-face conversations with toddlers. Adults let toddlers initiate language, and wait for a response, even from children whose language is limited. Adults label or name objects, describe events, and reflect feelings to help children learn new words. Adults simplify their language for toddlers who are just beginning to talk (instead of "It's time to wash our hands and have a snack," the adult says, "Let's wash hands for snack time!"). Then, as children acquire their own words, adults expand on the toddler's language.

Toddler-adult activities can include:

- setting out two or three familiar objects and asking the child to get one.
- calling attention to interesting things you see, hear, smell, taste, or feel.
- showing and labeling your facial features and the child's in a mirror.
- labeling and pointing to objects around a room.
- verbally labeling items of clothing as the child is dressing and undressing.
- labeling the people in the toddler's world.

Toddler-adult language and movement play are recommended. One classic play activity follows. Others are located in the Activities section.

### Take Your Little Hands

*Take your little hands and go clap, clap, clap.*
*Take your little hands and go clap, clap, clap.*
*Take your little hands and go clap, clap, clap.*
*Clap, clap, and clap your hands.*
*Take your little foot and go tap, tap, tap.*
*Take your little foot and go tap, tap, tap.*
*Take your little foot and go tap, tap, tap.*
*Tap, tap, and tap your foot.*
*Take your little eyes and go blink, blink, blink.*
*Take your little eyes and go blink, blink, blink.*
*Take your little eyes and go blink, blink, blink.*

*Blink, blink, and blink your eyes.*
*Take your little mouth and go buzz, buzz, buzz.*
*Take your little mouth and go buzz, buzz, buzz.*
*Take your little mouth and go buzz, buzz, buzz.*
*Buzz like a bumblebee.*
*Take your little hand and wave bye, bye, bye.*
*Take your little hand and wave bye, bye, bye.*
*Take your little hand and wave bye, bye, bye.*
*Wave your hand bye-bye.*

### Language With Music

Toddlers are music lovers. If a bouncy melody catches their ear, they move. They obtain plenty of joy in swaying, clapping, or singing along. Geist and Geist (2008) posit young children anticipate a pattern when a story or song is familiar first by recognizing its rhythm or beat and then its words. These authors suggest that children then move on to repeat the language present and, with teacher encouragement, improvise and make additions to the story or song.

Many can sing short, repeated phrases in songs, and some toddlers will create their own repetitive melodies (Figure 2–14). Words in

FIGURE 2–14 Toddler teachers sometimes sing nursery songs that include hand motions.

songs are learned when they are sung repeatedly. Adult correction is not necessary or appropriate. Playful singing and chanting by adults is a recommended language-development technique.

Educators can encourage young children's creativity with music. If teachers always focus on everyone singing the same words and/or doing the same actions, they may not be using music to promote creative expression. Fortunately, with the uninhibited and exuberant toddler this is not a problem; teachers are going to see some fantastic "moves" and hear some unique lyrics and takeoffs on songs and dances. The author enjoys remembering the time a 2-year-old composed his own song—"Zipper your do da."

The social component in musical games is also a language facilitator. Joining the fun with others gradually attracts even the youngest children (Figure 2–15). A toddler can be introduced to the joy of moving to a new song with others; mutual musical listening and participation in music experiences at small group times add new avenues for language growth.

One technique educators frequently engage in with music is to verbally describe how a particular child is moving to music. ("Johnny is lifting his knee high up to his tummy.") This encourages children's movement to music and should be used when appropriate. The adult can extend two index fingers for the shy or wobbly child to grip, thereby creating a dance partnership. This allows the child to release at any time. Gently swaying or guiding movements to the music may increase the child's enjoyment.

The following criteria for selecting sing-along songs, recorded music, and songbook selections are recommended.

1. a short selection for toddlers
2. repetitive phrases
3. reasonable range (C to G or A)
4. simple rhythms

FIGURE 2–15 Making music is a popular preschool activity.

Try to find pieces that represent the ethnic and cultural diversity of attending children and include folk music.

Suggested music resources are found in the Appendix.

## SYMBOLIC PLAY

At approximately 12 to 15 months, toddlers will begin to engage in symbolic (pretend) play. This important developmental leap allows the child to escape the immediate and firsthand happenings in her life and use symbols to represent past experiences and imagine future possibilities. Medina (2008) explains

Symbolic reasoning is a uniquely human talent. It may have arisen from our need to understand another's intentions and motivations, allowing us to coordinate within a group. (p. 47)

The acts of toddler pretend play observed by adults are widely diverse and depend in part on the child's life experiences. Greenspan (1999) describes a parent observing a young toddler's symbolic play:

. . . he tenderly puts his teddy bear to be inside an empty shoe box, and the parent recognizes the child is starting to grasp that one thing can stand for, or symbolize, another. Because he can picture what a bed looks and feels like in his mind, he is able to pretend that a hollow, rectangular box is really a symbol for a bed. When the parent comments that his teddy bear "is sleeping in his bed," he will eventually comprehend that the word "sleeping" stands for the bear's activity in the bed. As soon as he can articulate the sounds, the toddler will himself use the word symbol "sleeping" to describe an elaborate pattern of behaviors that he has observed. (p. 200)

One can always find toddlers who will talk into toy phones, spank dolls, grab the wheel of toy vehicles, and accompany motor movements with sounds, speech, and *vrooms*.

Some reenact less common past experiences that are puzzling to their teachers. Gowen (1995) suggests the teacher techniques listed in Figure 2–16.

1. <u>Mirror the child's sounds, words or actions.</u>
   (Child is rocking a doll while humming.)
   Teacher picks up a doll, rocks it, while saying "Go to sleep, baby."
   (Child is putting blocks together.)
   Teacher sits with child and puts one block on top of another and says "Blocks."

2. <u>Describe the child's actions.</u>
   (Child is climbing stairs.)
   Teacher says "One foot on the step, two feet on the step."
   (Child feeds doll with toy bottle.)
   Teacher says "You are giving your baby a drink of milk. Um, um, that tastes good."
   "Your ball is bouncing up, and down, up and down. Down it goes; up it goes. You picked up the ball, Will."

3. <u>Suggest a child action.</u>
   (Child has rolled a toy car across the rug.)
   Teacher says "Let's push our cars under the table and park them." as she grabs another toy car pushes it and parks it.
   (Child has picked up small floor pillows and is carrying them.)
   Teacher says "I'll get the wagon so you can put the pillows inside."

4. Request or suggest an action or vocalization.
   (Child is putting a plastic bowl on his head.)
   "Robin (child's name) has a new hat." teacher says.
   Then sitting next to him and picking up another bowl, she says,
   "Teacher needs a new hat too. Put it on my head, please."

5. <u>Make a positive statement.</u>
   (Child pats doll's back putting it upon her shoulder.)
   Teacher says "Your dolly feels better now. What a good mommy you are."
   (Child puts pretend play iron over the play ironing board.)
   "You are ironing your family's clothes so they look neat and pretty.
   (Child tries to feed teacher a plastic apple.)
   Teacher says "That apple tastes good. I was hungry. Thank you very much."

6. <u>Model an action or word(s) for the child to copy.</u>
   With stuffed dog and baby blanket, teacher says,
   "My dog is cold today. I'm going to wrap him up so he can take a nap."
   While on the play yard a loud airplane has attracted children's attention overhead.
   "I'm an airplane flying to grandma's house."
   Teacher pretends to fly.

FIGURE 2–16 Teacher response to toddlers' symbolic play.

## MAKING FRIENDS

Approximately 56 percent of infants and toddlers spend some time in early care and development programs (Women in the Labor Force & U. S. Bureau of Labor Statistics, 2005). Toddlers seem to have a strong need for both individual identity and autonomy and social connectedness. At times they display the ability to help others and are sympathetic or empathetic. They may venture out toward peers and retreat back to the security, closeness, physical comfort of caring adults. They are constantly learning from their first contacts and relationships with "other small people" and new adults.

Teachers, Wittmer (2008) believes, cannot underestimate the importance of their relationships with toddlers. Social competence and emotional control development predict school readiness. Caring adults can be instrumental in helping toddlers figure out, experiment, and understand new ways to interact and communicate with peers and also learn the rules of physical contact and socialization.

Each toddler entering group care differs not only in temperament, personality, capability, culture, and gender but also in past human relationships, memories, and their expectations of others. Past experience may or may not include attachment to significant adults or positive social interactions with other like-age children. Some toddlers may avoid peers, or express hostility and aggression, or ignore them. Toddler communication skills also vary. Vocal ability can range from utter silence to being a chatterbox.

Often, toddler play is side-by-side play. A toddler may watch what a neighboring peer is doing and may sometimes imitate the peer's actions. However, two toddlers playing cooperatively in an organized, shared-goal play situation is infrequent. Toddlers are usually in-their-own-world-of-discovery people, but they do at times pick up play ideas from one another. Social graces may be absent, yet some beginning empathy for others may be apparent when one toddler communicates by patting or hugging a crying peer or handing over a toy. Poole (1999) describes the difficulties toddlers face in building peer friendships;

It's hard work for toddlers to learn how to play with one another. At first, some may examine their playmates as if they were inanimate objects, such as a doll or a ball, pinching and poking without understanding that their actions can hurt. Toddlers also don't always have control over their strong emotions.

It takes time to learn not to hug too hard or to say "Hello" rather than swipe at a friend's face. Even when toddlers begin to sense that such behavior is frowned upon, they may continue testing the limits. (p. 37)

Wittmer (2008) reminds teachers that it takes time for toddlers to become interested in peers, feel comfortable playing with them, and develop their growing ability to be a caring friend.

Children's sense of *self* and other, which they bring to their interactions with peers, begins to develop in their first relationships with significant adults. A self that is full of confidence, capable of being intimate with others, and convinced that others are likely to be enjoyable and responsive (or not) emerges from these first relationships. Infants and toddlers develop their beginning sense of other as kind, trustworthy, helpful and fun in the embrace and enfolding (figuratively and literally) of the mother, father and other special adults. (p. 10)

By 15 to 18 months of age, many toddlers participate in joint physical activities and may more fully enjoy others' company. By age 2, they often pair off with a peer and have favorite companions. Young toddlers' emotions may erupt when sharing classroom playthings, causing friendships to change quickly. It is then, at age 2, that words can help children attract companions and repel others. Two-year-olds mimic increasingly and use words a friend uses.

## RECOGNIZING DIFFERENCES IN LANGUAGE GROWTH

Early childhood teachers are better able to identify accelerated, normal (average), and delayed speakers at about 18 months of age. What causes diversity is too complex to mention here, but some factors can be inferred, and others have been previously mentioned. Families' and caregivers' responses to children's nonverbal and verbal attempts to communicate toward the end of the first year and into the second year can be a determining factor.

Birckmayer, Kennedy, and Stonehouse (2010) urge caregivers to observe and discover each child's particular way of communicating which may be crying, smiling, making noises, hand and body actions, or other behaviors that the child employs to convey thoughts and feelings. Then responsive caregiver feedback should occur so the toddler learns making sounds and/or other overtures prompts the receiver (adult) to make sounds and/or actions back.

## INTRODUCING TODDLERS TO BOOKS

Toddlers show an interest in simple, colorful books and pictures and enjoy adult closeness and attention. Pointing and naming can become an enjoyable game. Sturdy pages that are easily turned help the toddler. A scrapbook of favorite objects mounted on cardboard individualizes the experience. Clear contact paper and lamination will add life and protection.

Board books (usually stiff, coated, heavy cardboard) for toddlers allow exploratory play and may offer colorful, close-up photographs or illustrations of familiar, everyday objects. These books promote the child's naming of pictures and active participation at book-reading times.

Toddler books are plentiful, and school collections include both fiction and nonfiction. Experts and librarians recommend volumes that are colorful, simple, inviting, realistic, and contain opportunities that encourage child involvement. With durable, glossy, wipe-clean page coating and smaller-than-average picture-book size, board books allow small and sometimes sticky hands to explore without tearing sturdy covers or pages.

Because a toddler may move on quickly to investigating other aspects of the environment, adults offering initial experiences with books need to remember that when interest has

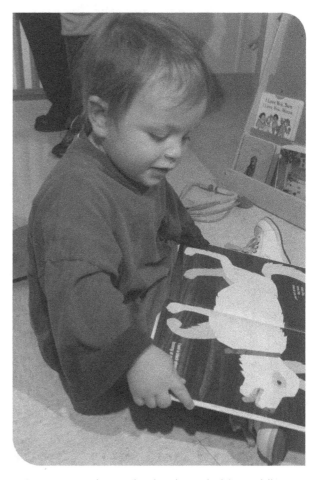

**FIGURE 2–17** The "right" book can hold a toddler's attention.

waned, it is time to respect the search for other adventures (Figure 2–17).

Other hints concerning the introduction of books, from Kupetz and Green (1997), are as follows:

- Do not expect to quiet a rambunctious toddler with a book.
- Pick a time when the child seems alert, curious, and interested.
- Establish a special reading time (although books can be read anytime).
- Use your voice as a tool to create interest.
- Be responsive.
- React positively to all of the child's attempts in naming objects, turning pages, or attempting any form of verbalization (Figure 2–18).

Toddlers with past experiences with picture books may have certain expectations for

**FIGURE 2–18** Toddlers often name what they see in book illustrations.

- Choose developmentally appropriate titles with simple text, larger size, familiar objects, and with available child "join in" opportunities.
- Adjust your expectations of toddler behavior. Coach patiently and offer needed support as they settle down.
- Use a routine signal to begin story time and be aware the shared reading time (or looking time) may be some children's initial experience. Slow down and urge assisting adults to offer the comfort of a lap.
- Pace reading to maintain child focus.
- Alternate active movement and quiet times during group time by using singing, finger play, or physical movement, which is suggested by oral or textual material. (p. 122)

What can toddlers begin to understand during the reading of picture books? Besides knowing that photographs and illustrations are between the covers of books, the toddler gathers ideas about book pleasure. As the child touches pictured objects, the child may grasp the idea that the objects depicted are representations of familiar objects. The toddler can notice that books are not handled as toys.

Very young children's reading-like behaviors may surprise their teachers especially when they observe the independent activity of toddlers with their favorite books. Almost as soon as the older toddler becomes familiarized with particular books through repetitive readings, he begins to play with them in reading-like ways. Attracted by the familiar object with which she has such positive associations, the toddler picks up the book, opens it, and begins attempting to retrieve some of the language and its intonations. Almost unintelligible at first, this reading-like play rapidly becomes picture-stimulated, page-matched, and story related.

Near 2 years of age, the toddler probably still names what is pictured but may understand stories. The toddler may grasp the idea that book characters and events are make-believe. If a particular book is reread to a child, the child can know that the particular stories in books do not change, and what is to be read is predictable. Sometimes the toddler finds that she can

adult-child book sharing. They may want to cuddle with a blanket, sit in adult laps, turn pages for themselves, point to and question book features, name objects, watch the adult's mouth during reading, and so on. Exhibiting flexibility and following the child's lead reinforces the child's social enjoyment of the book.

Educators should be cautioned about the practice of requiring a group of toddlers to sit and listen to a story together. The key words are group and require. Toddler group times are of short duration and planned for active child participation. As toddlers age, they maintain focus for longer periods. Educators of toddlers might try sharing a picture book with a few children. When they do so, they endeavor to keep the experience warm, comfortable, and intimate.

Jalongo (2004) suggests the following when reading to small group:

participate in the telling by singing, repeating character lines, and making physical motions to represent actions; for example, "knocking on the door" and saying "moo."

## Selecting Toddler Books

Books for toddlers should be:

- repetitive and predictable.
- rhythmical.
- illustrated with simple, familiar, easy-to-identify colorful objects, animals, toys, and so on.
- filled with feel, touch, and smell opportunities.
- sturdy, with easy-to-turn pages.
- set with few words on each page.
- relatively short, with simple, concise story lines about common, everyday life and environmental experiences.
- full of common, everyday activities toddlers can imitate such as waving goodbye, tooth brushing, face washing, using a spoon, wiping face with napkin, door knocking, stair climbing, or movement activities such as kissing, blowing, clapping, bouncing, stepping, jumping, stretching, and so on.
- simple and illustrate elementary concepts such as black and white, big and little, on and off, up and down, over and under, large and small, inside and outside, and so on.
- formatted with illustrations matched to the text on each page.

Bardige (2009) suggests selecting toddler books that include big, noisy things such as garbage trucks, airplanes, farm and zoo animals, or small intriguing things such as birds, bugs, butterflies, baby animals, and balls.

Additional desirable features of toddler-appropriate books often include simple, uncomplicated storylines; colorful, well-spaced illustrations or photographs; opportunities for the toddler to point and name familiar objects; sensory features; predictive books (ones allowing the child to guess or predict successfully); and strong, short rhymes or repetitive rhythms. "Touch and feel" books are particularly enjoyed, as are sturdy, heavy board pages. Novelty books that make noise, pop-up books, and books with easy-to-use moving parts capture a toddler's attention. Now is the time to also share the strong rhyming rhythms of Mother Goose and introduce two classics: *Mary Had a Little Lamb* and *Pop Goes the Weasel*.

Adults sing with toddlers, do finger plays, act out simple stories like *The Three Bears* with older toddlers participating actively, or tell stories using a flannel board or magnetic board, and allow children to manipulate and place figures on the boards.

This is an age when book-handling skills begin. This includes how to hold a book, where to look for illustrations, and how to open it. These skills can be modeled and discussed while adults point, ask questions, gesture, stress words, follow child interest or note lack of it, and enthusiastically enjoy the shared book experience.

## Electronic Books

Books with electronic features provide another way to engage toddlers with stories and print. Each book differs, but many have colorful illustrations that move, flash, "talk," or make musical sounds and noises. Pressing an area, button, icon, or symbol activates prerecorded features. But the research of Zimmerman and Christakis (2007) alerts early childhood educators to possible ill effects of early media exposure, particularly children's media viewing before the age of 3. Their study conclusions note that viewing of either violent or nonviolent entertainment television before age 3 was significantly associated with subsequent attentional problems 5 years later. The viewing of any content type at ages 4 to 5 was not associated with attentional problems. Another research study by the same researchers (Christakis and Zimmerman, 2007) examined violent television viewing during preschool years and its associated increased risk of children's antisocial behavior during school-age years. Other researchers (Dworak et al., 2007) have concluded that a link exists between television and computer game exposure and children's sleep patterns, diminished verbal cognitive performance, and their learning and memory abilities. Dworak and associates' research was conducted with a small group of school-age children. More extensive research is needed to probe preschooler's entertainment viewing and their educational game playing.

Most educators and parents agree that electronic books, games, and television programs do attract toddlers but that interest usually wanes quickly unless the media is shared with a responsive adult.

Educators understand how easily clever television commercials and television programs sometimes capture and engage toddlers. They advise families to limit or omit toddler viewing time. Toddlers may respond to catchy tunes, animation, and flashing colorful images with physical movement such as singing, dancing, and clapping. It looks like toddlers are learning, but the television program can't interact, build on a child's response, or expand interest with language-developing feedback. Overexposure to the medium actually crowds out and subtracts from time spent in more positive human contact and/or conversation in which language is really learned.

## Scribbling

In most home environments, toddlers see others writing and want to try it themselves. Large, chunky crayons and nontoxic markers are easily manipulated by toddlers at about 18 months of age. They usually grasp them in their fist and use a scrubbing motion. They have some difficulty placing marks where they might wish, so it is best to use very large sheets of sturdy paper taped to a tabletop. Brown bags cut flat or untreated shelf paper work well. The act of scribbling can serve several useful purposes, including enhancing small muscle coordination, exercising cognitive abilities, promoting social interaction, and allowing emotional release. It can also be seen as a precursor to an interest in symbols and print. An important point in development is reached when the child moves from linear scribbles to enclosed shapes and at a later age begins realistic, representational drawing. Some Asian families may place a high emphasis on drawing activities for young children, and their children's work at school often reflects more comfort and experience with art materials and writing tools.

## BEGINNING LITERACY

During toddlerhood, some children gain general knowledge of books and awareness of print. This is viewed as a natural process, which takes place in a literate home or early learning environment. Immersing toddlers in language activities facilitates their literacy development. It is possible to establish a positive early bonding between children and book-sharing times—a first step toward literacy. Some toddlers who show no interest in books will, when exposed to books at a later time, find them as interesting as other children. Parents need to understand that a literary interest can be piqued throughout early childhood. The fact that a toddler may not be particularly enamored with books or book-sharing times at a particular stage is not a matter of concern. It may simply be a matter of the child's natural, individual activity level and her ability to sit and stay focused in an environment that holds an abundance of features to explore.

### Musical Activities

Musical play with toddlers can help promote literacy skills. Activities can include:

- focused listening experiences.
- play that focuses on or highlights discrimination of loud and soft and fast and slow, rhythms, repeated patterns, tones, words, and so on.
- the use of repetitive beats, catchy melodies or words, clapping, tapping, rocking, galloping, marching, motions, and body actions.
- coordination of movement and music in some way.
- creative and imaginative opportunities.
- experiences with a variety of simple, safe musical instruments.
- the singing of age-appropriate songs.

Music activities often can be used to create an affectionate adult-child bond. Singhal (1999) describes toddlers participating in adult and child music activities:

Toddlers are beings in motion, and music is the perfect vehicle for directing and freeing their movements. They feel and internalize the steady beat of adult motions. Contrary to popular belief, toddlers can also be excellent listeners. They are fascinated by sound, whether it's a bee buzzing or a clarinet melody. The different shapes, feel and sounds of simple rhythm instruments also mesmerize toddlers. Being able to make a steady sound on his own on an instrument such as the drum is very empowering to a young child who wants to "do it myself!"

Even though at this age children may not be willing to echo back chanted tonal and rhythm patterns, it is still important that they hear them. The patterns are being "recorded" in their minds for future reference.

Singing, listening, and music-making are a completely natural and enjoyable part of a young child's being. (p. 22)

### Toys

Certain types of toys have a strong connection to toddlers' emerging language development (Figure 2–19). Musical toys, dolls and stuffed animals that make noises or talk, and alphabet toys, including magnetic alphabet letters, can be described as language-promoting toys. Noisemaking toys or recordings, both audio and visual, capture the toddler's attention. Manipulative toys for toddlers are becoming increasingly available.

### FREEDOM TO EXPLORE

Greenspan (1999) emphasizes how toddler problem solving develops and describes its relationship to "freedom to explore" (within supervised limits).

An ability to solve problems rests on the even more basic skill of seeing and deciphering patterns. It is the ability to understand patterns that lets a toddler know if she takes two steps here and two steps there that she'll be able

**FIGURE 2–19** Certain toys promote early scribbling behavior.

to reach her favorite toy. She becomes a successful navigator not only because her muscles are coordinated, but also because her growing brain now enables her to understand patterns. Toddlers learn to recognize how one room leads to another, and where you are in relation to them. They can meaningfully explore the world long before they are able to express their wishes and thoughts in words.

### The Comical Toddler—Exploring Humor

Adults may not realize that children begin honing their own comedic skills at impressively early ages. They point out that a child's reaction to physical stimuli, seen in activities such as tickling and bouncing, takes a new form sometime after the first birthday by becoming visual or oral rather than tactile. Toddler silliness or "joking" behavior can be seen as rudimentary attempts at humor and can be appreciated as child-initiated attempts to get others' reactions to the ridiculous and unexpected. They may playfully mimic adult words or actions, wear a pot for a hat, make funny face, or wholeheartedly enjoy participating in an "All Fall Down" activity.

## ADVICE TO TODDLER TEACHERS

Bardige (2009), after reviewing current research, has concluded that the quality of care, especially language-developing care, for toddler-to-3-year-olds in the United States needs improvement.

> At the critical age for language learning, public investments in children's education are lower than they will be at any time during childhood. Caregivers and teachers on the frontlines, who are doing their best to provide safe, loving, growth-promoting care, are not doing enough talking. (p. 219)

She believes with appropriate supports caregivers and teachers will be able to maintain language-rich environments, and provide care attuned to the needs of the individual child and the group as a whole. Under these conditions children will thrive, but more financial program support is necessary.

## BRAIN-BASED TEACHING AND LEARNING

Brain-based teaching involves the active engagement of the child using purposeful teaching strategies based on principles derived from research and neuroscience (Jensen, 2008). Teachers and caregivers are encouraged to consider the nature of the brain to make better decisions concerning instructional methods useful in reaching more learners.

Teachers using a brain-based approach realize the brain is a mass of highly connected areas with one brain area affecting others. The brain is also a whole entity that is highly adaptable and designed to respond to environmental input.

Early childhood educators have made special efforts to plan and equip classrooms that provide language and literacy opportunities that are both functional and responsive to the developmental needs of children's bodies and minds. Carefully designed classrooms help teachers to fulfill job duties while promoting children's full potential.

Young children's brains are busy routing and filtering environmental input gained through their sensory organs. Input is sent to specific brain areas for processing. If the information gathered is deemed by the brain to be of sufficient importance, it is organized and indexed and stored. There is no single brain pathway but rather different shared and unique pathways for different types of learning such as emotional, social, spatial, vocabulary, and other brain areas. This statement should remind the reader of the work of Howard Gardner, a well known theorist and psychologist, whose work focused upon multiple intelligences.

No discussion of brain activity can exclude the fact that there are different types of brain cells. A brain neuron is a basic structural and processing unit of the nervous system. It continuously fires, integrates and generates information across gaps called *synapses* linking one cell to another and acts as a conduit for information. As a rule, the more connections ones cells make, the better (Jensen, 2008, p. 13). A 2-year-old has twice the number of neurons as an adult. Nelson explains how learning occurs.

> The development of neural networks of cells that have fired together often enough to "wire together" are activated by complex interactions between genes and our environment, and are modulated by countless biochemicals. Remember that to truly understand new content, we must move from micro to the macro and back to the micro world. In this process, information may become oversimplified and out of context, but as elaboration occurs, the pieces of the puzzle reunite to form an accurate picture that results in accurate learning. (p. 17)

Toddlers may seem cute and naïve when they refer to all males as daddy or when they attempt to bite a toy that resembles a banana. Their behavior illustrates toddler global (macro) thinking prior to their further experience when they notice details and exceptions that refine their understandings. The brain can be thought of as acting like a muscle. The more activity that takes place the larger and more complex it can become. What a child experiences intellectually and physically change what his/her brain looks like. The brain can wire and rewire depending on environment, life choices available, and also the individual choices that are made such as choosing to learn to play a musical instrument or learning how to move the body to play a physical sport (Medina, 2008, p. 58).

## ADVICE TO THE FAMILIES OF TODDLERS

Verbally responsive and playful people, and a "toddler-proof" home equipped with objects and toys the toddler can investigate, will help facilitate a toddler's emerging language skills. An adult sitting on the floor or on a low chair near a toddler at play can promote toddler communication and also help the adult see things from the child's vantage point.

Objects and toys need not be expensive and can be designed and created at home. Social contact outside the home is important also. Toddlers enjoy branching out from the home on excursions into nature and community with caring adults. Local libraries may offer toddler story hours, and play groups are increasingly popular and sponsored by a wide number of community groups. Exposing the toddler to supervised toddler play groups gives the child "peer teachers" and promotes social skills. Typically, toddlers play side-by-side rather than cooperatively, but beginning attempts at sharing and short give-and-take interactions take place.

Some toddlers may frequently ask for the names of things and can be insistent and impatient about demands. Words will be learned during real events with concrete (real) objects. Children continue to generate language when their early efforts are accepted and reinforced. Situations that involve positive emotions and those that involve multiple sensory experiences also evoke child language production.

Regularly involving toddlers in educative conversations with educational toys and simple books prompts language growth. Patience and interest—rather than heavy-handed attempts to teach—are best. Getting the most from everyday experiences is a real art that requires an instructive yet relaxed attitude and the ability to talk about what has captured the child's attention. A skilled adult who is with a toddler who is focused on the wrapping paper rather than the birthday present will add comments about the wrapping paper. Or at the zoo, in front of the bear's cage, if the child is staring at a nearby puddle, the adult will discuss the puddle. Providing words and ideas along the child's line of inquiry, and having fun while doing so, becomes second nature after a few attempts.

Skilled adults tend to modify their speech according to the child's ability. They speak clearly, slowly enunciate and slightly exaggerate intonation, and pause between utterances. They may end their sentences with the "focused-upon" new word and emphasize it in pitch and stress. They also add to sentence length and complexity, providing that which is just a little beyond the child's level. Parent talk that sensitively and effectively suggests and instructs primes the child's language growth. If the home language is not English, Gonzalez-Mena (2006) suggests supporting children's development of that language, for it serves as a foundation for the later learning of a second language (in this case, English). This is aided by a strong school-home partnership.

The following two books contain a number of adult-child interactive games. They are good resources for parents and teachers.

Silberg, J. (2002). *Games to play with two-year-olds*. Bettsville, MD: Gryphon House.

Silberg, J. (2002). *Games to play with toddlers*. Bettsville, MD: Gryphon House.

Parents may need to become aware of the consequences that can result from home or center environments where toddlers experience chaos, unpredictability, violence, and frightening experience as a daily reality. Honig (1999) describes these toddlers as quick to be startled, aroused, angry, defiant, fearful, or withdrawn. She describes the chemical activity in their brains as abnormal. Building intimate, warm, trusting relationships is the best way to teach a child's brain that it need not send the body messages to release high levels of stress hormones. Honig recommends that nurturing providers offer each child interpretable, orderly, soothing, and loving experiences daily to support optimal brain development.

## SUMMARY

Language ability grows at its fastest rate of development during the toddler period. Young children accomplish difficult language tasks. They learn their native language sounds (phonetics) and successfully produce an increasing number of sounds. Grammar rules form and reform as the child gets closer to reproducing mature speech patterns. The child listens more carefully, noticing regularities and meanings (semantics) of words and gestures.

Concepts develop, serving as categories that help the child organize life's events. Many concepts are paired with words. Word symbols aid communication and language by allowing the child to speak and to be understood. Parents' conversations and the child's firsthand exploration through sense organs give depth to new words.

Toddlers are active in conversations, speaking and listening, sometimes correcting, trying to get the message across to whomever in the family will listen. Toddlers talk to themselves and their toys in one-word and then two-word (or more) sentences. These sentences are barely recognizable at first but gain more and more clarity as children age.

Differences between children's speech output may be noticed, and responsive, sensitive adults are language-promoting companions. Toddler books are enjoyed and plentiful, but researchers suggest non-educational electronic media viewing may produce undesirable effects for children under age 3.

Brian-based teaching involves using strategies based upon what neuroscientists have discovered concerning how young children learn.

## ADDITIONAL RESOURCES

### Readings

Acredolo, L. P., & Goodwin, S. W. (2000). *Baby mind: Brain-building games your baby will love to play.* New York: Bantam Books.

Fischer, B., & Medvic, E. (2003). *For reading out loud: Planning and practice.* Portsmouth, NH: Heinemann.

Medina, J. (2008). *Brain rules: Twelve principles for surviving and thriving work, home, and school.* Seattle, WA: Pear Press.

Owens, R. (2001). *Language development.* Boston: Allyn and Bacon.

### Toddler Books

Albee, S. (2003). *Blue's checkup.* New York: Simon and Schuster. (A visit to the doctor.)

Barton, B. (1986). *Trucks.* New York: Crowell. (Vivid color and objects that move.)

Blonder, E. (1988). *My very first things.* New York: Gossett. (Board book.)

Cousins, L. (1991). *Farm animals.* New York: Tambourine.

Cowley, J. (1999) *Mrs. Wishy-Washy.* East Rutherford, NJ: Philomel Books. (Board book.)

Darling Kindersley (2003). *Are lemons blue?* New York: Author. (Playful.)

Davenport, Z. (1995). *Mealtime.* New York: Ticknor & Fields. (Colorful illustrations.)

Davenport, Z. (1995). *Toys.* New York: Ticknor & Fields. (Common toys and objects.)

Dyer, J. (1996). *Animal crackers.* New York: Little, Brown. (A delectable collection of pictures, poems, and lullabies for the very young.)

Elya, S. M. (2006). *Beebe goes shopping.* New York: Harcourt.

Fleming, D. (2006). *The cow who clucked.* New York: Henry Holt. (Sounds and silliness that delight.)

Hoban, T. (1985). *What is it?* New York: Greenwillow.

Kunhardt, D. (1942). *Pat the bunny.* New York: Golden Touch and Feel Books.

Low, W. (2009). *Machines go to work.* New York; Henry Holt.

Lynn, S. (1987). *Farm animals.* New York: Macmillan.

Manushkin, F. (2009). *The tushy book.* New York: Macmillan

McCue, L. (1987). *Ten little puppy dogs.* New York: Random. (Board book.)

Newcome, Z. (2002). *Head, shoulders, knees, and toes.* Cambridge, MA: Candlewick Press.

Oxenbury, H. (1988). *Tickle, tickle.* New York: Macmillan.

Prelutsky, J. (Ed.) (1988). *Read-aloud rhymes for the very young.* New York: Alfred Knopf Publishers.

Scanlon, L. G. (2009). *All the world.* New York: Beach Lane Books.

Tafuri, N. (1987). *Where we sleep.* New York: Greenwillow.

Weeks, S. (2006). *Overboard!* New York: Harcourt (Bright, cheerful and fun.)

Whitford, R. (2005*). Little yoga: A toddler's first book of yoga*. New York: Holt, Henry Books for Young Readers. (Expect to try yoga positions with toddlers.)

## Helpful Websites

National Parent Information Network
http://npin.org
Provides related websites for parents and teachers.

Go to www.cengagebrain.com to access this text's Education Course-Mate website where you'll find helpful resource such as video activities, glossary flashcards, interactive exercises, quiz questions, and more!

# Review It and Use It

A. Match each word in Column I with the phrase it relates to in Column II.

| COLUMN I | COLUMN II |
|----------|-----------|
| 1. phonology | a. "Allgone cookie." "Shoe allgone." |
| 2. grammar | b. toddler goes through a naming or labeling stage |
| 3. dis? dat? | c. toddler unconsciously recognizes word order |
| 4. pivot | d. the sound system of language |
| 5. alphabet | e. each world language has its own |
| 6. symbol | f. as active as an adult |
| 7. toddler brain | g. a word represents something |

B. Write a brief description of experiences that could promote a toddler's learning the word *hat*. (Example: Parent points to a picture of a hat in a book and says, "Hat.")

C. List five identifying characteristics of the following concepts: van, rain, needle, and giraffe.

D. Return to question B. How many of your examples involved the child's sensory exploration of a hat? Why would this aid the child's learning?

E. Why is the toddler period called the prime or critical time for learning language?

F. Select the best answer.

1. Most children clearly articulate all English letter sounds by age
   a. 7 or 8.
   b. 6.
   c. 5.
   d. 24 months.

2. Most concept words used correctly by toddlers are
   a. labels and imitative echoing.
   b. fully understood.
   c. used because identifying characteristics have been noticed.
   d. rarely overused.

3. From beginning attempts, children usually
   a. reverse word order.
   b. use full simple sentences.
   c. use stress, intonation, and inflection in speaking.
   d. are always clearly understood.

4. One should _____ insist that the toddler pronounce "tree" correctly if he or she is saying "twee."
   a. always
   b. never
   c. usually
   d. tactfully

5. A toddler's one-word sentence, "Wawa," may mean
   a. "I want a drink of water."
   b. the child's dog, Waiter, is present.
   c. the child's father's name is Walter.
   d. any one or none of the above.

6. A child's first word is usually spoken between_____, and this is considered within the normal range.
   a. 10 and 22 months
   b. 9 and 20 months
   c. 11 and 25 months
   d. 8 and 18 months

## STUDENT ACTIVITIES

1. Make a book for toddlers from magazine illustrations or from photographs of common objects familiar to toddlers. Pages should be sturdy. Cut away any distracting backgrounds. If desired, outline objects with a wide-tip felt pen and protect pages with clear adhesive plastic or slip into page protectors. (An old binder works well to hold the pages.) Test your book on toddlers, and share your results.

2. Using only gesturing, get the person sitting next to you to give you a tissue or handkerchief or to tell you that one is not available.

3. Observe three toddlers (15 to 24 months old). Write down consonant sounds you hear. Record the number of minutes for each observation.

4. Using the following scale, rate each of the statements that follow. Talk about your ratings in a group discussion.

| 1 | 2 | 3 | 4 | 5 |
|---|---|---|---|---|
| Strongly Agree | Agree | Can't Decide | Mildly Disagree | Strongly Disagree |

   a. Toddlers can be best understood when adults analyze their words instead of their meanings.
   b. Some parents seem to have a knack for talking to young children and probably do not realize they possess this skill.
   c. The labeling stage is a time when children learn concepts rather than words.
   d. Learning language is really simple imitation.
   e. The study of semantics could take a lifetime.
   f. A toddler who does not like books is not progressing properly.
   g. After reading this chapter, I will not react to toddler grunts.
   h. Parents whose toddlers are speaking many words have purposely taught words to their children.
   i. It is a good idea to have a special place in the home where books are enjoyed with a toddler.
   j. It is best to give the toddler specific words for things, such as pickups instead of trucks, or bonnet instead of hat.

5. You notice your sister is ignoring her toddler's sign language attempts. What would you say or do? Be specific.

## Toddler Favorites

### Turtle

*There once was a turtle*
*that lived in a box.*
*He swam in the puddle*
*and climbed on the rock.*
*He snapped at a mosquito.*
*He snapped at a flea.*
*He snapped at a minnow*
*and he snapped at me.*
*He caught the mosquito.*
*He caught the flea.*
*He caught the minnow.*
*But he didn't catch me!*

Author Unknown

### Teddy Bear, Teddy Bear

*Teddy Bear, Teddy Bear, turn all around,*
*Teddy Bear, Teddy Bear, touch the ground.*
*Teddy Bear, Teddy Bear, read the news,*
*Teddy Bear, Teddy Bear, shine your shoes.*
*Teddy Bear, Teddy Bear, go upstairs,*
*Teddy Bear, Teddy Bear, say your prayers.*
*Teddy Bear, Teddy Bear, turn out the lights,*
*Teddy Bear, Teddy Bear, say*
*GOODNIGHT!*

Author Unknown

### The Little White Duck (Song)

*There's a little white duck sitting in the water,*
*A little white duck doing what he oughter;*
*He took a bite of a lily pad,*
*Flapped his wings and he said,*
*"I'm glad I'm a little white duck sitting in the water,"*
*quack, quack, quack.*
*There's a little green frog swimming in the water,*
*A little green frog doing what he oughter;*
*He jumped right off the lily pad,*
*that the little duck bit and he said*
*"I'm glad I'm a little green frog swimming in the water,"*
*glumph, glumph, glumph.*
*There's a little black bug floating on the water,*
*A little black bug doing what he oughter;*
*He tickled the frog on the lily pad*
*That the little duck bit and he said,*
*"I'm glad I'm a little black bug floating on the water,"*
*chirp, chirp, chirp.*
*There's a little red snake lying in the water,*
*A little red snake doing what he oughter;*
*He frightened the duck and the frog so bad,*
*He ate the little bug and he said,*
*"I'm glad I'm a little red snake lying in the water,"*
*sss, sss, sss.*
*Now there's nobody left sitting in the water,*
*nobody left doing what he oughter;*
*There's nothing left but the lily pad,*
*the duck and frog ran away. It's sad....*
*That there's nobody left sitting in the water,*
*boo, hoo, hoo.*

Author Unknown

## OBJECTIVES

After reading this chapter,
you should be able to:

- Identify characteristics of
  typical preschool speech.
- Describe differences in the
  language of younger and
  older preschoolers.
- Discuss the development
  of language skills in
  preschoolers.

## KEY TERMS

consonant
expressive
 (productive)
 vocabulary
metalinguistic
 awareness

overextension
receptive
 (comprehension)
 vocabulary
regularization
vowel

## On And On And On . . .

*Wilford is 4 and eager to speak in groups. He rambles, goes
on and on, and both bores and loses his audience. Renee,
his teacher, waits, patiently listening, but occasionally
interrupts him to say, "Thank you, Wilford, for sharing
with us." Sometimes this stops him, but often it does not.*

### Questions to Ponder

1. Is this "stream of consciousness" talking typical of
   4-year-olds? Is this a behavior found in some adults?

2. What teacher strategies might help Renee?

3. Describe three program activities that might help
   Wilford.

The preschool child's speech reflects sensory, physical, and social experiences, as well as thinking ability. Teachers accept temporary limitations, knowing that almost all children will reach adult language levels.

During the preschool years, children move rapidly through successive phases of language learning. By the time youngsters reach their fifth year, the most challenging hurdles of language learning have been overcome.

Teachers should skillfully interact with the children and provide appropriate learning opportunities and activities. An understanding of typical preschool speech characteristics can help the teacher do this.

Background experiences with children and child study provide a teacher with insight into children's language behavior. This chapter pinpoints language use during preschool years. Although speech abilities are emphasized, growth and change in other areas, as they relate to speech, are also covered.

In addition to the child's home environment, playing with other children is a major factor influencing language development. Finding friends in his age group is an important benefit of attending an early childhood center. In a place where there are fascinating things to explore and talk about, language abilities blossom (Figure 3–1).

It is almost impossible to find a child who has all of the speech characteristics of a given age group, but most children possess some of the characteristics that are typical. There is a wide range within normal age-level behavior, and each child's individuality is an important consideration.

For simplicity's sake, the preschool period is divided into two age groups: young, or early, preschoolers (2- and 3-year-olds) and older preschoolers (4- and 5-year-olds).

## YOUNG PRESCHOOLERS    **IRA**

Preschoolers communicate needs, desires, and feelings through speech and action. Close observation of a child's nonverbal communication can help uncover true meanings. Raising an arm, fiercely clutching playthings, or lying spread-eagle over as many blocks as possible may express more than the child is able to put into words. Stroking a friend's arm, handing a toy to another child who has not asked for it but looks at it longingly, and following the teacher around the room are behaviors that carry other meanings.

One can expect continued fast growth and changing language abilities, and children's understanding of adult statements is surprising. They may acquire 6 to 10 new words a day. Figure 3–2 displays children's stunning vocabulary growth from ages 1 through 7.

Squeals, grunts, and screams are often part of play. Imitating animals, sirens, and environmental noise is common. The child points and pulls to help others understand meanings. Younger preschoolers tend to act as though others can read their thoughts because, in the past, adults anticipated what was needed. A few children may have what seems to be a limited vocabulary at school until they feel at home there.

FIGURE 3–1 Children often share their ideas concerning how or what they might play.

## VOCABULARY GROWTH

| | | |
|---|---|---|
| 10–14 months | first word | First words are usually nouns instead of verbs. |
| 12–18 months | two words a week; close to 50 by 18 months | Child looks at something (or someone), points, and then says one or two words. Mispronunciations are common. |
| 18–24 months | 200 words | Some toddlers constantly ask "What dat?" or just "Dat?" They want objects named. |
| 2–3 years | 500 words | Questions, questions, questions! Mispronunciations still happen, and consonants may be substituted for one another in some words. |
| 3–4 years | 800 words | Preschoolers start to use contractions ("won't," "can't") as well as prepositions ("in," "on") and time expressions ("morning," "afternoon"). They may also make up words. |
| 4–5 years | 1,500 or more words | Children speak with greater clarity, can construct five- and six-word sentences, and make up stories. |
| 5–7 years | 11,000 words | Children retell and discuss stories. They have many words at hand and will know more than 50,000 as adults. |

**FIGURE 3–2** Vocabulary growth.

A difference between the child's **receptive** (or **comprehension**) **vocabulary** and his **expressive** (or **productive**) **vocabulary** is apparent, with the productive vocabulary lagging behind the receptive vocabulary. The receptive vocabulary requires that the child hears a word and anticipates or reacts appropriately; the production of a word means the child speaks the word at an appropriate time and place.

Children begin to acquire the more complex forms of grammar during this time period, including past tenses, embedded clauses, and passive constructions. Creative mistakes happen, such as "he breakeded my bike," which indicates that the child is noticing consistent patterns and applying them to the language system as he understands it.

The words used most often are nouns and short possessives: *my, mine, Rick's.* Speech focuses on present events, things are observed in newscaster style, and "no" is used liberally. As preschoolers progress in the ability to hold brief conversations, they must keep conversational topics in mind and connect their thoughts with those of others. This is difficult for 2-year-olds, and true conversational exchange with playmates is brief, if it exists at all. Although their speech is filled with pauses and repetitions in which they attempt to correct themselves, early preschoolers are adept at conversational turn taking. Talking over the speech of another speaker at this age occurs only about 5 percent of the time.

Speech may be loud and high pitched when the child is excited, or it may be barely audible and muffed when the child is embarrassed, sad, or shy. Speech of 2- and 3-year-olds tends to be uneven in rhythm, with comments issued in spurts rather than in an even flow like the speech of older children (Figure 3–3).

There seems to be an important step forward in the complexity of content in children's speech at age 2. They may begin making comments about cause and effect and sometimes use conjunctions, such as *'cause, 'ah,* and *'um,* between statements.

---

**receptive (comprehension) vocabulary** — the comprehension vocabulary used by a person in listening (and silent reading).

**expressive (productive) vocabulary** — the vocabulary a person uses in speaking and writing.

FIGURE 3–3 Speech can be limited when children are very interested.

Young preschoolers' talk is self-focused and mostly concerned with their intentions and feelings, why they wanted or did not want to do certain things, or what they wanted other people to do. Statements such as "I'm painting" or "I'm not climbing!" are commonplace.

Much of the time very young preschoolers' play focuses on recreating the work of the home and family—cooking, eating, sleeping, washing, ironing, infant care, and imitations of family events and pets (Figure 3–4). Play of slightly older preschoolers is more interactive. The child continues self-play but also explores other children, adults, environments, and actions. Eventually, most preschoolers understand that it is usually worth their while to share toys and take turns because when other playmates are around it is more fun. Two-year-olds may believe, as one preschooler remarked to his teacher, that "share means you give it away." When children begin exploring these other play options, "what's happening" in play becomes a speech subject, along with brief verbal reactions to what others are saying and doing.

A desire to organize and make sense of their experiences is often apparent in young preschoolers. Colors, counting, and new categories of thought emerge in their speech. There is

FIGURE 3–4 Teachers encourage the verbalizations of preschoolers.

a tendency for them to live out the action words they speak or hear in the speech of others. An adult who says "We won't run" may motivate a child to run; in contrast, an adult who says

"Walk" might be more successful in having the child walk. This is why experienced teachers tell children what they want children to do rather than what they do not want them to do.

### The Subdued 2-Year-Old

In any given group of young children, a few may appear subdued and quiet, having a tendency toward what many might call shyness. These children may possess a natural inclination that tends to inhibit spontaneous speech. Strong emotions can cause muscle tension, including tension in the larynx. Some adults asked to speak in front of a group experience this phenomenon. It can also affect speech volume. Most preschool teachers have worked with children whose speech was difficult to hear. Often, these children seem restrained when faced with unfamiliar situations. As older preschoolers they may become more outgoing and talkative or may continue to be less talkative and somewhat subdued when compared with their more boisterous counterparts. Teachers respect these children's natural inclinations and tendencies, but try to build the children's trust and their play opportunities with others.

### Verb Forms

In English, most verbs (regular forms) use -*ed* to indicate past tense. Unfortunately, many frequently used verbs have irregular past-tense forms, such as *came*, *fell*, *hit*, *saw*, *took*, and *gave*. Because the child begins using often-heard words, early speech contains correct verb forms. With additional exposure to language, children realize that past events are described with -*ed* verb endings. At that point, children tack the -*ed* on regular verbs as well as on irregular verbs, creating words such as *broked*, *dranked*, and other charming past-tense forms. This beautiful logic often brings inner smiles to the adult listeners. Verbs ending with -*ing* are used more than before. Even auxiliary verbs are scattered through speech—"Me have," "Daddy did it." Words such as *wanna*, *gonna*, and *hafta* seem to be learned as one word, and

stick in children's vocabulary, being used over and over.

A term for children's speech behavior that indicates they have formed a new internal rule about language and are using it is **regularization**. As children filter what they hear, creating their own rule systems, they begin to apply the new rules. An expected sequence in forming rules for past-tense verb usage follows.

- Uses irregular tense endings correctly (e.g., *ran*, *came*, *drank*).
- Forms an internal rule when discovering that -*ed* expresses past events (e.g., *danced*, *called*, *played*).
- Over-regularizes; for example, adds -*ed* to all regular and irregular verbs that were formerly spoken correctly (e.g., *camed*, *dided*, *wented*, *goed*).
- Learns that both regular and irregular verbs express past tense, and uses both.

In using plural noun forms, the following sequence is common.

- Remembers and uses singular forms of nouns correctly (e.g., *ball*, *dog*, *mouse*, *bird*).
- Uses irregular noun plurals correctly (e.g., *men*, *feet*, *mice*).
- Forms an internal rule that plurals have "s" or "z" ending sounds.
- Applies rule to all nouns (e.g., *balls*, *mens*, *dogs*, *feets*, *birds*, *mices*, or *ballsez*, *dogsez*, *feetsez*).
- Achieves flexible internal rules for plurals, memorizes irregular plural forms, and uses plurals correctly.

### Key-Word Sentences

The 2-year-old omits many words in sentences, as does the toddler. The remaining words are shortened versions of adult sentences in which only the essentials are present. These words are key words and convey the essence of the message. Teachers attempt to relate questionable child utterances to concurrent child activity to grasp a child's meaning. Sentences at this stage are about four words long. Some pronouns and

---

**regularization** — a child's speech behavior that indicates the formation and internalization of a language rule (regularity).

AGE

| | |
|---|---|
| age 2 | raises voice pitch at sentence ending: "Me go?" "All gone?" |
| | uses short "what" and "where" questions: "Whas dat?" "Where kitty?" |
| age 3 | asks yes-no questions |
| | begins to use "why" questions |
| | begins to use auxiliary verbs in questions: "Can I have gum?" "Will you get it?" |
| | begins to use "how" questions: "How you do that?" |
| age 4 | adds tag endings: "Those are mine, okay?" "You like it, huh?" "That's good, isn't it?" |
| | inverts auxiliary verbs in questions: "Why are you sad?" "Why aren't we staying with gramma?" |
| | begins to use complex and two-part questions and statements: "I will tell him how to do it if you like." "What can I do when he won't come?" "I don't know what to do." "Why does it fall down when the door slams?" |

**FIGURE 3–5** Question development.

adjectives, such as *pretty* or *big*, are used. Very few, if any, prepositions (*by, on, with*) or articles (*a, an, the*) are spoken. Some words are run together and are spoken as single units, such as "whadat?" or "eatem," as are the verb forms mentioned earlier. The order of words (syntax) may seem jumbled at times, as in "outside going ball," but basic grammar rules are observed in most cases.

Pronouns are often used incorrectly and are confused, as in "Me finish milk," and "him Mark's." Concepts of male and female, living things, and objects may be only partly understood, as shown in the example of the 3-year-old who says of a special toy she cannot find, "Maybe it is hiding!". This probably indicates she hasn't yet learned that hiding can be done only by an animate object.

### Questions

*Wh-* questions (where, what, why, who) begin to appear in the speech of the young preschooler. During the toddler period, rising voice inflection and simple declarative utterances such as "Dolly drink?" are typical. At this stage, questions focus on location, objects, and people. Occasionally, their questions display a special interest in causation (why), process (how), and time (when). This reflects more mature thinking that probes purposes and intentions in others. Figure 3–5 shows one child's question development. Questions are frequent, and the child sometimes asks for an object's function or the causes of

certain events. It is as if the child sees that things exist for a purpose that in some way relates to him. The answers adults provide stimulate the child's desire to know more. Questions about words and word meanings appear, such as "Why is his name Ang?"

Vocabularies of the young preschooler range from 250 to more than 1,000 words (Figure 3–6). An average of 50 new words enters the child's vocabulary each month. Gartrell (2007) notes

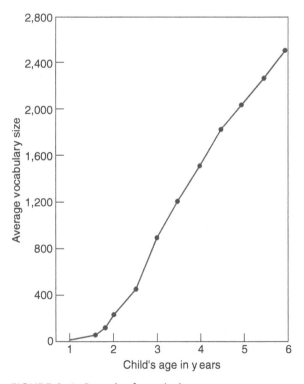

**FIGURE 3–6** Growth of vocabulary.

that children absorb information from the world around them and incorporate it into their growing beings.

## CATEGORIES IN CHILDREN'S THINKING

Children organize a tremendous amount of sensory data and information gained though life experiences by forming mental categories. Studies point out that young children can be quite sophisticated in how they group objects and think about their groupings. Young preschoolers' categories differ from those of older children. The young preschooler tends to focus on superficial properties such as the "look" of something and where it is found. A younger child may focus on the teacher's fuzzy sweater by wanting to touch and rub it and saying "soft." An older preschooler may talk about its number of buttons, or patterns, or its similarity to his own sweater or other sweaters he has seen. Preschoolers often put items together in terms of their visual similarities rather than grouping items according to more fundamental likenesses.

### Overlapping Concepts

Younger preschoolers commonly call all four-footed furry animals "dog," and all large animals "horse." This reflects **overextension**, in which the child has overextended and made a logical conclusion because these animals have many of the same features, can be about the same size, and therefore fit the existing word. This phenomenon is seen in the examples given in Figure 3–7.

Concept development, defined in Chapter 2 as the recognition of one or more distinguishing features or characteristics, proceeds by leaps and bounds during preschool years and is essential to meaningful communication. Details, exceptions, and discrepancies are often discussed in 4-year-olds' conversations. The younger preschooler can be described as a "looker and doer" who engages in limited discussion of the features of situations. The excitement of exploration and discovery, particularly of something new and novel, is readily apparent in preschool classrooms. Children typically crowd around to see, touch, experience, and make comments about objects and events. Teachers notice the all-consuming focusing and the long periods of watching or touching, usually followed by verbalizing and questioning an event or experience.

As they age, young children can find that learning not only brings them joy, but also perhaps mastery and satisfaction. Medina (2008) suggests this breeds the confidence it takes to take intellectual risks. A young preschooler who learns to button his sweater, tie his shoe, ride a bike, or count to five usually wants to share

| FIRST WORD | WORD WAS USED TO IDENTIFY AN OBJECT, PERSON OR EVENT | LATER WORD WAS APPLIED TO |
|---|---|---|
| dada | daddy | store clerk, doctor, mailman, football player, teenager. |
| moo | moon | cookie, melon, letter O, clock, pizza pan, button. |
| ah | soft | fuzzy sweater, dog's fur, flower petal, plush doll. |
| em | worm | pasta, caterpillar, licorice ropes, string, rice. |
| wh | sound of train | vacuum cleaner, mixer, wind, fast vehicles. motor noise. |
| ba | ball | oranges, meatballs, yarn, coconut, overhead light, lollypop, bubbles. |

FIGURE 3–7 Common overextensions used in child's first three years.

---

**overextension** — in the early acquisition of words and their meanings, the application of a word to include other objects that share common features, such as "water" being used to describe any liquid.

his accomplishment with anyone who will listen and will repeat the physical actions over and over just to prove he can do them.

## Running Commentaries

As children play, their actions are sometimes accompanied by a running self-commentary or "stream of consciousness" talking concerning what they are doing or what is happening (Figure 3–8). It can be described as a kind of verbal thought process, like mentally talking to oneself such as "Now, where did I put that key?"

It seems to increase in complex play situations as the child problem solves and talks it through.

Researchers suggest multiple reasons for preschoolers' private speech. These include the following: (1) talking to themselves is a way of giving themselves directions for their intended actions, (2) they need a sensorimotor activity as a reinforcer or "crutch" because their cognitive schemes are not yet well developed, and (3) it is more efficient for them to talk their ideas through in words rather than silently.

Self-talk may help children sequence actions, control their own behavior, use more flexible modes of thinking, and manipulate the goals they are trying to achieve in their play.

Talking to self and talking to another can occur alternately. Toys, animals, and treasured items still receive a few words. Statements directed to others do not usually need answers. Private speech rarely considers another's point of view. A conversation between young preschoolers may sound like two children talking together about different subjects. Neither child is really listening or reacting to what the other says. When a very young preschooler does wish to talk directly to another child, it is sometimes done through an adult. A child may say, "I want truck," to an adult, even if the child playing with the truck is standing close by.

Other researchers who have examined self-talk suggest a number of possible developmental benefits. These include:

● practicing newly recognized language forms.
● obtaining pleasure through play with word sounds.
● exploring vocal capacities.
● reliving particular significant events.
● creating dialogue in which the child voices all participants' parts, perhaps helping the child later fit into social settings.
● experimenting with fantasy, thereby accommodating the creative urge (Figure 3–9).
● attending objectively to language.
● facilitating motor behavior in a task or project.

Whatever its benefits, self-talk is natural, common behavior. By the age of 5, the child's self-talk is observed infrequently. As children approach the age of 3, both dialogue and monologue are apparent. Observers of play conversations find it difficult to determine just how much of each is present.

Teachers who conduct group times with younger preschoolers are familiar with children

Situation:    Four- and five-year-old girls playing with water

| | COMMENTARY | CHARACTERISTIC |
|---|---|---|
| Debbie: | "Two of those make one of these." (playing with measuring cups) | Talking to self. |
| Debbie: | "Two cups or three cups . . . whoops it went over." | Talks about what happened. |
| Tifine: | "Stop it or else I'll beat you up." (said to Debbie) | Does not respond to another's speech. |
| Debbie: | "This is heavy." (holding the 2-cup measuring container full of water) | Describes perception. |
| Christine: | "Is it hot?" (Christine just dropped in) | |
| Debbie: | "Feel it and see." "It's not hot." (feeling the water) | Hears another; answers appropriately. Child talking to self. |
| Debbie: | "I'm finished now. Oh this is awfully heavy—I'm going to pour it into the bottle." | Talking about what she perceives and what she is doing. |

FIGURE 3–8 Conversation during play activity.

**FIGURE 3–9** The teacher may assume the child is experimenting with fantasy play, or simply offering her a play toy, or waiting for the teacher to name the object.

who ramble on and on; the teachers deal with this behavior by using a variety of techniques. Teachers try to encourage "my turn, your turn" behaviors. Kitchen timers, a ping-pong paddle held by one speaker and then passed to another, or a turned-on flashlight used to signal a child that his speaking turn is over are strategies teachers have devised. Teachers also try to draw focus back to the subject at hand by saying, "Amy, yes, dogs do use their tongues when they drink. It is Jeremy's turn to tell us about his dog now."

### Repetition

Repetition in speech is common. Sometimes it happens randomly at play, and at other times it is done with a special purpose. A young child may repeat almost everything said to him. Most young preschoolers repeat words or parts of sentences regularly. Children's growing language skills allow them to create repetitions that rhyme, as in "oogie, woogie, poogie bear," which greatly please them. They quickly imitate words that they like; sometimes, excitement is the cause. Rhyming words or rhyming syllables may promote enjoyable mimicking and younger preschoolers are particularly fascinated and attracted to words that rhyme. Repetition of rhyming words seems to help children remember things such as "Get up at eight and you won't be late."

Free associations (voiced juggling of sounds and words) occur at play and at rest and may

sound like babbling. Many times, it seems as though, having learned a word, the child must savor it or practice it, over and over (Figure 3–10).

### Lack of Clarity

About one in every four words uttered by the young preschooler is not readily understandable. This lack of clarity is partially caused by an inability to control the mouth, tongue, and breathing and an inability to hear subtle differences and distinctions in speech. Typically, articulation of all English speech sounds, especially some

**FIGURE 3–10** Elsa Beth calls this "bussing" her teeth.

**consonant** blends, is not accomplished until age 7 or 8. Young preschoolers are only 40 to 80 percent correct in their articulation of words. This lack of intelligibility can be partly attributed to the complexity of the task of mastering the sounds. Although children may be right on target in development, their speech may still be difficult to understand.

The young preschooler may have difficulty with the rate of speech, phrasing, inflection, intensity, syntax, and voice stress. Faulty articulation and defective sound making can also contribute to the problem. The child who attempts to form the longest utterances is the one who is hardest to understand. The child who omits sounds is less clear than the one who distorts them. As a rule, expect omissions, substitutions, and distortions in the speech of 2- and 3-year olds, for they will be plentiful.

By 3 years of age, children's pronunciation patterns are not yet fully like those of adults, but the basic features of the adult phonological system are present. Most children can produce all of the **vowel** sounds and nearly all of the consonant sounds in at least a few words, but their productions are not 100 percent accurate.

Young children typically omit sounds at the ends of words, saying, for example, *ba* for "ball." Middle consonants in longer words are also passed over lightly—*ikeem* for "ice cream" or *telfone* for "telephone." Even beginning sounds may be omitted, as in *ellow* for "yellow."

Substitutions of letter sounds are also common, for example, *aminal* and *pasghetti*. Until the new sound is mastered, one consonant may even take the place of another; *wabbit*, *wun*, and *wain* are common examples. Children who cannot yet produce all of the speech sounds accurately can generally hear the differences between *w* and *r*, or *t* and *th*, when they are pronounced by others.

## Dramatic Play

Short play sequences that involve acting or imitating the behavior of family begin at home and school. Speech usually accompanies the reenactments. Although young children at this age play side-by-side, most of this dramatic play

**VIDEO ACTIVITY**

Go to the Education CourseMate website to watch the TeachSource Video entitled, *Preschool: Communication Development Through Language and Literacy Activities*. The video focuses upon preschoolers' dramatic play and role playing as well as songs, stories, and prewriting opportunities that are language and literary-building.

1. What dramatic play scenarios might be commonly initiated by a full classroom of preschoolers living in a rural farm community? And how might their teachers plan to accommodate it? How about a classroom full of intercity urban preschoolers?

2. In what way might early childhood educators connect alphabet letter recognition or print awareness opportunities with preschoolers' dramatic play?

starts as solitary activity. Common play themes include talking on the phone, caring for a baby, or cooking. Dolls, toys, and dress-up clothes are usually part of the action and may serve to initiate this type of play. Observers of 2- and 3-year-olds in classrooms find it hard to determine whether children are engaged in joint planning of play or are simply playing in the same area with the same kinds of playthings. Preschools purposely purchase multiple dolls so that many children can feed and rock "their babies" when they see others doing it.

## ADVICE FOR FAMILIES AND EARLY CHILDHOOD EDUCATORS

Families sometimes fret about a child who stops, stammers, or stutters when speaking. Calling attention to this speech and making demands on the child cause tension, making the situation worse. All children hesitate, repeat, stop, and start in speaking—it is typical behavior. Searching for the right word takes time, and thoughts may come faster than words. Adults need to relax and wait. Speech is a complex process of sending and receiving. Maintaining patience and optimism and assuming a casual "I'm listening" stance is the best course of action

---

**consonant** — (1) a speech sound made by partial or complete closure of the vocal tract, which obstructs air flow; (2) an alphabet letter used in representing any of these sounds.

**vowel** — (1) a voiced speech sound made without stoppage or friction of air flow as it passes through the vocal tract; (2) an alphabet letter used in representing any of these sounds.

FIGURE 3–11 "Me eatem!"

for the adult. Many schools routinely send home informational material to alert families to age-level speech characteristics.

Teachers frequently encounter child statements that are seemingly illogical and they suspect, if they acknowledge them, that the child will soon provide more information. Child logic is there, but teachers know that they are not privy to inner thought processes or children's past experiences. With more information, what at first appeared illogical turns out to have beautiful logic.

Frequently, a listening teacher will feel on the edge of understanding what a child is trying to say. This happens with both younger and older preschoolers struggling at times to put into words what they are thinking (Figure 3–11). Acceptance and interest are appropriate.

Attentive interaction with positive feedback is recommended for adults who live or work with 2- and 3-year-olds. Reacting to the intent of the child's message is more helpful than concentrating on correctness. In other words, focus on what is said rather than the way it is said. A lot of guessing is still necessary to determine what the child is trying to say. The adult's model of speech will override temporary errors as the child hears more and more of it.

By simply naming objects, adults can encourage children to notice how different items are similar and can help children gain new information about the world. Helping children see details and relationships in what they encounter

is useful if done in a matter of fact rather than a pressured way or an "I'm trying to teach you something" manner. Connecting past events to present events may aid their understanding.

Children's hearing should be checked regularly because even a moderate hearing loss may affect speech production. Preschoolers are particularly prone to upper respiratory infections and ear problems.

## BOOKS FOR YOUNGER PRESCHOOLERS

Many picture books are available for younger preschoolers. Experts suggest books for this age group that have:

- themes, objects, animals, or people that are familiar and within their range of life experience.
- clarity of content and story line.
- clear, simple illustrations or photographs with backgrounds that do not distract from the intended focus.
- themes concerning everyday tasks and basic human needs.

Most 2- and 3-year-olds enjoy actively participating in story reading, but they can be very good listeners as well. Participation can include pointing, making noise, repeating dialogue, or performing imitative body actions. Books that are repetitive and predictable offer the enjoyment of anticipating what will come next. For children who are used to being read to at bedtime, the calming effect of listening to the human voice becomes very apparent during story reading when heads nod or children act sleepy. Chapter 9 covers the topic of introducing preschool children to literature.

## OLDER PRESCHOOLERS

As younger preschoolers get older, adults can expect the following:

- longer sentences with more words per sentence
- more specificity
- more "ing" endings on verbs
- increased correctness in the forms of the verb "to be"
- use of more auxiliary verbs
- more facility with passive-voice verbs, including "did" and "been"
- changes in negative sentences, from "No want" to "I don't want"
- changes in question forms, from "Car go?" to "Where did the car go?"
- changes in mental categories
- additional clarifications in articulation of speech sounds

By the time they are between 4 and 5 years of age, most preschoolers' speech is similar to adult use; their sentences are longer, with almost all words present rather than only key words (Figure 3–12).

Preschoolers' play is active and vocal, and they copy each other's words and manner of speaking. A word such as "monster," or more colorful words, may swiftly become of interest and spread rapidly from child to child. Remember the joy that both younger and older children exhibited with the phrases: "zip-a-dee-doo-dah," "bibbidi-bobbidi-boo," "scoobidoobi-do," "blast off," "fuzzy-wuzzy," and "ooey-gooey"? Every generation of preschoolers seems to have their own favorite sayings, and new ones are constantly appearing.

The older preschooler's social speech and conversations are heard and interpreted to a greater degree by others of the child's age.

**FIGURE 3–12** Rene is explaining why she selected a certain puzzle piece.

The child learns and practices the complexities of social conversation, including (1) gaining another's attention by making eye contact, touching, or using words or catch-phrases like "Know what?"; (2) pausing and listening; (3) correcting himself; (4) maintaining attention by not pausing, so as not to let another speaker jump in; (5) taking turns in conversing by developing patience and trying to listen while still holding in mind what he wants to say.

## Friendships

The young preschooler may develop a new friend or find another he prefers to play near or with. At ages 2 and 3, friendships are usually temporary, changing from day to day. Friendships of older preschoolers are more stable and lasting. By ages 4 and 5, there seems to be a desire to remain compatible and work out differences, therefore creatively maintaining a type of play acceptable to both. Negotiation, clarification, and open-mindedness flourish during play. A friend's needs and requests are handled with sensitivity, and flexibility characterizes conversations. Needless to say, spats, "blowups," and the crushed feelings accompanying rejection sometimes occur. Verbal interaction between children adds a tremendous amount of verbal input and also promotes output.

## Group Play

Joint planning of play activities and active make-believe and role-playing take on new depth in older preschoolers. Most 4- and 5-year-olds' main concern seems to be interacting with age-mates. Twosomes and groups of play companions are typical in older preschoolers' classrooms and play yards (Figure 3–13). As speech blossoms, friendships blossom and disintegrate (Figure 3–14). Speech is used to discourage and disallow entrance to play groups when running from newcomers is impossible. Speech is found to be effective in hurting feelings, as in statements such as "I don't like you" or "No girls." Children find that verbal inventiveness may help them join play or initiate play.

In group play, pretending is paramount. Make-believe play appears to be at its zenith. Many children grow in the ability to (1) verbally suggest new directions and avenues of fantasy, (2) engage in verbal negotiation, (3) compromise, (4) argue, and (5) become a group's leader by using the right words. Popular children seem to be those who use speech creatively and become enjoyable companions to others.

Violent statements such as "I'm going to shoot you" or "cut you up" are sometimes heard, and these tend to reflect television viewing or media drama. The reality-fantasy dividing

**FIGURE 3–13** Group play encourages social development and social connectiveness.

**FIGURE 3–14** Emily is explaining why the rabbit in the book is naughty.

line may become temporarily blurred in some play situations, causing some children considerable anxiety.

Older preschoolers talk "in character" as they elaborate their dramatic play. If a scenario calls for a mother talking to a baby or teenagers talking, preschoolers adopt appropriate speech. Imitations of pop singers or cartoon characters are common. Role-taking is an important skill in mature communication, indicating that social and dramatic play and improvisation are effective means of facilitating growth in communicative competence.

Four-year-olds seem to boast, brag, and make lots of noise. However, apparently boastful statements such as "Look what I did" may just be the child's attempt to show that he is capable and to share his accomplishments. Although preschoolers enjoy being with their peers, they quickly and easily engage in quarreling and name-calling. Sometimes, they do battle verbally. Typically, 3- to 5-year-olds disagree over possession of objects or territory, and verbal reasons or verbal evidence may help them win arguments. Many conflicts are resolved and lead to continued play. Speech helps children settle their affairs with and without adult help.

As a child develops a sense of humor, giggling becomes part of the noise of play. Silliness often reigns. One preschool boy thought it hilarious to go up to a teacher named Alice and say, "What's your name, Alice?" and then run off laughing—quite mature humor for a 4-year-old! Preschoolers may distort and repeat what a caregiver says, making changes in sounds and gleefully chanting the distorted message. Teachers who want to cultivate children's ability to understand and appreciate humor try to plan activities and present materials that challenge children's ability to interpret humor.

Argument, persuasion, and statements aimed at controlling others are frequently heard during play. Older preschool children are able to state reasons (Figure 3–15), request information, give explanations, utter justifications for their behavior, and verbally defend themselves. At times, establishing authority in disagreements seems paramount to compromising.

## Inner Speech

A subtle shift takes place during the later preschool years, when inner speech becomes apparent and the child more frequently plans, monitors ideas, and evaluates silently. The child is still talking about his accomplishments and actions in a look-at-me fashion, but a greater portion of his self-commentary is unspoken.

FIGURE 3–15 Look at what I caught!

## EXPLORING THE CONVENTIONS OF CONVERSATION

Children learn language by reinventing it for themselves, not by direct instruction. They crack the code through exposure and opportunities to converse. They actively, although unconsciously, ingest and discover the rules of the system. Their speech errors often alert adults to the inner rules of language being formed.

Conversations have unwritten rules and expectations, the "you-talk-I-talk" sequence being the most apparent. Some preschoolers (3- and 4-year-olds) may delight in violating or "playing" with the conventions of conversation. Sometimes preschoolers deliberately mislead (usually to tease playfully) or use "taboo" bathroom talk, nonsense talk, or unexpected tone when they are capable of verbally responding at a more mature level. Most teachers sense the child may be asserting independence by rejecting conversational convention. One teacher

termed this "going into the verbal crazies" to reject what another child or adult is saying, therefore attempting to change or control the situation. By violating conversational convention, children may clarify how conversational interaction should take place.

### Relational Words

More and more relational words appear as the child begins to compare, contrast, and revise stored concepts with new happenings. The following teacher-recorded anecdote during a story-telling activity shows how the child attempts to relate previously learned ethics to a new situation.

> During story telling Michael repeated with increasing vigor, "He not berry nice!" at the parts of the story when the wolf says, "I'm going to blow your house down." Michael seemed to be checking with me the correctness of his thinking based on his internalized rules of proper moral conduct. (Machado, 2008, p. 16)

Perhaps because adults stress bad and good or because a young child's inner sense of what is and what is not proper is developing, teachers notice that preschoolers often describe feelings and people within narrow limits. One is pretty or ugly, mean or nice. Shades of meaning or extenuating circumstances seem yet to be understood. Preschoolers are focused on the here and now. Their senses actively probe by touching, smelling, observing, and listening to sounds. Around age 4, conceptual dimensions begin to be understood, and they question the function and use of items, make comparisons, and discover relationships. They are beginning to categorize their environment differently:

> Although the words "big" and "little" are commonly used by preschoolers, they are overused. Many other comparison words give children trouble, and one hears "biggerer," "big-big-big," and "bestus one" to describe size. Time words elicit smiles from adults as children wrestle with present, past, and future, as in "zillion days" or "tomorrower." Number words are difficult for some children to handle, and expressions such as "whole bunches" and "eleventeen" are sometimes heard.

Although 4-year-olds are able speakers, many of the "plays on words," double meanings, and connotative language subtleties that are important in adult speech are beyond children's understanding. Their creative uses of words at times seem metaphoric and poetic and are valiant attempts to put thoughts into words. Half-heard words and partially or fully learned words are blended together and are, at times, wonderfully descriptive. The author still laughs about the 4-year-old who called her "Mrs. Eye Shadow."

## Speech and Child Behavior

There is tremendous variety in the ways children can modify their voices, and they may speak in a different pitch or rhythm when speaking to different people. They can whine, whisper, change volume, and distort timing and pronunciation.

Some children discover that by increasing volume or changing tone they can affect others' behavior. They find that speech can show anger or sarcasm and can be used aggressively to hurt others.

Preschoolers may mimic the speech of "bad guy" media characters. Acts of aggression, clothed in the imitated speech and actions of a movie, television, or video character, can become part of this type of play. Purposeful echoing or baby talk can irritate or tease. Excessive talking is sometimes used to get one's way, and "talking back" may occur.

Some children find that silence can get as much attention from adults as loud speech. Tattling on another may simply be a way of checking for correctness, or it can be purposeful.

Through trial and error and feedback, the child finds that words can hurt, gain friends or favor, or satisfy a wide range of needs. Because preschoolers are emotion-packed human beings, their statements range from expressions of "you're my buddy" to "you're my enemy" within a matter of minutes.

What may appear to be violent statements may be just role-playing or make-believe competition. To some adults, preschooler speech may appear loud and wild. Their speech seems overly nasal and full of moisture that sprays outward. A young child may have frequent nasal colds and congestion during this period. Preschoolers tend to stand close to others and their volume increases when they feel strongly about their subjects.

## Impact Words

Not all speech used by older preschoolers is appreciated by adults. Name-calling and offensive words and phrases may be used by active preschoolers to gain attention and reaction from both adults and children. Children discover that some phrases, sentences, and words cause unusual behavior in others. They actively explore these and usually learn which of these are inappropriate and when they can be used. Children recognize that most of this type of talk has "impact value." If certain talk makes people laugh or gives the children some kind of positive reward, it is used over and over.

Bathroom words seem to be explored and used as put-downs and attention getters. As every parent and teacher knows, young children experiment with language related to the body, and particularly to the private parts, going to the bathroom, and sexuality. In fact, children's use of sexual words can make it seem as if they know more than they do. Giggles and uproarious laughter can ensue when these words are used, adding to the child's enjoyment, and new teachers may not know how to handle these situations. The school's policy regarding this matter can be a subject for staff discussion. Generally, newly spoken bathroom talk should be ignored unless it is hurtful, or the child should be told that the place to use the word is in the bathroom. This often remedies the behavior because the child's enjoyment of it is spoiled without an audience. Alternatively, it might suffice to firmly say, "That's a word that hurts. His name is Michael," or in a calm but firm voice, "That kind of talk is unacceptable." Preschoolers love using forbidden words, especially when they play together. What parents and teachers can control is what is said in their presence.

## Sound Words

In our culture, children are particularly fond of repeating conventionalized sounds reputedly made by animals ("arf-arf," "meow," "baa") as well as action sounds for toy vehicles ("putt-putt," "beep," "varoom"). When a child is playing the baby in home reenactment dramatic play, "wa-wa" will be heard frequently. Rough-and-tumble outside play may be accompanied by cartoon-strip sounds like "pow," "bam," and "zap." In addition, a good number of 4-year-olds can distinguish rhyming words, and they enjoy creating them.

## Created Words

Created words such as "turner-overer" for pancake turner, "mudpudders" for rain boots, or "dirt digger" for spade are wonderfully descriptive and crop up occasionally in child speech, perhaps as a means of filling in gaps in their vocabularies. Many cite young children's fascination with the functions of objects in their environment as the reason such words are created. Children enjoy nonsense words, and may revel in their newly gained abilities to use them.

## Displaying Creativity

Being creative is not a problem for most preschoolers. Most display their growing ingenuity and imaginative thought and see relationships outside of conventional categories as they manipulate, discover, and investigate their environment and the new experiences their teachers plan and introduce. Many school activities are carefully rigged for children's manipulation and first-hand exploration. In classrooms where children have learned their ideas are welcomed and listened to, discussion can lead to clarification and further dialog. In an activity planned to help children cross a street safely, a teacher will no doubt get many practical and illogical suggestions including asking an adult for help, looking and listening carefully, and perhaps creative solutions such as riding an elephant borrowed from the zoo.

## WORD MEANINGS

During later preschool years children often become focused on what words mean and they begin to think and wonder about words. They begin to understand that words are arbitrary symbols with no intrinsic connection to their meaning but rather are representatives of meaning. The young child who says, "Templeton has a big name; my name is small," is displaying a recognition of word length or number of syllables.

## Reality and Nonsense

Some preschool children can enjoy the absurd, nonsensical, and ridiculous in their experiences and find humor in the unexpected. Others, at a different stage in their cognitive development with another orientation, insist on knowing the right way—the real, the accepted, the "whys and wherefores"—and will see no humor in what confuses them or contradicts the "usual order of things."

A number of preschoolers view life and surroundings seriously, literally. Others can "play" in speech with the opposite of what they know to be true. We know this is true in some adults also. Some simply do not seem to enjoy what most of us may find humorous.

There is considerable "language play" in nursery rhymes, fairy tales, and classic stories and children discover wonderful, fun ways to repeat things that story characters say. They may gleefully stomp up a hallways saying, "Fee, f, fo, fum, here I come!". They may build bridges with blocks and make play figures "trip, trap, trip, trap" across them. Teachers are careful not to suppress a child's delight in absurdity by insisting on exact or literal renditions of things. Teachers encourage nonsense play by appreciating a child's inventions or nonsensical propositions. They may model some silliness or nonsense themselves. For example, the teacher might invert words in a sentence well known to the children to evoke child laughter by saying, "And the dogs go meow and cats say bowwow." And then the teacher would hope the children would either correct her or join in the game, producing their own inversions.

## Myths Concerning Speech and Intelligence

A large and mature vocabulary at this age may tend to lead teachers to think a child has superior intelligence. Making conclusions about children based on language ability at this age has inherent pitfalls considering the many factors that could produce limited or advanced vocabulary, particularly when one considers cultural differences, bilingualism, and the child's access to "language-rich environments." At later ages language usage does seem to be related to school success.

## Common Speech Patterns of Older Preschoolers

Four-year-olds often rhyme words in their play and speech, as previously mentioned. Older preschoolers engage in less frequent self-chatter. They continue to make errors in grammar and in the use of the past tense of verbs ("He didn't caught me"), adjectives ("It's biggerer than yours") (Figure 3–16), time words ("The next tomorrow"), and negatives ("I didn't did it").

## CHILD'S AGE

| 2–2½ years | joins words in sentences of two or more words<br>knows name<br>has vocabulary of more than three words<br>understands long spoken sentences and simple<br>  commands<br>begins using plurals and past tense<br>changes pitch and/or loudness for specific meaning<br>begins using forms of verb "to be"<br>uses a few prepositions<br>uses "I," "me," and "you" | uses about 25 phonemes<br>articulates about 10 to 12 vowel types and<br>  about 12 to 15 consonants<br>points to and names objects in pictures<br>names five to eight body parts<br>enjoys rhythm in words, nursery rhymes,<br>  finger plays, and simple stories<br>understands and responds to almost all<br>  of adult speech<br>generalizes by calling round objects ball,<br>  and so on |
|---|---|---|
| 2½–3 years | begins to use negatives, imperatives, and<br>  commands<br>shows variety in question types<br>adds as many as two to three words to<br>  vocabulary daily<br>names items in signs and books<br>uses three- or four-word sentences<br>enjoys fun with words | follows simple directions<br>points to body parts when asked<br>names many common objects<br>uses an increasing number of nouns, verbs,<br>  and pronouns<br>draws lines and circular forms in artwork<br>knows words or lines from books, songs,<br>  and stories |
| 3–4 years | asks why, what, where, how, and when questions<br>loves word play<br>makes closed figures in art<br>begins using auxiliary verbs<br>tells sex and age<br>utters compound sentences with connecting<br>  "and . . . er . . . but," and so on<br>engages in imaginary play with dialogue and<br>  monologue<br>says full name<br>follows two- and three-part requests<br>relates ideas and experiences<br>uses adverbs, adjectives, and prepositions<br>answers who, what, and where questions<br>names some colors and is interested in counting | looks at books while alone and enjoys<br>  reading times<br>talks about relationships<br>memorizes a short song, poem, finger play,<br>  or story<br>repeats three digits and two to three<br>  nonsense syllables if asked<br>uses adjectives and pronouns correctly<br>can copy a recognizable circle or square<br>  well if shown a model<br>can imitate a clapping rhythm<br>starts to talk about the function of objects<br>can find an object in group that is different<br>can find missing parts of wholes<br>can classify using clear, simple distinctions<br>knows names of common shapes |
| 4–5 years | has vocabulary of more than 1,500 words<br>uses sentences of five to six (or more) words<br>may use impact, shock, and forbidden words<br>may use words of violence<br>argues, convinces, and questions correctness<br>shares books with friends<br>acts out story themes or recreates life<br>  happenings in play<br>has favorite books<br>likes to dictate words<br>notices signs and print in environment<br>uses etiquette words, such as "please," "thank<br>  you," and so on<br>enjoys different writing tools<br>knows many nursery rhymes and stories | may add alphabet letters to artwork<br>creates and tells long stories<br>can verbally express the highlights of the day<br>knows many colors<br>can repeat a sentence with six or more<br>  words<br>may pretend to read books or may actually<br>  read others' name tags<br>holds writing tools in position that allows<br>  fine control<br>traces objects with precision<br>classifies according to function<br>asks what words mean<br>is familiar with many literary classics for<br>  children<br>knows address and phone number<br>can retell main facts or happenings in stories<br>uses adultlike speech |

**FIGURE 3–16** Developmental language-related milestones at ages 2 through 5.

But preschoolers' skills increase, and their use of forms of the irregular verb "to be" improves such as "I am so," or "Mine are hot, and yours are cold." Sentence structure comes closer to adult usage, including use of relative clauses and complex and compound sentence forms. Articulation of letter sounds is still developing; about 75 percent of English letter sounds are made correctly. Omissions of letter sounds ('*merca* for "America") and substitutions (*udder* for "other") are still present.

Older preschoolers may have a vocabulary larger than 1,500 words. They are learning new words and new concepts while they also enrich and solidify their knowledge of known words by establishing multiple links among words and concepts. Four-year-olds' attention and memory improve as they gain a greater understanding of concepts, strategies, and relationships that are associated with their first-hand manipulation and real experiences (Thomlinson & Hyson, 2009).

Many older preschoolers are very concerned about the correct names of things and detect errors in the speech of others. Being an active explorer, his questions can indicate his interest in natural phenomena such as "Why is the moon in the sky?". The 4-year-old becomes a problem solver and tends to explain things through visually noted attributes; for example, "A cow is called that 'cause of its horns."

Preschoolers may not be able to talk about their solutions to problems. Although they can respond to and solve questions posed verbally, they may not be able to explain their thinking.

Most 4-year-old children enjoy books, stories, and activities with words. More and more of their time is spent on these pursuits. Some teachers have promoted this interest by making favorite word lists or a "My Box of Words" collection with individual children.

The 4-year-old may still stutter and clutter and stop speech when there is stress or excitement. The less-mature speech of a best friend might be copied, and nonverbal gesturing is most often a part of conversations.

Children's basic mental categories become elaborated as experience provides details and specifics are noticed and understood. The basic category animals eventually includes a subcategory, cats, and then may include a smaller category such as Persian or Siamese, as learning takes place.

A wide range of individual speech behavior is both normal and possible. Some younger preschoolers may have the speech characteristics of older preschoolers, whereas some older preschoolers have the characteristics of younger preschoolers or kindergarteners. Each child is unique in his progress and rate of acquiring language skills.

## Metalinguistic Awareness and Brain Growth

Teachers and parents hope that preschool language arts experiences will, when the time comes, help children learn to read and write with ease. Preschoolers may begin to notice words as objects. **Metalinguistic awareness** can be defined as a child's knowledge of the nature of language as an object. Children begin to notice words as objects and later become able to manipulate them to learn to read and write and to accomplish a host of other ends, such as using metaphors, creating puns, and using irony. Pan and Gleason (1997) observe:

> Before children can engage in flexible uses of words, they must have an implicit understanding that words are separate from their referents. Young children often consider the name of an object another of its intrinsic attributes. They believe, for instance, that if you called a horse a cow, it might begin to moo. Later children learn that words themselves are not inherent attributes of objects, which allows them to move beyond literal word use and adopt a metaphoric stance. (p. 327)

A critical restructuring of the brain begins at about age 4 when a surge in learning is

---

**metalinguistic awareness** — a conscious awareness on the part of a language user of language as an object in itself.

happening. The brain is beginning to eliminate weak connections but is still eagerly seeking information from the senses. Early childhood educators and many researchers are urging that a national emphasis and priority be given to early childhood education, especially in the key areas of language learning, mathematics, music education, and problem-solving skill development.

## SUMMARY

Knowing typical and common language development characteristics helps the teacher understand that children are unique individuals. Rapid growth of vocabulary and language skills is part of normal growth. Errors in the speech of young preschoolers (aged 2 to 3) make verbalizations partly understandable. Key words in the correct order give adults clues to what is intended. Self-talk during the child's play usually describes what the child is doing and may alternate with social comments.

Teachers can use their knowledge of early childhood language development in many ways, such as alerting the staff about a child's need for hearing tests or special help and helping parents who are concerned with their child's speech patterns.

The speech of older preschool children (aged 4 to 5) is very similar to adult speech. Children in this age group explore words and begin to understand their power. Make-believe peaks and is often accompanied by a child's imitation of the speech used by others in their lives. Some newly learned speech may be irritating to school staffs and families, but it can indicate intellectual and social growth. Exploring and enjoying books occupies more of the children's time. Exploring the real and fantasy worlds with words becomes children's active pursuit during the early childhood years.

There is no "average" child when it comes to language development; individual differences exist and are treated with acceptance and optimism.

Added interest and emphasis on language fundamentals during preschool years has occurred in light of research on brain growth and function.

## ADDITIONAL RESOURCES

### Readings

Clay, M. M. (2001). *Change over time in children's literacy development.* Portsmouth, NH: Heinemann.

Genishi, C., & Dyson, A. M. (2009). *Children, language, and literacy: Diverse learners in diverse times.* New York: Teachers College Press.

Jones, E., & Cooper, R. M. (2006). *Playing to get smart.* New York: Teachers College Press.

Paley, V. G. (1988). *Bad guys don't have birthdays: Fantasy play at four.* Chicago: University of Chicago Press.

Paley, V. G. (1988). *Mollie is three: Growing up in school.* Chicago: The University of Chicago Press.

Singer, D. G., Golinkoff, R. M., & Hirsh-Pasek, K. (Eds.) (2006). *Play = learning.* New York: Oxford University Press.

### Helpful Websites

National Child Care Information Center (NCCIC)
http://nccic.org
Staff will research your questions and connect you with information on young children's language and literacy.

National Network for Child Care
http://www.nncc.org
For the ages and stages of 3- and 4-year olds, select Articles & Resources and then select Child Development.

 Go to www.cengagebrain.com to access this text's Education Course-Mate website where you'll find helpful resource such as video activities, glossary flashcards, interactive exercises, quiz questions, and more!

# Review It and Use It

A. Associate the following characteristics with the correct age group. Some may seem to fit both categories; choose the most appropriate one. Write the characteristics under the headings "Younger Preschooler" (2- and 3-year-olds) and "Older Preschooler" (4- and 5-year-olds).

"Look, I'm jumping."  
telegraphic speech  
rhyming and nonsense words  
name-calling  
nonverbal communication  
vocabulary of more than 1,500 words  
talking about what one is doing  
stuttering  
talking through an adult  

repetitions  
omission of letter sounds  
adult-like speech  
bathroom words  
substitutions  
role-playing  
planning play with others  
arguing  

B. Select the best answer.

1. The younger preschool child (2- to 3-years old)
   a. may still grunt and scream while communicating.
   b. always replies to what is said to him by another child.
   c. articulates most sounds with adult-like clarity.
   d. speaks mainly in complete sentences.

2. A truly typical or average child
   a. would have all the characteristics of his age.
   b. is almost impossible to find.
   c. is one who speaks better than his peers.
   d. learns about 20 words in each day.

3. Repetition in the speech of the young child
   a. needs careful watching.
   b. is common for children aged 2 to 5.
   c. indicates higher intelligence.
   d. happens for a variety of reasons but usually means a hearing problem exists.

4. Name-calling and swearing
   a. may take place after the preschool years.
   b. can gain attention.
   c. shows that children are playful.
   d. happens only with poorly behaved children.

5. A word like "blood" or "ghost"
   a. may spread quickly to many children.
   b. has impact value.
   c. can make people listen.
   d. all the above.

6. Most younger preschoolers
   a. cannot correctly pronounce all the vowels.
   b. omit some letter sounds.
   c. have similar-to-adult speech.
   d. none of the above.

7. Stuttering during preschool years
   a. happens infrequently
   b. should be drawn to the child's attention.
   c. may happen when a child is excited.
   d. means the child always needs professional help to overcome it.

8. "Me wented" is an example of
   a. pronoun and articulation difficulty.
   b. a sentence spoken by an older preschooler.
   c. verb incorrectness that is typical.
   d. the speech of 5-year-olds.

9. Joint planning in play with two or more children is found more often with
   a. 2- to 3-year-olds.
   b. 4- to 5-year-olds.
   c. slowly developing children.
   d. male children.

## STUDENT ACTIVITES

1. Observe a group program for preschoolers without interacting but just recording or taking written notes. Stay at least 15–20 minutes. Share any type of child speech that was mentioned in this chapter during your next class meeting.

2. Read the following from Justice and Pence (2006) with a peer. Then role-play a situation in which a seasoned early childhood educator is instructing a new classroom assistant by giving examples concerning reaching the goal of helping preschoolers learn new words or understand a word's meaning. Then switch roles. Share some of your examples with the total group.

   Justice and Pence (2006) point out children's acquisition of a new word moves from broad, shallow understanding to greater specificity and deeper understanding over time with ongoing exposures to the word in different contexts. Educators support deeper understanding when children hear words many times such as hearing repetitive words in stories, or through hearing the same word or words in varying classroom circumstances, or when adults frequently connect words to real objects, actions, or illustrations. (p. 19)

3. Write definitions for the following:

   | consonant | metalinguistic awareness |
   |---|---|
   | egocentric speech or private speech | overextension |
   | expressive vocabulary | running commentary |
   | impact words | vowel |

# Growth Systems Affecting Early Language Ability

## OBJECTIVES

After reading this chapter, you should be able to:

- Describe sequential stages of intellectual development.

- List three perceptual-motor skills that preschool activities might include.

- Discuss the importance of an early childhood center's ability to meet young children's social and emotional needs.

## KEY TERMS

| | |
|---|---|
| accommodation | mental image |
| assimilation | metalinguistic |
| classify | skills |
| conceptual | reflective |
| tempo | social |
| impulsive | connectedness |

## An Unexpected Remark

*Leisel entered the classroom on her first day of work as an assistant teacher for a class of 4-year-olds. The morning went well until Paynter, a boy, said, "You sure are ugly." Leisel thought, "All right, how should I answer this? Should I just ignore it, believing he is just having a bad day, and let it go until I know more about him?" Instead Leisel said with good humor, "I'm very ugly when I wake up in the morning. My eyes are half awake, and my hair sticks up and goes in spikes. Sometimes I look in the mirror and say, 'Oh no.' "*

### Questions to Ponder

1. Which way would you have chosen to answer? Would your response have been similar to Leisel's? If not, why?

2. How do you think Paynter might have responded to Leisel?

3. How many 4-year-olds know words can be powerful? Few, many, most, or is this more characteristic of older elementary schoolchildren?

The child is a total being, and language growth cannot be isolated from physical, mental, and social-emotional well-being. All body systems need a minimum level of movement (exercise) to keep the body in good working order and to stimulate brain growth. A proper intake of nutritious foods and living conditions that provide emotional security and balance can affect the child's acquisition of language and her general health and resistance to disease. A preschool, child center, or learning center intent on developing language skills focuses on satisfying both physical and emotional needs while also providing intellectual opportunity and challenge by offering a variety of age-appropriate activities (Figure 4–1).

## PHYSICAL GROWTH

Physical development limits or aids capabilities, thereby affecting children's perceptions of themselves, as well as the way they are treated by others. Early childhood teachers are aware of these fundamental physical changes that take place in young children. For instance, a slightly taller, physically active, strong, and well-coordinated child who can ride a two-wheel bike and drop-kick a football may be admired by her peers. These two skills are not often witnessed during preschool years, but occasionally a child possesses such physical skills. A wide range of physical abilities in individual children exists within preschool groups as in all developmental areas. Bergen, Reid, and Torelli (2001) describe children's physical development of the late toddler period:

> Children of this age show great achievements in gross- and fine-motor development. They are now stable walkers and enjoy going for walks of short duration. Running is a new thrill, and they may seem to go everywhere at a run. Most can climb purposefully to get a desired object out of reach, walk up and down stairs, use riding wheel toys by pushing with their feet, and "dance" to music. They can throw a ball using their whole arm but can't yet catch it. (p. 92)

Preschoolers grow at the rate of 2 to 3 inches in height and 4 to 6 pounds in weight a year. At about 18 to 24 months, the child's thumb is used in opposition to just one finger. The ability to use tools and drawing markers with a degree of skill emerges. The nutritional quality of the child's diet exerts an influence on both body

**FIGURE 4–1** Outdoor structures can involve different types of physical activity.

and neural development. Monitoring nutrient intake, height, weight gain, and emotional well-being can alert parents to possible deficiencies.

Illness during accelerated growth may produce conditions affecting language development if it damages necessary body systems.

Hearing loss and vision difficulties impair the child's ability to receive communications and learn her native language. An impairmed brain may hinder the child's ability to sort perceptions, slowing progress.

Preschools and early learning programs plan a wide range of motor activities; much of the children's time is devoted to playing with interesting equipment in both indoor and outdoor areas (Figure 4–2). The well-known benefits of a healthy mind in a healthy body should be planned for by incorporating daily physical activities that promote well-exercised and well-coordinated muscles into young children's daily programs.

Planned physical movement opportunities and activities prepare children for academic learning. Movement stimulates learning physiologically, and also helps young children to experience concepts so they can process them cognitively. Teachers often offer children opportunities to solve movement problems by urging them to invent their own solutions. Activities can make abstract concepts (like over and under) concrete when children physically experience

**FIGURE 4–2** Outdoor climbing structures can promote development of both large and small muscles.

them. Teachers can and should ask children to talk aloud about the motor task at hand while they are performing it, according to a study by Winsler, Manfra, and Diaz (2007):

> Findings from a present study showed overall that children from both groups (kindergarten and preschool) do indeed respond to teacher's speech instructions and that performance on motor sequencing and counting tasks improved when children are asked to speak out loud. (p. 28)

Brain-based learning advocate, Eric Jensen (2008) emphasizes children's physical movement needs and benefits. He urges early childhood educators to:

- facilitate hand movements each day with clapping games, dancing, puzzles, and manipulative objects.
- engage learners in cooperative activities and group work.
- offer novel activities in a variety of learning locations, and plan child activities and choices connected to the learning that require moving the body in some way. (p. 39)

He believes exercise triggers the release of brain-derived neurotrophic factor (BDNF), a natural substance that enhances cognition by boosting the ability of neurons to communicate with one another. Jensen cites the 2004 research of Griesbach, Hovda, Molteni, Wa & Gomez-Pinilla as the basis of his recommendations.

## PERCEPTION

An infant's physical actions are the vehicle of knowledge. Seeing and trying to touch or act upon the environment are the work of infancy. This early physical stage precedes and develops into the child's **mental image** of her world, and this makes later verbal labeling and speech possible.

As the child matures, perceptual acuity increases; finer detail is seen. Most children achieve 20/20 vision (adult optimum) at age 14. From ages 2 to 5, vision is in the 20/45 to 20/30 range. It is estimated that 20 to 25 percent of preschoolers have some eye problem that, if

---

**mental image** — a "perceptual representation" or mental picture of a perceptual experience, remembered or imagined.

uncorrected, could delay learning or cause vision loss. Experts advise families and teachers to watch for an eye that slightly turns in or out, squinting, eye closing or head turning when the child is focusing, avoidance of coloring activities or books, and clumsiness or frustration during play. Unfortunately, many eye screening tests performed by school staffs, instead of pediatric eye specialists or professionals, miss an accurate diagnosis.

Hearing acuity increases from birth through ages 4 and 5. At this point, the hearing mechanisms are essentially mature and will not change greatly except through disease or injury. Ohl (2002) points out the importance of hearing ability in infancy.

> Both oral language and reading require the same types of sound analysis. The better babies are at distinguishing the building blocks of speech at 6 months of age, the better they will be at other more complex language skills at 2 and 3 years of age, and the easier it will be for them at 4 and 5 years to grasp the idea of how sounds link to letters. (p. 2)

Kotulak (1996) describes what happens to a child who is born deaf:

> In a child who is born deaf, the 50,000 nerve pathways that normally would carry sound messages from the ears to the brain are silent. The sound of the human voice, so essential for brain cells to learn language, can't get through and the cells wait in vain. Finally, as the infant grows older, brain cells can wait no longer and begin looking for other signals to process, such as those from visual stimuli. (p. 27)

Young children are noted for their desire to get their hands on what interests them. If a new child with particularly noticeable hair joins a group, hands and fingers are sure to try to explore its texture. If a teacher wears bright or shiny jewelry, some children will want to touch it. Perceptions are gathered with all sense organs. Experts believe that the main purpose of receiving, organizing, and interpreting what one encounters perceptually is to achieve constancy—a stable, constant world. Development involves changes or shifts in the way a person organizes experience and copes with the world, generally moving from simpler to more complex, from single to multiple and integrated ways of responding.

Researchers exploring infant visual preferences have pinpointed a series of changes in attention-drawing features from infancy to age 5. At approximately 2 months of age a change occurs. The child shifts from having attention captured by movement and edges of people and objects to active search and explore. Later, from age 2 to 5, children change from unsystematic exploring to systematically examining each feature carefully.

Children get better and better at focusing on one aspect of a complex situation: they become selective in focusing their attention, and they ignore the irrelevant and distracting. Life events that cause tension and anxiety can interfere with children's emerging abilities. In complex situations children do best when perceptual distractions are minimized, allowing deep concentration.

Individual differences have been noted in the way children explore their environment and react to problems. Kagan (1971) has described **conceptual tempo** to contrast the **impulsive** child, who answers quickly and may make mistakes, with the **reflective** child, who spends considerable time examining alternatives. A second difference in perception identifies field-independent and field-dependent styles of perceiving. Field-independent children are those good at ignoring irrelevant context, whereas field-dependent children tend to focus on the total context.

### Visual Literacy Skill

Educators interested in visual literacy (viewing skill) describe it as a primary basic human capacity that aids learning and problem solving

---

**conceptual tempo** — a term associated with Jerome Kagan's theory of different individual pacing in perceptual exploration of objects.
**impulsive** — quick to answer or react to either a simple or complex situation or problem.
**reflective** — taking time to weigh aspects or alternatives in a given situation.

and that is useful across many educational disciplines—math, science, music, art, language, and so on. Visual literacy, as discussed here, involves young children's understanding and use of symbolic representation. It is not unlike Gardner's spatial-kinesthetic intellectual theory (Gardner, 2000), which focuses on relationships and the ability to notice characteristics and details that lead to ideas and conclusions.

Visual literacy refers to a group of vision competencies a human being can develop by seeing and at the same time having and integrating other sensory experiences. The development of these competencies is fundamental to normal human learning. When developed, they enable a visually literate person to discriminate and interpret the visible actions, objects, symbols, natural or man-made, that she encounters in her environment. Through the creative use of these competencies, she is able to communicate with others. Through the appreciative use of these competencies, she is able to comprehend and enjoy the masterworks of visual communication.

A preschool example of visual literacy skills at work would be the 4-year-old boy who said sadly, "Katrin (a fellow teacher and gifted story-book reader) won't be here for story time." "Why?" his teacher asked. "She's all dressed up," the boy answered. Katrin had previously left school for a series of dental appointments. On those days the boy noticed she was dressed differently and would then leave school.

The process of visual perception involves several basic parts, including the sensing of information along dual pathways in the brain. An understanding of this process is essential to realizing the power of visual images to move us emotionally and behaviorally and to influence our conscious thought.

The educational philosophy known as the Reggio Emilia approach encourages educators to use visual literacy concepts. Educators who use this approach promote children's expression of ideas through graphic arts, using diverse media and symbol systems to make children's learning visual. The children's work can then be talked about, reflected upon, and refined. This can lead to new perspectives, new avenues of exploration and discovery, and deeper understanding.

Burmark (2002) believes visual literacy is a learned skill and discusses the learning process:

> The process of becoming visually literate is not unlike the process of learning to read. When a child first looks at words on a page, the letters and spaces are meaningless. They appear to be nothing but random shapes—little curves and lines that big people keep pointing at all the time. In time, the child begins to associate those shapes with the sounds coming out of parents' mouths, and is soon able to crack the mysterious code of meaning behind the words on the page. Verbal literacy involves a person's ability to interpret and use spoken and written language to decode the world of words. Likewise, visual literacy relates to a person's ability to interpret and create visual information—to understand images of all kinds and use them to communicate more effectively. (p.79)

The primary literacy of the twenty-first century will be visual—pictures, graphics, images of every kind—and students must learn to process both words and pictures and shift back and forth between them. Teachers can help children become more knowledgeable and more skilled in their use of verbal communications, and can also help them gain skill in using and understanding visual images. Some authors suggest early childhood educators give preference to verbal literacy and written text and de-emphasize visual thinking and learning in their curriculum planning (Karchmer, Mallette, & Leu, 2003). Children will need to know how to make meaning not just from text but also from vast amounts of information conveyed through images.

## Perceptual-Motor Skills

Perceptual-motor, or sensory-motor, intelligence has been defined as an action-oriented knowledge, not to be confused with the intelligence that involves thinking and logic. The latter grows during preschool years and beyond, when children can think about and know without acting out in a physical way.

Piaget, the noted Swiss psychologist and researcher, greatly affected early childhood

FIGURE 4–3 Dancing can involve lots of body movement.

educators' interest in perceptual-motor activities. Piaget and others observed that automatic movements such as crying, sucking, and grasping in infants became controlled, purposeful body movements as the child grew. He speculated that physical movement served as a base for later mental abilities (Figure 4–3).

During the preschool years, the development of motor skills is as important as the development of language skills. Just as there is gradually increasing control over language, movement, and body control in the preschool years, there is also a similar continuing increase in the ability to scan new material, organize one's perception of it, remember it, and perhaps refer to it by some label or assign meaning in some other way. The close ties between motor activities and thought processes indicate that the child needs motor activity involving the five sense organs, as well as large muscle use. Exactly how much of a child's mental activity is dependent on or promoted by physical activity is unknown. Most educators of young children believe that a definite, strong connection exists between development of mental and physical skills (Figure 4–4).

Motor skill develops in an orderly, predictable, head-to-toe fashion. Head, neck, and upper-body muscles are controlled first (large muscles before small muscles), and center-of-body muscles are coordinated before extremities (fingers and toes). Handedness (left or right) is usually stable by age 5 or 6. Child limitations can occur if motor experience is limited.

FIGURE 4–4 Both motor and mental skill is being used as the child decides what should be placed in the big, medium, and small categories.

A child who has had limited experience to run around, to climb, to use her body effectively in activities that demand gross motor skill, may not be ready for the finer adjustments that are required in the motor skills of eye movement and hand-eye coordination in her early grades in school.

Montessori's approach (1967a) to educating young children stresses direct manipulation of real objects presented in sequenced form. She designed and constructed many tactile (touching) exploring materials for the young child. She explains her motives:

> The training and sharpening of the senses has the obvious advantage of enlarging the field of perception and of offering an ever more solid foundation for intellectual growth. The intellect builds up its store of practical ideas through contact with, and exploration of, its environment. Without such concepts the intellect would lack precision in its abstract operations. (p. 117)

Preschools are full of appealing equipment and programs that offer a planned approach to the development of sensory-motor skills. They are seen as integral parts of the curricula. School success in later elementary years may also be influenced by the development of perceptual-motor skill.

There seems to be no clearly accepted or defined separate place within the preschool curriculum for sensory-skill development. Some centers identify a series of sequential activities and label them perceptual or sensory-motor activities; their main goal is skill development. In other centers, every activity is seen as developing perceptual-motor skill. Commonly, music activities and physical games deal with physical coordination and endurance.

Peterson and Thaut (2007) believe ample and convincing research evidence exists to support the idea that when children's physical actions are coupled with music experiences, such as singing, dancing, or learning to play a musical instrument, brain development is enhanced.

Programs plan for perceptual-motor activities within their language arts curriculum. What remains important is that this type of emphasis be part of every center's program.

This list of objectives designed to refine perceptual-motor skills is drawn from a number of schools' and centers' goal statements.

- awareness of self in space
- awareness of self in relation to objects
- flexibility
- body coordination
- posture and balance
- awareness of spatial relationships
- rhythmic body movements
- ability to identify objects and surfaces with the eyes closed
- awareness of temperatures by touch
- ability to trace form outlines with fingers
- ability to discriminate color, shapes, similar features, different features, sizes, textures, and sounds
- ability to match a wide variety of patterns and symbols
- ability to identify parts of figures or objects when a small part of a whole is presented
- eye-hand coordination
- familiarity with the following terms: same, different, long, longer, longest, small, smaller, smallest, big, little, tall, short, wide, narrow, high, low, above, below, on, in, hard, soft, sweet, salty, sour
- ability to identify food by tasting
- ability to identify smells of various items
- ability to identify common sounds

## Activities for Perceptual-Motor Development

It is difficult to think of one piece of preschool equipment or one activity that does not address some aspect or component of perceptual-motor development. Figure 4–5 lists perceptual-motor development activities and equipment, gathered from a broad range of early childhood books and sources. It can serve as a beginning.

EXPERIENCES
DEALING WITH:                          POSSIBLE MATERIALS AND EQUIPMENT

**Visual Discrimination**

long, longer, longest                  felt or paper strips; sticks; ribbons

small, smaller, smallest               nested boxes; blocks; buttons; measuring cups

big, little                            blocks; jars; buttons; balloons; toys

tall, short                            felt figures; stuffed toys

wide, narrow                           pieces of cloth and paper; scraps of wood; boxes

high, low                              jump rope; small ball; see-saw made from small board with tiny block in middle

above, below                           felt pieces to place above and below a box with colored stones

**Auditory Discrimination**

quiet, noisy                           two boxes: one containing something that rattles (such as stones or beads)
                                         and one containing cloth or paper

bell sounds                            bells of varying shapes and sizes for a variety of tones

falling sounds                         feather; leaf; stone; block of wood; cotton

shaking sounds                         maracas; baby rattle; pebbles inside coffee can

musical sounds                         variety of rhythm instruments

**Tactile Discrimination**

textures                               sandpaper; tissue; stone; waxed paper; tree bark; velvet; wool; fur; cotton

outline of shapes                      thin wooden circle, square, triangle, rectangle; letters cut from sandpaper

recognition of objects                 four different-shaped objects, each tied in end of sock—children guess what
                                         each is by feeling it (change objects often)

hard, soft                             handkerchief; rock; cotton batting; nail; sponge

**Taste Discrimination**

identifying food: sweet,               small jars: filled with salt, sugar, unsweetened lemonade
  salty, sour

trying new foods                       variety of vegetables children may not know; samples of fruit juices; honey,
                                         molasses, maple syrup

**Smell Discrimination**

identifying object by smell            cake of soap; vial of perfume; pine sprig; onion; vials of kitchen spices; orange

**Kinesthetic Discrimination**

lifting, racing downhill, swinging,    yard and motor play materials
  throwing, running, jumping,
  climbing, bending, stretching,
  twisting, turning, spinning,
  balancing

FIGURE 4–5 Perceptual activities.

 **VIDEO ACTIVITY**

Go to the Education CourseMate website to watch the TeachSource Video entitled, *Infant and Toddlers: Communication Development*.

1. Can you estimate how many words that the teacher offered were paired with real actions or objects in the clothes washing sequence? Cite examples.

2. Did you think there was enough repetition of new words or reinforcement of words for the children to use them in a like situation?

3. It's obvious this toddler teacher was focused on children's language development, but could the clothes washing activity also be classified as a perceptual-motor activity? Explain.

## COGNITIVE DEVELOPMENT  IRA

There are major, opposing views concerning the link between language and thought. One view is that language is the foundation of thought and vital to a person's awareness of the world. Another view suggests that language is dependent on thinking; as intelligence grows, language grows, reflecting thoughts. Vygotsky (1980) has influenced early childhood educators' beliefs by theorizing that language is an actual mechanism for thinking, a mental tool. Language makes thinking more abstract, flexible, and independent from immediate stimuli. It is difficult to determine which of these ideas is closer to the truth, but most educators will agree that language and thought are closely associated.

Researchers believe very young children, including preschool children, are much more capable of learning than previously thought. The reason that young children's cognitive development and rapid learning curve may have been underestimated is that young children are learning seemingly ordinary things encountered in everyday activities and play. Many educators believe that children will not simply soak up needed knowledge from their environment. They provide focusing activities, that attempt to build language skills and basic numerical understandings (Figure 4–6). Other educators, who disagree with their view, believe that children are capable learners. These educators attempt to provide an opportunity for children's self-discovery.

As the child's brain grows, it is reorganized by experience. Experience changes the brain, but then those very changes alter the way new experience affects the brain. Children who have been passive viewers of life (through electronic media or unfortunate circumstances) rather than active listeners (explorers and conversationalists) may lack practice in both auditory analysis and logical and sequential reasoning skills.

Greenspan (1999) believes the most critical role for emotions is to create, organize, and orchestrate many of the mind's most important functions. He states:

> In fact, intellect, academic abilities, sense of self, consciousness, and morality have common origins in our earliest and ongoing emotional experiences. (p. 197)

Greenspan presents educators with what he perceives to be the fundamental sequential building blocks of mental growth based on

FIGURE 4–6 The adult's words accompany the child's activity choices at times.

human beings' capacity to experience emotions. They include the ability to

- attend.
- engage.
- be intentional.
- form complex, interactive, intentional patterns.
- create images, symbols, and ideas.
- connect images and symbols.*

The idea that the reciprocal emotionally charged interactions between infants and young children and caregivers influence their cognitive development is not new, but increasingly it is given close attention by anyone caring for the very young.

Problem solving has been associated with "literacy behaviors" that come before conventional reading and writing. Once children become higher-level symbolic thinkers, they are able to piece together the mental processes used in everyday problem solving with the symbols needed for reading and writing.

## Classifying Information

Intellect is rooted in each particular child's stored perceptual and sensory-motor experiences. Each child interprets happenings and attempts to connect each to what she already knows. If it fits, the child understands and it all falls together. An example of this might be seen if one watches a 9-month-old learn to make noise come out of a toy plastic horn. At first, the child has no knowledge of how the horn works. When she first blows into it and it makes a toot, the child blows into it repeatedly (and usually happily). After that, the child knows how to toot the horn. Infants, toddlers, and preschoolers can be thought of as having mental groupings (classes and categories). They **classify** what they encounter, including events, people, and objects, before they have words for them. The 9-month-old just described probably has no word associated with what the child knows about the horn. Each mental

* From Greenspan, S. I. (1997). Growth of the mind and the endangered origins of intelligence. Copyright © 1997. Reprinted by permission of Da Capo Press, a member of Perseus Books Group.

grouping is distinguished by a set of distinctive features, and objects yet to be classified are examined for the presence of these features. If the horn-blowing infant reacts by trying to blow into a new toy horn of a similar shape, one can be relatively sure the child is forming a class of "horn" mentally. One can expect that this infant will try blowing into any horn shape that comes her way. Later, a word or language symbol can be attached to a class or category, which makes it possible for the child to communicate about what the class or category means to the child or how the child feels about it. Simple words like mama, *milk*, or *ball* may be among children's earliest categories of the world around them.

Preschool teachers readily see differences between the feelings and meanings expressed by each child. For example, the way that a child reacts when meeting a new large animal may demonstrate what she knows and feels about large animals. Another child's reaction might be entirely opposite.

Putting events and experiences into classes and categories is innate—a natural mental process. The motivation to engage actively with the environment—to make contact, to have an impact, and to make sense of experience—is built into human beings. The mind yearns for order, and knowledge is built within from what is experienced. Children construct theories or hypotheses about objects and phenomena by putting things into relationships. A child's knowledge is constantly changing, for children are curious and are constantly searching for a variety of experience, fighting to overcome boredom. A new or novel idea or event may greatly affect a child by adding to or changing all a child knows and feels on a particular subject.

As a child's language ability develops, mental classes, categories, and concepts are represented symbolically by words. Words become an efficient shortcut that eliminates the need to act out by gesturing or signaling to make something known to another. Thoughts can be analyzed and evaluated internally as the child grows older. If there exists a common language system between the child and others, it can be used to reveal the child's unique self (Figure 4–7).

Piaget's (1952) terms **assimilation** and **accommodation** describe what happens when

---

**classify** — the act of systematically grouping things according to identifiable common characteristics, for example, size.
**assimilation** — the process that allows new experiences to merge with previously stored mental structures.
**accommodation** — the process by which new experiences or events change existing ideas or thought patterns.

FIGURE 4–7 Group play exposes children to the ideas of others.

infants and children experience something new. Each individual unconsciously structures (internally builds and organizes) what is perceived. If a new experience or event is perceived, it is assimilated into what already mentally existed. If it changes or modifies those existing structures (ideas or thought patterns), the new is accommodated. In other words, children attend to features that make sense to them, and learning involves adding to what is already known or modifying (changing) what is known.

An example of a child trying to make sense of her experience follows:

> . . . after a visit to the hospital to see her dying great-grandmother who was over 90, Amy (age 4) commented, "Ya know, Dad, the Brooklyn Bridge is pretty old. It's going to die soon!" In her struggle to understand life and death, Amy had made a connection between the Brooklyn Bridge and her great-grandmother.

Although children use words that adults know and recognize, the knowledge behind children's words often carries quite a different meaning and understanding.

 **VIDEO ACTIVITY**

Go to the Education CourseMate website to watch the TeachSource Video, *Piaget: Sensorimotor Stage.* Using infants, the video presents Piaget's sensorimotor development stages.

1. Pretend you are watching a young preschool child discover, perhaps for the first time that the yellow and blue paint he is using makes green when mixed. He is repeating the process again and again silently. As his teacher, you might interact with him to increase his language development. Describe your actions or conversation.

2. Does the video reinforce the idea that educators whenever possible relate a learning opportunity to a child's past experience? If yes, explain. If no, state your reasons.

## Different Levels of Maturity

The human brain's cortex contains two differently specialized hemispheres. Each hemisphere appears designed for unique functions, different abilities, and styles of thought, including verbal and spatial thinking. Different brain areas are well defined and possess a rich concentration of certain abilities that are not equal among children (Figure 4–8). Naturally, the brain structures of some children may be developing more

1. seeking information (focusing)
2. seeking word labels (concept building)
3. naming, classifying, categorizing, and grouping experiences mentally—objects, ideas, etc. (general to specific; revising concepts)
4. responding and remembering (memorizing and recalling)
5. comparing and contrasting information (abstracting)
6. making inferences and predicting in general ways (predicting)
7. generalizing (inductive thinking)
8. applying known information to new situations (transferring)
9. making hypotheses (educated guesses) and predicting in specific ways (deductive thinking)

FIGURE 4–8 The child's emerging intellectual skills.

FIGURE 4–9 DelJon's pretend cell phone is his shoe.

slowly than those of others, which might affect their ability to learn and may cause teachers to compare them unfairly with children of the same age who have developed more quickly. Consequently, teachers need to pay special attention to how they act when comparing children. Competitive, pressurized lessons can create an unhealthy "I'm not good (smart) enough" attitude that can be self-perpetuating.

Preschool children's statements that seem to be "errors in thinking" on the surface can, on deeper analysis, be seen as quite mature and understandable, not just random guesses. When a child says a camel is a horse with a hump, she should be given credit for seeing the similarity rather than merely corrected.

The child's fantasy world, which appears and is expressed in speech, should be seen as a giant intellectual leap (Figure 4–9). Make-believe is internal intellectual creation and/or recreation. A preschooler may say she is someone else—most often this someone else is a hero of sorts or an admired personage, usually from the movies, videos, television, or real life. There may be days when the child wishes to assume the name and identity of a friend or animal. Many children during preschool can readily follow story sequences and identify with book characters. An in-depth discussion of preschoolers and books is found in Chapter 9.

Teachers need to realize that there are differences between adult concepts and child concepts. The child's view of the world is usually based on immediate, present happenings and beginning thought processes. A child's speech is full of many unique misconceptions, conclusions, and errors (as judged by adult standards). These errors arise because of each child's unique way of sorting out experiences—a continuous process of trying to make sense and order out of daily events. Errors based on just a few happenings may be quite logical conclusions. For example, a child may conclude that milk comes from the store, or, when looking at an *n*, that it is a "baby n."

## The Teacher's Role

Teachers who work with infants, toddlers, and preschoolers realize that sensory-motor experiences and opportunities with people, toys, and room environments are early intellect-building events. Exploring and experimenting are enhanced by adult provision of materials and equipment. At some point, teachers realize that some actions look as though the child thought first and then acted. At about 10 months, some infants seem to be majoring in dropping and emptying. They drop things from high-chair trays and watch the objects fall, or put things into containers, drawers, or boxes and empty and refill these over and over. One has to smile and think of very young infants as active scientists.

A "zone of proximal development" is what Vygotsky (1980) calls the area between what the child can solve alone when faced with problems and experience, and what the child can possibly solve or come to know with the help of adults or more experienced, knowing children. When adults name and explain happenings and talk about relationships, this is seen as a stimulant to both language and mental growth. A teacher trying to put into practice Vygotsky's  theories would try to talk with children, becoming a catalyst who names, discusses, and prompts children's exploration and expression of what they have discovered or formulated (Figure 4–10). It is also important that adults know when not to interrupt children's thoughts when they are deeply engaged in play. Dialogue makes much more sense when children seek adult help or when they are companions in activities.

In promoting what children will store (learn and remember), teachers deal with both meaning and feelings. Each intellect-building encounter and interaction with children starts with the adult's supportive acceptance and caring. Purposeful teacher dialogue is often part of child-teacher exchanges. Its goal is to advance further discovery or to help put the discovery or experience into words. A teacher listens and observes closely. This listening may expose aspects of the child's thinking, logic, inner concepts, and feelings.

As children try to make sense of happenings and experiences, teachers can expect to be asked questions. Four-year-olds can ask hundreds of questions on any given day. Teachers sometimes answer a question with a question. Skillful questioning and sensitive responses from the teacher preserve a child's feelings about expressing worthwhile ideas and make the child more willing to speak and share. These are some examples:

- "I can see you want to have a turn talking too, Emma, and I want to hear you."
- "Would you tell us, Jacob, about the boat you put together this morning?"

**FIGURE 4–10** Teachers may act as an interested "sounding board" that encourages the child's expression of what he has discovered.

- "You thought of a different way to make a hole in your paper; perhaps your friends would like to hear about it."

- "Shayne, you wanted to know how our hamster got out of his cage. Can you see an opening he might have squeezed through?"

- "Did anyone see what happened to Yang's shoe?"

- "I wonder if there's a way for three people to share two pairs of scissors."

Teachers can support children as they converse by encouraging them to step outside their own perceptions to become aware of larger, more generalized patterns in the things they observe. The processes of questioning, predicting, and testing possibilities can be learned firsthand as children solve their own problems. Early childhood educators facilitate children's ability to come to their own conclusions and relate those conclusions to observable evidence, if possible. A teacher may also ask children to compare their ideas with one another in group conversations.

Children may gain **metalinguistic skills** during the preschool years. They are then able to "think about language." Many play with language and words and make comparisons between spoken and written words. Others may be able to analyze words into individual parts and judge what is correct word usage and what is not.

## SOCIAL AND EMOTIONAL GROWTH

Interaction with other people is always a major factor in a child's language learning. Children who have positive feelings about themselves—feelings of self-value and security—speak frequently. New contacts with adults outside the home run smoothly as the child branches out from the home.

Gallagher and Mayer (2008) suggest the school day should begin with a feeling of warmth and comfort as children transition from family. This is a time when responsive teachers make an effort to recognize each child's individual presence by welcoming and greeting them. Throughout the day teachers keep in touch with children's interests, moods, and feelings of

well being. They engage, converse, and find joy in daily interactions. Educators model caring, provide opportunity and feedback, and build individual teacher-child relationships, while maintaining high expectations.

How to be in a relationship may be the most important skill children learn (Gallager and Mayer, 2008). Research suggests children able to form high-quality and secure relationships with adults and other children display better language usage, problem solving ability, social connectedness, and they acquire harmonious play skills. Young children watch and learn from teachers and others' behaviors. The tone set in a caring and supportive school environment can lead to feelings of acceptance. Each child should feel he/she is a valued member of a group of others.

During preschool years, children form ideas of self-identity. It becomes difficult for children to believe in themselves—or their language abilities—if self-esteem is constantly undermined. Figure 4–11 suggests teacher behavior and response in communicating with children to promote social growth.

---

In communication, the teacher:

- cares and is ready to give of self.
- listens, intent on understanding.
- adds simple words when the child cannot.
- does not correct speech when this might break down willingness to speak further.
- is available for help in clarifying ideas or suggesting new play and exploring possibilities.
- senses child interests and guides to new real experiences.
- is available when problems and conflicts happen.
- enjoys time spent in child activities.
- establishes friendships with each child.
- talks positively about each child's individual uniqueness.
- is an enthusiastic and expressive communicator.
- offers friendly support while redirecting undesirable social behavior or stating rules.
- notices and respects each child's work.

**FIGURE 4–11** Teacher behaviors that are helpful to the child's social growth.

---

**metalinguistic skills** — the ability to think about language as a separate entity.

Erikson (1950) identified a series of social-emotional developments in the young child, which are presented in a shortened form here.

- (Infants) Trust vs. Mistrust. Trust develops from consistent care, which fulfills basic needs (food, warmth, physical contact, and so on), leading to stable and secure feelings rather than anxiousness. A positive view of life forms.

- (Toddlers and 2-year-olds) Autonomy vs. Shame and Doubt. Children get to know themselves as separate persons. What they control, decisions they can make, and freedom they may have while still being very dependent become apparent. Awareness of inabilities and helplessness is sensed. Behavior may be testing and full of the word "no."

- (Preschoolers) Initiative vs. Guilt Feelings. Experimentation and active exploration of new skills and directions occur. There are strong emotions at times in resistance to authority figures and rules, yet children are still dependent on adult approval. (p. 145)*

Social development must not be ignored in planning and conducting language activities or in trying to manage groups. Structure and rules are necessary for group living. An individual child's status in the eyes of the group can be enhanced through the sharing and appreciation of the child's ideas and accomplishments and by providing frequent opportunities for the child to lead or help lead the group in activities, which is almost always a confidence and status-building experience.

Teachers should be concerned with a child's **social connectedness**—a term that has been defined as characteristic of people with stable and secure lives, supportive families and friends, and close ties to community and who are accepted as a worthy part of a group and are able to weather life's stresses with a sense of individual identity. A teacher is in control of a school's atmosphere and works with the home and community, thus plays a large role

* From Erikson, E. (1950). *Childhood and society*. Copyright © 1950, © 1963 by W. W. Norton & Company, Inc., renewed © 1978, 1991 by Erik H. Erikson. Used by permission of W. W. Norton & Company, Inc.

in the development of this aspect of a child's personality.

Preschoolers begin to learn labels for feelings, such as happy, sad, jealous, fearful, and so on. They begin to think of others' feelings. The conscience is forming, and interest in right and wrong is expressed. Teachers who speak of their own feelings as adults set an example and provide a climate in which children's feelings are also accepted and understood.

Most children explore social actions and reactions. They have a strong desire to spend time with their peers (Figure 4–12). They want to have friends, and in play, they learn to make plans, negotiate, and communicate. Strong emotions accompany much of children's behavior; their total beings speak. When a child feels

FIGURE 4–12 Being left out feels like the end of the world.

**social connectedness** — a term associated with the following human characteristics: is stable and secure, develops close relationships with others, has supportive family and friends, and is deemed a worthy individual by others. Often seen by others as able to transcend stress and possess an individual identity.

left out, life becomes an overwhelming tragedy; on the other hand, a party invitation may be a time to jump for joy.

It is through symbolic and pretend play that young children are most likely to develop both socially and intellectually. Opportunities for spontaneous child-initiated social play need to rate high on a center's agenda. The following list identifies activities that can help children develop a sense of self. These are just a few suggestions; many more are possible.

● activities using mirrors
● activities using children's photographs and home movies
● tracings of the child's outline
● activities that involve making name tags and placing names on belongings, drawings, lockers, and projects
● activities that identify and discuss feelings
● activities concerned with personal opinions
● activities that show both similarity to others and individual diversity
● activities that build pride or membership in a group
● activities that identify favorite pursuits, objects, or individual choices
● small group activities involving cooperation

The following is a list of social abilities that serve as a strong foundation for future schooling. Children should be able to

● get and hold the attention of adults in a variety of socially accepted ways.
● express affection or mild annoyance to adults and peers when appropriate.
● use adults as resources after determining that a task is too difficult to handle alone.
● show pride in achievement.
● lead and follow children of the same age.
● compete with age-mates.

Teachers strive to supply a center atmosphere in which a sense of trust and security thrives. Children need to learn to trust people in their world, or else they reject all that these people want to teach them. They need to have faith in those who respect them and accept their feelings, and learn to trust themselves.

As children age, self-acts can be talked about and judged by the child. The author once met a young 3-year-old boy who would sit himself in a chair if he thought he had misbehaved (for example, if he had purposely bumped another with a bike, pushed another, taken another's toy). He would sit only a few moments, and then jump up and happily resume play. This type of guidance technique was not used by the staff, but at home, sitting in the "thinking chair" was a common occurrence. The center staff respected the child's behavior and watchfully intervened when behavior warranted urging the child's use of words to solve problems. The child's self-imposed chair-sitting behavior slowly disappeared as he learned to ask for a turn and gained new social skills.

Whether young children see themselves as "valued identities" depends on their interactions with others.

## SUMMARY

Physical, intellectual, and social-emotional growth proceeds concurrently with the child's speech. Understanding these growth systems allows teachers to use appropriate techniques and behaviors. Child characteristics and teacher-provided growth opportunities are included in Figure 4–13.

Perceptual-motor activities are an integral part of many centers' language arts programs. Many educators believe that there is a strong correlation between physical activity during this period and mental growth. Some educators present visual literacy activities to preschoolers, believing visual literacy is a learned skill (Figure 4–14).

Adults need to react to and sense the correctness of what seem to be errors in children's thinking. Guiding the child's discovery of concepts is an integral part of early childhood teaching.

A child who trusts can learn. Teachers must accept children's feelings and concentrate on establishing bonds between themselves and the children. This encourages growth of abilities. The feeling tone that lies beneath each human contact and conversation creates a setting for learning.

| CHILD CHARACTERISTICS | TEACHER-PROVIDED GROWTH OPPORTUNITIES |
|---|---|
| • curiosity<br>• ability to learn<br>• interest in what affects the child personally<br>• focus on here and now<br>• intellectual activity<br>• social involvement<br>• physical energy<br>• symbolic thinking<br>• language growth<br>• emotionally "charged"<br>• growth is in spurts with parallel and uneven growth possible in different growth areas | • varied, firsthand experience with abundant sensory materials, objects, and media<br>• teacher enthusiasm for learning<br>• time to explore and make own discoveries<br>• language arts activities<br>• planned program with developmentally appropriate activities and age-suitable classrooms and play yards<br>• supportive assistance when pursuing a line of inquiry<br>• an environment that encourages the development of the child's sense of trust<br>• caring adults and a safe, secure environment<br>• activities and routines to satisfy physical, intellectual, social, and emotional needs<br>• cultural respect and dignity<br>• play with peers<br>• knowledgeable adults who take a personal interest in each individual child's welfare and growth<br>• opportunities for child-initiated project work |

*Note: This figure is not intended to be complete but rather to offer highlights of chapter text.

**FIGURE 4–13** Growth and opportunity.

## VISUAL LITERACY ACTIVITIES

- Read Ellen Stoll Walsh's *Mouse paint* (1999, New York: Harcourt/Red Wagon Books [board book]), which discusses how useful color can be.
- Chart color choices. Offer shell pasta that has been colored with yellow, blue, red, and green food coloring. Chart children's choice of the best one to eat. Discuss.
- Display child art with a word in 2- to 3-inch letters that closely connect. Ask children for a word that "talks" for her art. "Does your artwork need a word to go with it?" "If your painting could talk, what would it say?"
- Make graphs. Example: How many came to school in a car or bus, walked, or biked? What kind of pets do we have—dog, cat, bird, turtle?
- Use visual cards as a transition devise. The card selected by the child is the place she chooses to go next. (Book for library area, block for block area, paint can with brush for art area, etc.)
- Find round, square, and triangular objects in illustrations or photos.
- Create a flower garden wall display with a photo of a child's face or child's name in the center of each flower. Children can make flowers using various media.
- Make a "Guess-What-I-Am?" flannel board set using simply shaped objects such as a house, tree, scissors, hat, and so on. Make all shapes with no details and use the same color.
- Line up three photos and have children guess what story they tell.
- Post photographs or images representing honesty, empathy, kindness, helpfulness, beauty, work, responsibility, and so on, that expand children's understanding of human characteristics. Discuss one characteristic daily.
- After a story is read and is familiar, decide how it could be told with pictures, in dance, or with clay instead of using words.
- Collect photos or illustrations of happy, sad, frightened, and so on, multicultural faces. Discuss ones that go together and what emotion is present.

**FIGURE 4–14** Visual literacy activities.

## ADDITIONAL RESOURCES

### Readings

Burmark, L. (2002). *Visual literacy: Learn to see, see to learn*. Alexandria, VA: Association for Supervision and Curriculum Development.

Darling-Kuria, N. (2010). *Brain-based learning activities: Connecting theory and practice*. St. Paul, MN: Redleaf Press.

Jensen, E. (2000). *Learning with the body in mind*. San Diego: The Brain Store.

Notari-Syverson, A., O'Connor, R. E., & Vadasy, P. F. (2007). *Ladders to literacy*. Baltimore, MD: Brookes Publishing Co.

### Helpful Websites

International Visual Literacy Association (IVLA)
http://www.ivla.org
Contains articles and information on research and conferences.

National Child Care Information Center (NCCIC)
http://www.nccic.org
Lists ages and stages of growth.

National Institute of Mental Health
http://www.nimh.nih.gov
Outlines risk factors affecting social and emotional development and readiness for school. Search the site by using key words Good Start.

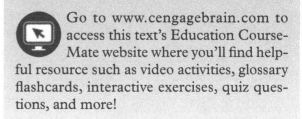

Go to www.cengagebrain.com to access this text's Education Course-Mate website where you'll find helpful resource such as video activities, glossary flashcards, interactive exercises, quiz questions, and more!

# Review It and Use It

1. Describe children's development of physical skill, and react to the statement "Physical skills have little effect or influence on young children's language skills."

2. Choose the category that fits best, and code the following words with the following headings (1) perceptual-motor development, (2) social-emotional development, or (3) mental development.

   trust
   concepts
   tasting
   self-awareness
   self-image
   categorizing
   predicting
   avoiding people
   eye-hand skill
   body image
   security
   generalizing
   balance
   conscience
   abstracting

   Check your answers with a peer. If you differ on a rating explain your selection.

3. Read the following teacher behaviors and verbalizations. Write the numbers of those you think would help a child develop healthy social-emotional skills.

   a. Recognizing each child by name as the child enters.

   b. Pointing out (to others) a child's inability to sit still.

   c. Telling a child it is all right to hate you.

   d. Keeping a child's special toy safe.

   e. Encouraging a child's saying, "I'm not finished," when another child grabs his or her toy.

   f. Saying, "Jerome (child) thinks we should ask the janitor, Mr. Smith, to eat lunch with us."

   g. Saying, "Hitting makes me angry. It hurts."

   h. Planning activities that are either "girls only" or "boys only."

   i. Encouraging children who show kindness to others.

   j. Allowing a child to make fun of another child and then neglecting to speak to the first "fun maker" about it.

k. Changing the rules and rewards often.

l. Ignoring an irritating behavior that seems to be happening more frequently.

4. Choose the best answer.

   a. Most centers agree that perceptual-skill development belongs
      i. somewhere in the program.
      ii. in the language arts area.
      iii. in the music and physical education area.
      iv. to a separate category of activities.

   b. The younger the child, the more the child needs
      i. demonstration activities.
      ii. to be told about the properties of objects.
      iii. sensory experience.
      iv. enriching child toys.

   c. Trust usually _____ being able to risk and explore, when considering early childhood school attendance.
      i. follows
      ii. combines
      iii. is dependent on
      iv. comes before

   d. Young children's thinking is focused on
      i. first-hand current happenings.
      ii. abstract symbols.
      iii. pleasing adults for rewards.
      iv. the consequences of their behavior.

   e. There is a _____ relationship between language and thought.
      i. well-understood
      ii. well-researched
      iii. clear
      iv. cloudy

## STUDENT ACTIVITIES

1. Using the chalkboard or a large piece of newsprint (or shelf paper), list, with a small group of other students, the teacher behaviors that might develop a sense of trust and build children's self-esteem.

2. Plan and conduct two activities with preschool children that concentrate on a perceptual-motor skill. Report your successes and failures to the group.

3. Study a few solitary, unengaged preschoolers who seem to want to join in a play relationship with a peer or group of peers. Record any verbal overtures and describe any nonverbal actions. Then assess each child's degree of success in gaining a social connection. Share your notes with classmates.

4. Pair with another student. Taking turns, have one person take three personal articles and place them on the table or desk in front of the other person. Try to categorize these articles. How many objects can you put in the same category? Can you find a category that includes all of the items?

5. Collect a few common visual icons such as a poison warning, a raised open hand symbol meaning stop, an arrow indicating a direction or other icons. Test with a child or small group of children asking "What might this mean if you saw it . . . (on a bottle, etc.)? Share results.

USE IT IN THE CLASSROOM

### Visual Discrimination Games

1. Children find hidden objects in illustrations or photographs in this activity. Hide cutouts of different shapes made from any adhesive paper in illustrations or photographs. Example: Cut out geometric shapes and simple object shapes (dog, cat, hat, glove, ball, bat, flower, and so on); then stick shapes in a scene cut from a magazine or in a drawing you have created. Ink stamping set shapes or commercial stickers also work. Make a key sheet using duplicate hidden shapes on a blank sheet so that children know what they are looking for. Children can circle or color the object when found.

(Note: Outlining the shapes with a dark colored felt pen makes it easier.)

2. Find objects in the same category, such as food, clothing, shoes, hats, flowers, bugs, cars, and so forth, in a picture book, magazine, or catalog. Example: "Let's see how many different hats we can find."

3. Make a set of index cards onto which you have pasted pictures of food items. Make other categories on other index cards. Mix them up. Paste an item from each category into a medium-sized department-store gift box lid, then sort the index cards into the box lids according to category. Try the activity with a small group of children. What did you discover?

CHAPTER

# 5

# Understanding Differences

## OBJECTIVES

After reading this chapter, you should be able to:

- Discuss Standard and non-Standard English.

- Describe the teacher's role with children who speak a dialect.

- Discuss early childhood centers' language programs for second-language learners.

- Identify common speech problems.

## KEY TERMS

| | |
|---|---|
| accent | hearing |
| auditory | disabilities |
| processing | otitis media |
| bilingual | scaffolding |
| Black English | selective |
| cluttering | (elective) |
| culture | mutism |
| deafness | speech and |
| deficit | language |
| perspective | disabilities |
| dialect | Standard English |
| Ebonics | subculture |

## A Problem Solved

*It was the first song at circle time.*

> Good morning, I like the shoes you've got on. / In fact, I like 'em so much, I'm gonna put 'em in a song. / In a song, in a song, / I'm gonna put you and your shoes in a song.

*A boy asked if we could put hair in. "Good morning, I like the hair you've got on. . . ." The boy stopped singing. We finished the verse. The boy leaned toward me and said quietly, "But what about Mr. Baker?" "Who's Mr. Baker?" I asked. The boy lifted one hand from his lap and pointed to his left. I saw Mr. Baker, one of the father volunteers who came to tell stories. He was totally bald and trying not to laugh. None of the children found it funny. To leave Mr. Baker out was not funny. A girl whispered loudly to the boy, "Say skin." He leaned toward me and said, "Sing skin this time." The cloud left the boy's face. . . . and Mr. Baker gave him a thumbs-up, as if to celebrate another problem solved (Hunter, 2003).*

### Questions to Ponder

1. What is this reading an example of? What do you like about this song activity?

2. Could this vignette's song be used in a planned unit of study on diversity? If so, explain how?

The United States is a multicultural society. It is a vast array of people of different backgrounds and ethnicities. Members of families may be married, remarried, single, gay, straight, birthparents, adoptive parents, and/or unrelated individuals.

Children's families also differ substantially in size, resources, values, goals, languages spoken, educational attainment, child-raising practices, past experiences along with immigration status, countries of origin, and length of time in the United States. Families have broken almost all traditional rules for what makes a family but continue to affirm the most basic definition of family: a bond reinforced by love and caring.

Experienced teachers throughout the United States report that the children they teach are more diverse in their backgrounds, experiences, and abilities than were those they taught in the past. Projections suggest that by the year 2025, more than half of the children enrolled in America's schools will be members of "minority" groups, not of European-American origin. Genishi & Dyson (2009) suggest diversity and difference are the new "normal," and they point out immigrants are not settling exclusively in urban areas but also suburban and rural communities.

The National Assessment of Education Progress, known as the nation's report card, shows an alarming trend. The gap between affluent and poorer students in the United States has widened on important indicators, such as scores on reading, math, and science. In schools in high-poverty areas, 70 percent of children scored below even the most basic level of reading (Alexander, 2004).

Early childhood programs and elementary grade levels are experiencing an influx of Spanish-speaking children in parts of the country with little or no history of ethnic or racial diversity—a trend that is expected to continue at an increasing rate. Barnett, Yarosz, Thomas, Jung, & Blanco (2007) describe expected numbers of English language learners (ELLs):

> The number of children in the United States is growing rapidly, and the vast majority are from homes where Spanish is the primary language (Tabors,

Paez, & Lopez, 2003). This trend is even stronger at the preschool level. Hispanic children account for more than 20 percent of all children under five. (Collins & Ribeiro, 2004, p. 277)

More children enter school with addictions, diseases, and disorders such as fetal alcohol syndrome, and without having had sufficient sleep, food, or supervision at home. Teachers have found themselves virtually unprepared to deal with the vastly different linguistic and life experiences and abilities of language-diverse children (Figure 5–1).

Early childhood educators recognize that extra efforts made early in some young children's lives can prevent problems with learning to read. Children who are poor, nonwhite, and nonnative speakers are considered much more likely to fail to learn to read adequately. As with other educators, you will be searching for ways to meet young children's varied educational needs. Since play opens children to expression; it will be an integral part of any early childhood program.

Barrett (2003) has reviewed research concerning preschool enrollment and later reading achievement. A summary of his findings follows.

> Preschool programs can have an important short-term impact on general cognitive development and academic abilities including reading achievement. Effects appear to be larger for intensive, high-quality educational programs targeting children in poverty.

> Long-term findings included the following comments. School success (primarily grade repetition and special education placement) is dependent on verbal abilities; particularly reading plays an important role in accessing new knowledge from textbook readings and other school-work. (p. 57)

Barrett concluded that preschool education in a variety of forms improves general cognitive abilities during early childhood and produces

**FIGURE 5–1** Ethnic and cultural diversity is commonplace in America's classrooms.

long-term increases in reading achievement. He also notes that additional research on learning and teaching in the early years could provide more guidance for teachers.

## CHILD-FOCUSED AND CHILD-SENSITIVE APPROACHES

Au (2006) describes what is important to consider when a classroom includes children of diverse backgrounds. Establishing positive relationships with children is key:

> It may be helpful for the teacher to have an understanding of the students' cultural backgrounds and the values they bring to school. Once positive relationships and open communication have been established, students will accept the teacher as a role model and as a model of literate behavior. (p. 197)

Program planners are experimenting and refining instructional models. These new approaches are described as child-focused and child-sensitive approaches (Figure 5–2).

A safe classroom environment using these approaches is one that respects differences and uniqueness and energizes young children's ability to communicate desires, fears, and understandings.

### KIDS ARE DIFFERENT

Kids are different
They don't even look the same
Some kids speak different languages
They all have a different name
Kids are different
But if you look *INSIDE* you'll see
The one with brown hair, black hair, red hair
  or blond hair,
Is just like you and me.

Author Unknown

**FIGURE 5–2** Wall chart.

The NAEYC (1996) has recommended the following:

> For the optimal development and learning of all children, educators must accept the legitimacy of children's home language, respect (hold in high regard) and value (esteem, appreciate) the home culture, and promote and encourage the active involvement and support of all families, including extended and nontraditional family units. (p. 42)

Teachers realize that children whose language skills or patterns are different are just as intelligent and capable as those who speak Standard English. Before discussing language differences, it is important to clarify the intent of this book. The purpose here is to assist teachers (1) to help the children and (2) to help in such a way that it will not actually make matters worse. The teacher's sensitivity to and knowledge of a particular cultural group and its different language patterns can aid a particular child's growth. Preserving the child's feelings of adequacy and acceptance is the teacher's prime goal; moving the child toward the eventual learning of standard forms is a secondary goal.

Early childhood educators strive, through professional associations, individual efforts, and attention to standards, to increase program quality. In doing so, each center needs to examine its program to ensure language learning is not seen as occurring only at language time but from the moment teachers greet each child at the beginning of the day. Every child-adult interaction holds potential for child language learning. The key question is whether each child is receiving optimum opportunity during group care to listen and speak with a savvy adult skilled in natural conversation that reinforces, expands, and extends.

Language acquisition is more than learning to speak; it is a process through which a child becomes a competent member of a community by acquiring both the linguistics and sociocultural knowledge needed to learn how to use language in that particular community. It is particularly important that every individual have equal access to educational and economic opportunity, especially those from groups who have consistently been found on the bottom of the educational, social, and economic heap: African-Americans, Latinos, Mexican-Americans, and Native American people.

## STANDARD ENGLISH

**Standard English** is the language of elementary schools and textbooks. It is the language of the majority of people in the United States. Increasingly, preschool programs enroll children whose speech reflects different past experiences and a cultural (or subcultural) outlook. When attending a preschool or center, these children, by practicing and copying the enrolled group's way of speaking, become aware of the group's values, attitudes, food preferences, clothing styles, and so on, and gain acceptance as group members. Some theorize that group membership influences children's manner of thinking about life's experiences.

Standard English usage is advantageous and a unifying force that brings together cultures within cultures, thereby minimizing class differences.

**Dialect,** as used here, refers to language patterns that differ from Standard American English. Dialects exist in all languages and fall into two categories: (1) regional and geographical and (2) social and ethnic. Dialect has been defined as a regional or social variety of language distinguished by pronunciation, grammar, or vocabulary, especially a variety of speech differing from the standard literary language or speech pattern of the culture in which it exists. Two widely recognized dialects in the United States are a New England and a Southern accent. Diverse dialects include African-American English, Puerto Rican English, Appalachian English, and varieties

---

**Standard English** — substantially uniform formal and informal speech and writing of educated people that is widely recognized as acceptable wherever English is spoken and understood.
**dialect** — a variety of spoken language unique to a geographical area or social group. Variations in dialect may include phonological or sound variations, syntactical variations, and lexical or vocabulary variations.

of Native American English, Vietnamese English, and others. Dialects are just as highly structured, logical, expressive, and complex as Standard English.

Boser (2006) notes that experts have been predicting the imminent demise of American dialects for decades because of increased mass media exposure, but the opposite seems true. Boser notes his conclusion is drawn from the work of a group of expert linguists who are compiling a new atlas of North American English. This first work to plot all major speech patterns in the continental United States and Canada shows that regional dialects have become more pronounced. Boser points out that although mountains of data have been collected on *how* dialects are changing, understanding of *why* they change remains elusive.

African-American preschoolers who speak **Black English** (African-American English) use advanced and complex syntax, such as linking two clauses, as do their Standard English–speaking peers. Black English is a systematic, rule-governed dialect that can express all levels of thought. African-American English, Black English, and the term **Ebonics** refer to a grammatically consistent speech whose key features include not conjugating the verb "to be" and the dropping of some final consonants from words (Figure 5–3). In the past, many debated whether African-American English is a distinct language or a dialect; the controversy still exists today. Elevating African-American English to the status of a language has evoked emotional reaction nationwide from both African-Americans and others. Early childhood professionals have mixed opinions. Many educators believe that the professional teacher's primary task is to preserve children's belief that they are already capable speakers and that teachers also should provide the opportunity for children to hear abundant Standard English speech models in classrooms. Linguists and educators do agree on the desperate need to teach some African-American children Standard English,

1. extreme reduction of final consonants ("so" for "sold," "fo" for "four," "fin" for "find," "ba" for "bad")
2. phonological contrasts absent, such as -th versus -f at word endings ("baf" for "bath," "wif" for "with")
3. "l" or "r" deleted in words ("pants" for "parents," "doe" for "door," "he'p" for "help")
4. verb "be" used to indicate extended or continuous time ("I be walkin")
5. deletion of some "to be" verb forms ("He sick" or "She talk funny")
6. deletion of s or z sounds when using third person singular verbs ("He work all the time" or "She say don't go")
7. elimination of s in possessives ("Mama car got crashed")
8. use of two-word subjects ("Ben he be gone")
9. use of "it" in place of "there" ("It ain't none pieces left" for "There are no pieces left")

**FIGURE 5–3** Some features of African-American vernacular English.

but there is little agreement on how best to do so. Although it has long been suggested that the dialectic features of African-American vernacular English and its phonology create additional challenges for learning to read English, limited efforts to test this hypothesis have been undertaken. It should also be made clear that many African-American children speak Standard English, not African-American English.

Actually, only relatively minor variations in vocabulary, pronunciation, and grammatical forms are apparent in most dialects.

Speakers of a particular dialect form a speech community that reflects the members' lifestyles or professional, national, family, or ethnic backgrounds. Certain common features mark the speech of the members, and no two members of a particular community ever speak exactly alike because each person's speech is unique. Unfortunately, to some, the term dialect can connote less-than-correct speech. Speech accents

---

**Black English** — a language usually spoken in some economically depressed African-American homes. A dialect of non-Standard English having its own rules and patterns, it is also called African-American English.
**Ebonics** — a nonstandard form of English, a dialect often called Black English that is characterized by not conjugating the verb "to be" and by dropping some final consonants from words.

differ in a number of ways and are fully formed systems. Children from other than mainstream groups enter school with a set of linguistic and cultural resources that in some respects differ from, and even conflict with, rather than resemble, those of the school culture.

Individuals react to dialects with admiration, acceptance, ambivalence, neutral feelings, or rejection based on value judgments. Most Americans have but a superficial acquaintance with stereotypes of American Southern or New York varieties of English, which have been experienced while listening to advertisements or entertainment media. People make assumptions about an individual's ethnicity, socioeconomic status, and competence based on the way he or she speaks, and unfortunately discrimination is not uncommon.

Just as a child who meets another child from a different part of the country with a different **accent** might say, "You sound funny!" so others may think of dialectic speech as crude or reflecting lack of education. Early childhood teachers are trained to remain nonjudgmental and accepting.

Dialect-speaking teachers, aides, and volunteers (working with children and families of the same dialect) may offer children a special degree of familiarity and understanding (Figure 5–4).

A Standard English–speaking teacher may sound less familiar but affords the child a model for growth in speaking the dominant language of our society, which is important to his life opportunities.

Although a dialect (or accent) may be an advantage in one's community, it may be a disadvantage outside of that community. When someone begins to learn English, others may feel betrayed because they feel the individual has denied his or her identity and joined forces with those who are rejecting group values.

Accented speech, for this discussion, is defined as distinctive, typical speech habits of an individual or group of individuals associated with a geographical location or region.

**FIGURE 5–4** An assistant teacher who speaks the same dialect can often form a special relationship with a child.

---

**accent** — prominence or emphasis given to a word or syllable through one or more of the following factors: loudness, change of pitch, and longer duration (Harris & Hodges, 1995).

## WORKING WITH DIALECT-SPEAKING FAMILIES

Many early childhood centers employ staff members who have dialects that the children can easily understand so that children feel at home. Teachers who speak the children's dialect may be eagerly sought and in short supply. Additional insight into the child's culture and the particular meanings of their words is often an advantage for teachers who have the same dialect as the children. They may be able to react to and expand ideas better than a Standard English–speaking teacher.

It is important for teachers to know whether the children are speaking a dialect and to understand dialectic differences. The four most common dialectic differences between Standard English and some common dialects occur in verb forms. These differences occur in the following areas.

- Subject-verb agreement
- Use of the verb "to be"
- Use of present tense for past tense
- Use of "got" for "have"

In some areas where a language other than English is spoken, part of the rules of the second language may blend and combine to form a type of English different from the standard. Two examples of this are (1) English spoken by some Native American children and (2) English spoken in communities close to the Mexican-American border.

There are differing opinions about the teaching of preferred Standard English in early childhood centers. In most centers, however, preserving the child's native dialect, while moving slowly toward Standard English usage, is considered more desirable than providing immediate, purposeful instruction in standard forms. Joint family and center discussions can help clarify program goals.

## THE TEACHER'S ROLE

Understanding dialectic differences is important to the teacher's understanding of each child. To give young children the best model possible, the early childhood teacher should speak Standard English. The federal government mandates that all children attending American public schools learn English, and instruction in English always begins at some point during the elementary school years.

Many successful teachers have speech accents and also possess other characteristics, abilities, and useful techniques that aid young children's development of language and literacy. It matters very little to children whether the teacher speaks a bit differently from the way they speak. The teacher's attitude, warmth, and acceptance of the dialect and the children themselves are very important considerations (Figure 5–5).

Teachers are in a unique position to build bridges rather than walls between cultures. Teachers' essential task is to create new and shared meanings with the children—new contexts that give meaning to the knowledge and skills being taught. The challenge is to find personally interesting and culturally relevant ways of creating new contexts for children, contexts in which school skills are meaningful and rewarding.

Competence is not tied to a particular language, dialect, or culture. Professional educators realize that language instruction or any other part of the planned curriculum should not reject or be designed to be a replacement of children's language or culture, but rather be viewed as language expansion and enrichment.

**FIGURE 5–5** "You are working very hard to thread the string through the small hole in that bead."

Genishi and Dyson (2009) are concerned about whether mandated curricular standards fit all children.

> But current standards and mandated curricula can be troubling. As we have argued herein, too often they imagine an idealized generic child, against whom all children might be measured, and that child is learning a generic language at a generic pace. The "different" children might need "explicit" instruction so that they, too, might sound generic. (p. 32)

They suggest "re-imagined" standards that contain reasonable goals for very young children, including the diverse and different ones.

Early childhood teachers may receive little instruction (teacher training) in the types of language behaviors to expect from diverse speakers; training in how to effect growth in language competencies also may be lacking. Teachers themselves will need to do their own classroom observation and research to identify cultural variations and differences that affect attending children's speech growth and development. Young preschoolers have learned the social speech expectations of their homes and possibly their communities. They know when to speak and when to be silent. At school they infer what is appropriate based on what they hear and observe there. When children begin to use a second language or second dialect, they tend to use words in syntactic constructions found in their native speech or dialect. Because many cultures, including Chinese, Vietnamese, and some Native American communities, expect children to learn from listening, young children from these cultures may be relatively silent compared with children encouraged to be verbal from birth. Hawaiian children observed by researchers often did not like to be singled out for individual attention and tended to give minimal answers when questioned.

Because impact and swear words are said with emotion and emphasis, it is not uncommon for these words to be learned first and used at the wrong time. In some cultures, children may be encouraged to use "yes" and interrupt adult speech to signify that they are in tune with the speaker.

Some facial expressions or gestures acceptable in one culture may be highly insulting in another. Even the acceptable distance between speakers of different languages varies. Teachers may interpret various child language (or lack of it) as disrespectful without considering cultural diversity. Misunderstandings between children, humorous as they may be to teachers, require sensitive handling.

A child may be a very good speaker of his particular dialect or language, or he may be just a beginner. Staff members working with the young child respect the child's natural speech and do not try to stop the child from using it. The goal is to promote the child's use of natural speech in his native dialect. Standard English can be taught by having many good speaking models available at the center for the child to hear. Interested adults, play activities, other children, and a rich language arts program can provide a setting where children listen and talk freely. Teachers refrain from correcting children's oral language errors and look for meaning and intention. They stress cooperation, collaboration, and frequent conversation.

The teacher should know what parts of the center's program are designed to increase the child's use of words. Teachers can show a genuine interest in words in their daily conversations with the children. Teachers can also use the correct forms of Standard English in a casual way, using natural conversation. Correcting the children in an obvious way could embarrass them and stop openness and enthusiasm.

Delpit (1995) points out that constant teacher correction and focus on correctness impedes the child's "unconscious acquisition" of a language by raising the child's anxiety level and forcing him to cognitively monitor his every word. She provides an example of one 4-year-old's resistance to being taught to answer the teacher's morning greeting with a specific "I'm fine, thank you" response. Delpit's example (1995) follows.

Teacher:   Good morning, Tony. How are you?

Tony:   I be's fine.

Teacher:   Tony, I said, How are you?

Tony: (with raised voice) I be's fine.

Teacher: No Tony, I said. How are you?

Tony: (angrily) I done told you I be's fine. I ain't telling you no more. (p. 94)

Careful listening, skillful response, and appropriate questions during conversations help the child learn to put thoughts into words. The child thinks in terms of his own dialect or language first and, in time, expresses words in Standard English. Delpit (1995) recommends that teachers provide students with exposure to an alternative form and allow children the opportunity to practice that form in contexts that are not threatening, have real purpose, and are intrinsically enjoyable.

Preschool teachers must face the idea that children's language and appearance may unconsciously affect their attitudes about those children and, consequently, teacher behaviors. A new or unsure teacher may tend to seek out and communicate with children whose speech and appearance is most similar to her or his own. Extra effort may be necessary to watch this tendency and converse and instruct all attending children. Staff-parent meetings and additional planning are musts to meet the needs of children with diverse language patterns. Pronunciation guides helping teachers say children's names correctly are gathered from families at admitting interviews. This is just a small first step.

Sensitive, seasoned teachers will not put some children on the spot with direct questions or requests at group times. They may include additional storytelling or demonstration activities with young children whose native cultures use this type of approach. "Rappin" and words-to-music approaches may appear to a greater extent in some child programs. Drama may be a way to increase language use in other classrooms. To be sure, with the great diversity in today's early childhood classrooms, teachers will be struggling to reach and extend each child's language competence. This is not an easy task. Teachers who work with other than mainstream children learn that their own views of the world, or ways of using language in that world, are not necessarily shared by others.

Suggestions based on the work of Soto (1991), though dated, still present accepted instructional strategies.

1. Accept individual differences with regard to language-learning time frames. Avoid pressures to "rush" and "push" children. Young children need time to acquire, explore, and experience second-language learning.

2. Accept children's attempts to communicate because trial and error are a part of the second-language learning process. Children should be given opportunities to practice both native and newly established language skills. Adults should not dominate the conversations; rather, children should be listened to.

3. Recognize that children need to acquire new language skills instead of replacing existing linguistic skills. Afford young children an opportunity to retain their native language and culture.

4. Provide a stimulating, active, diverse linguistic environment with many opportunities for language use in meaningful social interactions. Avoid rigid grammatical approaches with young children.

5. Valuing each child's home culture and incorporating meaningful active participation will enhance interpersonal skills and contribute to academic and social success.

6. Use informal observations to guide the planning of activities, interactions, and conversations for speakers of other languages.

7. Provide an accepting classroom climate that values culturally and linguistically diverse young children. (p. 102)*

## Additional Teacher Tips

A teacher should guard against

- correcting children in a way that makes them doubt their own abilities.

---

*From Soto, L. D. (1991, Jan.). Understanding bilingual/bicultural young children. *Young Children* 40(2):30–36.

- giving children the idea that they are not trying hard enough to correct or improve their speech.
- discouraging children's speaking.
- allowing teasing about individual speech differences.
- interrupting children who are trying to express an idea.
- hurrying a child who is speaking.
- putting children on stage in an anxiety-producing way.

## SECOND-LANGUAGE LEARNERS

Many English-language learners live in California, Texas, New York, Florida, and Illinois, but other areas are experiencing sudden growth in this population. Non–English-speaking children, like nonstandard dialect speakers, tend to come from low socioeconomic backgrounds and attend schools with disproportionately high numbers of children in poverty; however, many will not fit this description. A large group of professional, foreign-born technology workers' families reside in some urban areas. In the world today, in many countries it is "natural" to grow up speaking more than one language. More than 70 percent of the world's population does so.

Language-minority children (second-language learners) can be defined as children who speak their native language in social and cultural contexts out of school and have developed the necessary communicative competence. They also are being introduced, in substantive ways, to another language. In this discussion, it is English.

There are two main categories of second-language learners who speak no or very little English. The first category consists of those children who come to this country at a very young age or are born here to immigrants who have lived in areas of the world where language as well as the culture, systems of government, and social structures are quite unlike those of the United States. The second group of learners is native born, such as Native Americans or Alaskan native born children, but speak a different language and are members of a different culture than the mainstream American culture.

The following terms may be used in readings and research publications to describe second-language learners: **bilingual** learner, English as a second-language student, student with limited English proficiency, language-minority learner, English-language learner, and linguistically diverse student.

A bilingual child can be described as a child younger than 3 years of age who learns two (sometimes more) languages at the same time or a child who learns a second language after age 3. Sequential acquisition describes what occurs when a child starts to learn a second language after the first language is only partially established—such as when a young child enrolls in a school where his native language is not spoken.

Northwestern University researchers (2009) believe that some individuals may have a natural aptitude for learning language. Research emphasizes that the experience of becoming bilingual *itself* may make learning an additional new language easier (Marian, 2009). A bilingual advantage is also likely to be generalized beyond word learning to other kinds of language learning and an ability to better maintain verbal information.

It is not unusual to find enrolled preschool children who are learning English and also possess different degrees of proficiency in two or more other languages (Figure 5–6). Bilingual children initially might have smaller vocabularies when each language is considered separately. But when one considers that the memory capacity of young children is limited and this restricts their rate of vocabulary acquisition, it is understandable. Bilingual children have two sets of vocabularies to learn. At any particular point during development, one would expect them to know fewer vocabulary items in each language but approximately the same number when both languages are considered.

---

**bilingual** — refers to an individual with a language background other than English who has developed proficiency in the primary language and a degree of proficiency in English.

FIGURE 5-6 Arianne speaks Spanish, German, and English.

Many experts suggest that if more than one language is spoken in the home and both languages are spoken well, the infant should be exposed to both from the beginning. However, if, as is so often the case, the first language is spoken exclusively in the home, research indicates the child should be encouraged to develop expertise in a wide range of language functions in the first language, in the expectation that these will easily transfer to the second language (English). Learning his native language allows the child's phonemic sensitivity to develop, which may allow him to gain an alphabetic insight that is needed for learning to read with ease.

The most immediate question the teacher of a bilingual child must face is deciding how well the child is progressing in all the languages the child is learning. A full language assessment with respect to the child's first language and with respect to the child's knowledge of English will probably show that the child's difficulties are limited to the acquisition of English. The testing of young children in multicultural and economically diverse classrooms is a growing practice.

The phrase "culturally sensitive" refers to whether the test is responsive to social and cultural differences among test takers. Because tests of language always reflect aspects of culture, it is impossible to construct a single test that is absolutely culturally sensitive, and incorporates aspects of all cultures to which children belong.

What is very important, when working with English language learners, is that the learner receives input that is not only comprehensible but just slightly beyond his or her current level of competence.

Knowing common strategies that young children use to learn English as a second language helps teachers. Some follow.

## Children

- assume that what people are saying is directly related to the ongoing situation.
- learn a few stock expressions or formulaic speech and start to talk.
- search for patterns that recur in the language.
- make the most of the language they already have.
- spend their major effort on getting across meaning and save refinement for later.

The California State Department of Education (2009) recommends the following strategies to teachers of second language learners.

- Start with what the child already knows.
- Start slowly.
- Use a type of scaffolding in communications by combining words with some kind of gesture, action, direct gaze, etc.
- Provide safe havens. Plan room spaces and activities with no or minimal expectations of a child's having to speak.
- Get help from the English-speaking children, and show them ways to communicate and ask questions to encourage social interactions. Promote their modeling of language.
- Expand and extend the child's limited word use.
- Talk about the here and now.
- Do fine-tuning. Restate what you said in more simplified terms. Offer consistent routines.
- Ensure inclusion. Invite a child by name to small-group activities. (p. 54-55)

Most educators estimate that most second-language–learning children will require 4 to 6 years to become competent users of English, and some will take as long as 5 to 8 years.

The California Department of Education (2009) suggests achieving academic success in school includes developing a knowledge and mastery of formal schooling practices in addition to building on one's home or community language practices. All children, they believe, can have high levels of achievement if provided with a rich, challenging curriculum and appropriate forms of assistance.

An effective early childhood curriculum for second-language should provide for frequent and diverse opportunities for speaking and listening that offer **scaffolding** to help guide the child through the learning process. The curriculum also should encourage children to take risks when speaking, construct meaning, and reinterpret knowledge within comfortable social contexts.

The dilemma that second-language learners may face in early school experiences is likened to a situation in which you can't win. To learn the new language, one needs to be socially accepted by those speaking the language; however, to be socially accepted, one has to be able to speak the new language. Young children often hurdle this bind by using various strategies, including gestures to invite others to play and accept their company. Crying, whimpering, pointing, miming, and making other nonverbal requests may also be tried. Children collect information by watching, listening, and speculating. They may talk to themselves and experiment with sounds or rehearse what they have heard. Telegraphic and formulaic language develops and they may say "Hey!" or "Lookit" over and over to gain attention.

Monolingual and bilingual speakers make inferences about social and linguistic appropriateness based on continued interaction in diverse social situations. Learning a second language includes a number of difficult tasks. The child must

- produce sounds that may not be used in the native language.
- understand that native speech sounds or words may have different meanings in the new (second) language.

- learn and select appropriate responses.
- sort and revise word orders.
- learn different cultural values and attitudes.
- control the flow of air while breathing.

The California Department of Education (2009) describes four stages in learning English: (1) home language use, (2) an observational and listening period, (3) telegraphic and formulaic speech, and (4) fluid language use.

Researchers have identified many factors that may have an impact on how quickly young children acquire a second language: motivation, exposure, age, personality, aptitude, consistency, attitude, learning style, opportunity and support, and the individual characteristics of the home and family environment.

An important technique—admitting and recognizing that a child is a classroom resource when it comes to explaining other ways of naming and describing objects or other ways of satisfying human needs—should be utilized by educators. Printed word cards in both languages can be added to the classroom to reinforce this idea.

Research has promoted the idea that bilingual youngsters have not encountered a lifelong setback but instead they may be more imaginative, better with abstract notions, and more flexible in their thinking than monolingual children. They also have been described as more creative and better at solving complex problems. Compared with monolingual children, bilingual children may develop more awareness concerning the nature of language and how it works. Evidence suggests that being bilingual enhances cognitive development. It definitely is a job skill many employers seek.

Some English-only parents, particularly more affluent ones, seek tutors or early childhood programs that offer their monolingual children the opportunity to become second-language learners. Nationally many legislators believe bilingual programs should be available for all children, but this is yet to become a national priority.

---

scaffolding — a teaching technique helpful in promoting languages, understanding, and child solutions. It includes teacher-responsive conversation, open-ended questioning, and facilitation of children's initiatives. Also defined as instruction in which a teacher builds upon what the child already knows to help the child accomplish a task and/or suggests breaking a task down into simpler components to promote accomplishment.

Youngquist and Martinez-Griego (2009) conclude that when a *strong foundation* is developed in a child's native language he will learn to read, write, and speak in English faster than a child without one. These authors emphasize the importance of involving families and community to support the school's efforts. This *has* become a national priority recognized by professional associations such as NAEYC and the IRA. It is also considered a priority in Head-Start programs and the No Child Left Behind legislation, and is mentioned in most state standards that promote quality.

Researchers have noticed that bilingualism sometimes improves children's self-esteem and strengthens family ties. Other researchers state that it may cause family distress. Educators have raised concerns about placing bilingual children in English-only preschools and believe that this may result in the children losing the ability to communicate effectively in their native language. This might adversely affect family relationships and conceptual development.

## PROGRAM PLANNING FOR SECOND-LANGUAGE LEARNERS

Educators urge program planners who provide second-language learning opportunities to realize that the child's exposure, comfort level, motivation, familiarity, and practice in real communicative contexts are all important considerations. Curriculum developers in early childhood programs that enroll other-than-English-speaking children will have to decide their position on the best way to instruct. A debate rages. One end of the debate espouses native language use, native cultural instruction, and academic learning in the child's native language before instruction in English begins. At the other end, advocates would present English on the child's first day of schooling, with minimal use of the child's native language. Those on this later side of the argument believe that the earlier English is introduced and confronted, the greater the child's linguistic advantage. Others disagree saying no research evidence supports the idea that there is a neural window on second language learning, and deferring instruction for a year or two is not a disadvantage. Policy recommendations put forth by the National Institute for Early Education Research

in 2006 say that support for English language learners should be provided in both the home language and English where feasible.

Educators note the different points of view concerning English language learners, but may choose to create their own programs by using innovative curricula and other instructional techniques because no comprehensive studies clearly chart the right path for educators to take when teaching preschool ELLs (English language learners) (Freedson-Gonzales, 2008). Each teacher and each educational leader must decide what will work for the children they have enrolled in the context of the curriculum they use and the standards that guide them (Nemeth, 2009).

Above all, most educators agree that other-than-English-speaking children need to be perceived as intellectually able, and their teachers should hold high achievement and academic expectations for them as they do for all enrolled children. Teachers are aware that planning well for each child means gathering and knowing as much as one can about the child's culture, home environment, family, and community (California Department of Education, 2009).

Au (2006) recommends that in any curriculum approach educators need to realize that one factor that handicaps the academic advancement of English language learners is some teachers' tendency to be overly concerned about the surface features of language, such as correct pronunciation of English, rather than the content of the ideas students are trying to communicate. She also points out that if students believe that what they have to say is important, they will have the confidence to learn the language needed to express those ideas.

Most programs approach the differences existing between home and school cultures by promoting children's biculturalism. This allows children to have successful experiences both in their families, where one set of values and behaviors prevails, and in school, where another set of values and behaviors may be expected. In a culturally sensitive approach, early childhood professionals would use modeling with culturally diverse children and slowly introduce and increase the practice of teaching via direct inquiry, particularly using verbal questions while they continue to use modeling. This practice would help increase children's verbal skills and their ability to follow directions.

Planned activities that relate to the experiences of children's everyday lives are relevant and significant. Cooperative learning activities that involve a small group of young children working together can be planned. This helps develop social skills and positive group relations.

Selected findings of interest to early childhood educators from the *Report of the National Literacy Panel on Language Minority Children and Youth* reviewed by August and Shanahan (2006) follow. The National Literacy Panel on Language-Minority Children and Youth's mission was to identify, assess, and synthesize research on the education of language-minority children and youth with respect to their attainment of literacy.

- Findings suggest that oral language skills are an important dimension of literacy development (p. 13).

- Evidence suggests that vocabulary; listening comprehension, syntactic skills, and the ability to handle meta-linguistic aspects of language (such as providing definitions of words) are associated with reading comprehension (p. 14).

- It is difficult to achieve reading and writing fluency without achieving automaticity in English alphabet letter name knowledge (p. 14).

- Literacy outcomes are more likely to be the result of home (and school) language and literacy learning opportunities (p. 15).

- Schools underestimate and underutilize parents' interest, motivation, and potential contributions (p. 15).

- Research has failed to provide a complete answer to what constitutes high-quality literacy instruction for language-minority students (p. 16).

- Instruction focusing on key components, such as phonemic awareness, decoding, oral reading fluency, reading comprehension, vocabulary, and writing, has clear benefits.

- English-language proficiency as the basis for becoming literate in English argues for an early, ongoing, and intensive effort to develop this proficiency (p. 17).

- Beginning reading programs teaching non-English-speaking children to read in English are showing promising results (p. 17).

- Some researchers found that (alphabet) letter naming and tests of phonological awareness in English were good predictors of these students performance in English reading (p. 18).

- Given the available research, the 'bridging' of home-school differences in (home school) interactions can enhance students' engagement and level of participation in classroom instruction (Goldenberg, Rueda, & August, 2006, p. 256).

Within the field of early childhood education, there is a need for knowledgeable, trained, competent, and sensitive multilingual/multicultural early childhood educators. Early childhood educators who speak more than one language and are culturally knowledgeable are an invaluable resource in the early childhood setting. Many experts and researchers advocate recruiting teacher assistants and classroom volunteers who speak children's native tongue. The importance of opportunities for English language learners to engage in pretend play early in their preschool attendance period is emphasized by Roskos and Christie (2007) and Cheatham and Ro (2010). Teacher support can promote and extend children's play periods. When reading and writing play materials are suggested and supplied by teacher during child-selected (or teacher suggested) play scenarios, child play has a chance for added literacy depth. Many read-alouds lead naturally to possible pretend play and re-enacting the story. Role-playing, whether based on book characters or child-chosen scenario characters, provides an additional benefit resulting in higher measures of child creativity and enhanced ability to analyze situations from different perspectives (Bronson & Merryman, 2010).

The value of exposing second-language-learning children to quality books cannot be overlooked (Figure 5–7). Story times and one to-one,  adult-child book readings can supply vocabulary and meaning in a way that conversational models alone cannot accomplish. Songs and music can also present language-learning opportunities. Print use in the center environment is another vehicle to promote literacy development. Above all, opportunity for abundant play and interaction with English-speaking children is critical. The most successful methods for teaching a second language include the same

FIGURE 5–7 The introduction of English picture books benefit second-language learners.

FIGURE 5–8 Objects can be named when the teacher touches them.

techniques mentioned in the monolingual child's learning of his first language—warm, responsive, articulate adults involved with children's everyday, firsthand exploration of the environment.

Additional suggested teacher strategies and techniques follow.

- Provide a safe, accepting classroom environment.
- Listen patiently, maintaining eye contact.
- Give attention to child attempts.
- Respond to meaning rather than speech technicalities or specifics.
- Promote sharing and risk taking.
- Make classroom activities inviting, interesting, meaningful, and successful.
- Emphasize and repeat key words in sentences.
- Point at objects or touch them while naming them, when possible (Figure 5–8).
- Learn how to correctly pronounce the child's name.
- Include the child in small groups where there are other child models to follow.
- Help the child realize he is unique and special, exactly "as is."

- Learn a few useful words in the child's language (for example, *bathroom, eat, stop, listen*).
- Gesture and use objects and pictures that give children additional clues, such as a picture-based daily schedule.
- Provide activity choices in which the child does not have to interface with others—so-called safe havens.
- During activity times, provide enough staff so that teachers can work closely with children and materials.
- Use a running commentary technique in interactions. "Serena is painting with red paint." "I'm pinning a name tag on your sweater."
- Choose predictable books to share.
- Work with a small group at story-reading times.
- Use repeated presentations of the same songs at group times.
- Link up English-speaking "partners" in noncompetitive games.
- Use visual aids, photos, and pictures and point to clarify words (Nemeth, 2009).
- Take the time to look children in the eye showing you value your interaction (Nemeth, 2009).
- Check classroom noise levels to assure English language learners will have no difficulty distinguishing English speech sounds.

A number of researchers have found that when teachers work with second-language learners, they make adjustments similar to those families make when talking to their very young children; these include organizing talk around visual references (real objects, actions, happenings, people, and so on), using simple syntax, producing many repetitions and paraphrases, speaking slowly and clearly, checking often for comprehension, and expanding and extending topics introduced by the child.

Professional education associations recommend that teachers faced with many different languages in their classrooms consider grouping together, at specific times during the day, children that speak the same or similar languages so that children can construct knowledge with others who speak their home language.

Playmates of second-language learners can be encouraged not only to be aware and accepting of other children but to approach and invite them to play. Through discussion, example, and modeling, children can learn to use gestures, to use simple sentences, to speak slowly, and to repeat themselves or use different words when they think their "friends" do not quite understand. Teachers stress that these new classmates may need help. One classroom regularly scheduled a short picture book reading time when family members shared a book in a language other than English. Children could choose whether to attend. The book would then be repeated in English by their regular teacher, and a discussion period examined how children both attempted to understand and felt during the first reading.

As mentioned earlier, second-language learners can be ignored and left out of peer play. Even when trying to communicate nonverbally, they can be treated as "babies" or as invisible. They may be cast as the infant in dramatic play situations or be the object of a mothering child's attention—perhaps unwanted attention. Other children may speak to them in high-pitched voices and in shortened and linguistically reduced forms as they have observed adults sometimes do with very young children who are learning to speak. Teachers should monitor these peer behaviors and discourage them if necessary.

## Reaching Families

Home-school instructional support programs have provided books, electronic media, "borrowed" materials and equipment, and "take home"  suggestions for homes with limited access to English-language models and storybooks. Encouraging families to continue to maintain their first language and their home language literacy activities, and perhaps increase everyday conversations, is a common practice. Schools usually ask families questions about what types of language exposure a child has had since birth and what types of literacy experiences have been associated with them.

In some cases an interpreter may be necessary. Designing room features and planning curriculum activities that welcome a family's participation in classroom activities and show acceptance are important considerations.

## Behaviors Teachers Can Expect

When words are attempted, teachers can expect a Spanish-speaking child to have a problem producing consonant sounds that do not exist in his native language, such as *d*, *j*, *r*, *v*, *sh*, *th*, and *s*; beginning-of-word blends, such as *st*, *sp*, and *sm*; and word endings of *r* blends, such as *-rd*, *-rt*, and *-rs*. A few other word sounds also will be difficult.

Second-language learners may reach a stage at which they seem to repeat words, and focus intently and rehearse words. This happens not for the purpose of communication but rather so the child can practice through repetition, which is reminiscent of younger preschoolers' private speech or self-talk during play situations. These rehearsing-like behaviors are usually done at a low volume. The first unintelligible utterances that second-language learners issue may be sound experimentation.

## CULTURAL DIFFERENCES

Teachers interested in studying the cultures of enrolled children can start by identifying components of culture. These components include family structure; definitions of stages, periods, or transitions during a person's life; roles of

FIGURE 5–9 Teachers studying enrolled children's cultures may find that children's religious observances differ from their own.

**▶❙❙ VIDEO ACTIVITY**

Go to the Education CourseMate website to watch the TeachSource Video Case, *Multicultural Lessons: Embracing, Similarities and Differences*.

Shelley Outwater, a literacy coach, discusses her philosophy concerning how her pupils become aware of cultural similarities and differences in her classroom.

1. Discuss how multicultural learning and language learning can go hand-in-hand in a classroom such as Shelly's classroom or in a preschool classroom.

2. In the video's read-aloud segment, what teacher techniques and strategies were used in the adult-child conversation to increase child understanding and comprehension?

adults and children; their corresponding behavior in terms of power and politeness; discipline; time and space; religion; food; health and hygiene; history; traditions; holidays; and celebrations (Figure 5–9).

In some cultures it is believed that children are not appropriate conversational partners for adults. Children may not be encouraged to initiate conversations about themselves or their interests, and adult talk may not be child-centered. Children may have learned not to look directly at adults when talking. Some children grow up learning that cooperation is more highly valued than competition; others do not.

Cultures are complex and changing, so understanding cultural similarities and differences can be a life's study in itself. **Culture** is defined here as all the activities and achievements of a society that individuals within that society pass from one generation to the next.

Ethnic origin is often a basic ingredient in sub cultural groupings. **Subculture** is defined as

other than a dominant culture. Class structure also exists in societies consisting of upper, middle, and lower income groups. Often, patterns of child-rearing vary between cultures and classes.

What cultural differences can inhibit child speech? Adult models' lengths of sentences or their inability to modify their speech to child levels, neutral or negative environments, family arrangements that require children to be alone for long periods or in which children are expected to be quiet or cannot gain adult attention, and lack of books or early reading experiences are all factors that can affect speech growth. Families are the primary language teachers in the early years, and language competence grows out of familiar situations such as seeking help or establishing joint attention— situations that provide frameworks in which children learn to make their intentions plain and to interpret the intentions of others.

## PROMOTING ACCEPTANCE

Practitioners may have to field questions from children about another child's speech. Answering in an open, honest fashion with accurate information gives the adult an opportunity to

culture — all the activities and achievements of a society that individuals within that society pass from one generation to the next.
subculture — an ethnic, regional, economic, or social group exhibiting characteristic patterns of behavior sufficient to distinguish it from others within an embracing culture or society.

affirm diversity and perhaps correct a child's biased ideas. Negative stereotypes can be diminished or dismissed. Before answering, it is a good idea to clarify what the child is really asking. Examples of teacher statements follow:

"Yes, Paloma speaks some words you don't understand. Her family comes from Guatemala and they speak the Spanish language. Paloma is learning lots of new words at school in the language of her new country—English."

"Quan doesn't talk to you because he doesn't know our words yet. He speaks a different language at his house. He is listening, and one day he will speak. While he is listening and learning words to speak, he wants to play. Show him with your hands and words what you want him to do. He will understand."

Teachers working with culturally diverse children need to watch and listen closely. Children's behavior and movements will give clues to their well-being and feelings of safety in the group. Teachers may need to ease into situations in which unpleasant remarks or actions are directed at a newly enrolled child who speaks a different language and express sadness, such as: "Ricardo has heard some unkind and unfriendly words from you boys in the loft. He is new at school and doesn't know what our school is like. I'm going to try and help Ricardo enjoy his first day in our room."

## CULTURAL AWARENESS ACTIVITIES

In planning language activities of all types, every effort must be made to make children aware of cross-cultural similarities and to explore differences. Language arts programming should draw on the linguistic, cultural, and personal experiences of language-diverse children. When planning instructional activities, it is important to provide opportunities that are familiar to children from their family and community life. Parents and extended family members can be invited to share family stories and artifacts relating to theme units, learning centers, or other program components.

Young children can be exposed to the idea that people eat, sleep, wear clothing, celebrate, dance, sing, live in groups, and speak to one another in common languages, and that they do these things in ways that may be either the same as or different from the ways their families do these things. Planned activities can make comparisons, treating diversity with the dignity it deserves. Skin color, hairstyles, food preferences, clothing, and music are starting points for study. Modeling friendship and cooperation between cultures and planning activities showing dissimilar individuals and groups living in harmony is a good idea. Stories exist in all languages and in most dialects. Some centers ask children and parents to contribute family photos to use to construct a classroom "My Family" book. Each child is asked to dictate a caption for each family photo. The book is permanently placed in the class library collection. When a new child enrolls, new family photos are added. See the Additional Resources at the end of this chapter for related helpful readings.

Identifying quality multicultural and multiethnic picture books is discussed in Chapter 9. Room displays, bulletin boards, and learning centers should also reflect the cultural diversity of attending children.

It is important to plan language arts programs that incorporate different cultural styles of dramatic play, storytelling, and chanting. Librarians can help teachers discover picture books and other materials written in dialects or two-language translations.

### Families as Partners

A strong connection between home and school should exist, with families playing a role in program planning and as assistants or teachers in classrooms. When family literacy rates are less than desirable, teachers have to proceed carefully with suggestions concerning reading to their children. Wordless books and parent storytelling are alternatives. Reading books aloud at home in a bilingual child's primary language is also recommended. Family literacy programs are discussed in Chapter 19.

Volk and Long (2005) have the following suggestions that help educators honor children's home and school literacy resources.

- Guard against a **deficit perspective** that distorts the educator's vision when working with marginalized families.
- Gain the perspective that homes, families, cultures, and communities possess "funds of knowledge" literacies and individuals with valuable skills.
- Understand that children become literate in many ways.
- Recognize that most families value education and believe it is important.
- Recognize that families may use different yet various and effective methods to support literacy.
- Believe that children participate in many literacy interactions at home (Figure 5–10).
- Realize that children may be surrounded by abundant human and literary resources including networks of support and people of varying ages and abilities.
- Recognize that peers help each other and may clarify the teacher's statements.

## PROGRAM TYPES

Controversy exists concerning which type of program is best suited to the child learning English as a second language. A list of common program types follows.

- Bilingual program: Two languages are used for instruction.
- Transitional bilingual program: Children's first language is used as a medium of instruction until they become fluent enough to receive all of their instruction in English.
- Newcomer program: Recent immigrant children are provided a special academic environment for a limited period. They provide a welcoming classroom environment and use instructional strategies to orient children to American life and culture. Bilingual staffs are secured when possible.
- Developmental bilingual program: Equal status is given to English and another language, promoting full proficiency in two

A families' daily activities can be literacy-building and might include:
- Reading letters from their country of origin together.
- Consulting on children's homework.
- Jointly reviewing school assignments.
- Reading all school-home written communication with children.
- Reading and discussing all kinds of books such as phone book, dictionaries, encyclopedias, address books, recipe books, and reference books in their home language or English.
- Practicing new school skills or family skills that require reading such as instruction manuals, bills, announcements, advertisements, junk mail, milk and cereal cartons, and so on.
- Reading age-level appropriate books to their child in English or home language and discussing narrative, or naming actions or objects in illustrations.
- Discussing electronic or digital media they experience it together. Selecting educational content when possible.
- Playing games with and without electronic media especially games with cards, numbers, alphabet letters and rules.
- Participating in writing, singing, listening, viewing activities connected to their home or the American culture.
- Reading or listening to material concerned with the family's religious orientation and experience.
- Providing writing and art materials in a home area that is comfortable and supplied with a variety of paper, notebooks, coloring books, etc. and different kinds of writing tools—pens, markers, crayons, etc.
- Talking about print in the neighborhood such as street signs, house numbers, window ads, posted ads and announcements, menus, and so on.
- Enacting books, plays, events, or common and important family occasions with role playing.

FIGURE 5–10 How families increase child literacy with home activities.

**deficit perspective** — an attitude or belief that attributes children's school failures to children themselves, or their family or culture.

languages. Mixing and translating language is avoided but acceptable at social times.

- Two-way immersion program: This type of program provides integrated language and academic instruction for native English speakers and native speakers of another language. This enables English speakers to develop second-language proficiency. Both groups' families must have an interest in bilingualism.

- Tutor-assisted program: A special tutor (or teacher) works with a child for a portion of the school day.

A full-immersion program offers an age-appropriate curriculum in a language foreign to the child. Some parents, like Wardle (2003), believe the early years are the optimal time to learn a second language. August and Shanahan (2008) point out full immersion in English giving no attention to children's native language has not been shown to offer any advantage for later academic schooling.

Some classrooms combine approaches and program types, and identify elements common to successful English-language learner programs. These include the following, as identified by the Center for Research on Education, Diversity, & Excellence (2001):

- ongoing and guided parental involvement
- professional development for both specialized and mainstream teachers
- the promotion of proficiency in both first and secondary languages
- the use of assessment methods linked to instructional objectives to inform instructional planning and delivery
- developmentally appropriate curriculum
- high standards for language acquisition and academic achievement
- strong staff leadership
- sheltered instruction, an approach that integrates language and content instruction
- academic instruction in English
- special strategies to make content (in activities) meaningful and comprehensive*

Visuals and images (pictorial representations) used while the teacher is talking almost always improve student listening comprehension and reduce recall errors.

*From Center for Research on Education, Diversity, & Excellence. (2001). Some program alternatives for English language learning. Practitioner's Brief #3.

## ASSESSMENT FOR SPECIAL NEEDS

Assessment is usually undertaken when teachers suspect that a child has difficulty communicating and could profit from specialized instruction. The goal is to identify whether a child's language is more or less advanced than that of other children his age (delayed language) or is deficient when compared with performance on social and/or intellectual tasks (language deficit) or whether the child fits other categories. Screening tests should be conducted by trained professionals.

The California State Department of Education (2009) suggests teachers should team up with professionals knowledgeable about second-language acquisition to sort out which child behaviors are caused by second language learning and other causes. Behaviors that can be misinterpreted include the following:

- speaks infrequently
- speaks excessively (either in home language or in English)
- refuses to answer questions
- confuses similar sounding words
- is unable to tell or recall stories
- has poor general recall
- uses poor pronunciation
- uses poor syntax and grammar
- does not volunteer information (p. 64)

## CHILDREN WITH SPECIAL NEEDS

Special language-development preschool centers with expert personnel are available in most communities for children with easily identifiable communication deficiencies such as hearing loss, visual impairment, and obvious speech impairments. Other children in need of special help may not be identified at the preschool level and may function within the wide range of children considered to be average or typical for preschool ages. In language arts, learning disability is a term that refers to a group of disorders manifested by significant difficulties in the acquisition and use of listening, speaking, reading, or writing. Most programs are reticent to label children as having language learning problems because of their lack of expertise to screen and evaluate children in a truly professional manner. Referral to speech-language pathologists or local or college clinics is suggested to families when a question exists concerning a particular child's progress. Early childhood teachers are not speech or language pathologists and therefore should not be expected to diagnose language problems or prescribe therapy. Communication disorders are usually divided into two main categories.

**Hearing disabilities** are characterized by an inability to hear sounds clearly. Such disabilities may range from hearing speech sounds faintly or in a distorted way, to profound deafness. In the United States, approximately 1 out of every 300 children is born with permanent hearing loss (Eiserman, Shisler, Foust, Buhrmann, & White, 2007). It is estimated that by school age nearly 1 out of every 100 students have permanent sensory-neural hearing loss. Undetected hearing loss often results in language delay and language deficits. This not only can affect literacy, but also school achievement, degree of socialization, and readiness for both school and reading instruction. Identification of hearing loss and appropriate intervention before a baby is 6 months old can significantly improve language and cognitive development. See Figure 5–11, a resource published by the American Speech-Language-Hearing Association (ASLHA, 2001).

**Speech and language disabilities** can affect the way people talk and understand; these range from simple sound substitutions to not being able to use speech and language at all.

## SPEECH-LANGUAGE DISABILITIES AND PROBLEMS

More than 13 million people in the United States have some kind of expressive speech disability, the most common problem involving articulation—affecting an estimated 75 percent of people with these types of problems. The rest, approximately 25 percent, have language, voice, and fluency disorders, or a combination of these. Most articulation problems not caused by physical, sensory, or neurological damage respond to treatment.

A 2009 Chilean research team attempted to identify potential risk factors for speech disorders in 128 3- to-4-year-old preschool children (Barbosa et al, 2009). The study probed children's sucking behaviors (pacifiers and fingers) and infant feeding practices relationship to disorders. Mothers contributed data on children's infancy experiences. Preschoolers with identified speech disorders were three times as likely as other children to have used a pacifier for at least 3 years, the study found. In addition to the pacifier trend, children in this group were also 3 times as likely to have started bottle-feeding before nine months of age. Study conclusions suggest extended use of sucking, outside of breastfeeding, may have detrimental effects on speech development. Since this study was based on a relatively small number of children, further research is necessary.

Non-organic causes of problems can include:

- lack of stimulation.
- lack of need to talk.
- poor speech models.
- lack of or low reinforcement.
- insecurity, anxiety, crisis.
- shyness or lack of social confidence.

### Language Delay

Language delay may be connected to one or more of the following areas (Taylor, 2002).

- syntax (putting words together to create sentences)
- semantics (using words and understanding their meanings)
- morphology (using word endings, given the language context)
- pragmatics (using social language)

---

**hearing disabilities** — characterized by an inability to hear sounds clearly. This may range from hearing speech sounds faintly or in a distorted way, to profound deafness.
**speech and language disabilities** — communication disorders that affect the way people talk and understand; range from simple sound substitutions to not being able to use speech and language at all.

## WHAT SHOULD MY CHILD BE ABLE TO DO?

| Hearing and Understanding | Talking |
|---|---|
| **birth-3 months** <br> • startles to loud sounds <br> • quiets or smiles when spoken to <br> • seems to recognize your voice and quiets if crying <br> • increases or decreases sucking behavior in response to sound | **birth-3 months** <br> • makes pleasure sounds (cooing, gooing) <br> • cries differently for different needs <br> • smiles when sees you |
| **4–6 months** <br> • moves eyes in direction of sounds <br> • responds to changes in tone of your voice <br> • notices toys that make sounds <br> • pays attention to music | **4–6 months** <br> • babbling sounds more speech-like with many different sounds, including *p*, *b* and *m* <br> • chuckles and laughs <br> • vocalizes excitement and displeasure <br> • makes gurgling sounds when left alone and when playing with you |
| **7 Months-1 year** <br> • enjoys games like peek-a-boo and pat-a-cake <br> • turns and looks in direction of sounds <br> • listens when spoken to <br> • recognizes words for common items like "cup," "shoe," "juice" <br> • begins to respond to requests ("Come here," "Want more?") | **7 months-1 year** <br> • babbling has both long and short groups of sounds such as "tata upup bibibibi" <br> • uses speech or noncrying sounds to get and keep attention <br> • imitates different speech sounds <br> • has one or two words (bye-bye, dada, mama), although they may not be clear |
| **one to two years** <br> • points to a few body parts when asked <br> • follows simple commands and understands simple questions ("Roll the ball," "Kiss the baby," "Where's your shoe?") <br> • listens to simple stories, songs, and rhymes <br> • points to pictures in a book when named | • says more words every month <br> • uses some one- or two-word questions ("Where kitty?" "Go bye-bye?" "What's that?") <br> • puts two words together ("more cookie," "no juice," "mommy book") <br> • uses many different consonant sounds at the beginning of words |
| **two to three years** <br> • understands differences in meaning ("go-stop," "in-on," "big-little," "up-down") <br> • follows two requests ("Get the book and put it on the table") <br> • listens to and enjoys hearing stories for longer periods of time | • has a word for almost everything <br> • uses two- or three-words to talk about and ask for things <br> • uses *k*, *g*, *f*, *t*, *d*, and *n* sounds <br> • speech is understood by familiar listeners most of the time <br> • often asks for or directs attention to objects by naming them |
| **three to four years** <br> • hears you when you call from another room <br> • hears television or radio at the same loudness level as other family members <br> • answers simple "who?", "what?", "where?", and "why?" questions | • talks about activities at school or at friends' homes <br> • people outside of the family usually understand child's speech <br> • uses a lot of sentences that have 4 or more words <br> • usually talks easily without repeating syllables or words |
| **four to five years** <br> • pays attention to a short story and answers simple questions about them <br> • hears and understands most of what is said at home and in school | • uses sentences that give lots of details ("The biggest peach is mine") <br> • tells stories that stick to topic <br> • communicates easily with other children and adults <br> • says most sounds correctly except a few like *l*, *s*, *r*, *v*, *z*, *ch*, *sh*, *th* <br> • says rhyming words <br> • names some letters and numbers <br> • uses the same grammar as the rest of the family |

**FIGURE 5–11** Speech and hearing ages.

- sequencing (recalling and relating events in the correct order)
- vocabulary (comprehending and using new words)*

Language delay is characterized by a marked slowness in the development of the vocabulary and grammar necessary for expressing and understanding thoughts and ideas. It may involve both comprehension and the child's expressive language output and quality. It is wise for families to consult a speech-language pathologist if the delay is more than 6 months so language therapy, if recommended, can commence.

A complete study of a child includes first looking for physical causes, particularly hearing loss, and then examining other structural (voice-producing) conditions. Neurological limitations come under scrutiny, as do emotional development factors. Home environments and family communicating styles are also examined.

A language-delayed child may have a small vocabulary, and use short and simple sentences with many grammatical errors. He may have difficulty maintaining a conversation, and often talk about the immediate present rather than future happenings. He can have difficulty understanding others and in making himself understood.

Besides linguistic problems, a language-delayed child may have problems classifying objects and recognizing similarities and differences. He also may ignore opportunities to play with others.

Additional behaviors a teacher might notice in a language-delayed child include:

- less variety in sentence structure.
- simple two- and three-word sentences.
- less frequent speech.
- frequent occurrence of playing alone.
- less adept participation in joint planning with classmates.

Early childhood educators concerned about the speech and socialization of "late talkers" should discuss their suspicions with their teaching team and supervisors.

Teachers might readily agree with the following sample description of a language-delayed child: "Speaks markedly less well than other children of the same age and seems to have normal ability in intellectual, motor, sensory, and emotional control areas, but may be rejected by peers."

Researchers studying differences in the quantity of parent talk with their young children may find a wide disparity between two families—a child from one family could hear 700 utterances each day while a child from another family hears 11,000 utterances. Children in the first category can seem to possess lower-level language skills not caused by any innate problem but rather by an environmental situation.

Teachers working with language-delayed children use the following interactive techniques.

- gaining attention with tempting, interest-catching activities
- being at eye level, face-to-face, if possible
- establishing eye contact
- displaying enthusiasm and playfulness
- establishing a play activity involving "my turn, your turn" interaction
- verbalizing single words, short phrases, or short sentences depending on the child's verbal level
- pausing, waiting, and looking expectantly, encouraging the child's turn to talk
- repeating teacher statements and pausing expectantly
- copying the child's actions or verbalizations
- following the child's focus of interest with joint teacher interest
- probing the child's interest with logical questions
- maintaining close, accepting physical contact and a warm interactive manner

A few children may make a conscious decision not to try to learn Standard English or a new language when they are confronted with a language other than their native language or dialect. A number of reasons for their choice are possible. If others enrolled or teachers speak their native language, they may believe it is not necessary or simply not worth the effort. Families may not give a high priority to learning the new language, or children's enrollment may consist of only a few mornings a week. A child's decision can be temporary or long-term.

*From Taylor, R. (2002, Mar.). Helping language grow. *Instructor* 111(6): 25–26. Copyright © 2002 Scholastic, Inc. Reprinted by permission.

## The Cloistered Child

Some teachers and educators describe children with inadequate language due to lack of human interactive environments. To be "cloistered" connotes isolation, separation, limited experience, meager human contact, a narrow view of the world, small or sparsely furnished living quarters, and a time-consuming devotion to spiritual contemplation and prayer. In the cloistered child the spiritual contemplation and prayer have been replaced with the passive pursuit of hours and hours of never discussed screen watching.

The cloistered child is thought to display one or many of the following characteristics.

- limited attention span
- inability to express ideas
- limited language and vocabulary
- inability to draw on past knowledge
- inability to listen
- impulsiveness (says first thing that pops into mind)
- lack of perseverance ("It's work. It's too hard.")
- blunted interest and curiosity
- disorganization
- impatience, inability to wait
- poor conversation skill

To develop what is seen as "missing language and missing experience," experts recommend a curriculum that includes lots of talk, active involvement, time and play with others, and exposure to literature. Some educators recommend opportunities to play with peers and plan actions, which facilitate the child's seeing himself in control, along with the promotion of child resourcefulness in seeking help from others.

## The Overstressed Child

There are many different reasons why some children have stressful living situations. When young children's stress is connected to new adults, new situations, groups of peers, books and book-reading times, or conversations with an adult, teachers will notice child anxiety and aversion behavior. O'Leary, Newton, Lundz, Hall, O'Connell, Raby, and Czarnecka (2002) describe degrees of stress and possible causative factors teachers should avoid.

> Mild stress enhances conscious learning, but too much stress, especially for too long a time, prevents it. Stress speaks primarily to the emotional learning system, and there it works primarily in a negative way.
>
> Extreme stress, caused by too much different information, unrelated information, or information too rapidly introduced or presented within too short a space of time, adds to a negative emotional reaction and clicks in a fear response. This memory is engraved below the level of awareness and becomes conscious as an attitude toward or feeling about the situation or topic. (p. 46)

Fortunately, when no pressure and stress exist, and a safe school environment is experienced, many children who display an initial aversion to certain school activities, including language arts activities, venture forth slowly and their attitudes change. Most early childhood teachers have been acquainted with children who avoid book-sharing times yet listen from another area in the classroom. After a period, they move closer, and eventually they join the read-aloud group.

## Expressive and Receptive Language Difficulties

Educators begin suspecting problems in language development when they observe attending children in a variety of classroom situations, including group times, play times, adult-child exchanges, and social interactions. In lower elementary school grades, including kindergarten, the following characteristics are cause for concern. They are seen as behaviors indicating expressive-language difficulties.

1. limited use of language
2. trouble starting and/or responding to conversation
3. heavy reliance on gesture or nonverbal communication
4. limited or nonspecific vocabulary

**5.** inappropriate grammar

**6.** difficulty in sequencing rhymes or stories

Teachers handling preschoolers may think many of these characteristics are typical of younger preschoolers and that they will be corrected as the child approaches kindergarten age. Their program planning and teacher-child interactions aim to erase difficulties, and they would be concerned if growth in a preschooler's language ability and skill was not observable and apparent over time.

## Articulation

Articulation disorders involve difficulties with the way sounds are formed and strung together, usually characterized by substituting one sound for another, omitting a sound, or distorting a sound.

If consonant sounds are misarticulated, they may occur in the initial (beginning), medial (middle), or ending positions in words. It is prudent to point out again that normally developing children do not master the articulation of all consonants until age 7 or 8.

Most young children (3 to 5 years old) hesitate, repeat, and re-form words as they speak. Imperfections occur for several reasons: (1) a child does not pay attention as closely as an adult, especially to certain high-frequency consonant sounds; (2) the child may not be able to distinguish some sounds; or (3) a child's coordination and control of his articulation mechanisms may not be perfected. For example, the child may be able to hear the difference between *Sue* and *shoe* but cannot pronounce them differently. About 60 percent of all children with diagnosed articulation problems are boys.

Articulation characteristics of young children include the following.

● Substitution: One sound is substituted for another, as in "wabbit" for "rabbit" or "thun" for "sun."

● Omission: The speaker leaves out a sound that should be articulated. He says "at" for "hat," "ca" for "cat," "icky" for "sticky," "probly" for "probably." The left out sound may be at the beginning, middle, or end of a word.

● Distortion: A sound is said inaccurately but is similar to the intended sound.

● Addition: The speaker adds a sound, as in "li-it-tle" for "little" and "muv-va-ver" for "mother."

● Transposition: The position of sounds in words is switched, as in "hangerber" for "hamburger" and "aminal" for "animal."

● Lisp: The *s, z, sh, th, ch,* and *j* sounds are distorted. There are 2 to 10 types of lisps noted by speech experts.

Articulation problems may stem from a physical condition such as a cleft palate or hearing loss, or they can be related to problems in the mouth, such as a dental abnormality. Many times, articulation problems occurring without any obvious physical disability may involve the faulty learning of speech sounds.

Some children will require special help and directed training to eliminate all articulation errors; others seem to mature and correct articulation problems by themselves.

Teacher behavior that helps a child with articulation problems includes not interrupting or constantly correcting the child and making sure that others do not tease or belittle. Modeling misarticulated words correctly is a good course of action. Simply continue your conversation and insert the correctly articulated word in your answering comment.

## Voice Quality

Teachers sometimes notice differences in children's voice quality, which involves pitch, loudness, resonance, and general quality (breathiness, hoarseness, and so on). The intelligibility of a child's speech is determined by how many of the child's words are understandable. One can expect 80 percent of the child's speech to be understandable at age 3.

## Stuttering and Cluttering

Stuttering and cluttering are categorized as fluency disorders. Stuttering involves the rhythm of speech and is a complicated, many-faceted problem. Speech is characterized by abnormal stoppages with no sound, repetitions, or prolonged sounds and syllables. There may also be unusual facial and body movements associated with efforts to speak. This problem involves four times as many males as females and can usually be treated. All young children repeat words and phrases, and this tends to increase with anxiety or stress. It is simply typical for the age and is not true stuttering. A teacher should wait patiently for the child to finish expressing himself and should resist the temptation to say "slow down." An adult talking at a slow, relaxed rate and pausing between sentences can give a child time to reflect and respond with more fluency. Keeping eye contact and not rushing, interrupting, or finishing words is also recommended. Classmates should be prohibited from teasing a peer who stutters.

Trautman (2003) identifies the following causes of stuttering:

> There are four factors most likely to contribute to stuttering, *genetics* (approximately 59 percent of all people who stutter have family members who stutter); *child development* (children with speech, language, cognitive or development delays are more likely to stutter); *neurophysiology* (research has shown that some people who stutter process speech and language in different areas of the brain than people who do not stutter); and *family dynamics* (fast-paced lifestyles and high expectations can contribute to stuttering). (p. 49)

She notes that most stuttering starts between the ages of 2 and 4, and about 20 percent of children in that age group are affected. Many others in this age group go through a temporary lack of fluency and outgrow it. She points out that if stuttering lasts longer than 3 months and begins after the age of 3; the child will likely need therapy to correct it. Most children make a full recovery. The disorder continues in a few affecting about 1 percent of the adult population. Studies suggest that genetics plays a role in about half of stuttering cases (Rubin, 2010).

A speech-language pathologist is the appropriate person to evaluate and plan improvement activities. The National Stuttering Association (www.nsastutter.org) provides support, education, advocacy, and current research information.

**Cluttering** is more involved with the rate of speaking and includes errors in articulation, stress, and pausing. Speech seems too fast, with syllables and words running together. Listener reaction and good speech modeling are critical aspects of behavior for teachers when a child lacks fluency. Adults who work with a young child refrain from criticizing, correcting, acting negatively, or calling a speech problem to the child's attention. They create a warm adult-child relationship if possible, and try to eliminate any factors or conditions that increase problems in fluency. They work to protect the child's expectation of normal fluency and build the child's self-confidence as a speaker.

Approximately 25 percent of all children go through a stage of development during which they seem to stutter (or clutter) when excited or are searching for a word to express their thoughts. This may be temporary lack of fluency associated with learning to speak. Only a minority persists in early childhood stuttering, whereas in the majority of cases, stuttering is temporary and an often short-lived disorder that disappears without formal intervention, apparently on its own. Females evidence a higher recovery rate than do males.

## Selective (Elective) Mutism

Occasionally, early childhood teachers encounter silent children. Silence may be temporary or lasting, in which case it will be a matter for teacher concern. Children with **selective (elective) mutism** are described simply as children who can speak but do not. They display functional speech in selected settings (usually at home) and/or choose to speak only with certain individuals (often siblings or same-language speakers). Researchers believe selective mutism, if it happens, commonly occurs between ages 3 and 5 years. Because child abuse may promote delayed language development or psychological disorders that interfere with communication, such as selective mutism, teachers

---

**cluttering** — rapid, incomplete speech that is often jerky, slurred, spoken in bursts, and difficult to understand; nervous speech.

**selective (elective) mutism** — a behavior that describes child silence or lack of speech in select surroundings and/or with certain individuals.

need to be concerned. School referral to speech professionals leads to assessment and individual treatment programs. School administrators prefer that families make appointments and usually provide families with a description of local resources.

Teachers can help professionals DAP by providing observational data to describe the child's behavior and responses in classroom settings. Many factors can contribute to a particular child's silence or reduced speech. Consequently, teachers are cautioned to avoid a mutism diagnosis. A child's teasing or any other action that causes the embarrassment of a child with a language or speech difference should be handled swiftly and firmly by preschool staff members.

## OTHER CONDITIONS TEACHERS MAY CONSIDER PROBLEMS

### Frequent Crying

Occasionally, frustrated children will cry or scream to communicate a need. Crying associated with adjustment to a new situation is handled by providing supportive attention and care. Continual crying and screaming to obtain an object or privilege, on the other hand, calls for the following kinds of teacher statements:

"I don't understand what you want when you scream. Use words so I will know what you want."

"Sara does not know what you want when you cry, Ethan. Saying 'Please get off the puzzle piece' with your words tells her."

These statements let the child know what is expected and help him see that words solve problems.

### Avid Talkers and Shouters

Occasionally, children may discover that talking incessantly can get them what they want. In order to quiet children, others sometimes give in. This is somewhat different from the common give and take in children's daily conversations or children's growing ability to argue and state their cases.

Language for these children becomes a social weapon instead of a social tool. A child may find that loudness in speech can intimidate others and will out-shout the opposition. If a child

behaves this way, it is prudent to have the child's hearing checked. Teachers often change this type of behavior through discussions of "inside" (the classroom) voices and "outside" voices (which may be used on the playground), and also by mentioning how difficult it is to hear a "too loud" voice.

### Questioners

At times, children ask many questions, one right after another. This may be a good device to hold or gain adults' attention: "Why isn't it time for lunch?" or "What makes birds sing?" or "Do worms sleep?" The questions may seem endless to adults. Most of the questions are prompted by the child's natural curiosity or an attempt to gain attention. Educators' help children find out as much as possible and strive to fulfill the needs of the individual child. Along the way, there will be many questions that may be difficult or even impossible to answer.

### Learning Disabilities

It is estimated that over 5 percent of the nation's students are served in publicly funded learning-disabilities programs. The following signs during preschool years may indicate that a child has a learning disability.

- Starts talking later than other children
- Has pronunciation problems
- Has slow vocabulary growth; is often unable to find the right word
- Has trouble learning numbers, the alphabet, days of the week
- Has difficulty rhyming words
- Is extremely restless and easily distracted
- Has trouble with peers
- Displays a poor ability to follow directions or routines
- Avoids puzzles, drawing, and cutting

Experts point out that the sooner a problem can be identified and treated, the better the outcome is likely to be.

Most programs handling children with learning difficulties strive to pinpoint causative factors, and assess children's present level of functioning. Then programs and/or professional consultants develop individual learning plans (IEPs).

## Hearing Problems

A screening of young children's auditory acuity may uncover hearing loss. Rones (2004) estimates that 2 to 3 infants of every 1,000 are born with significant and/or permanent hearing loss and about 70 percent get their ears checked before leaving the hospital. The seriousness of hearing loss is related both to the degree of loss and the range of sound frequencies that are most affected. Because young children develop ear infections frequently, schools alert families when a child's listening behavior seems newly impaired.

**Otitis media** is a medical term that refers to any inflammation of the middle ear. There are two types of otitis media: (1) a fluid-filled middle ear without infection and (2) an infected middle ear. Researchers believe that otitis media may affect babbling and interfere with an infant's ability to hold on to a string of utterances in working memory long enough to draw meaning. Many preschoolers have ear infections during preschool years, and many children have clear fluid in the middle ear that goes undetected. Even though the hearing loss caused by otitis media may be small and temporary, it may have a serious effect on speech and language learning for a preschool child. The common cold outranks child ear infection, and a teacher can expect one child in three to be affected on any given day during some seasons of the year.

If undetected hearing distortion or loss lasts for a long period, the child can fall behind. One of three children enrolled in speech and language special treatment therapy is estimated to have a history of middle ear disease (Mody et al., 1999). General inattentiveness, wanting to get close to hear, trouble with directions, irritability, or pulling and rubbing of the ear can be signs a teacher should heed. Other signs to look for include:

- difficulty hearing word endings such as -*ed*, -*ing*, and -*s*.
- problems interpreting intonation patterns, inflections, and stress.
- distractibility.
- inattentiveness.

- asking adults to repeat.
- confusion with adult commands.
- difficulty repeating verbally presented material.
- inappropriate responses to questions.
- watching for cues from other children.
- complaints about ears.
- persistent breathing through the mouth.
- slowness in locating the source of sounds.
- softer or "fuzzier" speech than others.
- aggressiveness.
- loss of temper.*

Hearing loss can be temporary or permanent. Early detection and treatment are important.

Preschool staff members who notice children who confuse words with similar sounds may be the first to suspect **auditory processing** difficulties or mild to moderate hearing loss.

Mild hearing impairment may masquerade as

- stubbornness.
- lack of interest.
- a learning disability.

With intermittent **deafness**, children may have difficulty comprehending oral language.

Severe impairment impedes language development and is easier to detect than the far more subtle signs of mild loss. Most infected ears cause considerable pain, and parents are alerted to the need for medical help. However, if the ear is not infected or if the infection does not cause pain, the problem is harder to recognize.

## SEEKING HELP

If a child's speech or language lags behind expected development for the child's mental age (mental maturity), school staff members should observe and listen to the child closely to collect additional data. When speech is unusually

*Reprinted with permission from Mody, M., et al. (1999). Speech perception and verbal memory in children with and without histories of otitis media. *Journal of Speech, Language, and Hearing Research, 42*: 1069–1079. Copyright © 1999 by American Speech-Language-Hearing Association. All rights reserved.

---

**otitis media** — inflammation and/or infection of the middle ear.
**auditory processing** — the full range of mental activity involved in reacting to auditory stimuli, especially speech sounds, and in considering their meanings in relation to past experience and to their future use.
**deafness** — hearing is so impaired that the individual is unable to process auditory linguistic information, with or without amplification.

difficult to understand—rhythmically conspicuous, full of sound distortion, or consistently difficult to hear—this indicates a serious problem. Professional help is available to families through a number of resources. Most cities have speech and hearing centers and public and private practitioners specializing in speech-language pathology and audiology. Other resources include:

● city and county health departments.

● universities and medical schools.

● state departments of education offices.

● the American Speech-Language-Hearing Association.

Experts give the families of hearing-impaired children the following advice.

● Help the child "tune in" to language.

● Talk.

● Provide stimulation.

● Read picture books.

● Enroll the child in an infant-stimulation program during infancy.

● Schedule frequent doctor examinations.

● Join parent organizations with a hearing-impairment focus.

● See the child simply as a child rather than "a hearing-impaired child."

## SUGGESTIONS AND STRATEGIES FOR WORKING WITH CHILDREN WITH DISABILITIES AND SPECIAL NEEDS

The following suggestions and strategies are useful with typically developing children but also help children with disabilities and special needs. They apply to educators, administrators and families.

● Investigate whether a child is receiving supportive services at school and/or at an out-of-school location.

● Investigate equipment and media used or developed for specific problems or needs.

● Create and provide visual aids that depict or clarify instructional intent, such as posters and signs with pictures, drawings, or photographs.

● Use gestures that clarify words.

● Place children next to others who can provide help.

● Use cues such as a flashing light or music to gain attention, if necessary.

The Individuals with Disabilities Education Act, through federal and state mandates, ensures that children who have educationally significant hearing loss and certain other disabilities receive free, appropriate, public education. Programs develop a team approach that includes families or others familiar with the child's personality and interests, and professionals who are knowledgeable. This group creates individualized learning plans. Classroom environments are designed to promote learning and child comfort (Katz & Schery, 2006).

## ADVANCED LANGUAGE ACHIEVEMENT

Each child is unique. A few children speak clearly and use long and complex sentences at 2, 3, or 4 years of age. They express ideas originally and excitedly, enjoying individual and group discussions. Some may read simple primers (or other books) along with classroom word labels. Activities that are commonly used with kindergarten or first-grade children may interest them.

Singson and Mann (1999), researchers exploring possible factors associated with precocious reading ability, found that phonological awareness and parent's emphasis on letter sounds were significant predictors of early childhood ability. A few early readers may be sight readers with an exceptional memory for words. Educators aware of current research believe young children's knowledge of both alphabet letter names and sounds will aid their reading instruction.

Just as there is no stereotypical average child, language-talented children are also unique individuals. Inferring that these language-precocious children are also intellectually gifted is not at issue here. Young children with advanced language development may exhibit many of the following characteristics. They:

● attend to tasks in a persistent manner for long periods.

● focus deeply or submerge themselves in what they are doing.

- speak maturely and use a larger-than-usual vocabulary.
- show a searching, exploring curiosity.
- ask questions that go beyond immediate happenings.
- demonstrate avid interest in words, alphabet letters, numbers, or writing tools.
- remember small details of past experiences and compare them with present happenings.
- read books (or words) by memorizing pictures or words.
- prefer solitary activities at times.
- offer ideas often and easily.
- rapidly acquire English skills, if bilingual, when exposed to a language-rich environment.
- tell elaborate stories.
- show a mature or unusual sense of humor for age.
- possess an exceptional memory.
- exhibit high concentration.
- show attention to detail.
- exhibit a wide range of interests.
- demonstrate a sense of social responsibility.
- show a rich imagination.
- possess a sense of wonder.
- enjoy composing poems or stories.
- use richly descriptive expressions in talking.
- are highly attentive listeners who remember exceptionally well.
- read print in the classroom environment.
- write recognizable words or combinations of words.
- have sophisticated computer skills.
- express feelings and emotions, as in storytelling, movement, and visual arts.
- use rich imagery in informal language.
- exhibit originality of ideas and persistence in problem solving.
- exhibit a high degree of imagination.

Characteristics of possible giftedness for children under age 3 identified by Spencer and Stamm (2008) include:

- meeting verbal milestones early (speaking full sentences by 18 months, for instance)

- a long attention span (30 minutes is long for toddlers)
- being able to do complicated mental tasks early (like putting together puzzles with many pieces)
- creativity in thinking and problem solving
- an early, avid interest in books
- responsiveness to music
- an interest in sorting, organizing, and seeing patterns
- asking lots of questions
- memory for detail and how to get to many locations
- creative play (both in art and imaginative play, including having imaginary friends)
- a preference for older children
- a marked interest in people
- a less-than-typical need for adult help and guidance in activities

Preschoolers may recognize letters early and show an early focus on printed matter. They may be interested in foreign languages and also exhibit correct pronunciation and sentence structure in their native language. Young children may show an advanced vocabulary and may begin reading before they start preschool.

Unfortunately, young children who may be quiet, noncompetitive, and nonassertive; who are slow to openly express feelings; who rarely make direct eye contact, ask questions, or challenge something they know is incorrect; and who are acting appropriately according to their home culture may not be identified as gifted or talented. For indicators of outstanding verbal and linguistic abilities in Native American and Alaskan native children, see Figure 5–12.

Most experts recommend planning activities within the regular curriculum that promote advanced children's creative thinking. Suggestions include providing the following opportunities.

- Fluency opportunities: Promoting many different responses, for example, "What are all the ways you can think of to . . ."
- Flexibility opportunities: Having the facility to change a mind-set or see things in a different light, for example, "If you were squirrel how would you feel, . . ."

## INDICATORS OF OUTSTANDING VERBAL AND LINGUISTIC ABILITIES

knows signs and symbols of the traditional culture (at an earlier age and beyond the average child)

recalls legends in greater depth and detail after fewer hearings

is more aware of cultural norms and standards at an earlier age

has great auditory memory

remembers details of "everyday" events

makes up elaborate stories, songs, and/or poems

**FIGURE 5–12** Identifying outstanding talent in American Indian/Native American (AI/NA) students. (From U.S. Department of Education, Office of Educational Research and Improvement. [1994]. *Identifying outstanding talent in American Indian and Alaska Native students.* Washington, DC: Author.)

- Originality opportunities: For example, "Make something that no one else will think of."

- Elaboration opportunities: Embellishing of an idea or adding detail, for example, presenting a doodle or squiggle and asking, "What could it be?"

Some educators believe that teachers can help ward off problems for advanced students by grouping language-advanced children with others of high ability or shared interests. Other educators feel doing so robs peers of the sparkle and insight some peers possess.

Arranging situations in which the child's gifts or talents are seen as a group asset is another tactic, as is promoting individual special assignments and varied projects.

If teachers believe as does Gardner (1993, 2000) in the theory of multiple intelligences (one of which is linguistic intelligence) and in the occurrence of "crystallizing experiences," those teachers will notice the young children who take particular interest in and react overtly to some attractive quality or feature of a language arts activity. These children will tend to immerse themselves and focus deeply. This may be the child who loves to act roles in dramatic play, collects words, is fascinated with books or alphabet letters, creates daily rhymes, or displays similar behaviors. The child may persist and spend both time and effort on his chosen pursuit and displays a definite intellectual gift.

## SUMMARY

Teachers work with children who may differ greatly in language development. One of the teacher's roles is to carefully work toward increasing the child's use of words while providing a model of Standard English through activities and daily interaction. Teachers are careful not to give children the impression that their speech is less worthy than that of others.

Program goals should be clearly understood, as should the needs and interests of children who have developed a language that differs from the language of the school. Cultural differences exist, and teachers need to be aware of them to understand the young child. The teacher can provide activities that start at the child's present level and help the child grow, know more, and speak in both Standard English and his native language. Bilingual programs have become a political issue, and some states have eliminated them.

Speech differences require observation and study by a center's staff. Various language behaviors are considered speech and language disabilities. Families can be alerted to whether their children may need further professional help that a school is unable to provide.

## ADDITIONAL RESOURCES

### Readings

Cook, R. E., Klein, M. D., & Tessler, A., In collaboration with Daley, S. E. (2004). *Adapting early childhood curricula for children in inclusive settings* (6th ed.). Upper Saddle River, NJ: Pearson/ Merrill/ Prentice Hall.

Hanline, M. F., Nunes, D., & Worthy, M. B. (2007, July). Augmentive and alternate communication in early childhood years. *Young Children, 62*(4), 78–82.

Klein, M., Klein, D., & Chen, D. (2001). *Working with children from culturally diverse backgrounds.* Albany, NY: Delmar.

Meier, D. R. (2003). The young child's memory for words: Developing first and second language and literacy. New York: Teachers College Press.

Spenser, P., & Stamm, P.(2008). *Bright from the start: The simple, science-backed way to nurture your child's developing mind,* New York: Gotham.

Vukelich, C., & Christie, J. (2009). Building a foundation for preschool literacy: Effective instruction for children's reading and writing development. Newark, DE: International Reading Association.

## Helpful Websites

American Educational Research Association (AERA)
http://www.aera.net
Information on the academic achievement of second-language learners (search Publications).

ERIC Clearinghouse on Disabilities and Gifted Education
http://ericec.org
Includes information about gifted recent immigrant children and warning signs in preschoolers' language development.

Colorin Colorado
www.colorincolorado.org
Activities and advice offered to Spanish-speaking families and educators.

National Association for Bilingual Education
http://www.nabe.org
Association for teachers of bilingual children.

National Black Child Development Institute
http://www.nbcdi.org
Addresses issues concerning African-American children.

National Parent Information Center
http://npin.org
Provides information about communication disorders and English-language learners.

Go to www.cengagebrain.com to access this text's Education Course-Mate website where you'll find helpful resource such as video activities, glossary flashcards, interactive exercises, quiz questions, and more!

# Review It and Use It

A. Answer the following questions.

1. How can a teacher learn about the cultural background of a child?

2. What should be the teacher's attitude toward children whose speech is different from the teacher's speech?

B. Define the following terms:

1. dialect

2. bilingual

3. stuttering

4. auditory

5. cluttering

6. articulation

7. otitis media

8. subculture

9. Standard English

C. Select the correct answer.

1. Standard English is
   a. the language of textbooks.
   b. learned quickly by non-Standard English speakers.
   c. the same as spoken English.
   d. none of the above.

2. Early childhood centers try to
   a. insist that children speak Standard English during their first days of school.
   b. make sure each child feels secure and then practice English.
   c. plan activities in which language-different children have an interest.
   d. ignore each child's development of word use in his own dialect.

3. Teachers should be careful to guard against
   a. not correcting children's speech by drawing attention to errors.
   b. thinking that only Standard English is correct and therefore better than English spoken in a dialect.
   c. giving children the idea that they speak differently or "funny."
   d. giving special attention to children who come from low-income homes.

4. Young children with speech errors
   a. rarely outgrow them.
   b. need no special help or teacher attention.
   c. never hear as well as adults.
   d. can hear that what they say is different but do not have the ability to say it correctly.

5. Bilingualism in the young child is
   a. always a disadvantage.
   b. never an advantage.
   c. a challenge and unfortunate when the child is older.
   d. a problem when schools make children feel defeated and unaccepted.

D. Explain why designations such as Asian or Hispanic do not accurately describe a child's culture.

E. List five teacher techniques appropriate and useful in classrooms enrolling English-language learners.

F. Describe the speech characteristics of children who speak African-American English.

G. Provide 2 statements that are an example of a deficit perspective attitude.

## STUDENT ACTIVITES

1. Since vocabulary words can be more easily learned when teachers demonstrate, define, and present words in meaningful contexts, think of how many words might be associated with young English-language learners' body parts and body actions—such as nose, eyes, mouth or scratch, drink, jump, and so on. With a peer create a few activity ideas. Share with the total group. (Example: Building a face drawing with the child group by adding one feature at a time daily and printing its name adjacent to the drawing.)

2. Interview the director of a center that cares for bilingual and/or economically disadvantaged young children. Ask what techniques are used to increase a child's language ability. If there is no early childhood center in your community, give examples of goals or techniques used to increase a disadvantaged child's language ability that you have found from research at a library.

3. Knowing that it will be crucial that a newly enrolled 4-year-old English-language learner feels both welcome and special on his first day of school (which with this child happens to be in the second month of school), what will you, the teacher, do to prepare the class? (Example: Ask all enrolled children to practice introducing themselves at opening circle on Hermisio's first day by saying, "Hi Hermisio. Me llamo, Andrew. My name is Andrew.") Devise three other plans of action with a peer. Then share with the total group.

4. Tape your voice in a 5-minute conversation with a friend. Have the recording analyzed for dialect, accent, and Standard English usage.

5. Consider the following children. Which children would you suggest to the center's director as possibly needing further staff observation and expert assessment and help?

   a. Trinh seems roughly 2 years behind his age-mates in vocabulary.
   b. Rashad turns his head toward speakers frequently.
   c. Barbara rubs one ear constantly.
   d. Doan cups his hand behind his ear when spoken to.
   e. Tisha is 3, and one cannot understand her words.

f. Nelson says, "Why did his folks call him Rocky, when he can't say it? He says his name is Wocky Weed!"
g. Maria is always stressed and extremely tense when she has to speak.
h. Benji has a monotone quality to his voice.
i. Becky reads difficult books without help.

# Achieving Language and Literacy Goals through Program Planning

## OBJECTIVES

After reading this chapter, you should be able to:

- Define literacy.
- Describe emerging literacy in early childhood.
- Discuss program planning for early childhood language arts activities.
- Describe assessment's role in program development.
- Write an activity plan for a language arts activity.

## KEY TERMS

activity plans
assessment
behaviorism
child-initiated
  curricula
constructivist
  theory
cultural literacy
curriculum
curriculum models
early literacy
interactionists

literacy
nativists
nurturist
phonological
  awareness
psychosocial
  theory
social
  constructivist
  theory
visual literacy
webbing

## Questionable Language

*A group of Asian, English-language-learning boys often played only with each other. I was continually attempting to help them branch out and play with other children. It was slowly happening. At pick-up time, Mrs. Vu, Tan's mother, asked to speak with me. She had brought her neighbor with her as an interpreter. Moving out of the children's range of overhearing our conversation, her neighbor expressed Mrs. Vu's concern. Some of the Asian boys were using very inappropriate words in their native tongue, laughing and then running away. They had been careful in avoiding this activity when Phan, the bilingual assistant, was near. After assuring Mrs. Vu that we shared her concern and would monitor the children's behavior, I thanked her. Fortunately, we had an impending family meeting.*

### Questions to Ponder

1. Could some kind of planned child activity be used to address this problem?
2. What words would you use if you "caught" the boys in this behavior?
3. Should this behavior be discussed at a family meeting, or is this a private matter?

This text divides language arts into four interrelated areas—listening, speaking, writing, and reading—and also discusses **visual literacy** (viewing) as a primary, basic human capacity closely related to the other language arts areas. Increasing the child's understanding of how language arts combine and overlap in everyday preschool activities helps increase language use and **literacy**. Early childhood teachers realize that when children are taught to read or when a few children begin reading on their own before kindergarten, the learning of reading is dynamically concerned with the *interrelatedness* of the literacy skills of listening, speaking, and print (writing). Learning to read with ease happens more readily when young children listen, converse easily, think with and about words, and have rich vocabularies they have used to express their ideas.

To that end, a unified and balanced approach is recommended, one in which the teacher purposefully shows and stresses connections between areas (Figure 6–1). Past practice and program planning in schools attempted to promote literacy by dividing (segmenting) language arts into separate skills. Educators now believe separate, but integrated, skill activities can be part of a balanced language arts program.

The ages of the children and their past life experiences will decide the literacy activities a teacher plans and presents and the techniques and adult-child interaction the educator deems appropriate. Classes may include children who have been in group settings for 3 or 4 years, children with identified disabilities, children with exceptional abilities, children who are already independent readers, and children just beginning to acquire some basic literacy. Literacy knowledge grows and develops within human relationships with responsive adults and the other children.

## VISUAL LITERACY

As discussed in Chapter 4, a number of researchers and experts in the early childhood literacy field believe that, in addition to listening,

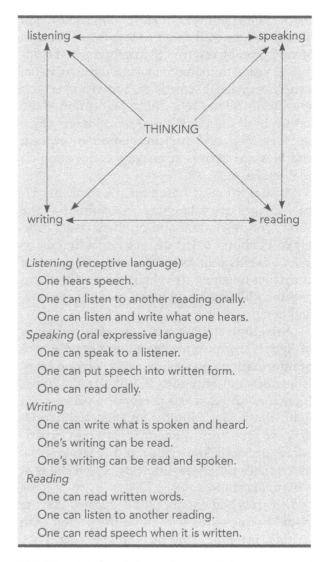

*Listening* (receptive language)
One hears speech.
One can listen to another reading orally.
One can listen and write what one hears.
*Speaking* (oral expressive language)
One can speak to a listener.
One can put speech into written form.
One can read orally.
*Writing*
One can write what is spoken and heard.
One's writing can be read.
One's writing can be read and spoken.
*Reading*
One can read written words.
One can listen to another reading.
One can read speech when it is written.

**FIGURE 6–1** Interrelations of early childhood language arts.

speaking, writing, and reading, a fifth language arts area exists—visual literacy, or viewing. The goals of instruction in the visual literacy area involve promoting young children's visual perception skills. This includes attending behavior, discrimination, identification, analysis, classification, sorting, and categorization of visual images. In other words, a conscious noting of differences in visual characteristics would be undertaken. These characteristics include line,

---

**visual literacy** — the ability to interpret and communicate with respect to visual symbols in media other than print.
**literacy** — involves complex cognitive interactions between readers and their texts and between background knowledge and new information. It involves both skill and knowledge and varies by task and setting. Different types of literacy are described—prose, document, quantitative, academic, workplace, and functional.

shape, color, number, texture, movement, and dimension, as well as other features. This area of study can be referred to in professional readings as visual thinking, visual intelligence, visual awareness, visual sensitivity, and visual arts. It specifically relates to a child's perception of the world; how she reacts to viewed images; how she sees, feels, and interprets emotions evoked; and how she arrives at insights concerning visual media.

Visual literacy, based on the idea that visual images are a language, is defined as the ability to understand and produce visual messages. Eckhoff (2010) defines visual literacy as a set of skills that help a viewer interpret and construct meaning. It is believed useful in improving children's cognitive, reading, writing, and creative skills.

Stieglitz (2008) points out that the sense of sight is the most important and basic source of information concerning one's surroundings. It involves not only the eye but also the brain. Elements of the visual perception process are light, the visual stimulus and its characteristics, eye receptors, the individual's past experiences, previous knowledge and ideas, and the individual's purposes, interests, and feelings at a particular time.

Morrow and Asbury (2003) suggest that the visual literacy area should be integrated with writing, listening, reading, and speaking. They also suggest using instruction that is spontaneous, is authentic, and involves children in problem solving. Instruction, they believe, should be direct, explicit, and systematic.

Telling stories using a photograph or drawing, eliciting the children's ideas about story content after viewing a picture book's cover, and discussing children's creative art and the details therein or the emotions they feel give teachers insights into what children are thinking. These activities also reveal children's ability to read visual cues and symbols.

When children and adults are in the process of viewing an image or living an event, they are not involved in the process of critical analysis. Rather, they are absorbing those images and events and actively seeking meaning. This would account for children's barrage of questions if they are interested in a new classroom animal, and also explains a good number of their other questions.

When children are encouraged to express their learning through the medium of graphic arts, they are "documenting" their understandings. They are encouraged to do this in the Reggio Emilia approach. Children trace and revisit their discoveries and actions, making them visible.

The exercise is an instrument for reflection and language development as the children discuss their creations. Reflection can lead to a refinement of ideas and further search and discovery. It can be likened to a scientist writing the results of her inquiry, which then leads to further questions.

The primary literacy of the twenty-first century will be visual. Pictures, graphics, and images of every kind will be processed.

## LITERACY GOALS—SKILL AND KNOWLEDGE

Any discussion of literacy begins with a working definition. Literacy can be defined as a demonstrated competence in communication skills that enables the individual to function, appropriate to age, independently of society and with a potential for movement in society. **IRA**

Literacy can be conceptualized as a relatively narrow domain of academic inquiry and educational practice (as in reading), or it can be viewed as an encompassing way of being that involves all forms of communication, including mathematical, scientific, and artistic forms. Literacy definitions change and reflect different historical, cultural, and technological development. New technology is enabling students to access the best information in the shortest time, which allows them to identify and solve problems and communicate this information to others. Reading and writing are but the initial layers of the richer and more complex forms of literacy required in Internet use.

Young children usually progress by developing knowledge of literacy that includes oral language skill and awareness that written (graphic) marks and words carry meaning. Early superficial understandings about picture books and reading aloud lead to a much deeper understanding of the purpose of reading. Psycholinguistic theory focuses on the unique nature of human language—humans' innate search for order, structure, and meaning. Using this theory as a basis, educators can see how children will initiate their own first steps toward literacy when exposed to language-rich environments in which positive attitudes develop toward language arts activities.

Cambourne's definition of literacy (1988) stresses one's ability to use language in daily life.

> . . . literacy is a word which describes a whole collection of behaviors, skills, knowledge, processes and attitudes. It has something to do with our ability to use language in our negotiations with the world. . . . Reading and writing are two linguistic ways of conducting these negotiations. So are speaking, listening, reflecting, and a host of other behaviors related to cognition and critical thinking. (p. 29)

**Cultural literacy** can be defined as the possession of the basic information needed to thrive in the current world. Children from poor and illiterate circumstances tend to remain poor and illiterate unless educational opportunities are available. Another definition states that an individual needs to be socialized to literacy and also develop behaviors such as knowing how and when to ask questions, how to hold a book or listen to a story, and when and how to participate.

## WHAT IS EARLY LITERACY?

The term **early literacy** refers to young preschool children's language arts behaviors, concepts, and skills that precede and can develop into a literacy that includes reading, conventional writing, and a larger body of literary knowledge at later ages. It considers change over time in how the child thinks about literacy and the strategies the young child uses in her attempts to comprehend or produce oral or written language.

The act of printing shapes with an underlying logic and children's "pretending to read" behaviors are viewed as early forms of reading

and writing. Many educators believe that additional research is necessary to understand exactly "what clicks into place" when young children make the transition from early reading and writing to conventional reading and writing. Instructional strategies and behavioral techniques based on that knowledge and the identification of what children understand, and which skills aided that transition, enhance a school's planning ability. Early literacy learning happens best in an atmosphere of social collaboration with peers and others who are more literate.

Figure 6–2 shows a set of particular accomplishments that a successful learner is likely to exhibit during preschool years (Snow, Burns, & Griffin, 1998). These authors state that the list is neither exhaustive nor incontestable, but rather it captures many highlights of the course of literacy acquisition revealed through research.

Early home-life activities start children's literacy development by providing early experiences, including parent and family models and attitudes. A home environment can be stimulating or drab, rich in literate activities or deficient. Children actively search for meaning, and many have lives in which print surrounds them and picture books are familiar. If children have observed and participated in home reading or writing activities, they often enter group care with interest and a positive attitude and an early head start in literacy. They are able to enjoy symbolic dramatic play and eventually attempt symbolic representation in art, block building, and a variety of other preschool pursuits. They communicate ideas; discuss meanings, and probe adults and other children for information. Preschoolers growing awareness and "knowledge of literacy" is evident and can include all language arts areas—reading, writing, speaking, listening, and visual representing.

Becoming literate is an extension and companion of language arts skill. Most children acquire spoken language without sit-down instruction; they all become speakers, although at different rates, unless disease, illness, or trauma interferes. Literacy, on the other hand, is not

---

**cultural literacy** — literacy that reflects a culture's knowledge of significant ideas, events, values, and the essence of that culture's identity.

**early literacy** — speaking, listening, print awareness and writing behaviors, reading of alphabet letters and words, and other skills that evolve and change over time, culminating in conventional literacy.

**Birth to 3-Year-Old Accomplishments**

- recognizes specific books by cover
- pretends to read books
- understands that books are handled in particular ways
- enters into a book-sharing routine with primary caregivers
- vocalization play in crib gives way to enjoyment of rhyming language, nonsense word play, etc.
- labels objects in books
- comments on characters in books
- looks at a picture in book and realizes it is a symbol for real object
- listens to stories
- requests/commands adult to read or write
- may begin attending to specific print such as letters in names
- uses increasingly purposive scribbling
- occasionally seems to distinguish between drawing and writing
- produces some letterlike forms and scribbles with some features of English writing

**3- and 4-Year-Old Accomplishments**

- knows that alphabet letters are a special category of visual graphics that can be individually named
- recognizes local environmental print
- knows that it is the print that is read in stories
- understands that different text forms are used for different functions of print (e.g., list for groceries)
- pays attention to separable and repeating sounds in language (e.g., Peter, Peter, Pumpkin Eater, Peter Eater)
- uses new vocabulary and grammatical constructions in own speech
- understands and follows oral directions
- is sensitive to some sequences of events in stories
- shows an interest in books and reading
- when being read a story, connects information and events to life experiences
- asks questions and makes comments demonstrating an understanding of literal meaning of story being told
- displays reading and writing attempts, calling attention to self: "Look at my story."
- can identify 10 alphabet letters, especially those from own name
- "writes" (scribbles) message as part of playful activity
- may begin to attend to beginning or rhyming sound in salient words

FIGURE 6–2 Developmental accomplishments of literacy acquisition. (Reprinted with permission from *Preventing reading difficulties in young children.* © 1998 by the National Academy of Sciences. Courtesy of the National Academy Press, Washington, DC.)

attained unconsciously or by all in our society. Literacy requires a shared body of understanding, much of which involves a common exposure to oral and written material and a level of proficiency in listening, speaking, reading, and writing. Currently, there is a national effort to help students who are not proficient readers, and surveys show many children experience literacy problems. Literacy acquisition involves a commitment of time and mental energy plus opportunity. At the preschool level, this commitment is a teacher's commitment to presenting a program that both promotes language arts skills and furnishes a shared body of understandings appropriate to preschoolers.

Elementary school reading textbooks in the early part of the twentieth century were collections of classics. The idea of reading levels was not in vogue, but rather the goal was to have every child learn information and skills that were common to the democratic literate public electorate of the time and necessary to the development of a truly educated man or woman. Literacy today is still seen by some as only referring to reading and writing, but many researchers and early childhood educators are concerned with the taproots of literacy, which may be developed during the preschool period (Figure 6–3).

To be considered functionally literate, one must have knowledge of shared, common information that is neither set down on paper nor explicitly stated in oral communication and that provides the basis for understanding what is heard or read. This idea is well illustrated by a similar phenomenon that occurs when outsiders listen to an in-group whose members have learned a specialized technical vocabulary. For instance, suppose we are having a difficult time understanding a group of computer buffs.

**FIGURE 6–3** Teachers are trained to encourage child speech during daily interactions and conversations.

We know they are speaking our language, but we cannot understand the bulk of their conversation. As they chat about bits, blogs, bites, DSL, or TCP/IP, they may not make any sense to us. We then might consider ourselves functionally illiterate in computer terminology.

Real access to concepts of cultural heritage comes from extended, personally meaningful conversations with adults, books read aloud at home, and children reading by choice for pleasure.

In programming, an integrated language/literacy approach that emphasizes child comprehension is suggested by current research. It is one of the goals of this textbook.

## LANGUAGE ARTS INSTRUCTION— HISTORICAL ROOTS

In examining the historical roots of language arts instruction one could start with the seventeenth-century theorist René Descartes (1596–1650), a French philosopher who theorized that God was responsible for the innate knowledge in children's minds, and the English philosopher John Locke (1632–1704), who expressed a contrasting position that suggested that children's minds at birth were blank and unfilled. Locke (1974) also emphasized the importance of experience in learning.

In the eighteenth century, Johann Pestalozzi (1846–1827) of Switzerland and Friedrich Froebel (1782–1852) of Germany presented yet another theory based on their personal interactions with young children. Both Pestalozzi (Rusk & Scotland, 1979) and Froebel (1974) recommend providing "natural environments" in which sensory experiences produce learning and a natural unfolding. Play, they suggested, was the route to learning and intellectual development, along with social, emotional, and physical development. Froebel introduced the notion of treating children with kindness, caring, and compassion. Many schools of the day offered sparse, sterile classroom environments, with young children seated in rows or at desks. Teachers required rote memorization, repetition, imitation, and strict adherence to rules.

## The Twentieth Century

At the turn of the twentieth century in the United States, schools for very young children imitated primary school practices, which included memorization and recitation by children, or they simply offered custodial care. Disciples of Froebel began to influence educators along the eastern seaboard. In the Midwest, John Dewey (1916) began experimenting with young children's educational environments. His beliefs promoted a curriculum of teacher-selected topics, themed units of study, and theme-influenced play areas. His ideas affected language arts instructional practices. Dramatic play and book (library) areas are still with us today, and theme instruction has not disappeared. Formal skill-building activities were avoided, but on-the-spot recognized learning moments (teachable moments) were capitalized upon.

Gesell (1940) was also influential. He suggested that developmental "norms" existed, and he believed that child growth and development were based on maturation. For teachers to be effective, they needed to determine children's readiness for learning on a child-by-child basis.

Maria Montessori (1967a), a physician-educator who in 1907 started her experiment by bringing education to children in a deprived area of Rome, captured the attention of some American early educators. Ideas concerning children's learning through sequenced manipulative materials and special teacher-child interactions were recognized. Some group lessons were believed necessary, but primarily, children self-selected from offered activities and decided their own pace, followed their own interests, and worked independently. Montessori instruction stressed order and self-contained tasks. Activities (tasks) had definite beginnings and endings, which included returning materials to shelves. Many of Montessori's activities approached learning in a sensory way; some were color-coded.

In the 1930s and 1940s, it was widely believed that early exposure to formal reading instruction should wait until the necessary skills had been achieved, which was believed to be somewhere around the age of 6½ (Morphett & Washburne, 1931). These prerequisite skills included auditory and visual discrimination, visual motor skills, and large motor skills.

A change occurred in early educational practice during the 1960s and the 1970s. Children were beginning to be seen as constructing their own knowledge of language from their experiences. Rather than moving children to higher levels of development, teachers were to match experiences to children's current levels. Piaget, a Swiss psychologist noted for his observations of his own children, studied children's cognitive growth. Piaget (1952) theorized that a child passed through several sequential stages and was unable to move to a higher stage unless she had mastered the stage before it. Learning took place as the child made sense of her environment through exploration and manipulation.

Chomsky (1968), who was concerned with language development, believed that acquiring language was a matter of the child's gaining facility with the rules that govern language. These rules were not learned but rather ingested as the child matured and interfaced with more mature speakers. Chomsky theorized that the human brain was uniquely equipped with a language facilitator that he called the "language acquisition device" (LAD).

Vygotsky (1978), considered a sociocultural theorist, suggested that learning took place through social contact and the development of what he termed "private speech." He emphasized the development of socially shared cognition with adults and peers. Adults (or others) assist the child to move ahead in development by noticing what the next logical step might be.

Morrow and Asbury (2003) have listed how different early constructivist approach theorists and philosophers influenced language arts program planning.

- Use of prepared and natural environments for learning
- Equal emphasis on social, emotional, physical, and intellectual development
- Supportive adults who encourage social interaction to aid learning
- A focus on learning rather than teaching
- Awareness that children must be actively involved to learn

Research in the twentieth century provided educators with additional data focusing on oral language, early writing attempts, development of early reading skills, and alphabet learning and/or alphabet sound learning. It emphasized early reading behaviors. This supported the idea that literacy began at birth. Educators tended to believe that a rich literary environment with activities that aided the development of literacy skills did more to promote children's natural interests than direct reading-readiness instruction did. The whole-language movement promoted young children's access to quality literature together with listening, discussion, and active participation in dramatizing, storytelling, poetry, and picture-book times. Early writing and print-related language arts activities gained wide acceptance.

The focus shifted to developmentally appropriate practice in the 1990s, and educators became aware of instructional strategies to prevent reading difficulties through the development of early skills during the preschool years. Much of early childhood language arts instruction changed. Many programs are working toward a balanced approach to programming, combining a developmental environment and appropriate literacy experiences with research-based, skill-building activities that equip children to make smooth transitions from nonreader to beginning reader to reader.

## In the Present

At no time in our history has the public eye been more intently focused on children's reading and writing achievement and classroom instruction in reading and writing. The National Reading Panel Report in 2000 urged an organized and systematic instructional approach with highly qualified teachers. Morrow and Asbury (2003) describe a comprehensive approach to early childhood literacy

> . . . grounded in a rich model of literacy learning that encompasses both elegance and the complexity of reading and language arts processes. Such a model acknowledges the importance of both form (phonemic awareness, phonics, mechanics, etc.) and function (comprehension, purpose, and meaning) of the literacy processes, and recognizes that learning occurs most effectively in a whole-part-whole context. This type of instruction is characterized by meaningful literacy activities that provide children with both

the skills and the desire to achieve proficiency and lifelong literacy learning.

> Teaching literacy skills and providing opportunities for learning literacy skills are appropriate for young children as long as the teaching methods are appropriate to the child being taught. In such a program, teachers provide numerous literacy experiences that include the integration of reading, writing, listening, speaking, and viewing. (p. 233)

Early childhood instruction may now include the task of assessing developing skills and making instructional plans based on **assessment** data.

In the many early childhood programs that are affected by the Elementary and Secondary Education Act that includes the No Child Left Behind Act (U.S. Department of Education, 2002), periodic assessment is the rule—not the exception—in kindergartens. Early childhood programs are being asked to be accountable by providing data that show young children's progress in the language arts.

The quest to identify the most appropriate and effective means to promote children's literacy development has remained elusive for the last half century (New, 2002). New believes the term *emergent literacy* has been replaced by *early literacy*. From this perspective, literacy begins at birth, is ongoing, and is influenced and interpreted by the surrounding sociocultural context. New suggests that as a nation, we are far from achieving common ground on considering the meanings, means, or purposes of early literacy. What we do know is that preschool educators will encounter children who arrive with research-identified risk factors including living in poverty, residing in single-parent homes, having a parent with low educational attainment, and having a home language other than English (Rimm-Kaufman, Pianta, & Cox, 2000). Early childhood educators will face the challenge of providing preschool experiences and activities that prepare children for kindergarten success in the crucial area of language arts. Children

---

**assessment** — a broad repertoire of behaviors involved in noticing, documenting, recording, and interpreting children's behaviors and performances. Testing is a subset of assessment behaviors in which performances are controlled and elicited in standardized conditions.

will especially need a background that ensures learning to read with ease when formal reading instruction begins. Goldenberg (2002) believes that productive and effective early childhood experiences and instruction must address the *interrelated* aspects of literacy. These follow.

● Understanding and use of print functionally (reading and writing for communication, expression, etc.)

● Understanding and use of the "alphabetic principle" **phonological awareness,** letter names and sounds, efficient and automatic decoding (i.e., writing)

● Motivation and interest in using print for a variety of purposes

● Language, cognitive skills, and knowledge necessary for comprehension and communication*

Although there is no consensus about how much of each aspect should be stressed, a successful literacy program addresses each of these in sufficient depth and breadth to promote literacy growth in the earliest and later years.

Goldenberg (2002) points out that although there is wide agreement that phonological awareness is an important aspect of being ready to learn to read, there is less agreement about whether children should receive direct instruction and training or whether phonological awareness should be accomplished in "natural language" activities such as poems, chants, songs, and so on. Proponents of strong phonics and phonological awareness training recommend a different set of practices than do those who emphasize the more contextual uses of literacy. Most early childhood educators search for meaningful and functional literacy activities, but many are introducing phonological skill-developing opportunities that encourage children to generate rhymes and segment phonemes within meaningful activities.

*From Goldenberg, C. (2002). Making schools work for low-income families in the 21st century. In S. Neuman & D. Dickinson (Eds.), *Handbook of Early Literacy Research.* Copyright © 2002 Guilford Press.

The joint position statement of the International Reading Association (IRA) and the National Association for the Education of Young Children (NAEYC), *Learning to Read and Write* (1999), serves as a guide for early childhood language arts program development. It describes developmentally appropriate language arts activities in infancy through the early primary grades. Recommended teaching practices and activities are categorized according to children's age levels. It promotes nurturing adult-child relationships; print-rich environments; daily reading and discussion of high-quality books; oral opportunities that focus on sounds and meaning; phonemic awareness activities; play that includes play with literacy tools; exposure to print, icons, and words in computer games; and firsthand activities that expand knowledge and vocabulary. No one teaching method or approach is likely to be the most effective for all children, according to the position paper. A variety of teaching strategies suited to child diversity and individuality is recommended.

**The National Early Literacy Panel.** The National Early Literacy Panel has studied literacy research findings extensively. McCardle (2006) points out the report of the National Reading Panel (NRP), National Institute of Child Health and Human Development (2002) identified five research-based elements that need to be present in any reading approach or program for children whose first language is English to develop the skills necessary to become successful life-long readers. These are phonics, phonemic awareness, reading fluency, vocabulary, and reading comprehension.

The panel believes that building young children's literacy skill is possible. The challenges facing early childhood educators are considerable. A number of variables that have strong and consistent relationships with later literacy outcomes have been identified by the report. After their review of a relatively large number of research studies with a large number of children, the following variables were found (Strickland, Shanahan, & Escamalia, 2004).

---

**phonological awareness** — the whole spectrum from primitive awareness of speech sounds and rhythms to rhyme awareness and sound similarities; at the highest level, awareness of syllables or phonemes.

### Strong Predictors of Positive Literacy Outcomes

- alphabet knowledge
- concepts about print
- phonological awareness
- invented spelling
- oral language (expressive, receptive, vocabulary)
- writing of name
- RAN (rapid automatic naming/lexical access)

In using the predictors, the panel cautions that they reviewed only existing research studies. Other predictors may yet be discovered when additional research becomes available.

### Putting Theories in Categories

Binding similar theories loosely together may help language arts program planners realize the theoretical basis for their language program decisions.

The **nativists,** those who believe in the natural unfolding of children without direct teaching from adults, include Rousseau, Pestalozzi, and Froebel. These educators can be conceived as thinkers who led later scholars and researchers to propose maturational theories with ages, stages, and normative behaviors.

**Psychosocial theory,** which stresses stages of human development, is associated with Freud. It can also be seen as a variant of the nativist tradition. Erikson's psychosocial theory stressed specific tasks to be resolved during stages of human development. The major tasks of toddlers and preschoolers were autonomy and initiative. Theory, along this line of thinking, may have evolved into a philosophy of child-directed learning such as traditional Montessori.

Locke's **nurturist** philosophy can be seen as a precursor of highly didactic preschool practices, although he also advocated offering children experiences to promote learning. Program models promote teachers as dispensers of knowledge, but activities might also be presented. These programs are based on the theory of **behaviorism.**

**Interactionists** view child development and learning as taking place between children and their environment. Program planners promoting this view subscribe to the **constructivist theory,** believing in children's creation of their own internal knowledge as they interact in both social and environmental pursuits. Piaget would describe this interaction as assimilation, accommodation, and equilibration. Vygotsky's **social constructivist theory** would emphasize the importance of language and socially shared cognition. He would recommend promoting assisted and scaffolded learning and encouraging children to use private speech to aid them in solving problems.

Although these theories differ in important ways, they share an emphasis on considering children as active learners who are able to set goals, plan, and revise. They recognize that children's cognitive development, which is so closely tied to language development, evolves gradually as children acquire strategies for remembering, understanding, and problem solving (Machado & Botnarescue, 2008).

---

**nativists** — those who adhere to the theory that children are born with biological dispositions for learning that unfold or mature in a natural way.

**psychosocial theory** — the branch of psychology founded by Erik Erikson; development is described in terms of eight stages that span childhood and adulthood.

**nurturist** — one who adheres to the theory that the minds of children are blank or unformed and need educational input or direct instruction to develop and "output" knowledge and appropriate behavior.

**behaviorism** — the theoretical viewpoint, espoused by theorists such as B. F. Skinner, that behavior is shaped by environmental forces, specifically in response to reward and punishment.

**interactionists** — those who adhere to the theory that language develops through a combination of inborn factors and environmental influences.

**constructivist theory** — a theory such as that of Jean Piaget, based on the belief that children construct knowledge for themselves rather than having it conveyed to them by some external source.

**social constructivist theory** — such as Vygotsky's emphasis on the importance of language and socially shared cognition in exchanges between adult and child when scaffolding was used, and encouraging children's use of private speech to aid problem solving.

## PHILOSOPHIES OF LITERACY INSTRUCTION

A variety of approaches to literacy instruction, representing different philosophical positions, have emerged, resulting in practices using widely diverse teaching techniques, materials, and assessment methods. Theorists do not all agree about what learning is or how it happens (Phillips & Soltis, 2009). Contrasting points of view will probably continue as they have in the past. Currently, educators debate the efficacy of academically oriented versus **child-initiated curricula.** Whole-language versus teacher-directed phonics instruction has also received considerable ongoing attention. Out of these debates the "balanced," "eclectic," "natural," and "centrist" philosophical positions have evolved and become often recommended positions.

In a child-initiated model of instruction, children's self-directed actions are facilitated by a teacher. A teacher facilitates learning by (a) providing children with a wide variety of experiences, (b) encouraging children to choose and plan their own learning activities, (c) engaging children in active learning by posing problems and asking questions that stimulate and extend learning, (d) guiding children through skill acquisition activities as needed, and (e) encouraging children to reflect on their learning experiences.

The staff of each early childhood center drafts a program based on the unique mesh of the staff's personal theories about what they believe is appropriate and effective. If a language arts program focuses on the correct form(s) of language, such as the planned and sequential learning of letter names, sounds, and so forth, the program could be described as traditional, or conventional. This text urges an approach to teaching language arts that is meaning-based, brain-based, and functional for children, literature-rich, and taught in a balanced and interrelated fashion. This type of program approach believes child knowledge and skill in language arts are reinforced and made meaningful when the reading, writing, listening, and speaking aspects of daily activities are encountered concurrently. A developmentally appropriate program first considers the unique group of children enrolled, their needs, their abilities, their interests, and their families' wishes concerning desirable educational outcomes.

Preschools and child centers have given special attention to developmentally appropriate practice guidelines published by the NAEYC. In designing programs for young children, developmentally appropriate practice has three recognized components: age appropriateness, individual appropriateness, and knowledge and honor of children's social and cultural contexts. Many centers depend on developmentally appropriate practice to form a framework for curriculum and adult interactions with children. Deeply embedded in developmentally appropriate practice is the idea that children have a natural disposition toward learning and actively construct their own knowledge through exploration and interaction with materials, peers, and adults. Educators also realize that low-achieving students often need planned and systematic instruction to acquire skills that will enable them to progress and eventually learn to read with ease.

Developmentally appropriate program planning may aim to strengthen what a child already knows and can do and/or may promote what a child can potentially discover or knows or can newly accomplish.

Researchers trying to identify the effect of developmentally appropriate practice on children's cognitive development conclude that children's receptive language was better in programs with higher-quality literacy environments and when developmentally appropriate activities were more abundant. Many educators believe that outdated views, including extensive whole-group instruction and intensive drill and practice of isolated language arts skills, are not suitable or effective with preschoolers. In terms of cognitive development, the use of developmentally appropriate instructional strategies

---

**child-initiated curricula** — a basic tenet underlying this type of curriculum is the belief that true growth occurs when children are free to develop intrinsic interests naturally.

appears to facilitate children's creativity, is associated with better verbal skills and receptive language, and contributes to higher levels of cognitive functioning.

Figure 6–4 offers a possible sequence of children's language learning in both planned and spur-of-the-moment classroom activities.

Child has experiential background observing and participating in a rich language arts school environment.

Child gives attention to classroom activities, demonstrations, behaviors modeled by others, new happenings, teacher presentations, or other classroom events. Child perceives activity to be useful, interesting, or worthwhile.

Child feels comfortable and safe in this situation and feels capable and likely successful. Child understands that teacher expects appropriate classroom behavior.

Child continues focus and concentration on activity that is unfolding and progressing.

Child gathers and selects information and data; develops beginning ideas; may ask questions; and looks, listens, touches as if investigating or trying to find out.

Child may see or state relationships and form hypotheses or conclusions and may discuss points of view.

Child may test ideas or check ideas with teacher or others present.

Child may receive feedback from teacher and/or other children. Child may be uncertain or puzzled.

Child may develop a definite idea and "fit" the newness experienced in the activity into what she already knows. Learning occurs.

**FIGURE 6–4** Possible sequence in language learning.

## FEDERAL LEGISLATION AFFECTS LANGUAGE ARTS CURRICULA

In July 2001, the White House Summit on Early Childhood Cognitive Development met and focused on the chain of negative educational events that can result when children are unable to master reading in the lower grades of elementary school. An increased federal emphasis exists on not only reading instruction but also what prepares young children and precedes their kindergarten enrollment (Love, 2003).

The federal No Child Left Behind Act (U.S. Department of Education, 2002) sections dealing with guidelines for reading are designed to improve children's reading in publicly funded schools from kindergarten through third grade. Pushing formal reading instruction into preschool classrooms was not recommended and was not the legislation's intent. The idea that literacy experiences during preschool years are critical for successful learning during elementary school years was a central concern.

The assessment of preschool children and programs recommended in the NCLB Act is a "hot button" topic for many early childhood educators. Educators and professional teacher organizations worry that testing will label very young children, and they are concerned about assessment validity and unfair judgments of programs working with disadvantaged children or second-language learners. They fear standardized testing tends to lead to standardized teaching—one approach fits all—the opposite of the kind of individualized diagnosis and teaching that is needed to help young children continue to progress in reading and writing (IRA & NAEYC, 1999).

**More about the No Child Left Behind Act (NCLB).** The No Child Left Behind Act's provision that federal grants be contingent on the fact that all enrolled children at primary schools make "adequate yearly progress" in reading created shock waves throughout public educational systems. As a result, regional areas, states, cities, local communities, school districts, and professional organizations and groups have made attempts to identify age-level literacy characteristics. They have also developed standards and goal statements, pinpointing the literacy skills gained in the early years that may ease children's learning to read. Written standards statements and prescribed curricula can include mandating the time children are to spend in daily classroom literacy-promoting activities. Groups working to address the requirements of the No Child Left Behind Act have also developed, refined, or examined testing alternatives; initiated teacher training and retraining; and pursued various additional efforts. Reading scores for elementary school students, including minority students, didn't budge in 2009 according to the National Assessment of Education Programs (NAEP) and achievement gaps among white, African American, and Hispanic students has changed only slightly since 2007 (Toppo, 2010).

Early childhood centers attempt to design curricula that are culturally relevant. Child observation and documentation activities are now part of the teacher's responsibility in many preschools as well as elementary schools. Child journals, child portfolios, teacher checklists, testing sessions, recording, and observations are commonplace as teachers struggle to identify the literacy growth of each child.

Many educators are involved in debates concerning the wisdom of some or all of the practices that are a result of this federal legislation. Most commonly, they express fears and frustrations involving "pushed down" curriculum formerly introduced in higher grades, literacy or academic activities "crowding out" playtime or other curricular activities, bilingual instructional techniques, and "fairness" in testing.

Early childhood educators are as worried as some families are about skill-and-drill sessions, work sheets, and lessons that have no connection to children's backgrounds or interests. Many early childhood educators realize that they may be failing the children who need them the most. Multiple studies show many children from low-income families enter kindergarten a year to a year and a half, on average, behind middle-class children in their language development, as well as other cognitive skills. This is a gigantic lag that dramatically affects children's success in the first grades of primary school and perhaps their entire educational future.

The field is searching for palatable techniques and strategies to incorporate code-related components of literacy mentioned in the No Child Left Behind Act into language arts program planning, particularly for children most in need. The easy part may be intentionally incorporating skill building into daily conversations and daily activities. The hard part may be overcoming teachers' reticence concerning systematic planned skill-based instruction and effectively identifying at-risk children. Educators believe teachers do not need to make children ready for learning; most are quite eager learners.

Arne Duncan, U.S. Secretary of Education criticizes the effectiveness NCLB because he believes some states have "dumbed" down their Standards of Proficiency (Will, 2009). Guernsey (2009) points out that academic kindergarten practices have developed in the wake of new science. She suggests that all children, not just a select few children of above average and advantaged circumstances, are able to learn earlier that once believed. She advocates the following: (1) training teachers to blend play with learning in planned activities, (2) making preschool affordable for working families, (3) encouraging full-day kindergarten (as 10 states do), and

---

 **VIDEO ACTIVITY**

Go to the Education CourseMate website to watch the ABC News Video entitled, *No Child Left Behind (NCLB): Good Intentions, Real Problems.*

Quite a bit of this video dealt with labeling "failing schools" at elementary school level and little dealt with early childhood centers' role in helping children gain the skills they will need when they transition into elementary school.

1. Do "failing" early childhood centers exist? Schools with deficiencies in language arts programming and instruction? Discuss this.

2. Use Chapter 6 to help you identify what areas of instruction preschool program planners should not ignore in young children's language arts development. List 5. What books, websites, associations or public agencies should schools consult if they need expert professional help in language arts program planning?

(4) building a bridge between preschool and kindergarten. She suggests

> The first day of kindergarten shouldn't feel like plunging into a pressure cooker. These steps would help turn kindergarten classrooms into the blooming gardens of learning they're supposed to be. (p. 11A)

## State Standards, Head Start Performance Standards, the Head Start Child Outcomes Framework, and Other Frameworks

According to Kendall and Marzano (2004), at least three principal reasons exist for the development of standards. These are (1) to establish clarity of curriculum content; (2) to raise expectations for achievement; and (3) to ensure accountability for public education. Most states have state initiatives and standards aimed at preparing preschoolers for kindergarten. Many states have developed accountability programs that they hope will indicate how well children in individual programs are performing relative to the skills and behaviors identified by the state as prerequisites for effective kindergarten performance. The skills and behaviors include pre-reading skills including phonological awareness, letter knowledge, and vocabulary; numeracy; and social-emotional competence. The State of California's *Preschool Learning Foundations* (2009) includes standards for listening, speaking, reading, writing, and English language development.

Curriculum planners and developers in early childhood schools and centers keep standards in mind while preparing a school's program of activities if they receive public funds. Standards adopted at a particular school represent what that school and its teachers expect children to recall, replicate, manipulate, understand, or demonstrate at some point in time—in this case, prior to kindergarten entry.

Early childhood programs nationwide, depending on their state's decision to mandate or recommend their standards, may not be able to design their program of activities, for they may be spelled out in law. Some written standard statements provide examples of child behaviors teachers can observe that indicate child accomplishment or progress toward mastering a particular standard statement. Many state standard statements are in draft or final written form and are available on the Internet or available by contacting a state's Department of Education. The National Institute for Early Childhood Research (NIEER) has a directory of states that have downloadable early childhood (preschool) language and literacy standards (http://www.nieer.org). Another source is http://www.educationworld.com.

Head Start, reauthorized by Congress in 1998, augmented its Head Start Performance Standards, a document that guided language arts program planning along with other curricular areas. In 2000, the Administration for Children and Families (ACF) issued guidelines for devising and implementing outcome-based education plans. Consequently, the Head Start Child Outcomes Framework (U.S. Department of Health and Human Services, 2003) is available. The framework involves eight basic learning and development "domains." Two domains are identified as language development and literacy. Each domain is composed of domain elements and examples of specific indicators of ability. Head Start has shifted from its original focus on social competence and play to literacy and discrete academic outcomes.

The framework gives definition to learning objectives for Head Start and Head Start teachers. The objectives include five federally mandated indicators of learning achievement that were set as requirements for Head Start children graduating their programs and entering kindergarten.

The framework also emphasizes the importance of parents' understanding of their vital out-of-school function in promoting language and literacy development. It promotes parents' understanding that children's cumulative life experiences and adult-child interactions from birth on affect language and literacy growth.

To obtain a copy of the Head Start Performance Standards or the Head Start Child Outcomes Framework, go to http://www.hsnrc.org.

The National Association for the Education of Young Children's *Standards and Accreditation Performance Criteria for Early Childhood Programs* (2007)) has been developed through a national effort to identify language and literacy standards. To review language and literacy standards, and performance criteria, search online at http://www.naeyc.org. Proceed to *Academy* for additional NAEYC accreditation information.

Figure 6–5 is checklist of language and literacy standards for preschool classrooms developed by Enz and Morrow (2009). Your employment classrooms may use its own created set of standards or those goals created by the federal government, a state department or licensing agency, a local school district or a school's standards list may have been developed by a national organization such as NAEYC or IRA (The International Reading Association). A few private schools use standards developed through joint home, school, and community consultation and agreement.

Many educational practitioners and experts have worried about how standards, whether local, state or national, will affect the quality of their early childhood instructional programs. Some have adopted a pro-standards stance while others feel there are inherent dangers in predetermined standards that are mandated and forced upon them. They may feel others are unaware of the needs and characteristics of their particular child group.

Possible positive benefits accrued by standards' use cited by pro-standards advocates include:

● Recognized standards have been developed using the best information and research available by well known and respected groups of educators.

## LANGUAGE AND LITERACY STANDARDS FOR PRESCHOOL CHILDREN

Listening Comprehension
__ Listens with increased attention
__ Understands simple oral directions
__ Listens to and engages in conversation

Vocabulary
__ Shows an increase in listening and speaking vocabulary
__ Uses new vocabulary in daily communication
__ Refines understanding of words
__ Increases listening vocabulary

Verbal Expression
__ Uses language for a variety of purposes
__ Uses sentences of increasing length, grammatical complexity
__ Uses language to express routines
__ Tells a simple personal narrative
__ Asks questions
__ Begins to retell stories in sequence

Letter knowledge and Early Word Recognition
__ Begins to associate letter names with their shapes
__ Identifies 10 or more printed letters
__ Begins to notice beginning letters in familiar words
__ Begins to make some letter sound matches
__ Begins to identify some high-frequency words

Knowledge of Literacy Forms
__ Predicts what will happen next in a story
__ Imitates special language in a book
__ Asks questions about the information/events in a book
__ Connects information and events in books to real life

Speech Production and Discrimination
__ Identifies differences between similar sounding words
__ Produces speech sounds with increased ease and accuracy
__ Experiments with language

Phonological Awareness
__ Begins to identify rhymes
__ Begins to attend to beginning sounds
__ Begins to break words into syllables or claps with each syllable
__ Begins to create words by substituting one sound for another

Print and Book Awareness
__ Understands that reading/writing are ways to obtain information
__ Understands that reading/writing communicates thoughts/ideas
__ Understands that illustrations carry meaning but cannot be read
__ Understands that letters are different from numbers
__ Understands that a book has a title and an author
__ Understands that print runs from left to right and top to bottom
__ Begins to understand basic print conventions

Motivation to Read
__ Demonstrates an interest in books and reading
__ Enjoys listening to and discussing books
__ Requests being read to and re-reading the same story
__ Attempts to read and write

Written Expression
__ Attempts to write messages
__ Uses letters to represent written language
__ Attempts to connect the sounds in a word with their letter forms
__ Begins to dictate words/phrases for an adult to record on paper

FIGURE 6–5 Language and literacy standards for preschool children.

- Standards identify clear and explicit goals for early childhood programs.

- Standards are designed to prepare enrolled children with the abilities and skills necessary to enable them to learn to read with ease when formal instruction in reading begins.

- With all or most schools using the same standards transferring from school to school is not a problem.

- Teachers and teaching staffs are provided with guidelines for planning curriculum and daily activities.

- Standards' use is bound to add status to the early childhood teaching profession as well as the programs themselves.

- Families can examine school standards and determine if the program meets their needs.

- National standards promote uniformity of instruction nation wide.

- Standards at preschool level may more easily meld into kindergarten standards.

Standard disadvantages and possible dangers listed by opposing educators include

- Standards' use may promote adopting teaching practices that emphasize passing assessments or tests that measure standards' accomplishment.

- Early childhood curriculum areas that encompass art, music, or other more creative pursuits will be slighted.

- Physical development and exercise will be given a lower priority.

- Some schools will be labeled 'failure factories'.

- Emphasis on standards may cause teachers to ignore the individual and unique talents of some children while they concentrate on 'strugglers'.

- Teaching methods may not be identified in standards.

- Increased public pressure on schools and teachers may take place.

- Children's socio-emotional development may take a back seat to intellectual and academic growth.

Stott believes that standards in the field of early education are an essential first step for designing a more effective preschool curriculum.

## LANGUAGE USE IN ALL CURRICULUM AREAS

Every planned preschool activity uses language in some way. Past experience is basic to all language arts because a child's success often depends on her understanding of what is happening. Language helps children learn, retain, recall, and transmit information. Messages are received through words and nonverbal means. The teacher's speech, behavior, and use of words in planned activities are discussed in the following chapters.

In addition to the early childhood center's planned program, daily sequence of activities, play with peers, and unplanned happenings also stimulate language. Teachers use every opportunity to add meanings in a natural, conversational way during the preschool day. This generally begins with the teacher's personal greeting or affectionate physical contact as the child enters the center. The "hello" and comments are part of the rituals in preschools that aim to recognize each child's presence each arrival time.

Daily routines are the regular features of a school's program that occur about the same time every day—snacks, toileting, and group activities—in which language is an associate function. Language-related activities are included in both small and large group times; these activities can range from short announcements to literacy-oriented activities the teacher presents or prepares.

Planned activities should have a purpose children can understand and in some way connect to what they already know (Figure 6–6). Most, if not all, learning can be made applicable to the child's life. Early childhood practitioners provide real, hands-on experiences in their classrooms when possible. Secondhand activities are second best. If classroom charts, posters, and graphic representations are used, teachers consider using bold colors.

Concrete vivid images are most influential. Neuroscientists theorize that this is because (1) the brain has an attentional bias for high contrast and novelty; (2) 90 percent of the brain's

FIGURE 6–6 Many new words can be connected to an activity with growing plants.

sensory input is from visual sources; and (3) the brain has an immediate and primitive response to symbols, icons, and other simple images. (Jensen, 2008), p. 56

With real object exploration in children's activities, the learner's brain may be focusing upon location, property differences, color, form, weight, and other unique properties.

In an activity planting spring seeds, signs or labels adjacent to planted seeds have a practical purpose. The teacher could read the seed packet instructions to the children to find out about planting particulars. If individual planting pots are used, the children and/or teacher could print their names to label them.

Educators are encouraged to use number and measurement terms in preschool activities in which counting, comparing, adding, or taking away is encountered in planned or unplanned daily happenings. Participation in preschool activities that touch on math knowledge and terminology dramatically reduces the disparities between children from low-income and middle-income families.

 **VIDEO ACTIVITY**

Go to the Education CourseMate website to watch the TeachSource Video entitled, *Preschool: Guidance*. The teacher in the video is conducting a teacher led activity about feelings, personal space, good and not good touches, and seeking help when the child's efforts fail. Although this could be classified as a guidance lesson, it was also a language lesson.

1. How did the teacher personalize the activity?
2. Were new vocabulary words reinforced visually and physically? In other ways, also?
3. Could you comment on the clarity of this teacher's words, her eye contact, and her speech pacing during her presentation of new concepts?

## LANGUAGE ARTS PROGRAMMING

Preplanned language arts programs develop from identified goals: the knowledge, skills, and attitudes that the school intends to teach (Figure 6–7). Early childhood teachers also base teaching techniques on what they believe is best, right, appropriate, and prudent. This, in turn, is connected to views they hold about how, what, when, and where children learn to

FIGURE 6–7 The school's staff meets often to assess whether the school's program is achieving standards and serving each child's individual needs.

communicate and use language. The following views about language learning are commonly expressed or implied by staff members involved in planning language arts programs.

- Language permeates all planned and unplanned activities.
- A dynamic, rich-in-opportunity classroom stimulates communication and exchanges of ideas.
- Real experiences are preferred to vicarious ones when practical and possible.

- The reciprocal nature of exploring and discovering together should be promoted by teachers.
- Play provides many opportunities to learn language (Figure 6–8).
- Teachers' instructional techniques should be skilled and alert to child readiness.
- Stressing relationships between objects, events, and experiences is a useful teaching technique.
- Individual planning, as well as group planning, is desirable.
- Program activities should center on the children's interests.
- Literary classics (preschool level) are an important planned-program component.
- The entire teaching staff should be committed to and enthusiastic about their planned program and should understand the stated objectives.
- An integrated approach to language arts instruction helps children experience the "connectedness" of language arts areas.
- Reading and writing is better conceptualized as a developmental continuum.

The best type of planned literacy-promoting program is one that is captivating enough to

FIGURE 6–8 Outdoor play can also provide language-learning opportunities.

hold the imagination, engaging enough to sustain active involvement for a period of time, and stimulating enough to motivate further literacy exploration.

Early childhood teachers realize that goals for attending children may be much different than families' goals. Rather than telling families what they ought to be doing, it is the school's job to support and complement families' efforts. There is sometimes a need to find community translators to help bridge the gap between home and school.

One can envision an ideal language arts curriculum starting at birth and continuing throughout the child's lifetime. The author sees it as a program of home and life experiences supporting learning and self-discovery in which colorful, interconnected strands of language arts knowledge and skill thread through early childhood and come together in an "'aha' rainbow" when the child successfully decodes her first word, first sentence, or first book. The child then passes through a door equipped to move on into a vast amount of stored human knowledge, discovery, inspiration, creativity, and fantasy. These milestones in development are hopefully accompanied by understanding, rich personal life experiences, natural inquisitiveness, and a belief in the child's own ability and self-worth.

The ideal early childhood curriculum in language arts offers quality child-relevant speaking, listening, early writing, and reading activities in addition to literature opportunities. These activities encourage, sustain, and provide growth, ensuring the necessary foundational knowledge and skill for an easy transition to school and a successful kindergarten year and beyond.

## Teacher Training

Your classes in early childhood education, self-study, and your life experiences will influence the early childhood literacy program you will attempt to offer young children. Many times, your ideas will be incorporated into a teaching team's effort to design a planned curriculum.

Your training should have encouraged you to continually improve instructional practice and to analyze what is working and what is not. Questioning and researching are parts of the joy of teaching and can lead to new techniques

and insights. When looking for program ideas, be open-minded and look inside to remember what inspired your own literacy development. Do not discount your ability to really focus on children and discover their agenda or your ability as an "innovator" of a language arts program that addresses the needs and interests of each child. The specific teaching behaviors that an early childhood educator working toward language arts and literacy goals should possess are listed below. It cities both knowledge and skills. Research has identified the following "critical" teacher behaviors:

● using new words with children;
● extending children's comments through questioning;
● focusing children's attention on an analysis of books read to them;
● engaging in intellectually challenging conversations;
● placing an importance on child engagement during group time;
● obtaining and maintaining children's attention;
● believing academic and social goals are both important;
● providing literacy-learning opportunities and being intentional in instructional efforts to stretch children's thinking;
● supporting children's writing attempts;
● providing knowledge, promoting phonological sensitivity, and instilling child familiarity with the basic purposes and mechanisms of reading, especially to preschoolers with less prior knowledge and skill (at-risk children);
● giving individual children adequate time to speak;
● planning and implementing small group activities;
● engaging in extensive conversations;
● joining individual children or small groups in the library or writing areas;
● creating a literacy-rich classroom environment with accessible materials;
● ensuring careful organization and management of materials;
● providing opportunities for children to practice skills taught;

- giving guidance in structured lessons for acquisition of skills; and

- providing opportunities for children to work independently or in collaborative groups.

## Programs for At-Risk Preschoolers

The U.S. Department of Education defines a linguistically and culturally diverse child (an educational term) as a child who is either non-English proficient (NEP) or limited-English proficient (LEP). Educators recognize the difficulties many young children may face when entering child care centers or preschools and attempting to learn an unfamiliar language. High-quality educational programs recognize and promote all aspects of children's development and learning Nemeth (2009) has identified strategies based upon best early childhood practice. She urges educators to provide some degree of daily support in each child's home language and to

- extend learning by maintaining themes for days at a time;

- use key words for each theme;

- repeat and emphasize important words in English;

- include visual aids as part of communication whenever possible;

- use body language, gesture, facial expressions, and American Sign Language to augment your communication with DLL (dual language learners) children;

- make adaptations all around the classroom (multi-ethnic and multicultural representations and models);

- conduct home language surveys (regional area of families' language and culture);

- use authentic props and real items to connect with each child's prior experience; and

- use the talents of bilingual staff, volunteers, family, and children (pp. 20–22).

## Culturally Diverse Musical Experience

The songs and music of childhood are a part of our cultural heritage. The folk songs and ballads that have survived to the present day and the regional tunes parents and teachers offer are part of each child's cultural literacy. Early childhood programs attempt to provide the music of various ethnic groups. Most of these musical experiences give young children the opportunity to form beginning ideas concerning the music and language of diverse peoples.

Musical activities have gained new status and are viewed as language-developing activities. Studies suggest that in cultures in which musical play is actively encouraged, children acquire heightened competencies in motor and communication skills at early ages.

## Classroom Environment

Classrooms should be designed to reflect the rich literate environments in which children are immersed outside of school. The use of teacher-made signs that label children's materials, furnishings, or equipment or areas where children store their belongings and books are helpful, but other educators feel labeling is not an effective practice if labels are not talked about or if there is no recognized purpose for labeling items. Available paper in various sizes, shapes, and colors that children can write on in their theme play or their independent-time activities encourage child use. All learning experiences should be organized so that they invite children to participate in literacy events.

Authentic literacy events need to become the focus of the school day as children:

- are signed in daily so that the teacher knows who has arrived in school;

- put away their materials in an appropriate setting, using the signs in the room or their names on their cubbies;

- read recipes and menus as they cook, eat, and learn about healthy nutritional activities;

- write prescriptions at the play hospital or take phone messages in the house corner; and

- read storybooks, write letters, and record observations.

Creating a warm, cozy, friendly environment where children are in a state of relaxed alertness is the goal of educators.

## Determining Program Effectiveness

Goals pinpointed through staff meetings and solicited parent input can be finalized in written form to serve as a basis for planning. For one child or many, goals are achieved when teachers and staff plan interesting and appropriate activities for daily, weekly, monthly, or longer periods. In addition to the actual program, materials, and classroom equipment and arrangement, teacher techniques and interactions and other resources aid in goal realization.

Teacher observation and assessment instruments—both commercial instruments and those designed by teachers—add extra data that help in planning programs (Figure 6–9).

Assessment may be defined as an ongoing process of gathering evidence of learning in order to make informed judgments about instructional practice. Many educators believe assessment of children's growth and development is an essential component of all high-quality preschool programs (Enz & Morrow, 2009)

> Assessment allows teacher and parents to see how a child is progressing and helps teachers to prepare instruction for their students' ever-changing language development and literacy needs. (p. 2)

Carefully planned, recorded, and well-conducted teacher observation is an assessment tool that is hard to beat. Standardized tests all too often do not tell observant teachers anything they do not already know about children. Some assessments attempt to determine ability and accomplishment in a number of language and communication areas; others may be limited to one language skill.

School assessment and testing strategies can include the collection of daily performance or work samples, making anecdotal observations, using checklists, identifying benchmarks or milestones, accomplishments, or conducting testing with norm or criterion-referenced instruments. Literacy portfolio development is initiated in many programs to begin a documented and on-going collection of child performance.

Standard tests are defined as tests in which a prepared script is read verbatim to the one tested. They are usually commercially published (see Appendix) and referenced to a select and accepted set of norms or standards. Norms reflect the average accomplishments or performance of a large group of children at a particular age or grade level. Standardized tests may cover a wide range of topics such as listening skill, auditory memory, and vocabulary but rarely test all skills, knowledge, and ability associated with emergent literacy or early reading ability.

Enz and Morrow (2009) report that one of the most high-profile users of standardized tests with preschoolers is Head Start with the Head Start National Reporting System (NRS), which measures a set of skills that include expressive and receptive English vocabulary, uppercase letter naming, and early math skills.

There is a national interest in ensuring that every child has high levels of skills. A school that embraces testing is often labeled a place for drilling students, filling their heads with memorized facts, and showing them that nothing in the learning process has much fun or joy (Mathews, 2010, p. 182). This does not have to happen, and many early childhood centers test children so they can both individualize their instruction and find out if attending children are progressing by being exposed to their standards-based planned curriculum and their staffs' guidance and teaching strategies. How is a teacher otherwise to know if she and the curriculum are effective? Great teachers are always excited about learning new ways they can help students (Canada, 2010). At successful schools there is a constant focus on getting real information about students' performance early and often, using data to have a much better picture of student's ability and then creating an action plan to target individual students' deficiencies. . . (Canada, 2010), p. 19.

## Literacy Portfolios

A number of centers and programs create individual literacy portfolios in an effort to track individual children's literacy development and to complement the school's standardized assessment and reporting methods. A first step is identifying educational goals and purposes that a portfolio might satisfy. Usually this deals with both school and home language arts activities and opportunities. What types of items

## SAMPLE OF STAFF-DESIGNED LANGUAGE AND LITERACY CHECKLIST

Child _____ Age _____ (Check if present) Date _____

1. can distinguish illustrations, photographs, and so on from print
2. identifies front/back of books    F_____ B_____
3. notices print in the environment
4. is interested in a book's content and illustrations
5. realizes illustrations can tell a story
6. realizes adults are reading printed text in a storybook
7. realizes print contains names and ideas (storylines)
8. realizes books are authored by people
9. realizes a story she creates can be put into print
10. recognizes her name in print
11. can find her printed name in a group of names
12. chooses books regularly in book areas
13. pretend reads
14. makes up stories
15. can act out stories
16. asks or answers questions about books being read
17. listens to a book attentively
18. handles books with care
19. pretend writes
20. uses alphabet letters in art or constructions
21. knows first letter of her name
22. tries to print name or other words
23. can name a few or many alphabet letters
      few _____ many _____ all _____
24. demonstrates she can hear rhyming words
25. creates a rhyme
26. tells a story with a beginning, middle, and end
      beginning _____ middle _____ end _____
27. has a favorite book
28. can identify words with the same beginning sound
29. knows reading starts at the top left on a page
30. knows there are spaces between words
31. wants her name printed on her work
32. can visually discriminate between alphabet letter shapes
      few _____ many _____
33. can discriminate between two different speech sounds
34. can perform two- or three-part commands
      Two part _____ Three part _____

35. can predict what might happen in a story based on the cover and illustrations
36. can identify and clap how many syllables are in a three-syllable word
37. recognizes that a letter can be written in uppercase and lowercase form
38. recognizes silly orally spoken mistakes are illogical. (The mouse ate an elephant. The cup fell off the table and hit the ceiling.)
39. can predict what would come next in a simple pattern (AooAo?)
40. controls a writing tool with small motor movement
41. has the ability to attend to and understand conversations, stories, poems, and other oral presentations
42. has a vocabulary (three years, more than 2,000 words; four years, more than 4,000 words; five years, more than 5,000 words)
      average_____ complex _____ varied _____
43. asks questions
44. tells feelings, opinions, ideas, needs, desires, and so forth
      often _____ infrequently _____
45. is a good conversationalist
      initiates _____ listens _____ responds _____
46. pronounces words clearly as expected for age
      clearly _____ average for age _____
47. has increased length of oral sentences
48. uses complex sentences at times
49. discriminates between sounds in words
50. can identify whether a sound in a word is the same or different from another word
51. knows the beginning sound of her name
52. makes an attempt to copy familiar words
53. prints name
54. recognizes common environmental or human symbols
55. is beginning to realize her name is a series of sounds blended together
56. sees visual differences in printed alphabet letters
57. knows the alphabet is a special category of visual graphics
58. can maintain focus of attention in small group instruction (appropriate to age and attention span)

**FIGURE 6–9** Sample of a staff-designed language and literacy checklist.

SAMPLE OF STAFF-DESIGNED LANGUAGE AND LITERACY CHECKLIST—cont'd

59. has group social skills such as raising hand, taking turns, asking questions, staying on topic, waiting for answers to her questions, and so on

60. can understand group time rules and participates in formulating them

61. uses language to initiate play with peers

62. makes choices and decisions and verbalizes them

63. can articulate sounds according to developmentally appropriate expectations

64. has developed divergent thinking skills

65. has an adequate grasp of meaningful concepts that are appropriate to age

66. has been exposed to capital alphabet letters used correctly in her name

67. is aware of and/or understands up, down, across, top, bottom, right, and left

68. uses visual cues; for example, follows directions on picture cards

69. is aware computer icons have meanings and knows meanings of a few

70. can find commonalities and differences in oral stories and visual representations

71. can create verbal labels for common objects

72. is aware of some punctuation marks in text

73. has been exposed to the use of computers

74. participates in singing

75. knows about a culture other than her own

76. attempts to write words

77. is familiar with graphs and charts and understands their use in visualizing data

78. understands that symbols are used for objects and events

79. can identify sounds in the environment

*Note: This was gathered from a wide collection of individual state standards and goal statements. It is not intended to be a complete or comprehensive list, but rather a sample of one school's efforts to assess its children's readiness for kindergarten. Some duplication of questions is present.

FIGURE 6–9 (continued)

might be collected is next considered, and then home-school collaboration particulars. Often literacy portfolio development is a joint project undertaken by both teachers and families. Items are collected over time and dated. These can include child work samples, child-dictated text, artwork with recorded comments, photographs of child work or dramatic play, a favorite book list, adult-child interviews, child-created stories or dictation, early writing attempts, alphabet-related examples, word lists; in short, records of child activities related to speaking, listening, pre-reading and reading skill development, print awareness, or any activities concerned with child literacy growth.

The portfolio usually travels from school to home and back. This activity informs families about what is happening at school and affords families a review and then insertion of home-collected items. Often children's portfolios become a special book from which children and their families derive pride and pleasure in a child's accomplishments and progress.

Large, album-sized binders are used to accommodate children's artwork in some programs, and many schools use page protectors or clear plastic kitchen storage bags to protect inserts. Items are filed in chronological order when dated. Reviewing a child's portfolio with the child generates considerable interactive conversation and promotes feelings of accomplishment. Some schools create digital files of students' work.

### Teacher Observation

Many child care centers encourage teachers to continually observe the language skills of attending children. Each child and group may have different needs, and the center attempts to fulfill needs and offer a language arts program that will be growth producing and enriching. Many different observation methods and instruments can be used. Some may be school-designed; others may be commercially produced.

A teacher who is a keen observer and listener gathers information, which guides teacher actions and planning. In their efforts to make an activity relevant, teachers observe attending children's needs, desires, and interests and make individual judgments regarding children's already acquired knowledge, attitudes, and language skills. Educators believe that assessing beyond children's level of performance by looking at ways children learn and interact provides a much richer portrait of children than just identifying levels of skill. As teachers observe, some try to answer the following questions.

- What individual language characteristics are present?
- How can activities be planned that capture and hold children's interest and enthusiasm?
- How do my actions and behaviors affect the children's language arts behaviors?
- Which children are interested in which indoor and outdoor areas?
- What patterns of language behavior have I noticed?
- What do children seem eager to talk about or explore?
- What can I do to provide experience or exploration just beyond what they already know?
- Which children readily express their ideas?
- Which children are socially adept and learn language in play with others?

Assessment is a continual, ongoing process. Observation information is confidential and often useful in program planning. Running accounts of child conversations are difficult to obtain because an adult's presence may affect a child's spontaneity. Also, the child's attention span and mobility make it almost impossible to capture more than a few minutes of speech with preschoolers. Many teachers note a few phrases or speech characteristics on a writing pad they carry with them throughout the day. For many teachers, having time just to observe children is considered a luxury. However, observation is important and can be considered an ongoing teacher responsibility in all areas of instruction.

To ensure a language program's quality, plans are changed, updated, and revised based on both the children's progress and staff members' evaluations and observations. Keeping a planned language arts program vital, dynamic, appealing, and appropriate requires continual revision and overhaul.

## GOAL STATEMENTS

A particular center may have many or few goal statements, which can be both general and specific.

If standards exist and affect an early childhood program, goals are often identified and listed. Privately funded early childhood programs in most states may choose to look at standards statements but some schools may decide to not incorporate them into their planned program goals and instead develop their own.

### Goals for Children's Writing Development

In the process of literacy development, young children can profit from an understanding of the role of the printed word. The uses of writing, including recording and transmitting information, recording self-authored creations, and providing entertainment, are important to the quality of human life. Knowing and understanding how writing is used may lead to a realization of the value of learning to read. Writing and reading open each individual to the thoughts, creations, and discoveries of multitudes of people, living and deceased. This discussion is not intended to promote formal early printing instruction but rather to point out that there are basic ideas about writing that must be considered when planning a language arts curriculum that promotes literacy. Figure 6–10 displays one activity that introduces

**FIGURE 6–10** Printed words may accompany new objects in early childhood classrooms.

children to print. Chapter 16 covers print and writing development and programming ideas in detail.

There is a strong connection between the child's familiarity with books (and her book-reading experiences) and literacy. Illustrations of the reasons for writing and how writing can satisfy everyday needs can be incorporated into any center's goals for promoting literacy growth.

Most schools concentrate on exposing children to printed words rather than beginning actual writing skill practice in alphabet letter formation.

## Prereading Goals

Reading skills are multiple and complex and they often involve the coordination of other skills and abilities. Some reading goals that will facilitate later reading skills follow.

- Reads pictures
- Shows an interest in and enjoyment of stories and books
- Is able to arrange pictures in a sequence that tells a story
- Finds hidden objects in pictures
- Guesses at meanings based on contextual cues
- Reads own and others' names
- Predicts events
- Recognizes letters of own name in other words
- Senses left-right direction
- Guesses words to complete sentences
- Chooses favorite book characters
- Treats books with care
- Authors own books through dictation
- Sees finely detailed differences
- Recognizes and names alphabet letters at times
- Shows interest in libraries
- Shows interest in the sounds of letters
- Watches or uses puppets to enact simple stories
- Has background in traditional literature appropriate for age and ability
- Develops phonemic awareness

## Goals That Promote Early Literacy

Preschool teachers planning and conducting programs that promote language development in young children try to provide a "classic" literary experience, featuring appropriate age-level materials collected from many cultures and eras. Such a curriculum would serve as a basis of human cultural understanding and would include a wide range of oral and listening materials and activities: books, poetry, language games, puppetry, and storytelling. Most teachers believe that early exposure to and familiarity with literary classics can help the child understand what might be encountered later in literature, media, or schooling.

At present, a widely circulated list of classics for preschool children has not been available, but a list of these works has existed in the minds and hearts of individual teachers. Mother Goose stories are undisputed classics. Two other agreed-upon classic stories are *Goldilocks and the Three Bears* and *Peter Rabbit*. Chapters 9 and 17 present in-depth discussions in this planning area. Whether a story, play, rhyme, or song is considered a "classic," however, is usually a matter of judgment by individual teachers.

## Sociocultural Language Goals

Are there important goals teachers need to consider in a democratic society? Many sources suggest the following:

Goal #1: All students are able to communicate effectively with all persons within a multicultural, diverse society.

Goal #2: All students learn to value linguistic diversity and celebrate the cultural expressions of those who are different from themselves.

Goal #3: All students see the value of language and literacy for their own lives.

Early childhood educators can lay the groundwork and monitor attitudes and feelings that in any way degrade other-than-mainstream-language speakers.

A language arts curriculum should include language activities that celebrate cultural diversity. Family and community literacy activities are important considerations. Family stories and literacy-promoting activities and events can be included in center planning. Collaboration with parents reinforces the unique contributions families and neighborhoods make to child literacy growth.

## LANGUAGE ARTS CURRICULA

Many early childhood **curriculum models** exist. Some are well known; others are little known. Models usually provide well-defined frameworks to guide program implementation. Child development theories are their underlying foundation. Whether a particular model, a combination of models, or an eclectic model is used, early childhood educators are constantly challenged to examine, reflect, and improve children's daily language arts experiences.

Schools and centers differ widely in **curriculum** development; however, two basic approaches can be identified. In the first, a unit or thematic approach emerges from identified child interest and teacher-selected areas, such as families, seasons, animals, and so on. Using this approach, some centers use children's books or classic nursery rhymes as their thematic starting topic. Others introduce a proposed theme (unit) topic to small discussion groups of children. This offers input from attending children and lets teachers explore children's past experience, knowledge, and interests. Questions children ask and vocabulary used may aid teachers' thematic unit development. Staff and parent group discussion can also uncover attitudes and resources. Goals are considered, and activities are then outlined and scheduled into time slots. Many teachers believe this type of program approach individualizes instruction by providing many interrelated and, consequently, reinforced understandings while also allowing the child to select activities.

The second common instructional approach is to pinpoint traditional preschool subject areas, such as language arts, science, mathematics, art, cooking, and so forth, and then plan how many and what kind of planned activities will take place. This can be done with or without considering a unifying theme. Some teachers believe that this is a more systematic approach to instruction.

In both approaches, the identification of goals has come before curriculum development.

Ages of children, staffing ratios, facility resources, and other particulars all affect planning. After planned curriculum activities take place, teachers evaluate whether goals were reached and modifications and suggestions are noted. Additional or follow-up activities may be planned and scheduled for groups or individual children.

### Thematic Inquiry Approach to Language Instruction

Imagine a classroom turned into a pizza parlor or a flower garden. There would be a number of activities occurring simultaneously—some for small groups, others for large groups, and some for individuals. Teachers would be involved in activities, and classroom areas might be set up for continuous, or almost continuous, child exploration. Art, singing, number, movement, science-related, health-related, safety-related, and other types of activities would (or could) be preplanned, focusing on the two themes mentioned previously. Bintz (2010) reminds teachers that singing has long been used as an instructional strategy in literacy development.

The sensory activities could be included so that children could experience the smells, sounds, sights, tastes, and so on, associated with each theme. Planning language arts instruction using this approach allows teachers to use creativity and imagination.

It is an integrated approach to curriculum and takes advantage of the natural relationship between developmental domains and between content areas (Koralek, 2008), Koralek explains

> When curriculum is integrated, children can explore a theme in depth, achieve early learning standards, and apply their knowledge in meaningful ways. They learn facts related to a specific topic, ways to find information, and how content areas are related. p. 10.

---

**curriculum models** — refers to a conceptual framework and organizational structure for decision making about educational priorities, administrative policies, instructional methods, and evaluation criteria.
**curriculum** — an overall plan for the content of instruction to be offered in a program.

Theme instruction requires planning time to gather and set up material that might not be found in the school storeroom or supply area. It is easy to see that there could be many opportunities for children's use of speech, listening, reading, and writing, and the natural connection among these activities might be more apparent to the children. Most teachers believe that using a thematic approach is an exciting challenge that is well worth teacher time and effort. They see this approach as one that encourages child-teacher conversations and consequently expands children's language usage and knowledge.

Teachers should not limit their program to traditional themes but should explore and discover beyond the familiar. Teachers can follow children's curiosity and their own childhood interests. Many centers believe that real teaching is found when each staff member gives children what she individually has to offer from the heart as well as the mind.

Considerable staff brainstorming and discussion takes place when deciding which theme topics are suitable, feasible, appropriate, and educationally advantageous for their particular child group and facility.

In constructing a theme, the following steps are usually undertaken.

1. Observe and record a child's interest and/ or teacher drawing from past experience.

2. Identify a topic. (It could be a book, poem, drama, or another category.)

3. Try to discover what children know and want to know.

4. Imagine possible activities (in and out of school).

5. Decide on attempted goals of instruction.

6. Pinpoint range, scope, vocabulary, main ideas, and activities.

7. Discuss room environment, staffing, visitors, and helpers. (What will take place in the classroom or yard or in learning centers?)

8. Make specific plans for individual and group activities.

9. List the necessary materials and supplies.

10. Decide on a culminating activity (usually a recap or "grand finale").

11. Set a timetable if necessary. (Daily schedules may be prepared.)

12. Pinpoint evaluation criteria.

Nemeth (2009) suggests pinpointing key vocabulary words in any instructional theme, and then creating a key word list (with a pronunciation guide) in each attending children's home language. This may sound a daunting task but doing so enables the teacher to connect a word a child already knows to a new English word and, learn a few new words in another language herself.

Williams (1997) uses a four-step child-teacher interactive process to jointly plan unit (theme) activities for a group of 4-year-olds. A description of these steps follows.

1. The teacher asks, "What do you wonder?" or "What do you want to know about— (a particular topic, example: the ocean)?" Then the teacher records each child's answer or question in a different color on a wall chart that is posted at the children's eye level. Then the teacher adds her own questions.

2. The teacher asks, "What can we do to find out?" Then the teacher records the children's ideas on a second piece of chart paper. If no one responded, that is acceptable. The teacher instead develops a list of children's questions or ideas that might come up while the unit is in progress, and these are added to the chart.

3. The teacher asks, "What materials do we need?" on a prepared third chart. Materials suggested by the children that do not seem directly related are gently probed by teacher. A child may have a connection to the topic of study not readily seen by the teacher.

4. The teacher asks, "What will you bring (do)?" and "What would you like me to bring (to do)?" The teacher checks with parents about objects and materials suggested by their child. A parent newsletter invites parents to share or bring in additional topic-related items to the classroom.

To promote literacy, teachers think about how each theme activity involves listening, speaking, reading, and writing and how to logically connect these areas during ongoing activities.

With current public and educator interest in standards and accountability, an increasing number of programs must document theme goal attainment and identify successful instructional strategies. Although this can be done many ways, it most frequently involves the collecting and recording of multiple pieces of evidence of theme activities, lessons, events, and classroom experiences. Children's work samples and participation might be captured using a variety of strategies including the technology available. Before, during, and after photos, videos, slides, movies and artifacts together with teacher observations of groups and individual children may illustrate children's engagement and learning. Seltz (2008) defines a documenter as a researcher, collecting as much information as possible to paint a picture of progress and outcomes. He believes that often the documentation provides insights into children's thinking and helps drive further curriculum planning.

## Brain-based Learning and Theme Instruction

What should teachers keep in mind while using a theme instruction approach, traditional approach or a brain-based learning approach?

1. Periodic repetition of theme information and ideas can aid children's learning. Medina (2008) suggests reviewing newly learned material. He states

   Memory may not be fixed at the moment of learning, but repetition, doled out in specifically timed intervals, is the fixative. p. 130.

2. Talking about an event *immediately* after it has occurred helps children's memory of the event. Teachers can promote children's recollections by suggesting they talk about a discovery or learning event that has just occurred.

3. Offer real objects or second-best, pictures that accompany new vocabulary words during theme instruction. Students learn better with pictures or real objects present than from words alone (Medina, 2008).

4. It is best not to interrupt a child trying to complete a task. Wait until a child looks for help or there is a level of frustration to intervene.

5. Children need time to digest information especially when there is lots of new information. Providing time to think things over is a good idea, then revisit new learning.

6. The brain is unable to pay attention to two things at once. Learning stations, centers, or separate room area can be the best way to prepare the learning environment. Eliminate visual and sound room distractions when child focus or concentration is expected.

7. Create attention-attracting activities or centers. Children do not pay attention to boring things.

8. Planning for children's sensory involvement in activities is a good idea. Children learn best if their sense of sight, hearing, touching, feeling, and even their sense of smell is present. In other words, teachers should consider stimulating several senses at once (Medina, 2008).

## Thematic/Literature-Based Instruction

Literature-based instruction, now mandated or recommended in elementary schools in many states, is very similar to what early childhood educators call thematic instruction. Both levels realize the value of literature and its relationship to literacy. A theme in early childhood could be any topic of interest to children. A literacy-based approach uses a classic book or informational book as its central core. A preschool educator would have no problem using a book as a starting place and could plan discussions, drama, art, music, puppetry, and other language arts activities to strengthen various concepts encountered.

## Curriculum Webs and Webbing

The use of curriculum webs (or **webbing**) in program planning is popular with some preschool teachers (Figure 6–11). A web can be thought of as a graphic overall picture of what

**webbing** — a visual or graphic method of mapping a possible course of study.

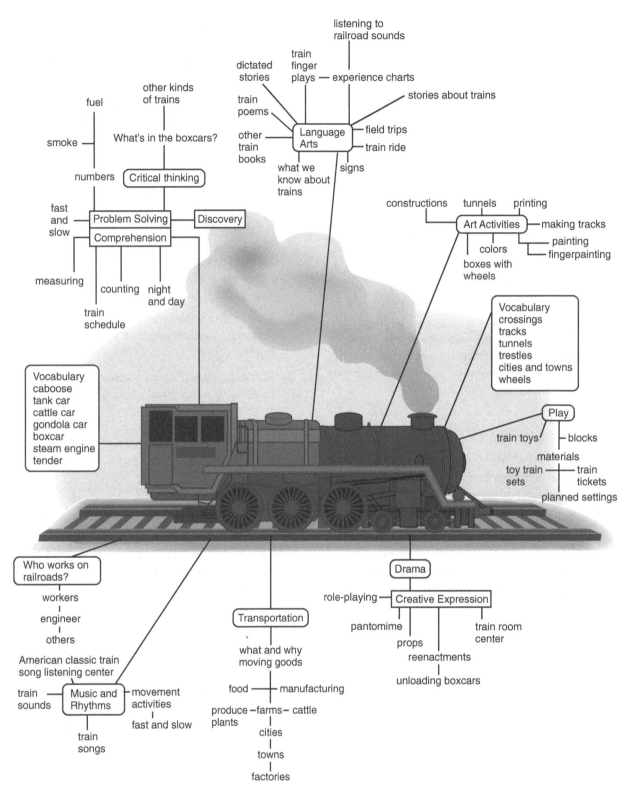

**FIGURE 6–11** This webbing example suits a theme based on a picture book about trains, such as Donald Crew's book, *Freight Train*.

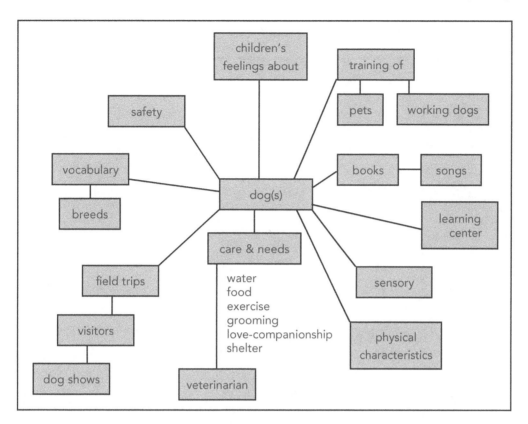

**FIGURE 6–12** Topic web—dog(s).

might be included in a theme or unit approach to instruction. Figure 6–12 shows a skeleton web designed for the study of dogs. Under the box "care & needs" one can think of a number of items that could be listed. In fact, the web could become highly detailed as the teacher using it listed concepts associated with the subject—dogs. The object of creating a web is for the teacher to define and refine the web based on the interests and needs of the particular enrolled group. The plan (web) is then translated into planned daily happenings with children's active exploring and participation (Figure 6–13). The goal is to offer activities to engage the students' interest and imagination and to spark their desire to seek out answers, ponder questions, or create responses). One of the rewards of teaching is to present or set up an activity that children eagerly select, and perhaps ask a million questions about; in other words, one that has "captured" them and engaged their minds (Figure 6–14).

Webbing is described by one staff member as follows: "To create a plan we choose an idea, brainstorm hands-on activities, and put them on a web. This gives us a sort of road map. It's a process rather than a product."

Translating a web into a week by week teaching overview or plan is the next step and is unique to each program. If daily lesson plans are developed, activities or lessons would be written in greater detail and could include the following steps.

● Naming the activity;
● Naming the curriculum area;
● Identifying room location and set up necessary;
● Identifying the number of children and teaching staff present;
● Listing necessary preparation;
● Identifying a goal or objective or standard involved (an example of a multiple goal approach is seen in Figure 6–15);
● Identifying the developmental skills necessary for child success;
● Describing opening teacher statements;
● Describing key concepts, facts, skills, vocabulary, etc.;

## OPENING: CHOOSE ONE DOG STICKER FOR YOUR NAME TAG OR TAKE-HOME FILE (STICKERS OF DOG BREEDS)

**Large-group Instruction**

a. Discussion

Update and review of theme findings and discoveries so far

b. Chart introduction

Different dog breeds have names

Checking opening stickers

Finding similarities and differences

c. Composing

Writing an invitation to a guest speaker—the dog groomer

Requesting a description and, when possible, a demonstration of the dog-care techniques and tools.

d. Song: "Bingo"

Chant: "The Diners in the Kitchen" by James Whitcomb Riley

Poem: "My Puppy" by Aileen Fisher

**Small-group Instruction**

a. Story time: "Harry the Dirty Dog" by G. Zion or "Dogs" by Dorling Kindersley (2005)

Discussion

Care of dogs

Can dogs do small jobs or work?

Working dog photos

**Discovery Time Choices**

a. Art

Construct a dog and label using clay or body-part cutouts to paste and label them with the teacher's help

b. Sorting

Assorted dog bones by color, size, and shape

c. Science

How do dogs differ from one another? Examining hair from a variety of dogs and giving each a descriptive label—curly, black, spotted, long, etc.

d. Construction

Making and decorating a large-box doghouse with the teacher's help

e. Cooking and measurement

Making homemade dog bones by reading a recipe chart

f. Writing center

Dictation of a story about a dog, or choosing to do a naming-seven-puppies activity

g. Listening Center

Firehouse dog story on tape

"Bert the Bird Dog" recording

h. Library Center

A selection of books about dogs

i. Yard activities

Exploring walking on all fours

Making dog prints on long paper rolls using sponges or potato prints (teacher directed and supervised)

Hiding-rubber-bones game

Trying to lap water from a bowl (teacher supervised)

Playing with a doghouse construction

**FIGURE 6–13** One-day plan during a weekly theme study of dogs (4-year-olds' classroom).

● Describing how the activity will proceed to conclusion;

● Describing how practice or applying or reinforcing learning might take place;

● Planning clean up;

● Planning a transition; and

● Describing how the activity, teacher or child learning might be assessed or evaluated.

To examine a sample language activity planning form see Figure 6–16.

Theme planning needs to take into account the English language learners in the class. Nemeth (2009) urges teachers to allow extra theme days for children not only learning new theme words, concepts, and skills but also English. She points out themes can contribute to the scaffolding of language learning while also encouraging the use of English. She suggest adding home language words to classroom labels by color coding them, such as Spanish words in red ink, Chinese in green and so on. This system of coding by color, Nemeth suggests, can also be used with stickers in the classroom book storage and reading areas to identify other than English-only books.

### Reggio Emilia

Early childhood educators studying the Reggio Emilia approach to program planning are re-examining their curriculum. Gandini (1997)

**FIGURE 6–14** Creating a sense of wonder and discovery is among the goals of a quality program.

describes the teacher's role in the Reggio Emilia approach.

> To know how to plan or proceed with their work, teachers observe and listen to the children closely. Teachers use the understanding they gain in this way to act as a resource for them. They ask questions and discover the children's ideas, hypotheses, and theories. Then the adults discuss together what they have recorded through their own notes, or audio or visual recordings, and make flexible plans and preparations. Then they are ready to enter again into dialogues with the children and offer them occasions for discovering and also revisiting experiences since they consider learning not as a linear process but as spiral progression. (p. 216)

Gardner (1999) identifies how a Reggio Emilia curriculum develops.

> The educators of Reggio Emilia have developed and continuously improved a set of techniques for taking the ideas and actions of young children seriously. Much thought is devoted to the opening exposure to experiences that might constitute themes to be developed in the coming weeks. But it is not possible to plan such a curriculum in advance. Rather, the particular reactions of particular children to particular experiences become the bedrock, the driving force of the "curriculum." The activities of next week (sometimes even the next day) grow out of the results, problems, and puzzles of this week; the cycle is repeated so long as it proves fruitful. Children and teachers are continually reflecting on the meaning of an activity, which issues it raises, how its depths and range can be productively probed. (p. 202)

## The Project Approach

The project approach involves integrated teaching and learning. It encourages meaningful, first-hand, relevant study of child-teacher–developed and child-teacher–chosen activities. This program approach is valued by teachers for its flexible and creative aspects, which fit diverse child groups and geographical communities. Children are involved in decision making, program planning, implementation, and evaluation through active teacher-child shared discussion, brainstorming, and project outlining. Teachers also

NOTE: This is a portion of a longer description. The words in italics show how the teacher works toward a variety of goals.

This episode is an account of a sequence of planned activities culminating in a cooking experience for four four-year-old children. Part 1 of the episode details the preparation in the classroom for the purchase of the food and the group's trip to a local store. Part 2 describes the cooking.

The fresh pears at lunch evoked the excited comment "Apples!" from Spanish-speaking Fernando.

"Well, this is a fruit," said Miss Gordon, encouragingly, "but it has another name. Do you remember the apples we had last week?"

"They were hard to bite," said Joey.

"And we made applesauce," said Rosina.

"This fruit is called a pear, Fernando; let's taste this pear now. We'll have apples again."

*The teacher responds to what is correct in the child's response, valuing his category association. First, she wants to support communication and willingness to experiment with language; later she gives the correct name. The children strengthen the experience by relating it to previous experience in which they were active.*

"Mine's soft," said Joey.

"Can we make applesauce again?" begged Rosina.

The teacher replied, "Perhaps we could do what Janice wanted to do. Remember? To take some home to her family?"

"To my mommy, and my grandma, and Danny."

"Not to my baby," said Rosina. "He's too little. Him only drink milk."

"Tomorrow we'll buy lots of apples," said Miss Gordon.

*The teacher is building a sense of continuity by recalling earlier intentions that had been expressed by the children.*

*She rarely corrects use of pronouns for four-year-olds. She knows the child will learn through greater social maturity and hearing language.*

After rest, Miss Gordon asked the children how they could take home their applesauce. "What can we put it in?"

Rosina ran to the house corner and returned with two baby food jars. "I bringed lots," she said. Miss Gordon remembered that Rosina had come to school lugging a bag full of baby food jars, many of which she had put away. "A good idea! And your mommy said she would keep more for us. Let's write a note to tell her we need them tomorrow."

Rosina dictated a note: "I got to bring bunches of jars to school. We are going to make applesauce. I love you, Mommy." Rosina painted her name with a red marker.

*The teacher helps children to think ahead to steps in a process.*

*The use of a tense form, although incorrect, represents learning for the child. The teacher does not correct at this moment, when she is responding to the child's pleasure in solving the practical problem that had been posed. She is strengthening the connection between home and school.*

*The teacher helps the children learn that writing is a recording of meaning and a way of communicating.*

The next day was jar washing and arranging time. Each of the four children put his or her jars on a tray on which there was a large card with the child's name.

Janice put on one jar for her mother, one for her grandmother, one for her brother, and after a pause, one for herself.

Rosina changed her mind. "My baby can have a little tiny bit," she said. So she needed a jar for her father, her mother, her baby, and herself.

Joey and the teacher figured out that he needed six, and that Fernando needed nine!

*The children are actively involved in the steps preparatory to the planned activity—an experience in organization that has personal meaning.*

*The teacher's plan calls for recognition of one's own name and one-to-one counting of family members.*

The teacher turned their attention to a chart near the cooking corner. She had made a recipe chart, pasting colored (magazine) pictures next to the names of the items they would need to make the applesauce and had taped a stick of cinnamon to the chart.

Miss Gordon said, "Let's look at the recipe chart. I have a list so we can remember to buy everything."

The children said, "Apples."

Miss Gordon checked her list.

Then, "Sugar."

The children were silent as they looked at the stick of cinnamon taped to the chart.

Miss Gordon suggested, "Smell it. Have we had it before?"

Joey remembered: "Toast! What we put on toast!"

"Yes," said Miss Gordon, and then gave the word, "cinnamon."

*The children are having a dual experience—pictorial representation and formal symbol usage.*

*The teacher supplies the word after the children have revived their direct experience with the phenomenon.*

(Biber, Shapiro, & Wickens, 1977).

**FIGURE 6–15** Multiple-goal approach.

## LANGUAGE ACTIVITY PLAN GUIDE

1. Language activity title _____

2. Materials needed _____

3. Location of activity (to be used when plan is developed for a particular classroom or area) _____

4. Number of children _____

5. Language goal or objective _____

6. Preparation (necessary teacher preparation, including getting materials or objects, visual aids, etc., ready) _____

7. Getting started (introductory and/or motivational statement) _____

8. Show and explore (include possible teacher questions or statements that promote language ability) _____

9. Discussion of key points, discoveries, conclusions, subjects for further study (what vocabulary and/or concepts might be included?) _____

10. Apply (include child practice or application of newly learned knowledge or skill when appropriate) _____

11. Transition statement (needed if activity plan is to terminate or if a second activity immediately follows) _____

12. Evaluation: (1) activity; (2) teacher; (3) child participation; (4) other aspects such as setting, materials, outcomes, etc. _____

**FIGURE 6–16** Sample activity plan form.

plan activities and experiences. Children are urged to explore and investigate and become testers of ideas as individuals and in study groups. Teachers using thematic unit instruction may feel the project approach best suits kindergarten and elementary-aged children. Others have incorporated projects into preschool curriculum.

## COMMITMENT TO GOALS AND OBJECTIVES

A number of factors determine whether program goals are met.

- Enthusiasm and commitment of staff
- Staffing ratios
- Staff ingenuity and resourcefulness
- Methods and techniques used
- Resources available
- General feeling or tone of center
- Examination of sequence (easy to complex)
- Parental and community support

Effort and staff creativity translate goals into daily activities.

### Daily Activity Plans (Lesson Plans)

Recognizing children's interests stimulates activity-planning ideas based on what captures and holds the children's attention. Part of the challenge and excitement of teaching is finding ways to be creative in daily activity planning.

Although two staff members work toward the same goal, they may approach the task in different ways. Lesson plans are more frequently used in schools using approaches other than the thematic (unit) approach described earlier but can also be used for individual teacher-conducted activities within theme planning.

Lesson plans (or **activity plans**) enable teachers to foresee needs—settings, materials, and staffing. The time that children spend waiting can be minimized. Some teachers pinpoint exactly what words and concepts will be emphasized or what questions asked; other teachers prefer a more spontaneous approach.

Some activities in language arts may require teacher practice beforehand. Others may require visual aids or materials that must be gathered in advance. Planning time is time well spent. Preparation reduces teacher tension and results in child activities that run smoothly.

Teachers must strive to be always aware of child safety and comfort. They must also try to maintain a reasonable level of stimulation somewhere between not very interesting and overly exciting activities so that children are encouraged to process information in a manner that is both pleasurable and efficient. Experienced teachers know when children are interested and are actively participating. Many teachers say this is one of the greatest joys of teaching.

Group size is an important factor in planning. It is easier for teachers to plan for an entire class group, and sometimes staffing demands it. However, many teachers have explored ways to keep children occupied and supervised while working with small groups. Small groups allow greater intimacy, conversational depth, and opportunity for feedback. Research substantiates the idea that both children and adults feel more comfortable sharing their thoughts when in small groups. "Instant replays" with small groups can be planned and coordinated. Beginning preschool teachers may not have seen many small group activities modeled by other teachers, but this text recommends them.

Teachers strive to maintain children's attention during activities. Teachers realize that attention is mediated by specific parts of the brain and that neural systems fatigue quickly. After 3 to 5 minutes of sustained activity, children need to rest, but they can recover within minutes too. In a familiar and safe classroom, if a child hears factual information for only 4 to 8 minutes and a teacher is not providing novelty, the brain seeks other stimuli. Perry (2000) recommends adding "emotional seasoning" like humor and empathy to teacher presentations and linking facts to related child concepts during activities, in addition to taking advantage of the novelty-seeking property of the human brain. He believes this is a challenging task for teachers of all-aged students. Medina (2008), the author of *Brain Rules*, urges educators using lesson plans to cover and explain one core concept at a time in clear and explicit terms and later connect details during

---

**activity plans** — written, detailed, step-by-step teaching plans, often including an evaluation section.

the activity or discussion. He suggests presenting key ideas in a hierarchical fashion and forming details around larger concepts. See Step 9 on Figure 6–16.

Brain research suggests educators provide down time lasting a few minutes in cognitive activities. This could be physical movement such as stretching, deep breathing or other movement (Jensen, 2008). Teachers should plan to do so when planned activities requiring focusing and concentration go beyond planned time estimates.

Activities based on teacher enthusiasm for life and growth, skills, talents, hobbies, and pursuits can fit beautifully into language arts goals. Family and community resources, including borrowed items and field trips, increase the vitality of programs.

## Evaluation

Thinking back over planned activities helps teachers analyze the benefits and possibly leads to additional planning along the same line or with the same theme. Oversights in planning frequently occur, and activities may develop in unexpected ways. Hindsight is a useful and valuable tool in evaluating activities (Figure 6–17).

Often, centers evaluate their planned programs by asking themselves questions such as the following:

● Do children share personal interests and learning discoveries with teachers and/or other children?

● Can teachers enter conversations without diminishing children's verbal initiative?

● Do children become involved in planned activities and room centers?

● Are there times when children listen with interest?

● Are language arts areas (speaking, writing, reading, and listening) connected in a natural way during daily activities?

● Is child talk abundant?

Currently, the accountability of a program's quality and value has become an issue and has resulted in the development of content and performance standards. Consequently, programs are frequently required to develop some type of formalized method of assessment.

**THINKING BACK**

What I planned and how I went about it:

What effect my actions had:

What I could have done:

What effect this action would have had:

What I will do differently next time:

FIGURE 6–17 Thinking back.

## SUMMARY

Traditionally, language arts instruction and planning have been based on the educational theories educators believed to be the best and effective. Historically, theories have, over time, changed, evolved, and emerged. Theorists' and researchers' ideas have been accepted and then come into vogue. Currently, research and brain-based learning information has influenced federal legislation and publicly funded schools.

Language is part of every preschool activity. This text recommends an integrated approach to early childhood language arts, that is, a program that involves the areas of listening, speaking, writing, reading, and viewing.

Public centers identify language arts goals through a group process and consider standards. Activities are then planned. Approaches to activity planning are reviewed. Daily plans carry out what is intended. Assessment instruments are evaluated, and decisions are made concerning whether these instruments are to be used or not used. Staff observation provides data on children's abilities, interests, and skill levels, as well as additional insights that are useful in activity planning. Developing literacy portfolios is but one way to display and assess children's growth. Every center has a unique set of goals and objectives. Designing child experiences is done in a variety of ways. Program plans consider attending children's needs and interests.

Evaluating a planned activity after it is presented can pinpoint strengths and weaknesses. This also serves as the basis for further activity planning.

## ADDITIONAL RESOURCES

### Readings

Cassidy, J., Valadez, C.M., & Garrett, S. D. (2010). Literacy trends and issues: A look at the five pillars and the cement that supports them. *The Reading Teacher.* 63(8) 644–655.

Enz, B. J., & Morrow, L. M. (2009). *Assessing preschool literacy development.* Newark, DE: International Reading Association.

Labo, L. D., Love, M. S., Prior, M. P., Hubbard, B. P., & Ryan, T. (2006). *Literature links: Thematic units linking read-alouds and computer activities.* Newark, DE: International Reading Association.

Landry, S. H., Effective early childhood programs. Turning knowledge into action. In A. R. Tarlov & M. P. Debbink (Eds.).(2008). *Investing in early childhood development: Evidence to support a movement for educational change.* New York: Palgrave Macmillian.

Seefeldt, C. (2005). *How to work with standards in early childhood classrooms.* New York: Teachers College Press.

### Helpful Websites

National Association for the Education of Young Children
http://www.naeyc.org
Includes extensive information about standards and program planning.

National Reading Panel
http://www.nationalreadingpanel.org
Reports research-based instructional practices for young children.

International Reading Association
www.reading.org
Check out publications and position statements such as Developing Essential Literacy Skills (2008) or Assessing Preschool Literacy Development: Informal and Formal Measures to Guide Instruction (2009).

Go to www.cengagebrain.com to access this text's Education Course-Mate website where you'll find helpful resource such as video activities, glossary flashcards, interactive exercises, quiz questions, and more!

# Review It and Use It

A. Name the four interrelated language arts areas, arranging them in what you believe is their order of appearance in young children. Include the visual literacy area in your discussion.

B. Write three language arts goal statements (what you would want children to have the opportunity to experience and learn). These should be statements that would be included in a program where you are (or will be) employed.

C. Select the best or correct answer.

1. Assessment instruments can be
   a. a checklist.
   b. a child interest inventory.
   c. teacher made.
   d. all the above

2. Compiling and identifying a center's goal statements ideally involves
   a. children's input.
   b. each staff members ideas rather than consensus
   c. parents wishes only
   d. study and professional judgment

3. Early childhood language arts should be offered to children using
   a. an approach that helps children see relationships between areas.
   b. techniques that please teachers.
   c. separate times of day to explore reading and writing without combining these skills.
   d. lesson plan forms or a commercially planned course of study.

4. When goals are identified, a school (or center) should
   a. stick to its written goals even if parents object because the school's staff is qualified.
   b. lose its ability to fulfill children's individual needs if the same activity plans are used from year to year.
   c. keep its program "personal" by continually interviewing attending children.
   d. periodically take a close look at goals.

5. Using commercial assessment instruments
   a. is always best.
   b. serves as the only basis of professional programming.
   c. means using teacher-designed assessments is out of the question.
   d. none of the above.

6. "There is only one correct way to plan and present activities to children." This statement is
    a. true.
    b. false.
    c. true because each individual teacher strives to find the one plan that helps planned activities run smoothly and successfully.
    d. correct because the plan itself ensures success or goal realization.

D. List what positive advantages might be accomplished if a child's literacy portfolio is developed during the child's preschool years.

## STUDENT ACTIVITIES

1. Define literacy in your own words or discuss changes in what skills and knowledge are now required to function in the present "computer age." Share with the class.

2. Bintz (2010) urges preschool teachers to use singing activities as a strategy to increase vocabulary or content area learning. Using the theme trains (Figure 6–11) create a song that promotes vocabulary or concept learning. Make up your own tune or borrow a common melody and write lyrics. Be ready to teach your creation to your classmates

3. Form two groups of five students. Each group takes from 5 to 10 minutes preparing their reaction to the reading that follows.

   Quote from Lily Casey Smith

   I never met a kid I could not teach. Every kid was good at something, and the trick was to find out what it was, then use it to teach him everything else. It was good work, the kind of work that lets you sleep soundly at night and look forward to the next day. (p. 63)

   (Walls, Jeanette. (2009). *Half Broke Horses*. New York: Scribner)

   Students in the audience are to identify key statements made by either group.

4. Using any activity plan form, make a written plan for a language development activity. Share your plan with others at the next class meeting. Rate the quality of your participation in the discussion using the following scale (or write a beginning outline for a theme of your own choosing or one that you believe would be of interest to a group of 4-year-old children). Then share your theme idea or lesson plan at the next class meeting.

   No Input
   Very Little
   Contributed about as Much as Classmates
   A Fair Amount
   Offered Lots of Ideas

5. Look back into your childhood before age 6. What classics, songs, rhymes, and language arts activities did you experience? If you do not remember, answer this alternative question: Which literacy-promoting language activities should not be missed by any child? Be specific, and name poems, books, rhymes, stories, or other literary experiences.

## Individual Activity:

### Understanding Locational Words

Note: This is a self-selected child activity set up during a study of transportation for a class of 3- and 4-year-olds. It is also a review activity for location words. A waiting list is available, so children are ensured a turn.

**Purpose:** The child will be able to place vehicle "under," "over," "behind," and "in front of" when given verbal directions after becoming familiar with the words in the play situation.

**Materials:** streets and a highway drawn on a large sheet of paper taped to a table; toy vehicles (car, truck, school bus, van, etc.); blocks, a box, or cardboard to make a highway overpass.

**Procedure:**

1. Place a box with toy vehicles inside in front of the child. "Tell me about what you find in the box." Verbally label each vehicle if the child does not.

2. Pause and let the child talk about the toy vehicles. Introduce overpass and discuss "under" and "over" the bridge.

3. "We're going to take turns. First, I'm going to ask you to put the vehicles in different places. Then, you tell me where you want me to place one of the vehicles."

4. "Can you drive the car under the bridge?" Encourage the child if necessary. Pause. "Which vehicle do you want me to drive under the bridge? Is it the bus or another one?"

5. "My turn. Drive the truck over the bridge." Pause. "Which one do you want me to drive over the bridge?"

6. "Put the bus in front of the car." "Which one do you want me to move in front of the bus?"

7. Proceed until all four location words are introduced and demonstrated. Then, "Tell me where you choose to drive or park the toys. I'll watch you."

8. Allow the child time to play as she wishes. As the child continues with the activity, add comments when appropriate, such as, "You drove the van under the bridge."

## Group Activity:

### Visual Perception*

**Purpose:** matching identical stockings game

**Materials:** enough matching pairs of stockings for each child in the group (more pairs if possible); socks of any size but different in color or pattern; two bags (separate, putting one sock of each pair in bags); plastic zip lunch bags

**Procedure:**
Additional activity ideas include:

1. Discussing stockings by examining the differences in socks children are wearing. Talking about how socks are kept together at home, whether a stocking has been lost, and if one visited their home, where stockings are found.

2. Introducing intact pairs in a basket. "To play our game, we need to select one pair from the basket, and then put one sock in one of the provided bags and the second in the other bag. We'll take turns. Mary, choose a pair of socks and tell us something about the pair you choose." Give each child a turn.

3. Putting socks in pairs. "Now we can start our game. I'm going to mix them all together and make a big pile of stockings, and then we'll try to find two stockings

*Activity from the theme—*Home Helpers.*

that are the same and put them in a plastic lunch bag so that we can keep each pair together. When you find two that match raise your hand. Here is the plastic lunch bag. Keep the socks you've found and put each pair in a plastic sack in front of you." Continue taking turns until all socks are paired. Count or discuss sock pairs, color, size, pattern, and so on.

**Reinforcement Activities:**

1. Turn this group activity into an individual activity in which one child can pair all the socks. A standing clothes rack or a clothesline can be used.

2. Mittens or shoes can also be matched in a similar group activity. The closer the distinctions are, the more difficult the task will be.

## OBJECTIVES

After reading this chapter, you should be able to:

- List three roles of a teacher in early childhood language education.

- Discuss the balances needed in teacher behavior.

- Describe ways a teacher can promote language growth.

## KEY TERMS

closure           explanatory talk
expansion       extension

## Children's Literacy Portfolios

*Miss Powell, a kindergarten teacher, planned a home visit to each entering child in her fall kindergarten class. At one home, a mother proudly shared the child's preschool literacy portfolio. Miss Powell was able to sit with both her soon-to-be student and the child's mother as they both commented on items in the binder. She found the child was reading a few words and had a huge interest in cats. Although she knew her district would test each child after school started, she was delighted with this home visit.*

### Questions to Ponder

1. How can Miss Powell put to good use the information she now has about this child?

2. Would you suggest that a child literacy portfolio be part of this child's kindergarten experience also?

A good description of a skilled early childhood educator is a "responsive opportunist" who is enthusiastic, who enjoys discovery, and who is able to establish and maintain a warm, supportive environment. An educator is also one who tries to build language, literacy, brain power, and emotional connection (Bardige, 2009). When a reciprocal relationship between a child and teacher is based on equality, respect, trust, and authentic dialogue (real communication), child language learning is promoted. Speech is at the foundation of a child's learning life. Teachers need to create a classroom atmosphere where children can expect success, see the teacher as a significant person, are allowed choice, and are able to make mistakes. Ideally, children should join in planned activities eagerly. These activities should end before the child's capacity to focus is exhausted. The child should be able to expect the teacher to listen and respond to the child's communication in a way that respects the child's sense of the importance of the communication.

In whatever preschool activities and learning experiences that a child encounters the following is taking place.

> There are events happening in the individual "cognitive apparatus" (child's mind) of the learner as he or she struggles to understand and remember the subject that is being learned; but it is also the case that much, if not most, effective learning occurs in social settings, as learners communicate or engage in collaborative activity with other individuals. Furthermore, when a person learns, or develops, or changes cognitively, these individual and social domains are intimately interrelated (Phillips & Soltis, 2009, p. 66)

Studies examining the quality of language environments in American preschools found that many preschools serving poor children scored in the inadequate range. High-quality group book experiences, cognitively challenging conversation, and teacher use of a wide vocabulary were associated with quality environments and young children's subsequent language and literacy development. It is impossible to underemphasize the importance of adult-child *interaction*. In schools and centers of questionable quality, some children may rarely interact with a preschool teacher and receive little or no individualized attention. They may be unable to make a socially satisfying and trusting emotional connection to the teacher or peers. These schools fail the children who most need a quality literacy environment to prepare them for later schooling.

## TEACHING STRATEGIES AND BEHAVIORS

Three specific teaching functions that encourage the development of language arts and literacy are discussed in this chapter.

1. The teacher serves as a *model* of everyday language use. What is communicated and how it is communicated are important.

2. The teacher is a *provider* of experiences. Many of these events are planned; others happen in the normal course of activities.

3. The teacher is an "*interactor*," sharing experiences and building a trusting connection with the children while encouraging conversation (Figure 7–1).

**FIGURE 7–1** Lucia is showing her teacher that she can make a big smile by pulling her cheeks up as her teacher has done herself to help define the word "smile."

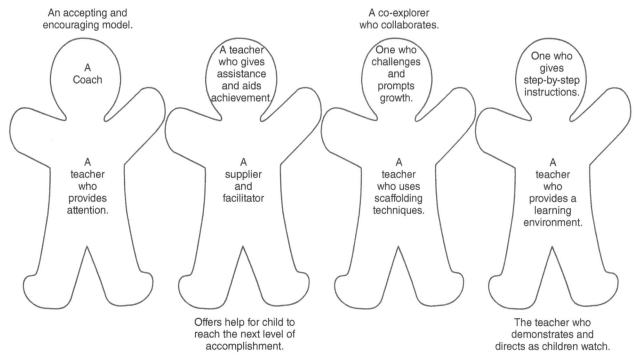

An accepting and encouraging model.

A Coach

A teacher who provides attention.

A teacher who gives assistance and aids achievement.

A supplier and facilitator

Offers help for child to reach the next level of accomplishment.

A co-explorer who collaborates.

One who challenges and prompts growth.

A teacher who uses scaffolding techniques.

One who gives step-by-step instructions.

A teacher who provides a learning environment.

The teacher who demonstrates and directs as children watch.

**FIGURE 7–2** Range of teaching styles.

These three functions should be balanced, relative to each child's developmental level and individual needs. The teaching role requires constant decision making: knowing when to supply or withhold information to help self-discovery and when to talk or listen (Figure 7–2). Basically, sensitivity can make the teacher the child's best ally in the growth of language skills. The importance of teachers' attitudes toward children's talk and teachers' recognition of children's thinking is critical. Researchers studying teacher-child interactions have found that teachers with more education are more responsive and sensitive. Newer, stricter licensing regulations and standards regarding the training of early childhood educators in most states aim to improve the quality of teacher-child interactions. Research consistently shows that training is an important predictor of involved, sensitive teacher-child conversation and discussion.

### The Observer Teacher

Observing all elements of a program, as well as children's behavior and progress, involves watching, listening, and recording. This can be the most difficult part of teaching because of time constraints and supervisory requirements. In-depth observation is best accomplished when a teacher is relieved of other responsibilities and can focus without distractions. Many teachers who do not have duty-free observation time must observe while on duty. Observation often unearths questions regarding children's difficulties, talents, and a wide range of special needs that can then be incorporated into plans and daily exchanges.

Learners are most likely to remember and understand what they are learning if they are challenged to make the connection to their own lives (Burman, 2009). Your role as the teacher is to provide experiences that challenge young learners thinking so new connections can be made. In the best situations, the teacher has background knowledge about each child's unique prior experience and knowledge so instruction can be individualized.

Knowing children's interests, present behaviors, and emerging skills helps the teacher perform the three aforementioned functions, based on group and individual needs. Teachers must be part detective and part researcher, sifting through the clues children leave, collecting data, testing hypotheses, and examining the way children really are to make a credible record of their growth and development.

Listening intimately is highly advisable. Providing an environment that is conducive to growth depends partially on being on a child's or group's wavelength. Conversations are more valuable when teachers try to converse and question based on the child's line of thought. Activities provided should increase children's ability to think and rethink and therefore make sense from what they encounter.

Unplanned teacher talk can be viewed as less important than talk in teacher-guided activities. If a teacher thinks this way, it can limit his ability to support problem solving, child discovery, and child expression of events important to the child. If a child brings you a leaf found in the play yard, that's the time for both of you to discuss its characteristics, where or how he found it, or some other features of the leaf. The listening and observing behavior of teachers increases the quality and pertinence of teachers' communicative interactions.

## THE TEACHER AS A MODEL

Teachers model not only speech but also attitudes and behaviors in listening, writing, and reading. Children watch and listen to adults' use of grammar, intonation, and sentence patterns and imitate and use adults as examples. Consider the different and similar ways teachers verbally interact with young children by examining Figure 7–3. Can you see how examples B and D offer the child more language growth?

An early and classic study by Bernstein, who studied British families in 1962, concluded that a recognizable style of verbal interaction based on social class exists. Working-class speakers, Bernstein believed, used a restricted code type of speech, whereas middle-class speakers used both elaborated code and restricted code speech in some verbal exchanges. Restricted code speech characteristics include the following:

● specific to a current physical context
● limited
● stereotyped
● condensed
● inexact
● nonspecific

**Example A**

| | |
|---|---|
| *Child:* | "It's chickun soup." |
| *Teacher:* | "That's right." |

**Example B**

| | |
|---|---|
| *Child:* | "It's chickun soup." |
| *Teacher:* | "Yes. I see chicken pieces and something else." |
| *Child:* | "It's noodles." |
| *Teacher:* | "Yes, those are long, skinny noodles. It's different from yesterday's red tomato soup." |
| *Child:* | "Tastes good. It's 'ellow." |
| *Teacher:* | "Yellow like the daffodils in the vase." (Pointing.) |

**Example C**

| | |
|---|---|
| *Child:* | "Baby cry." |
| *Adult:* | "Yes, the baby is crying." |

**Example D**

| | |
|---|---|
| *Child:* | "Baby cry." |
| *Adult:* | "You hear the baby crying?" |
| *Child:* | "Uh-huh." |
| *Adult:* | "Maybe she's hungry and wants some milk." |
| *Child:* | "Wants bottle." |
| *Adult:* | "Let's see. I'll put the bottle in her mouth." |
| *Child:* | "Her hungry." |
| *Adult:* | "Yes, she's sucking. The milk is going into her mouth. Look, it's almost gone." |

**FIGURE 7–3** Adult verbal styles.

● short in sentence length
● vague and indefinite

Elaborate code speech, in Bernstein's view, is

● more differentiated.
● more precise.
● not specific to a particular situation or context and affords opportunities for more complex thought.

Speakers' styles of communication were seen by Bernstein as powerful determining factors in the young child's development of cognitive structures and modes of communication. He believed that young children exposed exclusively to restricted code speakers are at an educational disadvantage in school settings where elaborated code speech predominates. The major assumption behind this view is that middle-class ways of talking with children support literacy development, whereas working-class ways of talking with children inhibit literacy development. Have you met others who typify these two styles?

Many other researchers have investigated verbal exchanges between families and children to pinpoint connections between adult talk and its relationship to child speech, thinking ability, brain growth, and literacy. More current studies describe parents' high-level and low-level distancing strategies in verbal exchanges. High-level distancing strategies include:

- drawing conclusions.
- inferring cause-and-effect relationships.
- planning together.
- evaluating consequences.
- evaluating effect.

These are strategies you will want to use.

Low-level distancing strategies include labeling, producing information, and observing. These are helpful and you will use them, but they may not be as growth producing especially if what you've discovered is not applied. Researchers hypothesized that social class alone does not predict children's cognitive and linguistic outcomes for families of many sorts produce successful and language adept students. Early childhood educators observing young children would agree.

It is suggested that early childhood teachers who aim to be good speaking models focus on studying their ability to use **explanatory talk** in child-teacher verbal exchanges. Explanatory talk consists of conversation concerning some connection between objects, events, concepts, and/or conclusions that one speaker is pointing out to another (Figure 7–4). Teachers commonly and typically explain their intent and actions to children and provide explanations in response to child comments and questions.

**FIGURE 7–4** Explanatory talk also occurs when a child explains her connection to a book's illustration.

This is a preferred behavior in early childhood teachers' verbal interactive exchanges. Some examples follow.

"The blocks go on the shelf. We will know where to find the blocks when we want to use them again, and no one will trip on them."

"The window was open, and the wind blew into our classroom. It knocked over the small cups where our seeds were planted."

"I'm putting my snack dish in the tub on the table when I'm finished. Mrs. Gregorio will come and get the tub after snack time."

This explanatory style sometimes carries over into teachers' personal lives. Teachers report family members often say to them, "Yes, I know why you're doing that!"

---

**explanatory talk** — a type of conversation characterized by a speaker's attempt to create connections between objects, events, concepts, or conclusions to promote understanding in the listener.

Adults should use clear, descriptive speech at a speed and pitch easily understood. Articulation should be as precise as possible. Appropriate adult models during infancy and the toddler period would have the following characteristics, which are also desirable in teachers of preschoolers.

> . . . being a good model involves more than merely speaking clearly, slowly, and appropriately. A good model uses a variety of facial expressions and other forms of nonverbal communication; associates talking with understanding and affection; provides happy, pleasant experiences associated with talking; and takes advantage of various timely situations. . . .

Teachers also need to be sure that reward in the form of attention is present in their teaching behavior as they deal with young children's attitudes, skills, and behaviors in language arts activities (Figure 7–5). Educators should use language patterns with which they feel comfortable and natural and should analyze their speech, working toward providing the best English model possible. Familiar language patterns reflect each teacher's personality and ethnic culture. Knowing what kind of model one presents is important, because knowing that there is room for improvement can help a teacher become more professional.

Modeling the correct word or sentence is done by simply supplying it in a relaxed, natural way rather than in a corrective tone. The teacher's example is a strong influence; when a teacher adds courtesy words ("please" and "thank you," for instance), these words appear in children's speech. Finishing an incomplete word by adding an ending or beginning may be appropriate with very young speakers. (The child may say "na na"; the teacher would provide "banana.") Completing a phrase or offering complete sentences in Standard English suits older speakers. Although adult modeling has its limits in facilitating spontaneous language, it is an essential first step in learning language.

After hearing corrections modeled, the child will probably not shift to correct grammar or usage immediately. It may take many repetitions by teachers and adults over time. What is important is the teacher's acceptance and recognition of the child's idea within the verbalization and the addition of pertinent comments along the same line.

To build children's vocabulary knowledge the classroom needs to introduce and expose children to new words, and provide these words in the context of situations. Definitions are offered using terms that are understandable and

**FIGURE 7–5** Giving attention can be a form of reward for some children.

relate when possible to children's past experience. Opportunities will arise because of children's innate curiosity and interest in the world around them. As children mature they develop independent strategies to figure out a word meanings. Dictionary use is introduced and educators provide assistance and are interested word collectors, themselves. Being "word" conscious happens when children's interest is piqued, and they seek new word meanings (Christ & Wang, 2010). Christ and Wang point out knowing a word's meaning includes knowing what the word refers to, and gaining the ability to use the word in accurate examples.

When adults focus on the way something was said (grammar) rather than the meaning, they miss opportunities to increase awareness and extend child interest. Overt correction often ends teacher-child conversation. Affirmation is appropriate; the teacher should emphasize the child's intended message.

Adults can sometimes develop the habit of talking and listening to themselves rather than to the children; it is hypnotic and can be a deterrent to really hearing the child. If one's mind wanders or if one listens only for the purpose of refuting, agreeing, or jumping to value judgments, it interferes with receiving communication from others. Teachers need not be afraid of silences and pauses before answering. The following listening suggestions are recommended.

- Work as hard to listen as you do to talk.
- Try to hear the message behind the words.
- Consciously practice good listening.

One teaching technique that promotes language skill is simple modeling of grammar or filling in missing words and completing simple sentences. This is called **expansion**. It almost becomes second nature and automatic after a short period of intentional practice. When using an expansion, the adult responds to the child by expanding the syntactic composition of the child's utterance. For example, the child's "It is cold" might be followed by "The window pane felt cold when you pressed your nose against it." The teacher's expansion is contingent and responsive, focusing on what the child was experiencing. Although using the strategy of expansion is a widely accepted and practiced teacher behavior, Crawford (2005) notes there is little research evidence that it has any positive effect. Evidence showing a negative effect is also yet to be found. Even without research validating the technique, many educators believe that the practice is still valuable, and when additional research takes place it will confirm their actions. While using expansion, the teacher can also promote wider depth of meaning or spark interest by contributing or suggesting an idea for further exploration. Additional conversation usually occurs.

The teacher is a model for listening as well as speaking. Words, expressions, pronunciations, and gestures are copied, as is listening behavior. A quiet teacher may have a quiet classroom; an enthusiastic, talkative teacher (who also listens) may have a classroom where children talk, listen, and share experiences. The way children feel about themselves is reflected in their behavior. When teachers listen closely, children come to feel that what they say is worthwhile.

Modeling good printscript form (classroom or center manuscript print) is important (Chapter 16 deals with this topic). Children seem to absorb everything in their environment, so it is necessary to provide correctly formed alphabet letters and numerals on children's work, charts, bulletin boards, and any displayed classroom print.

Teachers' use and care of books are modeled, as are their attitudes toward story and nonfiction book experiences. Through their observations of teachers' actions, children begin to develop ideas about how books should be handled and stored.

One teacher who wanted to model storytelling of personal stories divided a large paper into eight sections; in each section she drew a picture of different stages in her life. She showed this to her class and asked them to pick a picture, which she then related in storytelling. Teachers also model poetry reading and its use, dramatization, puppet play, and many other language arts activities.

---

**expansion** — a teaching technique that includes the adult's (teacher's) modeling of words or grammar, filling in missing words in children's utterances, or suggesting ideas for child exploration.

What we are communicates far more eloquently than anything we say or do. This is an old saying that was not written expressly for teachers of young children; nonetheless it is a good addition to this discussion. According to Au (2006), teachers must demonstrate the kind of literacy they want students to show. They must see themselves as readers and writers and convince students of the value of reading and writing. In doing so, they help young children gain an appreciation for literacy in their own lives. With picture books, some of the ways this is accomplished is by selecting and sharing books with an obvious enjoyment factor, by building on children's interests, and by discussing enjoyed book sections as these relate to individual children. An educator on any teaching day can model his or her thinking by talking aloud to promote children's thinking along the same lines. This is often done when sharing a book, but there are many additional opportunities.

"Today we have three boys sitting together in our circle whose names start with the letter 'J' . . . Jacob, Joseph and Joshua."

"You made a new color when your yellow paint touched the blue paint."

"I wonder what would happen if I put this sign that says 'Keep Out' on the door of the playhouse. Let's find out."

"This book says Bill and Will slid downhill. Those words rhyme—Bill, Will, downhill."

"I hear the same sound at the end of Emma, Olivia, and Isabella's names—Emma, Olivia, Isabella. And in Isabella's name I hear the sound two times."

"What a sad face Corduroy has. His mouth turns down at its corners."

"If I pour too much juice into this cup, it will spill. I don't want to do that so I'll stop a little way below the top."

## THE TEACHER AS PROVIDER

As providers, preschool teachers strive to provide experiences that promote literacy. Fortunately, the number of interesting language arts activities one can offer children is almost limitless. Teachers rely on both their own creativity and the many resources available to plan experiences based on identified goals and what they observe and feel necessary for child growth and needs. Early childhood resource books, other teachers, teacher magazines, workshops, and conferences all contribute ideas.

Gathering activity ideas and storing them in a personal resource file is suggested, because it is almost impossible to remember all the activity ideas one comes upon. An activity file can include new or tried-and-true activity ideas. Developing a usable file starts with identifying initial categories (file headings) and then adding more heads as the file grows. Some teachers use oversized file cards; others use binders or file folders. Whatever the file size, teachers find that files are very worthwhile when it comes to daily, weekly, and monthly planning. Often, files are helpful when ideas on a certain subject or theme are needed or when a child exhibits a special interest. A file collection is not used as the basis for activity planning but rather as a collection of good ideas or ideas you might like to try that might suit the particular needs of your group of children.

A large number of activity ideas are presented in following chapters. Your creativity can produce many others. Here are some suggestions for separate file headings (categories):

- Audiovisual Activities
- Bulletin Board Ideas
- Child Drama Ideas
- Children's Books
- Circle Time Ideas
- Classroom Environment Ideas
- Listening Centers
- Reading Centers
- Writing Centers
- Dramatic Play Stimulators
- Dramatic Play Theme Ideas
- Experience Stories
- Field Trip Ideas

- Finger Plays
- Flannel Board Ideas
- Free and Inexpensive Material Resources
- Language Game Ideas
- Listening Activities
- Listening Center Ideas
- Magazine (Child's) Activities
- Patterns
- Perceptual-Motor Activities
- Poetry
- Printscript Ideas
- Puppets
- Reading Readiness Ideas
- Rebus Stories
- Seasonal Ideas
- Conversation Starters
- Stories for Storytelling
- Visitor Resources

As a provider of materials, a teacher must realize that every classroom object can become a useful program tool to stimulate language. From the clock on the wall to the doorknob, every safe item can be discussed, compared, and explored in some way (Figure 7–6). Because most school budgets are limited, early childhood teachers find ways to use available equipment and materials to their fullest.

Most teachers are pleasantly surprised to see how avidly their classes respond to their personal interests. When the teacher shares enthusiasm for out-of-school interests, hobbies, projects, trips, and individual talents, he can help introduce children to important knowledge. Almost anything appropriate can be presented at the child's level. Whether the teacher is an opera buff, scuba diver, gourmet cook, stamp collector, or violin player, the activity should be shared in any safe form that communicates special interest and love of the activity, and the specific vocabulary and materials relating to the activity should be presented. Enthusiasm is the key to inspired teaching.

## Providing for Abundant Play

Abundant opportunities for play are important to the child's language acquisition. Considerable research shows that child's play is in fact more complex than it is commonly believed to be. It provides a rich variety of experiences: communication with other children, verbal rituals, topic development and maintenance, turn taking, intimate speech in friendships, follower-leader conversations, and many other kinds of language exchanges. Except when the children's

**FIGURE 7–6** Madison has an interest in insects so her teacher supplies both opportunity and equipment.

safety is in question, children's natural ability to pretend should be encouraged, and the flow of this kind of play should proceed without the teacher's interference. Children will want to talk to teachers about their play, and the teacher's proper involvement is to show interest and be playful themselves at times.

Intellectual conflict, Burman (2009) states, is a necessary requirement for learning. Something that conflicts with a learner's existing schema shakes up thinking. Teachers see preschool peers in frequent serious discussions. When this happens children may shift their understanding because a playmate has offered alternate perspective or a different idea. In the playhouse area this might be as simple as a child saying "Daddies don't cook!" and a peer replying "My dad cooks pancakes." They may even check the validity of their new understanding by running it by teacher for conformation and/or further discussion.

If a child has chosen to engage a teacher in conversation instead of play, or during play, the teacher should be both a willing listener and a competent, skillful conversationalist. As young children talk about their experiences, the talking itself aids their organization of thoughts. At times, younger ones monologue in our presence. They are not really asking for our reaction for they are listening to themselves think, while they also enjoy our physical closeness.

Young children explore constantly. They want to do what they see others doing. Play opportunities usually involve manipulating something. When deeply involved in play, children may seem to be momentarily awestruck in their search for meanings, but soon they will approach others with questions or comments.

They gain skills in approaching other children and asking if they can play, or just nonverbally joining a play group in progress. They begin to understand what attracts others to them, how to imitate another child's actions or words, how to express affection or hostility, how to assume a leadership role, how to negotiate, and how to follow or refuse playmates' requests. These and other play skills help them stay engaged in a play group for a longer period of time.

Preschoolers at play may even argue over correct language use. Some observers believe that the majority of language teaching that takes place in the 4-year-olds' classroom is child-to-child teaching.

A resourceful teacher will strive to provide a variety of play by regarding all of a center's area (and furnishings) as a possible place (or object) for safe and appropriate play. Creative use can be made of each foot of floor space. Children need large blocks of uninterrupted time to construct knowledge and actively explore their problem-solving options in an environment thoughtfully and carefully prepared by the teacher.

## Providing Accurate and Specific Speech in All Content Areas

Although this text concentrates on teacher-child interactions in the subject field, language arts, other content areas, such as mathematics (numbers), social studies, health and safety, art, music, movement, and so on, will be subjects of teacher-child conversations and discussions. The same teacher techniques that are useful in building children's language competence and vocabulary in language arts are equally useful for other content areas. Every subject area has its own vocabulary and common terms that can overlap other fields of study. For example, the teacher may discuss "applying" paints during an art activity and "applying" an antibacterial on a wound or scratch. If children are focused on the number of muffins on a tray, or whether there are enough scissors to go around, then teacher comments include number words.

There are more than two schools of thought concerning educator's role in offering vocabulary to preschoolers. It is possible for an educator to use both of the strategies. The first emphasizes a teacher's use of rich, specific and sometimes unusual words in daily instruction and conversation that are a little above children's common daily usage. Children adopt and savor them and incorporate them into their working vocabulary. If the teacher has an extensive knowledge of flowers, their names, care, and other information, she could add considerable vocabulary in a natural way without overdoing it. The second strategy involves consciously using or planning to use vocabulary root words or key words found in read-aloud books and themes. Root words are words, or parts of words, that children will encounter in early readers when their reading instruction begins. These are words identified as being words that are frequency used in beginning reading primers. Experts, such as

Dolch (1948), Biemiller and Slonim (2001), Dale and Chall (1948), have published word lists. Kindergarten teachers can also be good resources for beginning word lists. See Figure 7–7 for additional tips for increasing vocabulary.

Teacher comments should be as accurate and specific as possible in light of what the teacher believes the children might already know or have experienced. Purposeful teacher conversation adds a little more information than the children already know, and reinforces and adds depth to words already in the children's vocabulary. When working with numerals or other subjects, the teacher should use terminology that is appropriate to the subject area but at a level the children will understand. For example, the teacher might say "Let's count the muffins" or "The tool in your hand is a wire whip" or "The metal cylinder attached to the wall is a fire

extinguisher. Fire extinguishers have something inside that can be sprayed out to put out fires." In movement or music activities, many descriptive terms can be added to teacher directions, and conversations such as hop, jump, stretch or soft, loud, high, and low. These are easily understood while the child is in the process of experiencing them. The quality of the words children hear is crucial for their later school and language performance (Kalmar, 2008). Children build meaning as adults and teachers make comments, provide information, comfort them, guide them, praise and encourage their efforts, and display excitement and enthusiasm for the world around them. Sometimes, teachers are reluctant to use big, new words such as the word *hibernate* (Neuman & Roskos, 2007). Neuman and Roskos urge educators to remember that teacher words and phrases are one of the main

| INSTRUCTION METHOD | TEACHING TIP |
|---|---|
| Provide purposeful exposure to new words | Teach thematically to provide multiple exposures to words throughout the day, through read-alouds, conversations, centers, and projects.<br>• Select books for read-alouds in which illustrations and text provide clues to word meanings.<br>• Use an interactive read-aloud style and engage children in cognitively challenging discussions about books.<br>• Create media centers where children view DVDs, explore electronic books, and listen to interactive read-alouds on DVD that use new vocabulary. |
| Intentionally teach word meanings | Use a variety of direct teaching strategies.<br>• Ask eliciting and noneliciting questions during readalouds to prompt children to think about new words and their meanings.<br>• Provide an embedded definition when exposing children to a new word whose meaning is important for them to understand.<br>• Use extended instruction to help children gain a nuanced understanding of a word's meaning. |
| Teach word-learning strategies | Teach word-learning strategies while reading aloud.<br>• Use the three steps for strategy instruction: model, guide, and practice.<br>• Select books in which both text and illustrations give clues to a word's meaning. |
| Offer opportunities to use newly learned words | Provide a variety of opportunitites for children to use newly learned vocabulary.<br>• Use concept-mapping activities to organize pictures and props related to a classroom theme or project.<br>• Have children retell, buddy read, or act out texts that have been read in the classroom.<br>• Write down stories dictated by children that are related to a classroom theme or project.<br>• Develop art and craft projects in which children can apply newly learned concepts.<br>• Engage in inquiry projects related to the curricular theme.<br>• Provide props related to the theme that may elicit theme-related vocabulary use. |

FIGURE 7–7 Teaching tips for vocabulary instruction.

sources for giving children new knowledge. They stress giving explanations and examples and suggest saying,

> "When an animal goes to sleep for the winter, we say it is hibernating."

> Then, provide opportunities for children to practice their new language by saying "Do you remember what we call it when animals go to sleep for the winter? We call it hibernating." (p. 10)

The teacher prompts children's use of the words that the teacher provides. Most times a teacher is careful to define new words immediately after using the new terms. In number activities, number words are used in the presence of a corresponding number of objects. In movement activities, types of movement are discussed with quick demonstrations.

It is important to introduce new terms in a natural conversational tone rather than within the framework of an obvious lesson. Leading a child or groups of children to new discoveries offers the teacher an opportunity to use specific and accurate terms and also makes children feel like partners in the discoveries. A theme on birds could include many terms and specific names that a teacher might need to research.

## THE TEACHER—AN EDUCATOR WHO INTERACTS

An educator can be defined as a person who is always interested in what a child is saying or doing. This person encourages conversation on any subject the child selects, is never too busy to talk and share interests and concerns, and listens with the intent to understand. Understanding the child's message makes the educator's response more educationally valuable. Time is purposely planned for daily conversations with each child. When teachers talk about what they are doing, explain why particular results occur, and let children ask questions about procedures and results, children will have more exposure to and experience with extended forms of discourse. These private, personal, one-on-one encounters build the child's feelings of self-worth and open communications. Conversations can

be initiated with morning greetings such as the following:

> "Alphonse, I've been waiting to talk to you.

> "Tell me about your visit to Chicago."

> "How is your puppy feeling today, Andrea?"

> "Those new blue tennis shoes will be good for running in the yard and for tiptoeing, too."

Educators are aware of the "reciprocal opportunity" that is always present in work with young children. Teachers try to really hear verbal communications and sense nonverbal messages. They give undivided attention (if possible), which lends importance to and shows interest in children's ideas and also rewards children's efforts to use language and initiate social contact. A teacher can respond skillfully, first clarifying what the teacher thought she heard and then adding to the conversation and attempting to stimulate more verbal output, child discovery, some new feature or detail, or a different way of viewing what has captured the child's interest. The correctness of children's verbal expression of their thoughts, feelings, requests, or other intent is accepted and corrected only when it is socially unacceptable speech.

Studies of teacher-child interaction have discovered that some teachers were warm and accepting but offered children little invitation to talk. These teachers found it quicker and easier to anticipate students' needs and thus failed to seize opportunities that would make children want and need to talk.

Teachers can emphasize the symbolic component of an activity ("These words that you see on the handles say hot and cold.") and help children identify problems or dilemmas by suggesting that children put their ideas into words ("Adam, you wanted to give your scissors to Evan but couldn't. What happened?") Teachers may need to raise their own awareness of their interactions with children, in other words, rate themselves on their ability to expand children's verbal output and

**FIGURE 7–8** Teachers' comments are based on their knowledge of individual children.

accuracy (Figure 7–8). Tape recording daily conversation and analyzing them at times is recommended, even experienced teachers periodically do so.

It is wise to be aware and up to date on topics of special interest to preschoolers. Current popular toys, cartoon figures, community happenings, sports, recording artists, movies, and individual family events may often be the focus of young children's conversations. When a teacher has background knowledge, such as what current Disney characters are popular or familiar to her students or which children have a new infant sibling at home, her responses when children discuss these items could be more pertinent and connected to the reality of enrolled children's lives.

Early childhood educators use a technique called **extension**. Building on a child's statement, the teacher adds information, factual data, or additional meaning, and prompts the child to elaborate. This can both add vocabulary and clarify some aspect or concept encountered in the conversational interchange. The child's

"It spilled" might be answered with "Yes, Quan's hand knocked the cup over. I think maybe there was a time when you spilled something, too."

Many teachers have used a conversational interaction technique called **closure**. It involves pausing, specifically, hesitating in the middle of a sentence or at sentence endings. It is a technique that prompts guessing by the child, and the teacher is willing to accept any guess. Most often, children's guesses are logical but may not be what the teacher expected. Those children with a sense of the ridiculous may offer off-the-wall guesses equally acceptable to the teacher. It often promotes further dialogue. The teacher's saying "The sun disappeared behind a . . ." might elicit "hill," "mountain," "building," "tree," "cloud," or other possibilities from the child. The teacher's saying "Coats are hung in the . . . by the front door" is an example of middle-of-the-sentence closure or a fill-in statement. Using closure within a familiar context, like a well known story or song ("And he blew the house. . .?") is fun, and gives the teacher a chance to say "Emma, you guessed the *word* that

---

**extension** — a teaching strategy in which an adult expands the child's information by adding new, additional, related information or meaning.
**closure** — a conversation technique that prompts children to verbally guess and complete or fill in a teacher's sentence. The teacher pauses or hesitates, which prompts the child to finish a teacher verbalization.

I left out was down. Yes. It is the word." Teachers often also made lists of guessed words immediately so the children see the written word they guessed.

In looking at individual children, Covey (1989) reminds us of what we know in our hearts to be true, fair, and compassionate. Each child is to be valued for his identity as a person and for his unique individuality, separateness, and worth. Comparisons between children cloud our view. Traits teachers may see as negative can be fostered by the environment we offer and our own perceptions of correct student behavior. An educator's job, according to Covey, is to recognize potential, then coddle and inspire that potential to emerge at its own pace.

Waiting for a child's response is sometimes difficult for some teachers. When you wait, you give the child time to initiate or to get involved in an activity. You are, in effect, giving her this message: "You're in control—I know you can communicate, so you decide what you want to do or say. I'll give you all the time you need." Studies of adult-child interactions have shown that adults give children approximately one second in which to respond to a question. After one second, the adult repeats and rephrases the question or provides the answer. One second! Most children need much longer than one second to process the question and figure out their response.

Adult speech containing a relatively high proportion of statements or declaratives has been associated with accelerated language development in young children. Adult-child conversations tend to last longer if adults add new relevant information. If adults verbally accept and react to children's statements with "oh, really?" or "I see," when they are trying to grasp a child's meaning, additional conversation seems to be promoted.

When a teacher answers a child by showing interest, this rewards the child for speaking. Positive feelings are read internally as an automatic signal to continue to do what we are doing. Many experts suggest that teachers should guide and collaborate to promote children's independent problem solving in any given situation. Most often, teachers show their attention by listening to, looking at, smiling at, patting, or answering a child, or by acting favorably to what a child has said or done.

Experienced teachers know that children often will silently look for teacher's attention and approval across a busy classroom when they have accomplished a task or a breakthrough. They search to see if the teacher noticed. A busy teacher might give thumbs up or smile in response, if they can't offer words just then. The child by his behavior has indicated that he feels this is a teacher who cares about me.

In Figure 6–16 in the previous chapter there was a cooking activity that used a multiple goal approach to instruction. The teacher and children were jointly planning and participating. Children displayed interest and enthusiasm. This figure illustrates the teacher's thinking. She is guiding, providing, and interacting in a way that promotes children's verbal expression and use of writing. It is easy to see that children exposed to this type of interaction with an adult are learning far more than language. In the example, language and thought are paired. There are obvious growth opportunities in both. How many similar situations in joint planning and joint problem solving are possible in the average classroom? The opportunities are limitless!

Note also that in Figure 6–16 not once did the teacher interact in a test question manner by asking, "What color are apples?" or "What is this called on the recipe chart?" Rather, her verbal comments provoked children's discovery. When she prompted and it was obvious children were unfamiliar with a word (for example, cinnamon), the teacher offered it.

For those who want to ask thought-provoking questions, the work of Kucan (2007) provides another guide. As discussed earlier, teachers can get into the habit of primarily asking questions that call for a "right" answer, a memory question. This type of question does not call for interpretation, application, analysis, synthesis, explanation, evaluation, inference, prediction, comparison, contrasting or connecting ideas. Critical thinking, judgment, and problem solving are required to answer these questions.

Dangel and Durden (2010) urge educators to challenge children to thinking beyond the moment and analyze and conjecture. They suggest teachers use thoughtful questions and comments during teacher-child verbal exchanges that promote children's labeling, describing, or connecting the prior ideas and knowledge they possess to what is on hand or occurring during an activity. A teacher's question might also prompt child hypotheses, imaginations, or opinions. All involve higher level thinking skills.

Try to identify what is asked for in the following.

1. What might happen if Emma grabs Maria's paint without asking?

2. In our story, Josh carried all the eggs in a basket. Could we use something to carry our small blocks outside? We don't have a basket.

3. Saucedo said he was sorry when he knocked down Kai's block tower. What else might he have done to show Kai he was sorry?

4. What happened to make Ahmad so angry in our story? Would you do what Ahmad did?

5. Our pet, Missy, gets so frightened when people gather around her cage. What rules should we make?

6. Noah said, "The ant ate an elephant," and you all laughed. Why?

7. When Latanya said, "It won't work if you do that," what did she mean? Why wouldn't the scissors work?

Although some may seem to fit in more than one category, you should agree that all of these examples required much more thinking than a memory-checking question. Teachers trying to determine their questioning skills can test themselves using Figure 7–9.

Teachers often act as interpreters, especially with younger preschoolers. The child who says "Gimme dat" is answered with "You want the red paint." Do not worry about faulty teacher interpretations! Most children will let teachers know when they have interpreted incorrectly by trying again. Then the teacher has the opportunity to say, "You wanted the blue paint, Taylor."

Consider the dialog of the language-developing teacher below. Did the teacher's speech interactions accomplish the goal?

Goal #1: Use language slightly more complex than the child's.

Child: "Those are cookies."

Teacher: "Yes, they're called Gumdrop Mountains because they come to a point on the top."

## TEST YOUR QUESTIONING AND RESPONDING ABILITIES

Answer the following using A = always, S = sometimes, N = need to work on this, or U = unable to determine.

1. Do I respond to child-initiated comments 100 percent of the time? _____
2. Do I keep to the child's topic and include it in my response? _____
3. Do I ask questions that prompt children to see or discover an aspect that they might not have perceived or discovered? _____
4. Am I aware of the favorite subjects and interests of individual children and ask questions along these lines?

_____

   Are my questions appropriate in light of the children's development levels? _____
5. Do I often answer a child's comments using teacher echolalia?
      Child:   "I went to the zoo."
      Teacher: "Oh, you went to the zoo."
   Or would my answer more likely be, "What animals did you see?" _____
6. Are my questions usually open ended? _____
7. Are my questions thought-inducing, or are they merely seeking correct answers? _____
8. Do I provide a specific response to children's questions? _____
9. Do my questions take place in the context of mutual trust and respect, based on my genuine friendliness, unconditional acceptance, warmth, empathy, and interest? _____
10. Do many of my questions seem to put a child "on-the-spot" or fluster a child? _____

FIGURE 7–9 Assess your questioning and responding abilities.

Goal #2: Speak with young or limited-language children by referring to an action, object, person, and/or event that is currently happening.

Teacher: "You're climbing up the stairs."

Goal #3: Base your reactive conversation on the meaning the child intended. There are two ways to do this: (1) repetition ("Pet the dog" to child's "Pet dog"); (2) expansion (the child says, "play bath," and the teacher expands with, "You want to play with your toys in the bath tub").

Goal #4: Use recasting. (The child says, "You can't get in," and the teacher responds, "No, I can't get in, can I?")

Goal #5: Use "I see," "Yes," or a similar expression to indicate I am listening.

Encouraging children to tell about happenings and how they feel is possible throughout the preschool day (Figure 7–10). A teacher may find it harder to interact verbally with quiet and shy children or the ones that rarely stay in one place or sit down, but they keep on trying.

Teachers shift to more mature or less mature speech as they converse with children of differing ages and abilities. They try to speak to each according to his level of understanding. They use shorter, less complex utterances and use more gestures and nonverbal signals

with speakers trying to learn English. Whenever possible, it is professionally appropriate to interact in a way that displays a belief that all preschoolers are capable thinkers that are able to weigh complex ideas, and at times, use abstract reasoning as they strive to make sense of what happens around them.

The teacher who interacts in daily experiences can help improve the child's ability to see relationships. Although there is current disagreement as to the teacher's ability to promote cognitive growth (the act or process of knowing), attention can be focused and help provided by answering and asking questions. Often, a teacher can help children see clear links between material already learned and new material. Words teachers provide are paired with the child's mental images that have come through the senses. Language aids memory because words attached to mental images help the child retrieve stored information. Intellectually valuable experiences often involve the teacher as active participants in tasks with the child.

Pica (2007) urges teachers to combine concepts, and words with active physical movement and/or involvement. She believes young children still need to experience concepts physically, when possible, to fully understand them. Her book, *Jumping into Literacy*, abounds with early learning activities that promote language and literacy through music and movement.

**FIGURE 7–10** Bending or kneeling puts adults at an appropriate level to engage in intimate conversation.

The teacher interacts by supplying words to fit situations, It should be remembered that a new word often needs to be repeated in a subtle way. It has been said that at least three repetitions of a new word are needed for adults to master the word; young children need more. In some cases, when a new word is very salient and the child is highly motivated, a child may acquire the word after a single, brief exposure. This is called *fast mapping*, and children also more readily learn new words that are conceptually similar to words they already know (Wasik, 2006). Repeated exposure to a new word in the same and other meaningful contexts is still recommended in most situations. Walley, Metsala, and Garlock (2003) researched the ease with which children learn new words. They note that new words that are phonologically similar to a known word are also easier to acquire. If the child's vocabulary contains *hat*, *mat*, and *cat*, which contain similar morphemes, similar words may be learned readily.

Teachers often hear the child repeating a new word, trying to become familiar with it. To help children remember a new word, Bennett-Armistead, Duke, and Moses (2005) suggest making sure the words you say around the new word give clues to the word's meaning. For example, instead of saying "That is a fox," say "It is a furry animal called a fox. It looks like a small dog and has a big, fluffy tail." The best way to make a new word *real* to young children is to relate the new word to the child's own experiences and ideas.

There are times when a teacher chooses to supply information in answer to direct child questions. There is no easy way for the child to discover answers to questions such as "What's the name of today?" or "Why is that man using that funny stick with a cup on the end?" A precise, age-level answer is necessary; such as "Today is Monday, May 9" and (while demonstrating) "It's a tool, called a plunger. It pushes air and water down the drain and helps open the pipes so that the water in the sink will run out." As a provider of information, the teacher acts as a reference and resource person, providing the information a child desires. If the teacher does not wish to answer a question directly, she may encourage the child to ask the same question of someone else or help the child find out where the answer is available.

Child: "What's lunch?"

Adult: "Come on, we'll go ask the cook." *or* "Let's look at the menu. It lists all the food being served today. I'll read it to you."

Can teachers promote children's curiosity about words? By being aware that children sometimes ask about words they do not understand, educators can reward the child's interest with attention. Statements might include the following:

"You now have another word for car. It is the word automobile."

"I'm happy you asked what 'slick' means Josie."

"A new word in this book will be fun to say. The word is skedaddling and it means to move very quickly."

"When you hear a word that puzzles you, raise your hand. Ask about it, please."

"What a wonderful word that is!"

The teacher's reaction supplies children with feedback. The teacher is responsible for reinforcing the use of a new word and gently ensuring that the children have good attitudes about themselves as speakers.

Every day, the teacher can take advantage of unplanned things that happen to promote language and speech. The following provides an illustration.

While children were sitting in a story group, John noticed that a mobile, hung from the ceiling above, was spinning. "Look," said John pointing, "it's moving!" "How come?" said another child. "Someone must have touched it," said Mary. "Stand up, Mary, and see if you can touch it," added the teacher, standing up and reaching, herself, "I can't reach it either." "Maybe it spins itself," contributed Bill. "No, it can't spin itself," said another child. "Let's see," said the teacher. She got a piece of yarn with a bead tied to the end and held it out in front of the children. It was still. Then she held it near the mobile, which was in a draft of a window. The string swayed gently. "The window, the window is open," suggested the children. "Yes, the wind is coming through the window," said John. "And making it move," said all the children, pleased with their discovery. The teacher held the string so the children could blow at it. "Look,

I'm the wind," said one of them. That afternoon, outside, the children were given crepe paper streamers to explore wind direction. They were also read *Gilberto and the Wind*, which tells what can happen when wind blows the sail of a boat, the arm of a windmill, the smoke from a chimney, and a child's hat and hair.

Being able to make the most of an unexpected event is a valuable skill. Moving into a situation with skill and helping the child discover something and talk about it is part of promoting word growth (Figure 7–11).

## Teachable Moments

You have probably run across the phrase "teachable moments" in your training and perhaps have become adept at using this strategy. It involves a four- to five-step process.

1. Observe a child or a child group's self-chosen actions and efforts.

2. Make a hypothesis about exactly what the children are pursuing, exploring, discovering, and playing with, and so on.

3. Make a teacher decision to intervene, act, provide, extend, or in some way offer an educational opportunity to further growth or knowledge related to the child-chosen agenda.

This can be done a number of ways, so this step often involves teacher contemplation.

4. Determine exactly what you will do or provide. Take action. Often, this can be as simple as asking a question such as, "You are putting small pieces of torn paper in Andy's cage. What do you think Andy is going to do with them?" or by silently providing wedge-shaped blocks to a group of children racing small cars down a ramp. Or perhaps you decide to let a child who has been watching the kitchen helper hand-whip eggs try the hand-whip himself.

5. As a final step, consider having the children tell, act out, communicate, dictate, or in some way represent what has been experienced, if this is appropriate.

A watchful teacher, who is working to promote early literacy skills, may easily connect teachable moments to relevant opportunities involving literacy skills.

## Time Constraints

Comments such as, "You finished," "That's yellow," "How colorful," "It's heavy," "I like that too," or "A new shirt," may give attention, show acceptance, provide encouragement, and reinforce behavior. They feel like suitable and natural comments or responses, and they slip out almost unconsciously. In a busy classroom,

**FIGURE 7–11** Encouraging feuding children to express their feelings is a professional technique.

they often are said in haste when the teacher may have no time for an extended conversation because she is supervising a group of children. In other words, the best a teacher can do, time permitting.

Consciously trying to be specific and expanding takes focus, effort, and quick thinking, but with practice, it can become second nature with teacher statements such as, "You pushed your chair in under the table," "In your drawing I see red and blue," "You helped your friend Alejandra by finding her book," "Those are shoes with lights," "Tell me more about your kitten," and "Returning your crayons to the box helps others find them." Teachers' specific and/or descriptive comments promote literacy.

## SCAFFOLDING

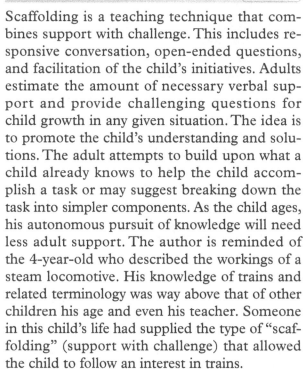

Scaffolding is a teaching technique that combines support with challenge. This includes responsive conversation, open-ended questions, and facilitation of the child's initiatives. Adults estimate the amount of necessary verbal support and provide challenging questions for child growth in any given situation. The idea is to promote the child's understanding and solutions. The adult attempts to build upon what a child already knows to help the child accomplish a task or may suggest breaking down the task into simpler components. As the child ages, his autonomous pursuit of knowledge will need less adult support. The author is reminded of the 4-year-old who described the workings of a steam locomotive. His knowledge of trains and related terminology was way above that of other children his age and even his teacher. Someone in this child's life had supplied the type of "scaffolding" (support with challenge) that allowed the child to follow an interest in trains.

It is believed that children need experiences and educational opportunities with adults who carefully evaluate, think, and talk daily occurrences through. What specific teacher verbalizations and behaviors are suggested in scaffolding? They include comments that offer responsive and authentic conversation, and facilitate child initiative. Educators ask open-ended questions. They prompt and, promote language by modeling slightly more mature language forms.

They help children express thoughts and feelings in words. An educator attempting to scaffold

- promotes longer, more precise child comments.
- invites divergent responses.
- offers specific word cues in statements and questions that help children grasp further information, for example, *what, who, why, because, so, and, next, but, except, if, when, before, after,* etc.
- provokes lively discussions and quests for knowing more about subjects that interest children.
- increases collaborative communication with adults and other children.

Scaffolding is not as easy as it first may appear to teachers. What is opportunity and challenge for one child may not be for the next. In scaffolding, teacher decision making is constant and complex. An educator using scaffolding believes understanding, discovery, and problem solving can be guided. Rather than always being dependent on adults for help, the child actually is moved toward becoming an independent thinker, advocates believe. Adults who accompany children at home or at school can use a scaffolding approach to talk through and plan activities as simple as setting the table, cleaning the sink, getting an art area ready for finger painting, or taking care of the needs of the school pet.

What is right or wrong becomes less important than the child's expression of his own conclusions. The child is encouraged to verbalize the "whys" of his thinking. For example, "Royal thinks the rabbit eats paper because he saw Floppy tearing paper into small pieces inside the cage."

Valuable teacher collaboration with children sustains the momentum of the search, actions, or exploration. Small group projects are often a natural part of children's block area play and can also be promoted in other aspects of daily play and activities. For example, a lemonade stand can be managed by a small group, or a present or card can be designed for a sick classmate at home and then completed and mailed by a small group of children.

## TEACHER INTERACTIVE STYLES

A central task for the educator is to find a balance between helping a child consolidate new understanding and offering challenges that will promote growth. Some educators believe that there are two teaching styles—transmission and interpretation. Transmission teaching is the traditional style, in which children's knowledge is thought to be acquired through the teacher talking, sharing books, and explaining classroom events and experiences. Interpretation teaching, on the other hand, is based on the understanding that children reinterpret information for themselves, and consequently, the teacher's role involves dialogues that support the children's efforts to verbalize their ideas and actual experiences.

One can easily see how easy it is to become a transmission teacher. It may have been overwhelmingly modeled in college student's own schooling. An interpretation teacher really listens and does not monopolize conversations by a display of what the teacher knows. Achieving balance between these two styles is the key. Educators both transmit and interpret.

In promoting developing language arts and literacy in early childhood, an interpretation style would not only help children talk about what they know but also help them put ideas and impressions in print by offering to take dictation or by using some other form of expression. The teacher's role is to provide the occasions, resources, and enabling climate for the pursuit of individual meaning.

Teachers can be fun-filled and playful companions at times, exhibiting their love and enthusiasm for life and the child's company. This side of teachers comes naturally to some adults and less easily to others. Perhaps many of us remember adults from our own childhood years that were able to engage themselves in adult-child interactions that could be described as joyful playing or companionable give and take.

## Interaction in Symbolic Play Situations

Pretend play (symbolic play) teacher interactions take both understanding and finesse. The teacher may wish to preserve the child's chosen play direction and not encroach upon self-directed imaginative activity but, at the same time, may wish to promote the child activity by giving attention, and therefore status, to the child's pursuit. There will definitely be many times when teacher interaction may be deemed intrusive because of the child's deep involvement. At those times teachers simply monitor at a distance. In other instances, particularly with younger preschoolers, teacher interaction may enrich the child's experience.

## Stressing Language Connections

The teacher interested in stressing connections between classroom language arts events and activities, as is done in an integrated approach or a whole-language approach, may often purposefully make the following comments.

> "I am writing down your ideas."
>
> "This printing I am reading says 'Please knock.'"
>
> "Do you want me to read what is printed on the wall?"
>
> "I can print that word."
>
> "What does the sign for your parking garage need to say?"
>
> "You seemed to be listening to the story I was reading."
>
> "Yes, *s* is the first alphabet letter in your name."
>
> "You want me to print your name on your work, right?"
>
> "I can read what this small printing on the box says."

## Accepting Approximations

Just as parents accept and celebrate inaccurate and incorrect language and writing attempts because they are seen as signs of growth, teachers also give attention to beginning attempts and provide encouragement. Lively, interesting environments and experiences where children offer their ideas and comments, feeling safe from criticism and insensitive grammar correction, help children risk and push ahead.

## Handling Interruptions

Children often interrupt adults during planned activities. When an idea hits, they want to share it. Their interruptions can indicate genuine involvement and interest, or they can reflect a variety of unrelated thoughts and feelings. Teachers usually acknowledge the interruption, accept it, and may calmly remind the one who interrupts that when one wants to speak during group activities, one should raise one's hand first. Other teachers believe preschoolers' enthusiasm to speak is natural and characteristic. These teachers believe asking children to raise their hands during group discussions is a practice best reserved for a later age. Interruptions give the teacher an opportunity to make a key decision that affects the flow of the activity. Will the interruption break the flow of what is going on, will it add to the discussion, or is it best discussed at a later time? The teacher may decide to defer a comment, or accept being sidetracked and briefly digress from the main subject, or develop the interruption into a full-blown teacher-group discussion. Examples follow:

Situation:  The teacher is telling a flannel-board story about a squirrel preparing for winter by hiding nuts in a tree.

Child:  "My cat climbs trees."

Teacher:  "Michael, I've seen cats climb trees."
(a short acknowledgment)

Teacher:  "Michael's cat climbs trees, and the squirrel is climbing the tree to hide the nuts he is storing away for winter."
(The teacher acknowledges, but refers listener back to the story line.)

Teacher:  "Michael, you can tell me about your cat that climbs trees as soon as we finish our story."
(The teacher defers discussion until later.)

Because preschoolers are action-packed, they enjoy activities that include an opportunity to perform the action words they encounter in books, discussions, or daily happenings (Figure 7–12). Teachers can promote "acting out" words with their own behaviors. Some action words are easily enacted include *pounce*,

| COMMON TEACHER STATEMENT | POSSIBLE CONSEQUENCES |
|---|---|
| "Tell me more." | expands |
| "Did you mean . . . ?" | clarifies |
| "Where did you see . . . ?" | specifying |
| "Who said . . . ?" | |
| "When did the bike . . . ?" | |
| "Whose name shall I write on . . . ?" | specifying possession |
| "This belongs to . . . ?" | |
| "Please tell Juan . . ." | conversing with others |
| "Choose one person to help you." | |
| "Can you show . . . ?" | provides information |
| "Tell me again . . ." | rephrase or repeat |
| "What would happen if . . . ?" | guessing or problem solving |
| "Thang thinks . . ." | valuing others' ideas |
| "Taylor says . . ." | |
| "What could we try . . . ?" | problem solving |
| "Where should we put . . . ?" | creative thinking |
| "What's a good name for . . . ?" | |
| "Who had the last turn to talk . . . ?" | turn taking |
| "Show me with your hands." | clarifies |
| "What will you need to . . . ?" | specifies |
| "What will you do first . . . ?" | |
| "Do you have a question for me?" | clarifies |
| "Did something happen that I didn't see?" | |
| "Did anyone hear a sound?" | listening skill |
| "Show me your hand when you want to tell us something." | turn taking |

*This is not meant to be a complete or comprehensive listing. Each language exchange with children is a challenge and opportunity.

**FIGURE 7–12** Sample teacher interaction verbalization.

*stamp, sneak, slither, creep,* and *slide. Enormous, droopy, sleepy, tired,* and other descriptive words can be connected to real examples or visual reproductions.

Incorporating the children's ideas and suggestions into group conversations and giving children credit for their ideas make children aware of the importance of their expressed ideas such as

"Kimberly's idea was to . . ." and

"Angelo thinks we should . . ." or

"Christal suggests that we . . .".

## Using Sequential Approaches to Instruction

Teachers need a clear understanding of how children learn words and concepts. Figure 7–13 includes guidelines for the teacher's words and actions to accompany the child's progress toward new learning.

One approach to teacher interaction during structured, planned, or incidental activities, described by Maria Montessori (1967b), is called three-stage interaction. It shows movement from the child's sensory exploration to showing understanding, and then to verbalizing the understanding. An example follows.

Step 1: *Associating Sense Perception with Words.* A cut lemon is introduced, and the child is encouraged to taste it. As the child tastes, the adult says, "The lemon tastes sour," pairing the word sour with the sensory experience. Repetition of the verbal pairing strengthens the impression.

Step 2: *Probing Understanding.* A number of yellow fruits are cut and presented. "Find the ones that tastes sour," the teacher suggests. The child shows by his actions his understanding or lack of it.

Step 3: *Expressing Understanding.* A child is presented with a cut lemon and grapefruit and asked, "How do they taste?" If the child is able to describe the fruit as sour, he has incorporated the word into his vocabulary and has some understanding of the concept.

| CHILD ACTIVITY | TEACHER ACTIONS |
|---|---|
| • focuses on an object or activity | • Name the object, or offer a statement describing the actions or situation. (supplies words) |
| • manipulates and explores the object or situation using touch, taste, smell, sight, and sound organs | • Try to help the child connect this object or action to his past experience through simple conversation. (builds bridge between old and new) |
| • fits this into what he already knows; develops some understanding | • Help the child see details through simple statements or questions. (focus on identifying characteristics) |
| | • Use "Show me . . . " or "Give me . . . " prodding statements that call for a nonverbal response. (prompting) |
| | • Put child's action into words. (Example: "John touched the red ball.") (modeling) |
| | • Ask the child for a verbal response. "What is this called?" "What happened when . . . ?" (prompting) |
| • uses a new word or sentence that names, describes, classifies, or generalizes a feature or whole part of the object or action | • Give a response in words indicating the truth factor of the response. "Yes, that's a red ball" or "It has four legs like a horse, but it's called a cow." (corrective or reinforcing response) |
| | • Extend one-word answers to full simple sentence if needed. (modeling) |
| | • Suggest an exploration of another feature of the object or situation. (extend interest) |
| | • Ask a memory or review question. "What did we discover when . . . " (reinforcing and assessing) |

FIGURE 7–13 Language learning and teacher interaction.

When using the three-step approach, Montessori (1967b) suggests that if a child is uninterested, the adult should stop at that point. If a mistake is made, the adult remains silent. The mistake indicates only that the child is not ready to learn—not that he is unable to learn. This verbal approach may seem mechanical and ritualistic to some, yet it clearly illustrates the sequence in a child's progress from not knowing to knowing.

The following example of a variation of the Montessori three-step approach includes additional steps. In this teaching sequence, the child asks the teacher how to open the tailgate of a dump truck in the sandbox.

| TEACHER INTENT: | TEACHER STATEMENTS: |
| --- | --- |
| 1. Focus attention. | "Look at this little handle." |
| 2. Create motivation, defined as creating a desire to want to do or want to know (note that in this situation this is not necessary because the child is interested). | "You want the tailgate to open." (Pointing) |
| 3. Provide information. | "This handle turns and opens the tailgate." (Demonstrating) |
| 4. Promote child's attempts or practice. | "Try to turn the handle." |
| 5. Give corrective information, feedback, or positive reinforcement. | "The handle needs to turn." "Try to push down as you turn it." (Showing how) Or, "You did it; the tailgate is open." |

Steps 1 through 5 are used in the following situation in which the teacher wants the child to know what is expected in the use of bathroom paper towels.

**1.** "Here's the towel dispenser. Do you see it?"

**2.** "You can do this by yourself. You may want to dry your hands after you wash them."

**3.** Demonstration: "First take one paper towel. Dry your hands. Then the towel goes into this wastebasket."

**4.** "You try it."

**5.** "That's it. Pull out one towel. Dry your hands. Put the towel in the wastebasket."

"Now you know where the dirty paper towels go. No one will have to pick up your used towel from the floor. You can do it without help now like some of your classmates."

Statements of this kind help the child learn both the task and the vocabulary. The ability to provide information that the child needs, without talking too much, is one of the skills required of a really excellent teacher. Most theorists believe that the successful completion of a task is a reward in itself. Others believe that an encouraging verbal pat on the back is in order.

The same dump truck scene detailed earlier could be handled using a discovery approach, instead of a teacher-directed sequence, with the following types of questions. "Did you see anyone else playing with this dump truck? Is there a button to push or a handle to turn that opens the tailgate? What happens if you try to open the tailgate with your hand?"

The goal of prompting in a child-adult conversation is to encourage the child to express ideas perhaps more precisely and/or specifically. It is used slightly differently with younger preschoolers, as shown in the following examples.

Young preschooler: "Cookie."

Adult: "You want a cookie?"

Child: "Dis cookie."

Adult: "You want this brown cookie?"

Older preschooler: "I want that cookie."

Adult: "You want one of these cookies. Which one of the cookies do you want? We have a chocolate cookie or a sugar cookie."

Child: "The chocolate one."

Can teachers really make a difference in the level and quality of children's language development? Very significant correlations have been found between both the frequency of informative staff talk, the frequency with which the staff answered the children, and the language comprehension scores of the children. Interaction does require teachers to "wonder out loud." They express their own curiosity while at the same time noticing each child's quest to find out what makes others tick and what the world is all about. How can teachers interact skillfully?

- Expand topics in which the child shows interest.
- Add depth to information on topics of interest.
- Answer and clarify children's questions.
- Help children sort out features of events, problems, and experiences, reducing confusion.
- Urge children to put what is newly learned or discovered into words.
- Cue children into routinely attending to times when the adult and child are learning and discovering together through discussion of daily events.

## Dealing with Children's Past Experiences

A teacher encounters a wide range of children's perceptions concerning the way children think they should communicate with adults. A child's family or past child care arrangements may have taught the child to behave in a certain way. With this in mind, the teacher can almost envision what it means to be a conversationalist in a particular family or societal group. Some families expect children to interrupt; others expect respectful manners. Wild, excited gesturing and weaving body movements are characteristic of

some children, whereas motionless, barely audible whispering is typical of others. Teachers working with newly arrived children from other cultures may see sharp contrasts in communication styles. Some children verbally seek help, whereas others find this extremely difficult. Some speak their feelings openly; others rarely express them. To promote child learning, a teacher needs to consider how she, their teacher, will interface to help each child understand that school may be very different than home.

Past child care experiences may have left their mark. A 4-year-old child named Perry seemed to give one teacher insight into how speech can be dramatically affected by past undesirable child care arrangements. The following is that teacher's observations and conclusions.

Perry sat quietly near the preschool's front door gnoring all play opportunities, and holding his blanket until his mom's return on his first day at school. He only spoke or looked up when teachers tried repeatedly to engage him in conversation and activities. He sat on adults' laps silently when they tried to comfort him, and ate food quickly and then returned to his waiting place near the door. The real Perry emerged a few weeks later as a talkative, socially vigorous child.

Our verbal statements and actions concentrated on rebuilding trust with adults and other children; only later was language-developing interaction possible.

It can be difficult for a child to engage an adult in conversation, as was the case with Perry. Seeking the availability of a teacher or caregiver and ensuring one's right to her attention and reply often calls for persistence and ingenuity in a poor-quality child care situation. Perry may have long before given up trying, and decided it was best to "just stay out of the way."

## Children's Inquisitive Honesty

Young children rarely limit their questions or modify their responses to the teacher for the purpose of hiding their ignorance, as older children sometimes do. During conversations, most young children intent on answers will probe enthusiastically for what they want to know.

 **VIDEO ACTIVITY**

Go to the video, *0-2 years: Module for Infants and Toddlers*, skip past the first segment with the crying infant and focus on the three caregivers comparing their vocal comments to the child who is exploring one or more play objects.

1. Which of the caregivers are providing a running commentary on what the child is doing at particular moments?

2. Which caregiver names objects and seems to encourage exploration, but does not direct the child's attention to toy features? Would you recommend pointing out to toy features to the child? Why or why not?

3. Which of the three caregivers seems to have more enthusiasm and involvement with her child? What makes you think so?

Teachers actively promote guesses and appreciate error making in an atmosphere of trust. They interact in conversations by focusing child attention, posing questions, discussing problems, suggesting alternatives, and providing information at the teachable moment.

### Outside Play and Literacy

Interacting to promote literacy during outdoor play challenges educators, but it is possible to offer some materials and activities that include a literacy feature. Probably the most common way is to try to read books on a blanket, in the shade, in the playhouse, or under a tree. Sidewalk chalk activities and games can be fun and might include printing names to jump on or over, or printing simple directions that read "Stamp your feet" or "Follow this line." Snapping instant photos and writing captions with the photographed child is a favorite activity. Occasionally labeling bikes A, B, C, etc. with hang-on cards might improve letter recognition, but caution is needed here. Overzealous teachers whose aim is to "teach on all occasions" should skip this discussion because children need lots of undirected time and freedom to pursue their own agendas, particularly when out of doors and using their own creative play ideas.

## THE TEACHER AS A BALANCER

In all roles, the teacher needs to maintain a balance. This means

- giving, but withholding when self-discovery is practical and possible.
- interacting, but not interfering with or dominating the child's train of thought or actions.
- giving support, but not hovering.
- talking, but not over talking.
- listening, but remaining responsive.
- providing many opportunities for the child to speak.
- being patient and understanding.

As is most often the case, when adults know the answer, many may find it difficult to be patient so children can figure out the answer for themselves. The teacher orally reflects and guards against being overly invasive and didactic.

There is an old story about two preschool boys who discover a worm in the play yard.

First child:     "Boy it tickles! Look at him!" (He holds the worm up to be seen.)

Second child:   "Let's show it to teacher."

First child:     "No way—she'll want us to draw a picture of it and make us print 'worm'!"

Teachers thoughtfully screen their comments and conversation to ensure they are free of sexist or biased attitudes, or stereotypes. If a teacher is talking about a stuffed teddy bear or the school's pet guinea pig (whose sex is yet to be discovered), use of the pronoun "it," rather than "he" or "she," is recommended.

## SUMMARY

Teachers function as models, providers of opportunities for language growth, collaborators, and interacting adults. Children copy behaviors and attitudes of both adults and peers. Educators realize the emotional connection they have which each child is important and it will influence the child's language growth. Teacher skills include extending and expanding child conversations and group discussions. Conversations that include having a child willingly express his ideas; actions, discoveries, and emotions are a key factor in the child's growing language competence. Using an extending technique means adding new information, and expanding concerns entails completing a child's statement so that it is grammatically complete.

Words are symbols for objects, ideas, actions, and situations. The teacher can increase children's vocabulary and understanding by helping children recognize links between the past and present and by using professional teacher strategies.

Teachers observe and listen closely so that teacher comments are pertinent and timely. An atmosphere of adult-child trust and acceptance of child ideas, whether valid or incorrect, is recommended.

The three teacher roles discussed in this chapter are model, provider, and interacting adult. A delicate balance exists in teaching functions. Every day decisions are made that affect children's language learning opportunities.

## ADDITIONAL RESOURCES

### Readings

Bennett-Arnistead, V., Duke, N. K., & Moses, A. M. (2005). *Literacy and the youngest learner: Best practices for educators of children from birth to 5* New York: Scholastic.

Burman, L. (2009). Are you listening? Fostering conversations that help young children learn. St. Paul, MN: Redleaf Press.

Denton, P. (2007). *The Power of our words: Teacher language that helps children.* Turner's Falls, MA: Northeast Foundation for Children.

Epstein, A. S. (2007). *The intentional teacher: Choosing the best strategies for young children's learning.* Washington, DC: National Association for the Education of Young Children.

Fassler, R. (2003). Room for talk: Teaching and learning in a multilingual kindergarten. New York: Teachers College Press.

Jones, N. P. (2005). Big jobs: Planning for competence. *Young Children, 60*(2): 86–93.

### Helpful Websites

National Association for the Education of Young Children
http://www.naeyc.org
Provides articles, publications, and other information.

National Parent Information Network
http://npin.org
Go to Virtual Library. Use "preschool language" as a search term. Sign up for free "Parent's Guide to Preschool" and find an article concerning talking to children about personal safety skills.

 Go to www.cengagebrain.com to access this text's Education Course-Mate website where you'll find helpful resource such as video activities, glossary flashcards, interactive exercises, quiz questions, and more!

# Review It and Use It

**A.** Name three functions of the language-developing early childhood teacher mentioned in this chapter. Omit balancer; if you remembered this function, there will still be another three.

**B.** List five examples of each of the functions you listed for question A.

**C.** Select the best answer.

1. The teacher is a model for
   a. speech.
   b. her political attitudes.
   c. speech that is more important than parents.
   d. speech only if she speaks perfect Standard English during planned activities.

2. It is more important for young children to
   a. like to speak than to speak correctly.
   b. sit quietly during activities than at circle time.
   c. speak rather than listen.
   d. have the teacher tell them about something than to explore it themselves.
   e. feel comfortable with a teacher rather than their peers.

3. Teachers reinforce learning by
   a. solving problems.
   b. giving attention to the child's use of a new word.
   c. motivating children to listen.
   d. asking about children's ideas.

4. When speaking, the teacher should
   a. attempt to use natural language patterns.
   b. speak loudly and clearly.
   c. make sure each child responds by speaking.
   d. refrain from giving child recognition for their good ideas.

5. Preschool children
   a. are also speech models.
   b. rarely teach others new words.
   c. play and mostly use newly learned words in play.
   d. have growing vocabularies only when teachers act appropriately.

**D.** Choose the one best answer.
1. Briana is staring at the wall clock. The teacher might say
   a. "You're wondering what time it is."
   b. "You are looking at our classroom clock. It tells us what time it is."
   c. "Tell me about the clock."
   d. "You've noticed our clock. Do you have one at your house?"

E. Write teacher statements that are an example of a teacher using (1) closure, (2) asking a child to demonstrate a word physically, (3) asking a child to relate a new word to past experience, and (4) a teacher defining the word whistle found in a story the teacher is reading. Example of a teacher putting into words what child is doing might be "You are using a paint brush by holding it in both of your hands."

## STUDENT ACTIVITIES

1. Pair up with a classmate. Switch between being the child and teacher in the following situations, and attempt to use strategies to help the child successfully solve his/her task or problem. Share your results with the total group.

   A. Rahjon (age 4) is trying unsuccessfully to pour sand through a large funnel.

   B. Margot (age 3½) is attempting to dress a large doll but seems to be unable to do so because the doll clothes have zippers and large buttons.

   C. Charlie's (age 4) job entails setting a small snack table with a plate, cup, napkin, and spoon for four children. It is his first time doing so and he is hesitating, somewhat bewildered, and looks to the teacher for help.

2. Pretend you are having a conversation about a teacher's car that the children observed being towed away for repair. You are attempting to extend the topic of discussion, wringing as much out of the experience as possible while monitoring child interest and knowledge. Create possible teacher conversational comments in b to g that follow after reading the example in a.

   a. Recap what you noticed and promote children's remembrance. Example: "I saw a tow truck driver climb out of the tow truck cab."

   b. Explain some aspect of the situation by giving reasons.

   c. Describe a cause-and-effect feature of the situation.

   d. Compare this situation with another.

   e. Talk about what might happen to the teacher's car.

   f. Comment about what the teacher could do in this situation besides calling a tow truck.

   g. Ask how the children would feel if it were their familys' car.

   h. List six other aspects of the situation that could be discussed.

   Compare your answers with those of a group of classmates. Now discuss further teacher-planned follow up activities that could increase and expand children's comments, questions, or understanding. Share with the entire group.

3. Listen intently to three adults. (Take notes.) How would you evaluate them as speech models (good, average, poor)? State the reasons for your decisions.

4. Tape-record or videotape your interaction with a group of young children for a period of 25 minutes. Analyze your listening, questioning, sentence structure, extending ability, and pronunciation.

5. Consider the following slogans. Explain and elaborate their meanings or create five other slogans that would mirror some of this chapter's ideas or suggestions, and then share them with the total group.

   Intent not correctness.

   Your topic, not mine.

The wrong answer is right.

Logic not mechanics.

Give them your eyes and ears.

Responsive opportunist here!

Shh! Here comes the teacher.

6. Read the following quote. Discuss its relationship to child language growth.

The small Zulu also didn't have just one daddy. He had the dadoos, his father's brothers and other male adults who talked to him about hunting, showed him how to make a little bow and arrow and all of this kind of stuff. They spent time with him and they "joyed in his presence," as someone once defined love. So on into adult life there was for both the boys and the girls this abundance of love and affection and attention and tenderness. (Lair, 1985)

7. Fill out the checklist in Figure 7–14 and compare your ratings with those of your classmates.

|  | AGREE | CAN'T DECIDE | DISAGREE |
|---|---|---|---|
| 1. Every center happening should encourage speech. | | | |
| 2. It takes considerable time and effort to have personal conversations with each child daily. | | | |
| 3. Each child is entitled to a personal greeting and goodbye. | | | |
| 4. "How are you?" is a good opening remark. | | | |
| 5. A child who bursts out with something to say that has nothing to do with what is presently happening must have something important on his mind. | | | |
| 6. Pausing silently for a few moments after speaking to a shy child is a good idea. | | | |
| 7. Most new vocabulary words are learned at group times. | | | |
| 8. Saying, "John stepped over the green block," is unnecessary, for the child knows what he has done. | | | |
| 9. All children have home interests that teachers can discuss with them. | | | |
| 10. At mealtimes, it is best to remain quiet while children enjoy their food. | | | |
| 11. If the child talks about a bathroom function, ignore it. | | | |
| 12. When Adam says, "Girls can't drive trucks," tell him he is wrong. | | | |
| 13. Teachers really need to talk more than they listen. | | | |
| 14. Saying, "Tell him you don't like it when he grabs your toy," is poor technique. | | | |
| 15. I don't think it's possible to use a lot of language-building techniques and still speak naturally and comfortably with a child. | | | |
| 16. Teachers should model a playful attitude at times. | | | |

FIGURE 7–14 Opinion poll.

# Developing Listening Skills

## OBJECTIVES

After reading this chapter, you should be able to:

- List five types of listening.
- Discuss teaching techniques that promote good listening habits.
- Demonstrate how to plan an activity that promotes a listening skill.
- Present a listening activity to a group of preschoolers.
- Tell a story that involves purposeful child listening.

## KEY TERMS

alliteration
continuant
grapheme
hearing
listening
listening
  comprehension
  level

onsets
phonemic
  awareness
rimes

## Unexpected Answer

*Claire, an early childhood teacher, circled her classroom of 4-year-olds during the first week of school, trying to make conversation and listen intently to each child at free choice time. When she noticed Anna painting at the easel, Claire stood by and admired her work before saying "I can see many different colors in your painting. There is blue paint and an alphabet letter, too. It looks like an 'a.'" Anna, a tiny child, barely able to reach the top of the paper with her paint brush, responded, "Actually, it is a lower case 'a' that makes a long vowel sound, and this color is aquamarine."*

### Questions to Ponder

1. When children know more than you expect them to know, what is a prudent course of action?

2. How should Claire respond to being corrected by Anna?

3. Anna has told the teacher a lot about herself, including . . . ?

**Listening** skill is the first language arts skill learned, and it develops before a child speaks. Many children develop the ability to listen carefully to the speech of others during infancy and early childhood; others do not. Because language growth has been described as a receiving process followed by a sending process, a child's listening ability is important to speaking and future reading and writing success.

Hearing and listening are quite different. **Hearing** is a process involving nerves and muscles that reach adult efficiency by age 4 to 5. Listening is a learned behavior, a mental process that is concerned with hearing, attending, discriminating, understanding, and remembering. It can be improved with practice. Listening affects social interactions, one's level of functioning, and perhaps one's overall success in life (Figure 8–1). Researchers estimate that we listen to 50 percent of what we hear and comprehend only 25 percent of that.

Listening skill can be described as passive and receptive, but it involves active thinking and interpretation. Lively conversations between adults and young children who feel free to verbalize reactions to life's happenings promote listening and speaking. Children offer more verbal comments in school settings in small, relaxed groups in which comments are accepted and appreciated. Young children sometimes learn that it is best to keep quiet in some classrooms. In other classrooms, every child's opinion counts and classroom discussions are frequent and animated.

There are usually many opportunities to listen in early childhood centers. Teacher-planned or child-created play is a source of many sounds. A quality program sharpens a child's listening and offers a variety of experiences. Listening is not left to chance; planned programs develop skills.

## RESEARCH ON LISTENING

Although current research is limited concerning both listening and whether direct instruction in listening skill is effective, studies conducted in the 1950s and 1960s showed that listening instruction led to measurable gains in listening comprehension. Active involvement during and following listening activities may help more than unconnected activities.

Listening is not a discrete skill or generalized ability, but a cluster of specific abilities closely related to those needed in the reading task. Early childhood professionals should be aware of the early development of a child's **listening comprehension level**.

## TYPES OF LISTENING

Listening occurs in many ways. A person does not always listen for knowledge but may listen to a sound because it is pleasing. The first time children discover the sounds made by pots and pans, they are fascinated. Preschoolers often make their own pleasurable or rhythmic sounds with whatever is available.

The human voice can be interesting, threatening, or monotonous to a child, depending on past experience. Silence also has meaning. Sometimes teachers suspect that a child has a hearing problem, only to find that the child was inattentive for other reasons.

FIGURE 8–1 The teacher bends and listens intently to understand what the boys are requesting.

---

**listening** — a mental process that includes attending, hearing, discriminating, understanding, and remembering.
**hearing** — the facility or sense by which sound is perceived.
**listening comprehension level** — the highest grade level of material that can be comprehended well when it is read aloud to a child.

*Appreciative listening.* The child finds pleasure and entertainment in hearing music, poems, and stories. It is best to begin with this type of listening because it is passive, but personal, for each child.

*Purposeful listening.* The child follows directions and gives responses.

*Discriminative listening.* The child becomes aware of changes in pitch and loudness. Sounds become differentiated in the environment. Eventually, the child is able to discriminate the speech sounds.

*Creative listening.* The child's imagination and emotions are stimulated by her listening experiences. Thoughts are expressed spontaneously and freely through words or actions, or both.

*Critical listening.* The child understands, evaluates, makes decisions, and formulates opinions. To encourage this critical listening, the teacher may pose such questions as "What happens when we all talk at once?" or "What if everyone wanted to play in the playhouse at the same time?" The child must think through the responses, decide the most logical solution to the problem, and present a point of view.

**FIGURE 8–2** Some of the ways a child listens.

| RESPONDING TO STIMULI | ORGANIZING THE STIMULI | UNDERSTANDING THE MEANING |
| --- | --- | --- |
| awareness | sequencing and | (classification; |
| focus | synthesizing | integration; |
| figure-ground | scanning | monitoring) |
| discrimination | | |

←———————————————— Memory ————————————————→

*Stage 1—Responding to stimuli.* Was there sound? Where was it? Which sound was it? Was there more than one sound? Were the sounds the same?

*Stage 2—Organizing the stimuli.* What was the sequence of the sounds? What was the length of time between sounds? Have I heard that sound before? Where have I heard it?

*Stage 3—Understanding the meaning.* What do the sounds and words mean?

**FIGURE 8–3** Stages of the listening process.

Children may listen but not understand. They may miss sound differences or listen without evaluating what they hear. Listening involves a variety of skills and levels. To provide growth opportunities, teachers should be aware of various listening skills, as shown in Figure 8–2. A child may rely on a combination of the skills described.

The goal of a good program in early childhood language arts is to guide the young child toward development of these listening levels. The listening process contains three stages the child moves through in efficient listening (Figure 8–3). When a sound occurs, it is remembered by thinking about its features: location, pitches, intensity, newness, and so on.

## TODDLER LISTENING EXPERIENCES

Families and center staff members can engage toddlers in a number of activities to stimulate listening. Body-action play of the old "coochee-coo" variety, "This Little Piggy," and simple rhymes and repetitions are recommended. Connecting noises and sounds with toys and objects and encouraging the child to imitate show the child that joy and sound making go hand in hand. Rhythmic clapping, tapping, and pan beating in sequence or patterns can be enjoyable (Figure 8–4). Musical toys and recordings add variety and listening pleasure. Encouraging children to watch facial expressions as different

**FIGURE 8–4** Drums capture interest quickly and provide listening pleasure.

human sounds are produced and locating environmental sounds together are techniques in developing children's listening skills.

Adults exercise care in classroom sound volume and quality; at all age levels, extra loud, shrill, vibrating, or emergency alert sounds can be frightening.

## Purposeful Listening Activities

The intent of purposeful listening practice is to increase the child's ability to follow directions and instructions, perform tasks, and respond appropriately in some fashion. Teachers can use a three-step method to help very young preschoolers gain skill in this type of listening. They tell children what they are going to tell them. Next, they say it; and last, they tell children what they told them.

**Example:**

1. "I'm going to give you an envelope, and tell you where to take it."

2. "Take the envelope to the cook, Mrs. Corelli, and then come back to our classroom."

3. "You took the envelope to Mrs. Corelli just as I said and returned. Thank you."

If you were attempting to tell a story to promote children's purposeful listening ability, you might start by saying, "I'm going to tell you a story about my dog. He is a very funny looking dog who makes people laugh. Laughing happens when people see my dog or hear his name. If you listen, you'll find out about Picasso. That is his name. When my story is finished, see if you can tell me one thing that Picasso does that makes people laugh."

Purposeful, attentive listening takes concentration. Teachers can perfect a "what I'm saying next is important" tone and consequently create a desire in children to listen. Statements such as "You might want to know how" or "You can listen closely to find out" or "If you'd like a turn, watch and listen" may also provide the motivation to listen closely.

Planned, purposeful listening activities can include activities that encourage children to listen in order to

- do something for themselves.
- tell another how to do something.
- operate some type of toy or equipment.
- carry a message.
- recall details.

- put objects in a special order or sequence.
- see how many names or facts they can remember.
- learn new skills, such as singing new songs or chanting or doing finger plays.

### Appreciative Listening Activities

Appreciative listening deals with light listening when enjoyment or pleasure is paramount. A wide variety of recorded and live appreciative listening experiences is possible. Background music can accompany favorite preschool pursuits. Chanting a remembered selection of words gives the children a double treat of hearing voices in unison and feeling part of a group. Some appreciative listening builds moods, touches emotions, and adds another dimension to experience. The world is full of beautiful and not-so-beautiful sounds. Programs attempt to offer listening experiences that are aesthetically pleasing environmental sounds such as familiar home and community sounds plus pleasant sounds in found in nature.

Possible appreciative listening activities include:

- moving to music.
- discussing music, rhythms, and sounds.
- talking about favorite sounds.
- talking about happy, sad, or funny feelings that sounds produce.
- tapping, clapping, or moving to music or rhythmic speech.

The benefits of introducing a music curriculum to young children are multiple as mentioned in previous chapters. Music offers another means of expression for children. It can build vocabulary, establish a sense of internal rhythm, develop an awareness of pitch and intonation in voice, and create an understanding of language concepts such as loud, soft, fast, and slow. Singing promotes the development of syntax and memorization skills.

There is a predictable pattern in children's learning of any song. Movements or words are learned first, then rhythms and other elements. Traditional nursery songs are plentiful, are appropriately pitched, and contain repetition of melodic and rhythmic patterns. Music is a "language builder."

### Favorite Children's Classics and Traditional Songs

A few classics and traditional American children' songs include *Old MacDonald Had a Farm, Dinah, Teddy Bear, Eensy, Weensy Spider,* and *I'm a Little Teapot.* Educators try to uncover traditional songs in attending children's home language and offer these tunes also.

### Partial Listing of Language Features Found in Songs

Music or a song may involve more than one of these learning opportunities—vocabulary development, predictability features in a story line or sequence, rhyming features, repetitions that reinforce, cultural literacy significance, concept development, appreciative listening features, purposeful listening aspects, discriminative listening opportunities, and creative listening experiences. Often, a coordination of words with physical movement also occurs in children's music.

## CRITICAL LISTENING ACTIVITIES

Critical listening requires the children's evaluation of what is heard and comprehended. It requires contemplation and reflection, and some preschoolers develop considerable skill in this area and use it frequently. These children seem able to weigh the new against what they already know and feel and are eager to discuss differences. Other children seem rarely to hold any opinion or particular viewpoint and are reticent to share thoughts. Activities that involve critical thinking can be ones in which

- a problem is discussed and solutions are offered and evaluated.
- a probable outcome or guess is prompted.
- a real or make-believe feature is pinpointed using some criteria.
- personal preferences or dislikes are discussed.
- group votes are reviewed and outcomes are anticipated.
- errors of some type are discovered or detected.
- feelings of others are predicted.
- inconsistencies are discovered.

## DISCRIMINATIVE LISTENING ACTIVITIES

Discriminative listening has gained increased attention as a result of current research and because of national legislative efforts to improve American children's reading ability. To discern whether a sound or sound pattern is the same or different, one uses discriminative listening skill. This skill is necessary when a child attempts to decode words in early reading.

The preschool teacher who plans a "Listening Detective" activity in which preschoolers catch the teacher in a mistake—such as "he huffed and he puffed and he blew the *tree* down" after the group is well acquainted with *The Three Little Pigs*—is presenting a discriminative listening exercise. Imitating a clapping pattern is another, as is finding rhyming sounds or matching xylophone notes.

## CREATIVE LISTENING ACTIVITIES

Many classroom literacy activities create an emotional response or reaction. Audiovisual media can do so also. Discussion after a read-aloud picture book or other literacy event may reveal children's feelings and imaginative ideas. Children may then be encouraged to recreate their feelings and ideas in subsequent art, drama, or other forms of expression.

Creative listening has been used as a strategy to unleash creative potential. Who among us hasn't had an "aha" or "light bulb turning on" experience when listening, or had a mental picture form while experiencing a piece of music or hearing a great storyteller?

## TEACHER SKILLS

Good listening habits are especially important in school situations. Teachers need to assess their own listening habits and abilities in their daily work with children. Jalongo (2009) has developed a listening skill assessment exercise for teachers. See Figure 8–5.

If teachers expect undivided attention from children, educators must also give undivided attention to them. Most of us have been told in teacher training to bend or lower ourselves to child eye level when we speak to

---

Ask Yourself these questions to help ou reflect on your habits as a listener in an inclusive classroom:

- How do I deal with children who seldom talk or are very soft-spoken? Do I encourage them to remain quiet to keep the level of children's talk in the classroom low, or do I make a genuine attempt to draw them into conversation?

- How do I deal with children who are exceptionally talkative or loud? Do I make assumptions about them and their families? Do my assumptions differ based on gender, race, or culture?

- Do I listen patiently to children who have difficulty expressing their ideas and struggle to be understood, or do I quickly move on? Do I make opportunities for them to be heard, not only by me but also by their peers?

- What do I do when children who have asked for a chance to speak fall silent when their turn comes? Am I sensitive to the fact that young children can forget what they were about to say, and do I ensure they have another chance to speak?

- How about when children's behavior is challenging—does everyone get treated fairly, or does the child skilled in verbal expression (e.g., a "smooth talker") avoid consequences more often?

- Do I ask many different types of questions, allowing more children chances to contribute, or do I play the "read the teacher's mind" game much of the time?

- When children say something of questionable accuracy, how do I handle it? Do I pounce on the statement as a "lie," or do I try to get further clarification? If I know it to be untrue or inaccurate, do I lose respect for the child, or remember that the line between fantasy and reality for young children is a dotted one? Do I consider that children sometimes express wishes as fact, and acknowledge this sensitively, with a comment such as, "Yes, wouldn't it be nice if we could . . . "

- How do I respond if a child shares something that makes me uncomfortable (e.g., "My cat got runned over by a car" . . . "My dad promised to take me camping, but I waited all weekend and he never came to get me"). Do I quickly move on, or do I acknowledge the feelings that underlie the message ("It is so sad to lose our pets" . . . "You were upset that a promise was broken")?

FIGURE 8–5 Do you listen to all kinds of children?

children, but how often do we do this when we listen to them?

Two factors may decrease teachers' ability to listen and model listening behavior: (1) they may not have had experienced teachers in their own schooling (including college professors) who listened with care and valued inquiry, and (2) teachers are so busy imparting information that they miss the profound questions and comments of children. This type of interactive style teaches children to sit passively and withdraw. It teaches most vividly what the teachers least suspect they have transmitted.

Instructions from teachers should be clear and simple, with a sequence of what comes first, next, and last. Usually, instructions need not be repeated when given clearly and simply.

Often, when the attention of the group is required, a signal is used. Any distinctive, easy-to-hear, pleasant sound or visual signal can alert children that it is time to listen. The silent pause before beginning an activity can be used effectively to focus attention on listening. Katz and Schery's (2006) suggestions for educators who handle young children with hearing loss also apply to teachers of younger preschoolers and English language learners. Suggestions include:

- Speaking using an ordinary tone/volume.
- Making sure the child's attention is focused on the speaker.
- Talking naturally and clearly and using simple phrases or simple but complete sentences depending on the child's language level.
- Clarifying idioms. Do so in context. For example, explain "It's raining cats and dogs" when you have used the expression after dashing inside during a cloudburst.
- Checking with the child to ensure comprehension. Sometimes asking "Tell me what I just said" provides information to the teacher about how much a child understands.
- Showing real-life pictures when reading or talking about a topic and using simple signs.

- Pointing, or having on hand an example of the object you're explaining.
- Being aware of background noise which can mask essential auditory information.
- Reducing classroom noise with acoustically treated low ceilings, carpet, and well-fitted doors.
- Putting rubber tips or old tennis balls on the bottoms of chair legs to reduce noise. (p. 95)*

Additionally Katz and Schery suggest positioning children to provide a hearing advantage and being sure that lighting is appropriate.

Teachers sometimes use a short song, finger play, or body-movement activity to stimulate interest and draw the group together (Figure 8–6). This helps children focus on what is to follow.

Encouragement and smiles at any time of the day can reward individual listening. Positive, specific statements, such as, "Ramon, you listened to what Jan had to say before you started talking" or "It's quiet, and now we can all hear the beginning of the story," give children feedback on expected listening behavior. The following are sample teacher statements that can promote a group's ability to listen.

## At the Beginning

- "When I see everyone's eyes, I'll know you're ready to hear about . . ."
- "We'll begin when we can all hear the clock ticking."
- "I'm waiting until everyone can hear before I start. We need to be quiet so that everyone can hear about . . ."
- "It seems everyone is listening; it's time to begin."
- "We take turns speaking. Skye is first, then . . ."

*From Katz, L., & Schery, T. K. (2006). Including children with hearing loss in early childhood programs. *Young Children*, *61*(1): 86–95. Copyright © 2006 NAEYC. Used with permission from the National Association for the Education of Young Children.

FIGURE 8–6 Starting a circle time with a "clapping song" can focus and engage the group.

## During the Activity

● "Wyatt had his hand up. Would you like to tell us about your idea?"

● "It's Maria's turn to tell us . . ."

● "We can hear better when just one person is talking. Louis, you go first, then Cristalee."

● "Ethan, it's hard to wait when you want to talk. Khesia is talking now; you can be next." (Later add, "Ethan, thank you for waiting for Khesia to finish. Now we will hear what you wanted to tell us.")

● "Everyone wants to tell us about their own pets. Raise your hand—I'll make a waiting list so that we can hear everyone." (Make the list quickly and hold it up.) "Isaac, your name is first."

## At Activity's End

● "We listened so quietly. We all heard every word of that story."

● "Everyone listened to what their friends said."

● "We listened and found out a lot about . . ."

Additional examples of teacher talk that promotes listening are as follows:

● "We are going to do two things right now."

● "Listen. Pick up your rug square; that's the first thing to do. Then put your square right here on this pile on the table. You were listening, Polly, thank you."

● "Listen and then you'll know who will hold the door open. Today it's Rudy's job. Whose job is it? Right, it is Rudy's job today."

● "Eyes open. Lips closed. It's listening time."

● "I can't hear when everyone is talking. Mario, it is your turn."

● "It's Adrian's time to talk now. That means no one else is talking."

● "Let's wait until it is quiet, then we are all ready to listen to the story."

● "When I see everyone's eyes looking in my eyes, I'll know you are ready to listen."

● "That was attentive listening. Everyone was quiet while Joni told us about her painting."

## A GROUP ACTIVITY

At group time, Rachel, a preschool teacher, gathered the children, and silently waited while they settled in before beginning. "Let's see who is with us today. If you hear your name, give me one clap. Gage." Gage claps one time. "Gage heard his name, and I heard one clap. I'll whisper the next name. If you hear your name give me two claps." Two claps are heard. "Good listening, Mara." Rachel continues until all in the group have been recognized by name.

Rachel then reaches for a story book. "In this book there is something Nathan and Nicholas Alexander want, but they can't see it. Let's look at the book's cover and I will read its title. Then I think you can guess." She places her hand under each word and reads *Nathan's Fishing Trip*. Children's hands shoot up, and Skylar guesses fish. Others agree. "Lulu Delacre wrote this story," Rachel continues. She turns to the title page and comments, "Look carefully at the pictures (illustrations), do you see Nicholas Alexander? He has a big two word name, but Nicholas Alexander is a very small mouse." She fans the book closer so that all can see. Rachel starts the story, but interrupts briefly to show a large drawing of a hook and a few colored fishing lures. When the word hook and lure are mentioned on the third page, she traces the hook shape as she talks about its sharpness. The book reading proceeds to its conclusion.

A discussion includes confirming that fish was a good guess. Rachel mentions it was a particular fish, a trout. She asks why Nathan and Nicholas Alexander may have decided to free the trout. Children's ideas are offered and discussed. Rachel then says, "Nathan and Nicholas Alexander have names beginning with the letter 'N' just like Nicole." She makes a quick "N" on a sheet of paper and holds it up.

A fishing game with fish shapes follows. This was prepared by Rachel beforehand. She explains some of the fish in the plastic washtub have the letter "N" printed on them, while other do not. "If you want a turn with the fishing game raise your hand." Rachel says. A waiting list is printed by Rachel, who selects one child and asks, "Do you want to choose a friend to play with you?" The child indicates a friend. Rachel lines out their names on the waiting list, and points to and reads the next child's name who is to have the next turn.

FIGURE 8–7 Rachel's group activity.

- "Josh has something important to say. Let's listen so that we all hear what he is going to tell us."
- "I know it's hard to wait, Cleota, but Rick is talking now. Wait. It will be your turn next."
- "What are we going to do after we pour the milk in the bowl? Yes, Brenda, we said we had to stir with the spoon. Good listening, Brenda."
- "Now let's think of another sound we might hear if we go to the window and listen."
- "It is my turn to speak, and your turn to listen."

Rewarded behavior is usually repeated and becomes a habit. Teachers should consistently notice correct listening behavior and comment favorably about it to the children.

How can one recognize good listening habits? Characteristics of children with listening skills follow. Good listeners look at a speaker's face, filter out distractions, concentrate on a speaker's message, and they can repeat back what was said. They rarely interrupt and may ask pertinent questions after mulling over what's been said.

Examine Figure 8–7. It is an example of a teacher attempting to promote listening skill and other language development skills. Can you identify a few of Rachel's listening promotion strategies?

## AUDITORY PERCEPTION

Ears respond to sound waves. These sounds go to the brain and become organized in relation to past experience. The same process is used in early childhood and later when the child learns to read. Language development depends on the auditory process.

Educational activities that give practice and help perfect auditory skills usually deal with the following objectives.

- sustaining attention span
- following directions or commands
- imitating sounds
- identifying and associating sounds
- using auditory memory
- discriminating between sounds (intensity, pitch, tempo)

The intensity of a sound is its degree of force, strength, or energy. Pitch is the highness or lowness of sound. Tempo is the rate of speed of a sound, in other words, the rhythm of the sound that engages the attention.

## Auditory Activities

A wide range of auditory activities can be planned. The following goals often serve as the basis for planning. Simple skills come before more difficult ones.

- recognizing own name when spoken

- repeating two nonsense words, short sayings, chants, poems, finger plays, or any series of words

- reporting sounds heard at home

- imitating sounds of toys, animals, classrooms, rain, sirens, or bells

- telling whether a sound is near or far, loud or soft, fast or slow, high or low, same or different

- identifying people's voices

- identifying and repeating rhythms heard

- retelling a story, poem, or part of either

- trying to perform first one-part and then two-part directions

 **LEARNING MODULE**

Go to the Education CourseMate website to complete the Wernicke-Geschwind module. This learning module involves the processing of language in the brain and language comprehension and production. You will gain detailed information and have some fun moving and labeling brain areas. A small ungraded test of your comprehension is included. The importance of the primary auditory and Wernicke area involves your ability to make speech sounds and words understandable as you work with young children.

1. The auditory area in the brain receives spoken language. Each child's listening ability is involved. What features of teacher planned activities will increase a child's ability to both hear well and understand?

2. When planning group activities, what room areas will be suitable if you wish the group to hear you and their peers?

3. Will you routinely assess whether you are able to listen closely and check if you heard correctly what a child says to you even when the message seems unclear or illogical? Provide a few examples of teacher statements checking to make sure they heard what they thought they heard.

- recalling sounds in sequence

- coordinating listening skills with body movements in a requested way

- enjoying music, stories, poems, and many other language arts, both individually and in groups

## SETTINGS FOR LISTENING

When preparing listening activities, the teacher can plan for success by having activities take place in room areas with a minimum of distracting sounds or objects. Screens, dividers, and bookcases are helpful (Figure 8–8). Heating and lighting are checked, and comfortable seating is provided. Decisions concerning the size of a group are important. In general, the younger the children, the smaller the group the teacher will attempt to instruct, and the shorter the length of the activity.

Listening cannot be forced, but experiences can be provided that create a desire to listen. Some schools offer children the choice of joining a group listening activity or playing quietly nearby. Teachers find that an interesting experience will attract children who are playing nearby. When activities are enjoyable and successful, the child who was hesitant may look forward to new experiences. A teacher may be able to turn on or turn off attention by ending, changing, or modifying activities when necessary. The teacher should watch carefully for feedback in children's gestures, actions, attentiveness, responsiveness, body position, eye focus, and other nonverbal clues. A skillful teacher will complete the learning activity before the group becomes restless. When an activity is planned for which listening is required, it is important to consider that an active preschooler may have to struggle to remain seated for any extended period.

### Evaluating Teacher Behaviors

Teachers planning activities need to consider the following questions. Why will a child listen to this activity? What factors or features could be included? What teacher behaviors, speech, or actions encourage child listening? How do I, as a teacher, develop "a listening habit" in

**FIGURE 8–8** Bookcases have been added to make this classroom area a quiet spot.

children and promote specific listening skills? Can I judge when I have captured child attention? Can I assess which children listen well and which children listen poorly? These are quite a few questions to be answered, and you may have thought of others. A good place to start is to analyze your own classroom experiences. Hopefully, you experienced a memorable class or teacher whose class you loved to attend. List the factors that made that teacher or class special. Usually mentioned are the teacher's personality, her style of teaching, and techniques that the teacher used to make students feel special, competent, smart, accepted, and so on. Also often mentioned are the teacher's uses of the classroom's physical space, enjoyed activities, and perhaps other adults or children in the classroom. The author remembers vividly the grammar school teacher who always skillfully read an interesting and exciting book after recess. She read with great enthusiasm, animation, and pleasure. Going back to the questions under discussion, we will take a closer look at each.

Why do children listen to an activity? A number of reasons are possible.

- The activity relates in some way to past experience.

- The children are curious about something new (Figure 8–9).

- There is a motivation to listen because of something the children want to know that personally affects them.

- The children enjoy the company of the people present.

- Something has happened to capture their attention.

- They can hear clearly without distractions and/or can easily see what is going on.

- They are physically comfortable.

- They have no physical, emotional, social, or personal distracting life situation upon which they are focused, such as hunger, lack of sleep, emotional pain, and so on.

What teacher behaviors, speech, or actions might influence child listening?

- enthusiasm

- animation (but not overly so)

- acceptance

- recognition of children by name

- establishment of a you-talk turn, I-talk turn interaction

- eye contact

FIGURE 8–9 Cracking an egg is a new experience for many children.

- listening skill
- patience
- clear and appropriately paced and pitched speech
- panning of a group with the eyes to gauge children's avid or waning attention and adjusting accordingly
- voice variety
- appropriate voice volume
- eye-level contact
- planning for enough time so that there is not a rushed feeling
- elimination of distractions such as two children sitting together who might "act up" or other noises in the classroom that interfere with listening
- lowered voice volume to gain attention
- stating of rules about turn-taking behavior, hand raising, and interrupting
- use of an attention-getting gathering activity at the beginning of the activity

Can I judge when I have captured attention or the activity has captured child attention? If you watch, you will know when they are with you, "all ears" so to speak. It is one of the joys of teaching. The feeling of communion never grows old. Ask any practicing teacher.

Can I assess which children listen well and which need help developing listening skill? If you are watchful, yes. However, there are days when even the best listeners will be distracted.

## Speak-Listen Group Times

Kindergarten and some early childhood programs are offering older preschoolers "talking-listening" social skill groups. The goal of this activity is to give children who desire to speak the chance to discuss child- and teacher-selected topics in a social setting. This structured activity promotes active listening. In elementary school, this group experience is usually termed "active listening" time or "community circle."

Children are seated in a circle so that they can look at the person speaking and easily hear everyone's comments. In preschools, the circle times ideally are kept short and intimate, with small groups of children.

Teachers structure this type of talking-listening time as follows:

1. The teacher announces a talk-listen circle as a choice of activity.

2. The teacher names the topic or elicits one from the group. It might be cats because a picture book has been shared, or worms

because one has been found, or it might be an open-ended statement like, "After school I like to go home and . . ."

3. A chart depicting expected talk-listen circle behavior is introduced or reviewed. "We'll be looking at the person speaking. We'll listen with our ears." The teacher may choose to introduce only looking at others during children's first circle, and listening another time.

4. The teacher states, "Each of us will have a turn to speak. If you don't want a turn to speak, you can say 'Pass'."

5. The teacher speaks first, modeling a short sentence—"My cat is gray and likes to sleep in a sunny window." Then she proceeds around the circle.

6. A very short group evaluation can take place when all have had a turn. Was it easy to wait for your turn? Did you see others' eyes while you were talking? (Children's answers are given in turn.)

Teachers may continue if discussion is still of interest with statements such as, "We've all had a turn. Raise your hand if you've something more to tell. Anyone can choose to leave our talking-listening time."

A number of common behaviors occur at preschool discussion times. An egg timer might have to be used with the child who drones on and on. The same children may pass day after day, or the same children may choose to participate in circle discussions. A child may not stick to the announced topic, but all comments are accepted and appreciated by the teacher.

Because listening closely and group discussion may be new to preschoolers and because individual developmental levels vary, children may either quickly or slowly grasp the social and listening skills offered. To encourage listening and speaking in turn, some programs use cardboard cutouts of lips and ears attached to tongue depressors. The speaker holds the stick with the lips while listeners hold ear sticks.

Of course, many unplanned discussions take place in most preschool classrooms. This type of structured group time encourages young children's social discussion—a skill useful in future classrooms.

## Listening Centers

Special listening areas, sometimes called listening posts, can become a part of early childhood classrooms. Enjoying a solitary time listening to recorded media while wearing earphones fascinates some children. Headsets plugged in to a jack or terminal help block out room noise. Partitions cut distractions. Clever listening places where children can settle into become favorite spots, such as large packing boxes, armchairs, a stack of pillows, or a climb-into bunk, nook, or loft.

Videos, audio cassettes, DVDs, CDs and CD players, photographs, picture sets, and books offer added dimensions to listening centers. Recordings of the teacher reading a new or favorite story can be available for children's use (Figure 8–10). These recordings are sometimes called read-alongs and are also available from commercial sources. Their quality varies widely,

**FIGURE 8–10** Listening with earphones puts this child into deep thought.

so it is recommended that they be reviewed before they are purchased.

When teachers realize how much future educational experience depends on how well language is processed through children's listening, listening activities and listening centers gain importance. Many of today's children have passively listened to considerable electronic media but may be particularly lacking in the practice of auditory analysis and logical sequential reasoning.

Children can record, with adult help, their own descriptions of special block constructions together with accompanying drawings or photos. "Why I like this book" talks can be recorded and made available to the whole class. Children can record comments about their pieces of art. A field-trip scrapbook may have a child's commentary with it. Recorded puppet scripts and flannel board stories can be enjoyed while the child moves the characters and listens. The child might explore small plastic animals while listening to a recorded story. Possibilities for recorded activities are limited only by preparation time, budget, and staff interest.

Children's ages are always a factor in the use of audiovisual equipment. Listening centers usually need teacher introduction, direction, explanation, and supervision.

## Recorded Media

Some companies specialize in recordings for children that are designed to improve listening skills. These recordings involve children in listening for a signal, listening to directions, or listening to sounds. Some recordings include body-movement activities along with listening skills.

Not all recordings contain appropriate subject matter for young children. Before purchasing the teacher should evaluate content. Tape recorders can fascinate children. They become valuable tools for listening activities. Under the teacher's supervision or after being given instructions for use, children can explore and enjoy a variety of audio material.

Books with themes concerned with listening are good springboards to discussions about listening skills. See books listed in the Additional Resources section at the end of this chapter.

## PHONOLOGICAL AWARENESS

Phonological awareness skills are believed to be predictive of a child's ease in learning to read. Researchers have begun to investigate how to enhance these skills before children enter kindergarten. Rhyming; segmenting morphemes and syllables in words; using discriminative and critical listening, phonemic contrasting, and phonemic games emphasizing beginning letter sounds in words; commenting on alphabet letter sounds; and engaging in other such sounds-of-language activities could all be categorized as phonological skill-building opportunities. These types of activities might aid all 4- and 5-year-olds and be particularly valuable for at-risk children. Making these activities relevant and interesting can be a teaching challenge. Activities can become an outgrowth of many daily planned and unplanned happenings. See the Listening Activities section at the end of this chapter for suggestions.

Phonological awareness is developmental—it develops in stages, the first and easiest being the awareness that our language is composed of words (Figure 8–11). Language learners progress and become aware that words are made up of word parts (that is, syllables), and in the last and most difficult stage, they become aware that syllables are made up of individual sounds (that is, phonemes).

1. Realizes language is composed of words
2. Can hear syllables in words
3. Can separate syllables or clap syllables
4. Identifies rhyming words
5. Can create rhyming words
6. Can recognize words beginning with the same alphabet sound
7. Can recognize ending sounds in words and match words that end with the same sound
8. Is able to blend sounds into words
9. Can create words by substituting or moving sounds

Note: Children's developing skills tend to follow a common progression, but some children can display a unique, individual progression.

**FIGURE 8–11** Phonological awareness and children's developing skills.

The 2002 National Reading Panel Report indicated that phonemic awareness instruction was more effective with focused and explicit instruction on one or two skills, rather than a combination of skills (Cassidy, Valadez, & Garrett, 2010). Phonetic awareness instruction was recommended for classes and to suit the needs of individual children. Instruction, the report noted, is best presented in print-rich classrooms that engage children as readers and writers, offers oral and written language experiences, and provides alphabetic principle exposure using a variety of strategies that entail authentic and purposeful uses of reading and writing.

As college student reading this part of the text you may need refresher concerning individual alphabet letter sounds. If so, consult the Appendix.

The research-based conclusions that follow are important to early childhood educators.

- Phonetic awareness instruction is effective in teaching children to attend to and manipulate speech sounds in words.
- Phonetic instruction is effective under a variety of teaching conditions and with a variety of learners.
- Teaching sounds in language helps children learn to read.
- Phonetic awareness helps children decode new words as well as remember how to read familiar words.
- Phonetic awareness boosts reading comprehension.
- Phonetic awareness helps all types of children, including normally developing readers, readers at risk for future reading problems, disabled readers, preschoolers, kindergartners, and first- through sixth-grade children learning to read English as well as other languages.
- Phonetic awareness helps some children learn to spell in English as well as other languages.
- Phonetic awareness instruction is most effective when children are taught to manipulate phonemes with alphabet letters, when instruction is explicitly focused on one or two types of phoneme manipulations rather than multiple types, and when children are in small groups.
- Phonetic awareness instruction should be suited to the child's level of development, with easier tasks being used for younger children.
- Teaching alphabet letters is important.
- Teaching children to blend phonemes helps them decode.
- It is important to teach letter shapes, names, and sounds so that children can use letters to acquire phonetic awareness.
- Phonetic awareness instruction is more effective when it makes explicit how children are to apply phonetic awareness skills in reading and writing tasks.
- Phonetic awareness instruction does not need to consume long periods of time to be effective.
- Computers can be used to teach phonetic awareness effectively.
- Phonetic awareness helps learners understand and use the alphabetic system to read and write.
- Phonetic instruction is a critical foundation piece.
- Phonetic instruction should be offered in short periods and be as relevant as possible.
- Early phonetic instruction cannot guarantee later literacy success.

Phonological awareness typically begins at approximately age 3 and improves gradually over many years. Phonological awareness refers to the general ability to attend to (listen to) the sounds of language as distinct from its meaning. A subskill, **phonemic awareness**, can be defined as understanding that spoken language can be analyzed into strings of separate words and those words can be analyzed in sequences of syllables and phonemes within syllables. English consists of approximately 41 to 44 phonemes, depending on the dialect (Ehri & Nunes, 2006). Few words have but one phoneme. Most words contain a blend of phonemes.

Young children begin to notice sound similarities in the words they hear. They enjoy

---

**phonemic awareness** — the insight that every spoken word can be conceived as a sequence of phonemes, and/or the awareness that spoken words are made up of sounds, and the ability to segment a word into its constituent sounds.

rhymes, language play with words, repeated syllables, and **alliteration**. Because children's books contain these features, close listening at story time is certainly one way to develop phonemic awareness.

Eventually, but usually not until kindergarten or early first grade, children can hear all the sounds in a word and can segment a word into each of its sounds, or phonemes. Is there a sequence in the development of phonemic awareness? Most educators agree that simultaneous learning is more characteristic. Activities associated with phonemic awareness are listed and described at the end of this chapter.

Learning about phonemes is not new. What is new is the importance assigned to phonemes. There is great pressure on teachers to make sure that young children know how to use them to decode words. Barone (2003) discusses successful implementation of phoneme instruction in kindergarten:

> . . . teachers built their instruction of phonemes around children's own language and experiences. They moved from what was known by the students to less familiar territory. They expected all of their students to participate and use whole-group sessions for assessment as well. From these activities, they moved to small groups in which individual student needs can be met. (p. 347)

Educators without a strong English language background need to be aware that phonemes are different from alphabet letters used in spelling words. Ehri and Nunes (2006) point out:

> Phonemes are different from the letters that are used as written units symbolizing phonemes in the spelling of words (Venezky, 1970, 1999). Letters that perform this function are called **graphemes**. Graphemes may consist of one letter for example, P, T, K, A, N, or multiple letters, such as CH, SH, TH, CK, EA, IGH, each symbolizing one phoneme.
>
> Graphemes and phonemes combine to form words. (p. 111).

And:

> If you find it difficult to distinguish the separate phonemes in words, this is because there are no boundaries in speech marking where one phoneme ends and the next begins. Rather, phonemes are folded into each other and co-articulated to produce seamless speech. (p. 111)

Can an early childhood program include the goal of developing phonemic awareness? Is phonological awareness training helpful for 4- to 5-year-old preschoolers who are at risk for reading difficulties? Research evidence points to a "yes" answer to both questions. A study by Brady, Fowler, Stone, and Winbury (1994) describe what was included in one well known phonemic awareness training program. Activities dealt with

- directing children's attention to rhyme
- segmenting morphemes and syllables (e.g., "Say a little bit of butterfly" and "Can you say 'butterfly' without the 'but'?")
- categorizing sounds (e.g., "Which word doesn't belong: mop, top, pop, can?")
- identifying syllables ("Do you hear 'doe' in window?"
- illustrating phonemic contrasts (e.g., /p/ vs. /b/)
- using segmentation and identification games at the phonemic level (e.g., "Say a bit of *boat*.")
- segmenting phonemes in two- and three-phoneme words using a "say it and move it" procedure

## PHONEMIC AWARENESS SKILL

A child with phonemic awareness may have phoneme segmentation skill, a skill that allows her to hear phoneme segments in a word. A phoneme is the smallest unit of speech distinguishing one utterance from another. Reading research findings support the idea that

---

**alliteration** — the repetition of the initial sounds in neighboring words or stressed syllables, for example, "The foam flowed free and fizzy."
**grapheme** — the sum of all written letters and letter combinations that represent one phoneme.

phonemic awareness predicts reading success. Research in this area is motivated by the accepted conclusion that a good number of children having difficulty learning to read cannot hear sound sequences in words.

One clever research team introduced a guessing game in which children listened to phonemic hints by a troll character concerning presents they would receive by guessing the word correctly. Hints were stretched-out phonemes in familiar words. In English, this might be done with *d-o-ll?*, *c-a-r?* or other short words. No alphabet letters need to be mentioned in this kind of activity.

Hearing individual phonemes is not an easy task. Hearing the "separate" words in a sentence is also difficult for children especially children whose home language is not English. When researchers and educators talk about developing children's phonemic awareness, they are talking about developing children's ability to hear such sounds, and particularly to analyze words into their separate sounds. Children hear and isolate letters with **continuant**, or sustainable, sounds first. The sounds articulated in the letters *a, e, i, o, u, f, l, m, n, r, s, u,* and *z* are easier to sustain than the stop sounds articulated in the letters *b, c, d, g, h, j, k, p, q, t,* and *x*. Therefore, it is easier for children to hear the continuant sounds in the word *mom* than the stop sounds in the word *bat*.

Five or more different levels of phonemic awareness have been identified (Adams, 1990).

1. The most primitive level—that measured by knowledge of nursery rhymes—involves nothing more than an ear for the sounds of words.

2. At the next level, the oddity tasks require the child to methodically compare and contrast the sounds of words for rhyme or alliteration; this requires not just sensitivity to similarities and differences in the overall sounds of words, but also the ability to focus attention on the components of sounds that make them similar or different.

3. The tasks at the third level, blending and syllable splitting, seem to require (a) that the child have a comfortable familiarity with the notion that words can be subdivided into these small, meaningless sounds corresponding to phonemes and (b) that she be comfortably familiar with the way phonemes sound when produced "in isolation" and, better yet, with the act of producing them that way by oneself.

4. The phonemic segmentation tasks require not only that the child have a thorough understanding that words can be completely analyzed into a series of phonemes but, further, that she be able to so analyze them, completely and on demand.

5. The phoneme manipulation tasks require still further that the child have sufficient proficiency with the phonemic structure of words that she is able to add, delete, or move any designated phoneme and regenerate a word (or a non-word) from the result.*

Phonemic awareness is required to make connections between single alphabet letters and sounds. It is therefore one of the first steps, or first skills, on the road to learning to read. Some preschool children can and do read the printed names of classmates and may have a large number of words memorized by sight, but tackling other words they see and sounding them out is impossible without phonemic awareness skill.

In-depth teaching in this area would focus on a number of language features including **rimes** and **onsets**, before single phonemes (other than onsets). In spoken syllables, onsets are any consonants before a vowel in a syllable; rimes are the vowel and any consonants after it in a syllable (Figure 8–12).

*From Adams, M. J. (1990). Beginning to read: Thinking and learning about print. Copyright © 1990 Massachusetts Institute of Technology. Used with permission from The MIT Press.

---

**continuant** — a consonant or vowel that may be continued or prolonged without alteration during one emission of breath.

**rimes** — the vowel and any consonants after it in a syllable.

**onsets** — any consonants before a vowel in a syllable.

| ONSET | RIME |
|-------|------|
| b- | -ack |
| st- | -ale |
| p- | -ick |
| s- | -ame |
| pl- | -ay |
| cl- | -ick |

FIGURE 8–12 Onsets and rimes.

Several researchers have shown that young children are competent at analyzing spoken words into onsets and rimes but not into phonemes when onsets or rimes consist of more than one phoneme. There is usually more than one phoneme in the onset, the rime, or both. An example of this is the fact that children can mentally analyze the word *smiles* into /sm/ and /ilz/, but not into /s/, /m/, /i/, /l/, and /z/. Educators have identified 500 primary-grade words that can be derived from a set of only 37 rimes. The fact that young children can split spoken words into onsets and rimes more easily than into phonemes (when phonemes are parts of onsets and rimes) raises the possibility that children use onsets and rimes rather than phonemes to pronounce new print words.

"Wait just a moment!" some readers of this text are saying, "I work at an early childhood center, and this type of language instruction isn't taking place." What questions will early childhood staff members discuss at their worksite before providing phonetic instruction or phonemic awareness activities? (1) Most certainly, is it developmentally appropriate? (2) Do children typically develop phonemic knowledge and phonic knowledge without direct teaching? The answer is yes to both questions. Direct and explicit instruction does not have to be intensive and systematic to be effective for a majority of children. At least three fourths of children typically develop phonemic knowledge and phonic knowledge without much direct teaching. Program directors may believe enrolled children would not profit from phonetic or phonemic instruction so may not offer it, or they may not feel they are not able to do so or may not be aware of its benefits for at-risk preschoolers. There may be other reasons also.

Various sources suggest that somewhere between 15 and 20 percent of children show a need for such additional instruction, whether it be provided in the classroom or not. Instructional techniques that help children gain phonics knowledge and phonemic awareness can be planned in the context of meaningful activities and language play. Many educators and phonics advocates recommend the following:

1. Read and reread favorite nursery rhymes, and enjoy tongue twisters and other forms of language play together.

2. Reread favorite poems, songs, and stories; discuss alliteration and rhyme within them; and play with sound elements (e.g., starting with *cake*, remove the *c* and consider what different sounds could be added to make other words, like *take, make, lake*).

3. Read alphabet books to and with children, and make alphabet books together.

4. Discuss words and make lists, word banks, or books of such words that share interesting spelling-sound patterns.

5. Discuss similar sounds and letter-sound patterns in children's names.

6. Emphasize selected letter-sound relationships while writing with, for, or in front of children.

7. Encourage children to play with magnetic letters and to explore letter-sound relationships.

8. Help children write the sounds they hear in words.

9. When reading together, help children use prior knowledge and context plus initial consonants to predict what a word might be, then look at the rest of the word to confirm or correct. This is especially important for helping children orchestrate prior knowledge with context and letter/sound cues in order to not merely identify words but to construct meaning from texts, which, after all, is the primary purpose of reading.

Phonological awareness activities should be embedded within a rich literacy context that also integrates reading, writing, and literature with the use of oral language across the curriculum. It requires children to be thoughtful, which does not happen when they passively complete worksheets or engage in drill sessions.

## More Phonemic Awareness Activities

Teachers of young children should recognize the important role they can play in contributing to young children's phonemic awareness and realize it can become a natural outgrowth of a wide variety of language-related activities and not become relegated to a "one-time-a-day" status.

These activities can take place in the daily context of a developmentally appropriate program. The goal of any phonemic awareness activity is to facilitate children's perception that speech is made up of a series of sounds. Activities that easily fall into the category of phoneme awareness activities are wordplay and word-game activities.

It is suggested that the reader study the references found in the Additional Resources section at the end of this chapter and search for other resources to uncover how educators have developed awareness programs for young at-risk children.

## Using Book Discussions to Develop Phonemic Awareness

A teacher's comments about a book the teacher is reading aloud can explicitly point out and analyze phonemic features, for example, "Those words start with the same sound: listen—*cap*, *cape*, and *coat*." See this chapter's Additional Resources section for a list of children's books that are helpful in developing phonemic awareness.

## OTHER LISTENING ACTIVITIES

Chapter 14 gives a great deal of encouragement and helps you conduct circle or group activities. If you will be trying out activities in this chapter, it is best to skip ahead and read Chapter 14 first.

Every classroom has some signal that alerts children to a change in activities or a new opportunity. This can range from a few notes on a classroom musical instrument to more creative signals. Usually, a short invitational and attention-getting statement will be used to pique children's curiosity, such as:

- "Gail has a new game for you in the rug area today."
- "Time to finish what you are doing and join us."
- "Madelyn is in the story-time center with a book about Clifford, the big, red dog."
- "Our clapping song begins in two minutes."

In some centers, children are simply asked to finish up what they are doing and join their friends in a particular room area. The enjoyment of already-started finger plays, chants, songs, or movement captures their attention and they are drawn in. This is a great time to recognize all children by name, as in the following (to the tune of "She'll Be Coming Round the Mountain").

> *Susie is here with us, yes, yes, yes.* (Clap on yes, yes, yes.)
>
> *Larry's here with us, yes, yes, yes.* (Continue until all children are recognized, and end with the following.)
>
> *We are sitting here together,*
>
> *We are sitting here together,*
>
> *We are sitting here together, yes, yes, yes.*

Early childhood programs that promote poetry, child dictation, storytelling, and authorship can institute a listening and discussion activity centered on what is called "an author's chair." Usually, the child-sized chair is specially decorated and used at one time of the day, or a sign is affixed—Author's and/or Reader's Chair. Children are invited to share their own efforts or share a favorite or brought-to-school picture book. Teachers may find a need to establish time limits for ramblers or may allow audience members to choose to leave quietly when they wish.

Riddles are another way to develop children's listening skills.

## LISTENING RIDDLES FOR GUESSING

### Rhyming Animal Riddles

*A tail that's skinny and long,*
*At night he nibbles and gnaws*
*With teeth sharp and strong.*
*Beady eyes and tiny paws,*
*One called Mickey is very nice.*
*And when there's more than one*
*We call them _____.* (Mice)

*He has a head to pat.*
*But he's not a cat.*
*Sometimes he has a shiny coat.*
*It's not a hog, it's not a goat.*
*It's bigger than a frog.*
*I guess that it's a _____.* (Dog)

*No arms, no hands, no paws, but it can fly in*
*    the sky.*
*It sings a song*
*That you have heard.*
*So now you know*
*That it's a _____.* (Bird)

*Sharp claws and soft paws,*
*Big night eyes, and whiskers, too.*
*Likes to curl up in your lap,*
*Or catch a mouse or a rat.*
*Raise your hand if you know.*
*Now all together, let's whisper its name*
*    very slow _____.* (Cat)

### Riddle Game

(Children take turns calling on others with raised hands.)

*I'll ask you some riddles.*
*Answer if you can.*
*If you think you know,*
*Please raise your hand.*
*Don't say it out loud*
*Till __?__ calls your name.*
*That's how we'll play this riddling game.*

### Guessing Game

*A beautiful flower we smell with our nose.*
*Its special name is not pansy but a _____.*
*    (Rose)*

*I shine when you're playing and having fun.*
*I'm up in the sky and I'm called the _____.*
*    (Sun)*

*If you listen closely you can tell, I ring and*
*    chime because I'm a _____.* (Bell)

*You've got 10 of me, I suppose, I'm on your*
*    feet and I'm your _____.* (Toes)

*I'm down on your feet, both one and two*
*Brown, black, blue, or red, I'm a _____.* (Shoe)

*I sit on the stove and cook what I can.*
*They pour stuff in me, I'm a frying _____.*
*    (Pan)*

It is helpful to have magazine pictures of a rose, the sun, toes, shoes, and a pan, plus a real bell to ring behind you as you speak. Riddles appropriate for young children who have little experience with rhyming follow.

### Body Parts Riddle

*If a bird you want to hear,*
*You have to listen with your _____.* (Ear)

*If you want to dig in sand,*
*Hold the shovel in your _____.* (Hand)

*To see an airplane as it flies, look up and*
*    open up your _____.* (Eyes)

*To smell a pansy or a rose,*
*You sniff its smell with your _____.* (Nose)

*When you walk across the street you use two*
*    things you call your _____.* (Feet)

*If a beautiful song you've sung, you used*
*    your mouth and your _____.* (Tongue)

*All these parts you can feel and see are*
*    parts of your _____.* (Body)

Tracing hands or drawing any body part they choose (on a picture with missing hands, feet, and so forth) is a fun follow-up activity for 4½-year-olds.

The following stories and games also can be used to enhance listening skills. These activities help specifically with the skill of listening and following directions.

### Sit-Down/Stand-Up Story

Say to the children, "Let's see if you can stand *up* and sit *down* when I say the words 'Listen: Stand *up!*' You all are standing. Sit *down!* Good listening; we're ready to start." Then, tell the children the following story.

> When I woke *up* this morning, I reached *down* to the floor for my slippers. Then I stood *up* and slipped them on. Next, I went *down*stairs to the kitchen. I opened the refrigerator, picked *up* the milk and sat *down* to drink. When I finished drinking, I tried to stand *up*, but I was stuck in the chair. I pulled and pulled, but I was still sitting.

> "Don't sit on the chairs," my dad called from upstairs. "I painted them."

> "It's too late! I'm sitting *down*," I answered.

> "Hurry and help me."

> Dad pulled and pulled, but I didn't come *up*.

> "I'll go get our neighbor, Mr. Green. Maybe he can help pull you, too," Dad said. Dad and Mr. Green pulled and pulled.

> "What'll I do?" I said. "The children will be waiting at school for me." Then I got an idea. "Go get the shovel," I said. Well, that worked. They pushed the shovel handle *down* and I came *up*.

> You know, I think I'm stuck in this chair, too. Look, I am. _____ (child's name) and _____ (child's name), please help me.

> Everyone else please sit.

Now, let's see if everyone can show how they can stretch way up with their hands and curl into a ball down on the floor.

A good follow-up is to talk about what can be seen in the room that is up above the children's heads and down below their knees, or say this poem together:

> *When you're up—you're up,*
> *And when you're down—you're down.*
> *But when you're halfway in between,*
> *You're neither up nor down.*

## SUMMARY

Listening skill is learned behavior. The ability to listen improves with experience and exposure, although young children vary in their ability to listen. Listening ability can be classified by type—appreciative, purposeful, discriminative, creative, and critical.

Planned activities, teacher interaction, and equipment can provide opportunities for children to develop phonetic and phonemic awareness.

Listening cannot be forced, but experiences can be provided so that a desire to listen is increased. Signals and attentive teacher encouragement can help form habits. Settings that limit stimuli and control the size of groups are desirable. When teachers are watchful and act when children seem restless or uninterested during planned activities, listening remains active. One of the responsibilities of the teacher is to plan carefully so that young children consistently want to hear what is being offered.

Phonetic instructional activities and phonemic awareness experiences during preschool involve children's understandings about words, word parts, and alphabet letter names and sounds. Learners become familiar with syllables and realize there are individual alphabet letter sounds. This aids their learning to read words on their own or when reading instruction begins in lower elementary school. Preschool activities in this area, if they take place, are suited to the children's level of development and are embedded within a rich literacy context that is as relevant to children's lives as possible.

## ADDITIONAL RESOURCES

### Children's Books with Listening Themes

Borten, H. (1960). *Do you hear what I hear?* New York: Abelard-Schuman. (Describes the pleasures to be found in really listening.)

Brown, M. W. (1951). *The summer noisy book.* New York: Harper and Row. (It can be easily made into a "guess what" sound game.)

Fisher, A. (1988). *The house of a mouse.* New York: Harper and Row. (Mouse poems can be read in a tiny teacher voice. It is full of rhyming text.)

Glazer, T. (1982). *On top of spaghetti.* New York: Doubleday. (Teacher sings a silly story.)

Guilfoile, E. (1957). *Nobody listens to Andrew.* Chicago: Follett. (The no-one-ever-listens-to-me idea is humorously handled.)

Johnson, L. (1967). *Night noises*. New York: Parents Magazine Press. (Discusses listening to noises in bed at night.)

Lord, C. (2010) *Hot rod hamster.* New York: Scholastic. (Promotes listening to make a choice, and prompts discussion.)

McDonnell, P. (2008). *South.* New York: Little, Brown. (Bird falls asleep and doesn't listen.)

Novak, M. (1986). *Rolling.* Riverside, NJ: Bradbury Press. (The sounds of a storm dominate this story.)

Showers, P. (1961). *The listening walk.* New York: Thomas Y. Crowell. (Good book to share before adventuring on a sound walk.)

Spier, P. (1971). *Gobble, growl, grunt.* New York: Doubleday. (Lots of variety in animal sounds, with brilliant illustrations included.)

Zolotow, C. (1980). *If you listen.* New York: Harper and Row. (This is a touching tale of a child who, missing her father, turns to listening.)

## Children's Books Promoting Phonemic Awareness

Bayer, J. (1992). *A, my name is Alice.* New York: Dutton. (Alliteration.)

Brown, M. W. (1991). *Good night moon.* New York: Harper. (Rhyming.)

Carle, E. (1994). *The very hungry caterpillar.* New York: Scholastic. (Blending and segmenting.)

Christelow, E. (2000). *Five little monkeys jumping on the bed.* New York: Clarion. (Rhyming.)

Guarino, D. (1997). *Is your mama a llama?* New York: Scholastic. (Rhyming.)

Hutchins, P. (1986). *The doorbell rang.* New York: William Morrow. (Blending and segmenting.)

Martin, B., Jr. (1997). *Polar bear, polar bear, what do you hear?* New York: Henry Holt. (Blending and segmenting.)

Peek, M. (1985). *Mary wore her red dress and Henry wore his green sneakers.* New York: Clarion. (Rhyming.)

Trapani, I. (1997). *I'm a little teapot.* Watertown, MA: Charlesbridge. (Rhyming.)

Urbanovic, J. (2007). *Duck at the door.* New York: HarperCollins. (The "d" sound repeats.)

## Readings

Adams, M. B., Foorman, B., Lundberg, I., & Beeler, T. (1996). *Phonemic awareness in young children.* Baltimore: Brookes.

Bennett-Armistead, V. S., Duke, N. K., & Moses, A. M. (2005). *Literacy and the youngest learner: Best practices for educators of children from birth to 5.* New York: Scholastic Inc.

Elster, C. A. (1994). I guess they do listen: Young children's emergent readings after adult read-alouds. *Young Children, 49*(3), 26–31.

Pica, R. (2007). *Jump into literacy: Active learning for preschool children.* Beltsville, MD: Gryphon House.

## Readings on Phonological Awareness

Ellery, V. (2009). *Creating strategic readers: Techniques for developing competency in phonemic awareness.* Newark, DE: International Reading Association.

Floyd, S., & Yates, W. (2001). *Curriculum-aligned thematic phonological awareness treatment.* Lake City, SC: Susan Floyd.

Opitz, M. F. (2000). *Rhymes and reasons: Literature & language play for phonological awareness.* Portsmouth, NH: Heinemann.

Paulson, L., Noble, I., Jepson, S., & van den Pol, R. (2001). *Building early literacy and language skills.* Longmont, CO: Sopris West.

Yopp, H. K., & Yopp, R. H. (2000). *Oo-pples and bonoo-noos: Songs and activities for phonemic awareness.* Orlando: Harcourt School.

## Game Making and Construction

Silberg, J., & Jones, R. (1995). *500 five-minute games: Quick and easy activities for 3-6 year olds.* Beltsville, MD: Gryphon House.

Silberg, J., & Noll, C. K. (1997). *300 three-minute games: Quick and easy activities for 2-5 year olds.* Beltsville, MD: Gryphon House.

## Helpful Websites

Learning Disabilities Association of America
http://www.ldanatl.org
Provides information on central auditory processing problems in children.

National Child Care Information Center
http://npin.org
Features child literacy and early phonetic awareness information.

Go to www.cengagebrain.com to access this text's Education Course-Mate website where you'll find helpful resource such as video activities, glossary flashcards, interactive exercises, quiz questions, and more!

# Review It and Use It

A. Five types of listening skills have been discussed. After each of the following statements, identify the listening type that best fits the situation.

1. After hearing an Indian drum on a recording, Brett slaps out a rhythm of his own on his thighs while dancing around the room.

2. During a story reading of *The Three Little Pigs*, Mickey blurts out, "Go get 'em, Wolfie!" in reference to the wolf's behavior in the story.

3. Kimmie is following Chris around. Chris is repeating, "Swishy, fishy co-co-pop," over and over again; both giggle periodically.

4. Debbie tells you about the little voice of small Billy Goat Gruff and the big voice of Big Billy Goat Gruff in the story of *Three Billy Goats Gruff*.

5. Peter has asked whether he can leave his block tower standing during snack time instead of putting the blocks away as you requested. He wishes to return and build the tower higher. He then listens for your answer.

B. Select the best answer.

1. Most parents unconsciously teach preschoolers
   a. to develop auditory perception.
   b. attitudes toward listening.
   c. to listen to their teachers.
   d. to ignore commands.

2. A teacher can promote listening by
   a. demanding a listening attitude.
   b. using a signal that alerts children and focuses attention.
   c. encouraging a child to repeat what he hears.
   d. telling a child she is not listening.

3. Critical listening happens when the
   a. child gives an answer that has nothing to do with his own opinion.
   b. child disagrees with another's statement.
   c. child makes a comment about how he enjoyed what he heard.
   d. teacher plans lots of questions where children can give imaginative answers.

4. Children come to early childhood centers with
   a. well-developed skills to listen.
   b. habits of listening.
   c. all the abilities and experiences needed to be successful in planned activities.
   d. a desire to listen.

5. Children's ability to follow a series of commands depends on
   a. their age.
   b. whether the commands were developmentally appropriate.
   c. their social skills.
   d. how well they can imitate the words of the commands.

C. Assume the children are involved in an activity when they are suddenly distracted by a red truck and a siren outside the window. List four things you could say to the children to draw their attention back to the activity. If you wished to use their focus on the siren for a spontaneous listening activity, how would you proceed?

D. What elements of music or singing a song might promote listening skills?

E. Describe two self-designed listening activities, stating the objective of each activity and giving a description of the activity. Be brief.

F. Define phonemic awareness, onset, and rime.

## STUDENT ACTIVITIES

1. Choose one of the listening activities found in this chapter, one from another source, or one you create. Present the activity to a group of preschoolers, modifying the activity to suit the child group if necessary. State what type(s) of listening behavior you are attempting to teach. Then answer the following questions.
   a. Was the activity interesting to the children?
   b. Were they able to perform the listening skill(s) involved ?
   c. Would you change the activity in any way if you presented it again?

2. Find two resources for additional listening activities. Cite the sources or state the title of the books, the authors, the dates of publication, and the publishers.

3. Practice the listening story in this chapter titled "Sit-Down/Stand-Up Story," or find another listening story. At the next class meeting, tell the story to a classmate. Share constructive criticism.

4. Create a recorded activity in which children will in some way analyze what they hear and share responses with the teacher. An activity that requires logical or sequential listening could also be attempted. Share your recording and accompanying objects and/or visuals at the next class session.

5. Watch a listening activity in a preschool center, and then answer the following questions.
   a. How did the teacher prepare the children for listening?
   b. What elements of the activity captured interest?
   c. How was the children's interest held?
   d. Did the teacher have an opportunity to recognize the children's listening skill?
   e. Did the children's listening behavior during the activity seem important to the teacher?
   f. Was this the kind of activity that should be repeated? If so, why?

6. Write a one-page paper concerning your feelings about phonological or phonemic awareness instruction for preschoolers. Consider that many other countries, including the United Kingdom, expect preschoolers to know both alphabet letter names and letter sounds before entering kindergarten. Bring your paper to class and pair up with three others to discuss each person's feelings and ideas. Share main points in your discussion with the entire class. Hand in your paper and your four-member discussion-group notes to the instructor.

7. Using a partner and the Appendix's Alphabet Pronunication Guide see if you both can pronounce the long, soft, hard, and short sounds of a, e, c, g, i, o, u, and supply an example word *for each sound not found on the page.* Note for some letters you will have to supply more than one example word.

## USE IT IN THE CLASSROOM

### Listening Activities

Note: The following activities will have to be evaluated for age-level appropriateness and use with a particular group of children. They are provided here as examples of listening activities but may or may not be appropriate for your teaching situation.

### Activities Associated With Phonological Awareness

- read-alouds, especially ones with repetition in words, phrases, and alliteration
- singing songs, especially those with repetitions or word play
- reading nursery rhymes and poetry
- engaging in language play—using silly words
- seeing words as separate entities
- noticing spaces between words
- labeling objects in the classroom; using word lists and charts
- counting words in a sentence or on a picture-book page
- raising one's hand on hearing a designated word
- clapping syllables
- counting syllables
- hearing different sounds in words and identifying them
- recognizing rhyming words
- using name tags; playing name activities and name games
- hearing sounds in their name by "stretching it out"
- playing with fun-to-say words—*rat-tata-ta, bibbity bobbity boo, licky sticky,* and so on
- rhyming a word with teacher's word
- allowing children to create their own rhyme

- thinking of words that start the same as teacher's word
- identifying beginning sounds in words
- associating sounds with written words
- matching sounds
- rhyming with children's names
- playing games with children's names
- making an 'A' stands for . . ." list and so on
- generating new rhyming words
- moving sounds to make new words

Note: These suggested activities are not presented in an age-level or skill-level order.

### Phonemic Awareness Activities

- using alphabet books, songs, rhymes, charts, toys, and games
- providing rhyming experiences—recognizing, identifying, and creating
- matching rhyming pictures
- clapping on rhyming words
- recognizing words beginning with the same letter—alliteration
- recognizing words beginning with the same sound
- hearing initial, middle, and ending sounds
- knowing the sounds alphabet letters make
- putting sounds together
- manipulating sounds
- naming words that start with the same letter
- counting sounds in words
- taking away sounds in words
- substituting sounds in words
- writing alphabet letters
- knowing the shapes of alphabet letters
- naming letter shapes
- trying to write words
- trying to read words
- making words with magnetic letters

- typing words or using alphabet stamp sets to form words
- grouping picture cards according to beginning, middle, and ending sounds
- making a list of same-sound beginnings
- matching sounds with alphabet letters
- comparing the number of syllables in words
- finding words with the same beginning and ending sounds
- playing with alphabet letter puzzles
- hunting for alphabet letters in the room
- making personal alphabet books

Note: These are not listed in sequential order, nor is the listing meant to be comprehensive.

### Recognizing Voices Guessing Game

**Purpose:** To practice discriminative listening and auditory memory skills

**Materials:** Individual snapshots of school personnel; and short recordings of different school staff members' voices reading a few paragraphs in a story book or describing the work they perform

**Procedure:** Line up snapshots in view of the children. After each is identified say, "Here are some snapshots of people we know. Now we're going to listen and try to guess who is talking. Raise your hand if you think you know."

A great follow-up is guessing children's voices using the same game format. This can be set up as an individually chosen activity after being introduced at a group time or can be used with a group.

### Build A Burger

**Purpose:** To practice purposeful listening

**Group size:** four to six children

**Materials:** Cutouts of photos or drawings of foods and dressings that are often added to hamburger buns—hamburger brown circles or meat patty imitations, onion slices, lettuce, tomato slices, cheese slices, pickles, salsa, bacon, mayonnaise, mustard, and catsup; cutout paper buns or clay bun halves; or bun size paper circles or small and large paper plates. Pencil and paper for waiting list.

**Procedure:** Ask children what kinds of food they like on their hamburgers. After the group discusses the things they like, say, "I'm going to show you pictures of some of the things you've said you liked on your hamburger. Here are onion slices." Go on to show and name all the cutouts. "You can build a hamburger for one of your friends in this game. You'll have to listen closely to find out what she/he chooses to have you put between the buns. "Choose a friend. Everyone who wishes will have a turn, but _____ will be first." Teacher can print each child's selection on chart paper, if desired. Make a waiting list. (Of course, the real thing would be more fun—provide plastic gloves or use individual plastic sandwich bags with food zipped inside for real food handling.)

### Sound Cans

**Purpose:** To match similar sounds by using discriminative listening skills

**Materials:** Cans with press-on or screw-off lids; cards large enough to hold two cans; outline of circles of can bottoms (made with dark pen); two circles for each card (large different color index cards work well); best to use cans that are impossible for children to open or to securely tape cans shut; pairs of cans filled with same materials, such as sand, paper clips, rocks, rice, beans, nuts, and bolts

**Procedure:** This is a solitary activity or one that children can choose to play with others. It can be used in a learning center. An introduction like the following is necessary. "Here are some cans and cards. The way you play this game is to shake one can and then shake all the rest to find the one that sounds the same as the first can. Let's listen to this can." Shake it. "Now I'm going to try to find the can that sounds just like this one when I shake it." Pick up another and ask, "Does this sound the same?" Shake the first and second cans. "No, this sounds different, so I'm going to shake another can." Go on until the mate is found and placed beside the first can on the card.

This activity is a classic one, and many sound sets are found in preschool programs. (Sets are also commercially manufactured.)

### "Can You Say It As I Do?" Activity

**Purpose:** To imitate sounds

**Materials:** None

**Procedure:** The teacher says, "Can you change your voice the way I can?"

"My name is (teacher softly whispers her name)." With changes of voice, speed, and pitch, the teacher illustrates with a loud, low, or high voice, speaking fast or slow, with mouth nearly closed or wide open, when holding nose, and so on.

The teacher then asks for a volunteer who would like to speak in a new or funny way. "Now, let's see if we can change our voices the way Kurt does. Do it any way you want, Kurt. We'll try to copy you."

The teacher then gives others a turn. This activity may be followed up with a finger play with voice changes, like the "Five Little Astronauts" activity in Chapter 14.

### "Listen, Oops A Mistake!—Interrupt Me Please."

**Purpose:** To associate and discriminate among word sounds and objects; to listen for inconsistencies

**Materials:** Four or five common school objects (such as a pencil, crayon, block, toy, cup, and doll) and a low table, or photographs or drawings of objects

**Procedure:** Talk about calling things by the wrong name, being sure to discuss how everyone makes mistakes at times. Begin with something like, "Have you ever called your friend by the wrong name?"

*Teacher:* When you call your friend by the wrong name, you've made a mistake. Look at the things on the table. I am going to name each of them. (Teacher names them correctly.) All right, now see if you can hear my mistakes. This time I'm going to point to them, too. If you hear a mistake, raise your hand and say, "Oops, a mistake!" Let's say that together once: "Oops, a mistake!" Are you ready? Listen: *crayon, ball, doll, cup.*

Change objects, and give the children a chance to make mistakes while others listen. This activity can later be followed with the story *Moptop* (by Don Freeman, Children's Press), about a long-haired red-headed boy who is mistaken for a mop.

### Errand Game

**Purpose:** To follow verbal commands

**Materials:** None

**Procedure:** Start a discussion about doing helpful things for family members. Include getting objects from other rooms, from neighbors, and so on. Tell the children you are going to play a game in which each person looks for something another has asked for.

*Teacher:* "Get a book for me, please." Or say, "Can you find a leaf?"

Items to ask for include a rock, a blade of grass, a piece of paper, a block, a doll, a crayon, a toy car, a sweater, a hat, clothes, a hanger, a blanket, and so forth. Send children off one at a time. As they return, talk to each about where the item was found. While the group waits for all members to return, the group can name the returned items. Put them in a row, ask children to cover their eyes while one is hidden, and then ask the children to guess which item was removed.

If interest is still high, the teacher can make a request that the items be returned and repeat the game by sending the children for new items.

### Blind Walk

**Purpose:** To depend on listening to another child's verbal directions

**Materials:** Scarves, bandanas, or cloth strips

**Procedure:** Discuss blindness and guide dogs. Pair children and blindfold one child. Ask the guide to hold the blindfolded child's hand and take a classroom walk. Ask the guide to talk about where they are going, and urge the blindfolded child to use her hands to feel objects, and so forth. Change blindfolds, giving the guide a chance to also go on a guided walk. (Some children may object to blindfolds or act fearful.

Respect their wishes. Let them be guides.) Conduct a brief follow-up discussion. (Activity courtesy of WICAP Head Start, Donnelly, Idaho)

### Jack-In-The-Box

**Purpose:** To discriminate sounds by listening for a signal and responding to it

**Materials:** None

**Procedure:** Recite the following rhyme in a whispered voice until the word pop is reached. Use hand gestures or hide your thumb in your fist and let it pop up each time the word pop is said.

*Jack-in-the-box, jack-in-the-box, where can you be?*

*Hiding inside where I can't see? If you jump up, you won't scare me. Pop! Pop! Pop!*

Suggest that children squat and pretend to be jack-in-the-boxes. Ask them to listen and jump up only when they hear the word pop. Try a second verse if the group seems willing.

*Jack-in-the-box, jack-in-the-box, you like to play.*

*Down in the box you won't stay. There's only one word I have to say. Pop! Pop! Pop!*

### Pin-On Sound Cards (Animals And Birds)

**Purpose:** To associate and imitate sounds and use auditory memory

**Materials:** Safety pins or masking tape; file cards (3-by-5) or self-stick memo paper with pictures of birds and animals (gummed stickers of animals and birds are available in stationery stores and from supply houses); suggestions: duck, rooster, chick, owl, goose, woodpecker, horse, cow, cat, dog, sheep, lion, mouse, turkey, bee, frog, donkey, seal

**Procedure:** Have a card pinned on your blouse or shirt before the children enter the room. This will start questions. Talk about the sound that the animal pictured on your card makes. Practice it with the children. Ask who would like a card. Talk about the animal and the sound it makes. Imitate each sound with the group. Have children imitate animal noises, and ask the child with the right card to raise her hand or stand up. Then prompt the child to finish "That's me; I'm a . . . ?" Children usually like to wear the cards the rest of the day and take them home, if possible.

### Funny Old Hat Game**

Gather a bag of old hats (such as new or discarded paper party hats). Pass the hats out to the children, or let the children choose them.

Say, "We're ready when our hats are on our heads. We're going to put our hats in some funny places and do some funny things. Listen."

"Put your hat between your knees."
"Put your hat under your arm."
"Put your hat over your shoes."
"Put your hat under your chin."
"Touch the top of your hat."
"Sit on your hat."
"Stand on your hat."

Encourage the children to choose a place to put the hat, and then say, "Where's the hat? Where's the hat, [child's name]. Can you see the hat, hat, hat?" (This can be chanted.) "Under the chair, under the chair—I can see the hat, hat, hat."

### See If You Can Game

Collect objects from around the classroom (for example, scissors, ruler, eraser, cup, chalk). Put them on a small table or on the floor on a large piece of paper. Say, "I'm not going to talk about one of the things you see on the table (floor). See if you can tell me what object I am talking about and say its name. Raise your hand if you know." (Keep giving hints until the children guess.)

"What has two circles for two fingers?" (Scissors)

"It's long and thin with numbers printed on one side." (Ruler)

"What makes pencil marks disappear?" (Eraser)

---

**Not suitable for programs having head lice problems.

"You can fill it with milk." (Cup)

"What's white and small and writes on the chalkboard?" (Chalk)

## Can You Do This Game?

Children imitate hand and body movements of teacher or other children. "Can you put your hands on your chin, knees, elbows, and so on?"

## What Has Changed Game Or Can You Keep A Secret? Game

**Purpose:** To listen for the purpose of correctly identifying a missing object or item.

**Materials:** A bag with hats, scarves, belts, pins, socks, gloves, shoes, and so on

**Procedure:** The teacher can ask a group to examine her closely because something is going to change or look different. The teacher asks the children to close their eyes or look down, or the teacher can turn her back to the children and quickly slip on one item from the bag. Begin by making changes obvious, then more subtle as they gain skill. "If you know what looks different or has changed, raise your hand. Keep it a secret, but you can give clues like "It is small and shiny." Teacher or child gives clues until the change is guessed. Child volunteers can be used to change things themselves after the game is learned.

CHAPTER

# 18

# Developing a Literacy Environment

## OBJECTIVES

After reading this chapter, you should be able to:

- Explain the need for materials in language development activities.

- Assist teachers in the care, storage, and replacement of materials.

- Describe early childhood language games.

- Design classroom literacy-building areas.

## KEY TERMS

| | |
|---|---|
| audiovisual equipment | listening center |
| language center | software |

## "Can I Have Another Turn?"

*Four-year-old Emma found computer use to be the high point of her day, and as her computer involvement grew her other interests narrowed. Her preschool teacher noticed she had lost interest in art projects, was socially less involved, spent less and less time with other children, and often tried to negotiate more time on the school's computer. Her teacher observed that Emma seemed distracted and restless, and she felt that Emma's gross-motor skills might be lagging. She also believed that Emma had shortened her attention span for everything else offered in class.*

*Emma's family noted that she immediately rushed to their home computer after school and had lost interest playing with neighborhood friends. Most of them stopped dropping by to ask her to play. Emma's interest in toys also seemed diminished.*

### Questions to Ponder

1. Is it possible that a 4-year-old could develop addictive behavior?

2. Emma's parents sought professional advice but wanted Emma to continue developing computer skills. What plan of action do you think might have been recommended to the parents?

3. What teacher plan of action would you suggest?

This text has emphasized the need to provide children with a variety of interesting classroom centers and areas, materials, objects, and furnishings.  Such settings, equipment, and materials are important in keeping programs alive, fascinating, and challenging.

The classroom environment can promote language skills in many ways for it provides the reality behind words and ideas. It also supplies opportunities for sensory exploration and increases children's knowledge of relationships.

It gathers or creates materials that capture attention, motivate play, and build communication skills. Familiar and favorite materials and furnishing are enjoyed repeatedly with the child deciding how much time to devote to each. Materials and settings can isolate one or more language or perceptual skills allowing for practice and accomplishment.

In language arts centers, related instructional materials are located in one convenient and inviting area. Stocking, supervision, and maintenance of materials, furnishings, and equipment by the teaching staff are easily accomplished. The classroom can be a place to grow, expand, test ideas, and predict outcomes, and ask questions. A prepared environment provides successful experiences for all children in a climate in which ideas and creative learning flourish.

The *physical* and *emotional comfortable level* of classroom areas and spaces are central to the literacy learning of all students and in particular, English language learners (Barone & Xu, 2008). Consequently, teachers consider this along with insuring children's health and safety.

A limited body of knowledge exists regarding how the physical features and equipment of a literacy-based classroom enhance learning. A preliminary study examining the impact of literacy-enriched play areas (especially ones with meaningful print) found that preschool children who played in such areas spontaneously used almost twice as much print in their play. Consequently, teachers are urged to experiment and creatively design language arts centers and other play centers and monitor the effect of the room and its furnishings on children's language arts skill development.

## SUGGESTIONS FOR PRINT-RICH ENVIRONMENTS

Suggestions for a print-rich classroom are abundant and depend on individual teacher innovation and creativity. Educators can label everything in the classroom that has a connection to current curriculum and post a picture or photo of the daily routine. Other ideas follow.

- Create a message center and classroom news bulletin where children can give and recieve a message from teacher and vise versa.
- Create a slogan, caption, question, or new idea for each school day. Print it and talk to children about it and also print child reactions.
- Innovate with individual child tickets or cards bearing children's names that stick to a board or fit in a slot in a play area that accomodates only a certain number of children at any given time.
- Use print and numerals in games or use symbols.
- Have an attendance chart that allows children to take off their names from the chart and place them in a basket as they enter the classroom.
- Use graphing activities with children's names, physical features or their selected preferences or choices.
- Add print to imaginative or dramatic play areas by monitoring conversation and suggesting labels.
- Highlight the functional use of print in daily classroom life by pointing it out to individuals or groups.

## THE LANGUAGE ARTS CENTER

Full of communication-motivating activities, every inch of floor and wall space of a language arts center is used. Small areas are enlarged by building upward with lofts or bunks to solve floor-space problems in crowded centers (Figure 18–1). Adding areas that children can climb into is another useful space-opening device.

A **language center** has three main functions: (1) it provides looking and listening

---

**language center** — a classroom area specifically set aside and equipped for language arts–related activities and child use.

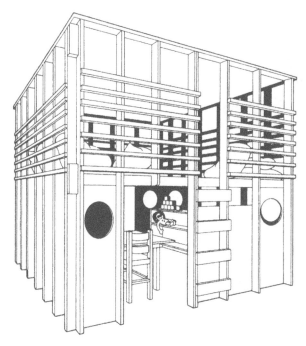

FIGURE 18–1 Solving space problems.

FIGURE 18–2 A crawl-into listening area for quiet language activities furnished with headsets.

activities for children, (2) it gives children an area for hands-on experiences with communication-developing materials, and (3) it provides a place to store materials. Barone and Xu (2008) suggest creating an inviting area that easily accommodates five to six children at one time.

The ideal area has comfortable, soft furnishings with ample work space, proper lighting, and screening to block out other areas of active classrooms. Teachers sometimes make centers cozy and inviting with pillows, a covered crib mattress, or a bean bag chair or two. The area can become a place of refuge for the child who needs to get away from the bustle of the group or the child who wants to interact with friends, and it can be a nice place for the teacher to spend time with children individually.

Language arts centers should be quiet places that are separated from the more vigorous activities of the average playroom. Suggested furnishings are listed by category.

*General-Use Materials*
    one or more child-size tables and chairs
    shelving dividers or screens
    soft-cushioned rocker, easy chair, or couch
    soft pillows
    crawl-into hideaways, lined with carpet or
       fabric (Figure 18–2)

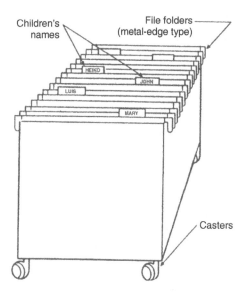

FIGURE 18–3 Children's work file box.

    individual work space or study spots
    audiovisuals and electrical outlets
    book racks that display book covers
    chalkboard
    storage cabinets
    flannel board
    pocket chart
    children's file box (Figure 18–3)
    bookcase (Figure 18–4)

**FIGURE 18–4** Bookcases can be used as room area boundaries.

bulletin board

carpet, rug, or soft floor covering

chart stand or wall-mounted wing clamps

waste basket

*Writing and Prewriting Materials*

paper (scratch, lined, newsprint, and typing paper in a variety of sizes)

table

file or index cards

paper storage shelf

writing tools (crayons, nontoxic washable felt markers, and soft pencils in handy contact-covered containers)

primary school typewriter

small, sturdy typewriter table or desk

word boxes

picture dictionary

wall-displayed alphabet guides

cutouts of colorful alphabet letters

tabletop chalkboards with chalk

blank book skeletons

scissors

tape

erasers

alphabet letter stamps and ink pads

tracing envelopes, patterns, wipe-off cloth

chart paper

magnet board with alphabet letters

hole punch

yarn

write-on, wipe-off boards

stick-on notes

notepads

pencil sharpener

envelopes baskets, desk trays, and flat boxes

stationery

brass paper fasteners

set of printscript strips with attending children's and staff's names

stickers

glue sticks

stencils

*Reading and Prereading Materials*

books (including child-made examples)

book and audiovisual combinations (read-a-longs)

cutouts of favorite story characters

rebus story charts

an alphabetized chart of enrolled children's names

catalogs, television guides, and newspaper advertising (Barone & Xu, 2008).

*Speech Materials*

> puppets and puppet theaters
>
> flannel board sets
>
> language games

*Audiovisual Equipment*

> overhead projector
>
> record, tape, or CD/DVD player; headsets; and jacks
>
> story records
>
> language master, recording cards
>
> picture files
>
> television screen and VCR
>
> computer and printer
>
> video camera
>
> digital camera

Adults usually supervise use of **audiovisual equipment** in a language center, and a number of the simpler machines can be operated by children after a brief training period. Tape recorders, CD/DVD players, electronic media, and headsets require careful introduction by the teacher.

## The Teacher's Role in Language Centers

Teachers are congenial, interested companions for the children: sharing books; helping children with projects; recording children's dictation; playing and demonstrating language games; making words, word lists, signs, or charts (Figure 18–5 and Figure 18–6); and helping children use the center's equipment.

Teachers slip in and out as needed and monitor equipment use. Vigorous or noisy play is diverted to other room areas or outside yard areas. Children who have been given clear introductions to a language center's materials and clear statements concerning expectations in use of the center's furnishings may need little help. It may be necessary, however, to set rules for the number of children who can use a language center at a given time.

The teacher explains new materials that are to become part of the center's collection. Many materials are demonstrated before they are made available to the children.

**FIGURE 18–5** Stickers, words, or children's work may be added to charts.

---

**audiovisual equipment** — any mechanical or nonmechanical item useful in offering sight or hearing experience.

Hurt no living thing:

Ladybug nor butterfly,

Nor moth with dusty wing,

Nor cricket chirping cheerily

Nor grasshopper so light of leap,

Nor dancing gnat,

Nor beetle fat,

Nor harmless worms that creep.

**FIGURE 18–6** Language center chart.

Posting children's work on the center bulletin board and planning chalkboard activities and printing messages that may catch the children's attention motivate interest in and use of the center. Plants and occasional fresh flowers in vases add a pleasant touch. To help children use equipment, materials, and machines on their own, teachers have become inventive, using step-by-step picture charts posted above or near materials. Color-coded dots make buttons or dials stand out. Some centers control machine use by giving training sessions in which children obtain "licenses." Children without licenses need to have adult companions.

Another task the teacher may want to undertake is making read-along recordings to accompany favorite books. The popularity of read-alongs cannot be denied, nor can the educational benefits. Children who use read-alongs are learning word recognition as well as some of the more advanced reading skills. For fun and pleasure, the lure of read-alongs makes them another gateway into the world of books. Teachers should consider the following when making recordings:

A narrator's pacing is important. It cannot be too fast, or the child trying to follow along will be lost. If it is too slow, the child will become bored. The inflection and tone of the voice are also vital. The narrator cannot be condescending or patronizing; neither should there be an attempt to "act out" the story and run the risk of making the story secondary to the performance.

Besides these factors, a teacher needs to estimate audience attention span and use a pleasant page-turning signal. With story recordings, either on tape or CD (with or without a story visual), the child may be a passive listener or can be an active, responsive participant. Some commercial manufacturers and teachers have cleverly designed interactive features, but these, though enjoyable and educational, cannot match what is possible with a "live" book reading and are a second-best activity.

## HOUSEKEEPING AND BLOCK AREAS

Educators emphasize the importance of housekeeping and block areas, both of which encourage large amounts of social interaction and the use of more mature, complex language. High levels of dramatic play interaction are also encouraged in theme (unit) centers. Teachers design spacious, well-defined, well-stocked (theme-related) partitioned room areas for block play and dramatic play.

## DISPLAYS AND BULLETIN BOARDS

Interesting eye-level wall and bulletin board displays capture the children's attention and promote discussion. Displaying children's work (with children's permission), names, and themes based on their interests increases their feelings of accomplishment and their sense of pride in their classroom. Displays that involve active child participation are suggested. Many can be designed to change daily or weekly.

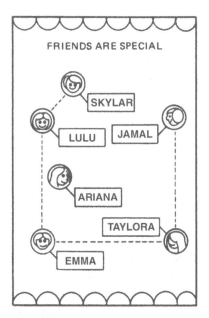

FIGURE 18–7 Bulletin board ideas.

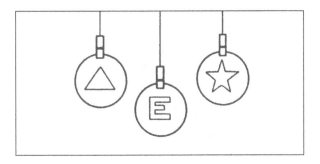

FIGURE 18–8 Plastic lid chalkboard activities.

Printscript is used on bulletin boards with objects, pictures, or patterns. Book pockets, picture hooks, ¼-inch elastic attached to clothespins, and sticky bulletin board strips allow pieces to be added and removed.

Figure 18–7 shows one bulletin board idea. The child selects a spot to paste her picture (photo) and name. A colored line is drawn between the photo and name. Later, colored lines can be drawn, connecting friends' pictures.

## CHALKBOARD OR WHITE BOARD ACTIVITIES

One of the most underutilized instructional items in early childhood centers can be the chalkboard or white board. The following chalkboard activities are suggested to help children's language development.

**Tracing Templates and Colored Chalk.** Using a sharp tool, cut large plastic coffee can lids into a variety of patterns (Figure 18–8). Suspend the patterns on cord or elastic with clothespins over the chalkboard.

**Pattern Games.** Draw Figure 18–9 on the chalkboard. Ask the children what shape comes next in the pattern. Then draw Figure 18–10 and see whether the children can make a line path from the dog to the doghouse.

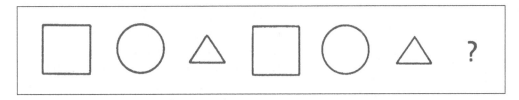

FIGURE 18–9 What comes next in the pattern?

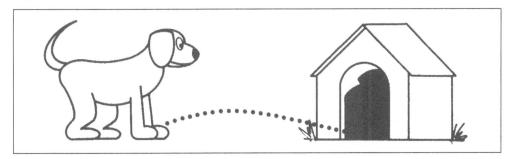

FIGURE 18–10 A left-to-right skill builder.

## AUDIOVISUAL EQUIPMENT

Budgets often determine the availability of electronic items and materials in an early childhood center. Care of equipment and awareness of operating procedures are important. Special fund-raising projects, rental agreements, borrowing arrangements, or donations have secured audiovisuals for some programs. The machine's or item's instruction manual should be studied for the proper care and maintenance necessary for efficient use.

The following audiovisual equipment enriches a center's language arts program activities.

- *Camera* (including Polaroid, cell phone, and video cameras). A camera can be used to provide images and photos that are useful in speaking activities, displays, and games.

- *Projector and Screens.* Common home, school, field trip, and community scenes can be discussed, written about (experience stories), or used for storytelling.

- *Lite-bord™.* This is a special display board that uses nontoxic erasable crayons for making colorful drawings and words that glow.

- *Video Cameras.* Children enjoy being recorded while displaying and explaining their creations. It has multiple uses.

- *Overhead Projectors, Screens, and Transparencies.* Stories with silhouettes or numerous transparency activities can be designed. Small patterns and alphabet letters can be enlarged and copied by teachers for a variety of uses. A number of teachers have used drawings or have placed images on the screen while storytelling or reading poetry (for example, using a "Humpty Dumpty" picture sequence while reciting the rhyme). Meier (2004) recommends supplying children with overhead projector sheets, or other kinds of plastic sheets, so that they can project their images and words onto a large screen. Some, but not all, picture books work well with this instructional technique. If text and illustration appear on the same page, this type of sharing is recommended. Teachers may have access to equipment used to make transparencies. The author strongly recommends this type of alternative storybook reading. Illustrations can be enlarged and enjoyed. Text appears giant-sized.

- *Opaque Projector.* Pages of picture books can be projected on wall areas to offer a new way to read books. Guessing games are also possible. Characters from picture books can become life-size companions.

### Listening Center Equipment

The following equipment is useful for the center's **listening center**.

- *Headsets and Jack Boxes.* Accommodating up to eight children at one time adapt to cassette, CD, and record players. Volume control is set on the jack box.

- *CD Players.* Most centers have this piece of equipment. Commercial suppliers of story CDs are plentiful.

- *Digital Camera.* Classroom photographs can be displayed on the computer, and prints can be made for display. Photo printers are available from many manufacturers.

- *Digital Camcorder.* Classroom action photography can be displayed on television sets and computers, or prints can be made.

- *Pocket Wall Charts with Stands.* This handy teacher's aid displays alphabet letters, words, sentences, shapes, pictures, colors, names, and so on. It is easy to use. Teachers prefer see-through pocket styles. These can be teacher-made.

- *Big Book Storage Rack.* See-through individual hanging bags can be used for big books and oversized materials; this visual solves the problem of storing large items.

- *Write and Wipe Boards and Easels.* Colored markers glide on and wipe off quickly. They are useful for teacher activities or child use. They are made in free-standing or tabletop styles, and some are magnetic, so plastic alphabet letters and numerals with magnets will stick.

- *Computer.* Besides computer use with software programs and use as a word processor, the computer has become a versatile piece of equipment.

- *Tape Recorders.* This is still a popular audiovisual aid that is used in early childhood centers. The tape recorder opens up many activity ideas. Suggestions for language development activities with tape recorders follow.

---

**listening center** — a classroom area designed to accommodate children's listening experiences.

- Record children's comments about their artwork or project. "Tell me about . . ." is a good starter. Put the tape and artwork together in the language center so that it is available for the children's use.
- Let the children record their comments about a group of plastic cars, human figures, animals, and so on, after they arrange them as they wish.
- Have children discuss photographs or magazine pictures.
- Record a child's comments about a piece of fruit that she has selected from a basket of mixed fruit.
- Record a "reporter's" account of a recent field trip.
- Gather a group of common items, such as a mirror, comb, brush, and toothbrush. Let the child describe how these items are used.
- Record a child's description of peeling an orange or making a sandwich with common spreads and fillings.
- Record a child's comments about her block structures. Take a Polaroid photo and make both tape and photo available in the listening and looking area.
- *Television Sets and VCRs.* These can be purchased as separate units or as combined machines. Children's classic literature is available. Local video rental stores and public libraries stock a variety of titles. Active teacher-child discussion of what is viewed is recommended.
- *Discussion or Study Prints.* A collection of large posters, photographs, mounted magazine pictures, and life-size book characters can be used in activities. Visuals can increase child verbalization and serve as creative "jumping off" spots.

## The Use of Picture Files

Picture files consisting of collections of drawings and photographs are made available to children in classroom language centers. Teachers find that they are invaluable motivators for many language-related child activities. Some of the most puzzling and outlandish images can get the most attention and discussion. Magazine photos and photos showing classroom scenes or attending children are popular with children. Images can be rotated and used to supplement a present course of study. Think about creating categories such as animals or fire engines and so on.

It is a good idea to start with enlarged photographs of each child and staff (affix to a firm backing). Resources for pictures include coloring books, shape books, inexpensive children's books, calendars, catalogs, trade journals, travel folders, and toy advertisements.

Suggested activities include:

- writing captions.
- storytelling from a series of pictures.
- giving names to animal pictures.
- finding hidden objects.
- categorizing pictures.
- finding objects that have alphabet letters printed on them.
- putting illustrations in a sequence and telling a story.
- matching pictures with related objects.
- finding alphabet letters in signs.
- identifying logos or outdoor signs from familiar fast-food restaurants or other local businesses.
- singing or creating a song to go with a picture.
- rhyming with pictures.
- finding things of the same shape, color, and category.
- classifying pictures by season.
- making a sound to fit a picture.
- writing a letter to someone shown in a picture.
- finding an object in the classroom that looks like something in a picture.
- choosing a favorite from a picture collection of food or other objects.
- labeling everything in a picture.
- finding things that start with the same alphabet letter sound.
- making an alphabet book as a group project or promoting each child's creation of an individual alphabet book.

It is easy to see that there are many possibilities. Teacher ingenuity creates others. Teachers often protect images with clear contact paper or lamination. Classrooms may have a teacher's set and a children's set. Smart teacher substitutes pack them along for "filler" or "spur of the moment" activities.

A special column in NAEYC's *Young Children* reports on early childhood classrooms that are trying to integrate technology into their learning program. Following are described language arts ideas and suggestions for teachers interested in bookmaking activities.

- Create multimedia book-making centers.
- Promote child authored and illustrated books with scanned images of children's drawings combined with audio files of child storytelling.
- Use computer printouts of stories typed by teacher from children's dictation.
- Help children create blended stories featuring a combination of child-written text and dictated text with printed digital photographs taken by the child (NAEYC, 2008).

### Technology, Electronic Equipment, and Literacy Learning

What do early childhood educators believe concerning the use of technology? Most will agree that machines, whether computers, audiovisuals or other technology, can teach, support, assist, motivate, and be used for the practice and application of literacy skills. Technology cannot "be the teacher of literacy," but it can be a useful tool in assessing and tracking children's literacy skill development.

More academic research is necessary to help educators and families understand how both school and home electronic media affect the informal learning of young children. Some manufacturers and associations, such as Microsoft and the national PTA (Parent-Teachers Association), are urging parents to use "PACT" to determine what types of media are appropriate for young children.

> The "P" stands for parental involvement. The "A" is for determining what a child can access on line. "C" is for selecting content deemed appropriate for little ones. And "T" stands for time, as in how long children can play a game console, TV or computer. (*USA Today*, 2008)

New products are building in features that encourage children's group play (e.g., Nintendo) and other features such as co-viewing. A new website, WhatTheyPlay.com, helps families examine ratings of children's program titles. IBM

and Zula USA are developing "educational virtual worlds" that attempt to teach 4-year-olds about math and science. PBS has created online neighborhoods for preschoolers (Snider, 2008). The site allows 3- to 6-year-olds to play and learn with the help of characters such as Curious George and the Berenstain Bears. Homes and schools will decide whether subscription fees and program content is suitable.

## PLANNING LANGUAGE CENTERS AND COMPUTER CENTERS

Once rooms or areas are designated as language centers, staff members classify materials into "looking and listening" or "working with" categories (Figure 18–11). Display, storage, working space, and looking and listening areas are determined. Activities that require concentration are screened off when possible. Enz and Morrow (2009) have a checklist for evaluating classroom literacy centers. See Figure 18–12. Many different

FIGURE 18–11 Writing tools are always found in classroom language centers.

## LITERACY CENTER

— manipulatives (roll movie or puppets with related books)
— children participate in designing the center (develop rules, select a name for center, and develop materials)
— area placed in a quiet section of the room
— visually and physically accessible, yet partitioned from the rest of the room
— rug, throw pillows, rocking chair, bean bag chair, and stuffed animals
— private spot in the corner, such as a box to crawl into and read
— the center uses 10% of the classroom space and fits 5 or 6 children

## THE LIBRARY CORNER

— bookshelves for storing books with spines facing outward
— organizational system for shelving books
— open-faced bookshelves for featured books
— 5-8 books per child
— books represent 3 to 4 grade levels of the following types:
    (a) picture books, (b) picture storybooks, (c) traditional literature,
    (d) poetry, (e) realistic literature, (f) informational books,
    (g) biographies, (h) chapter books, (i) easy to read books,
    (j) riddle/joke books, (k) participation books, (l) series books,
    (m) textless books, (n) television-related books, (o) brochures,
    (p) magazines, (q) newspapers
— 20 new books circulated every 2 weeks
— check-out/check-in system for children to take out books daily
— headsets and taped stories
— felt board and story characters with the related books
— materials for constructing felt stories
— other story manipulatives
— system for recording books read (e.g., cards hooked onto a bulletin board)

## THE WRITING CENTER (THE AUTHOR'S SPOT)

— tables and chairs
— writing posters and a bulletin board for children to display their writing by themselves
— writing utensils (pens, pencils, crayons, felt-tipped markers, colored pencils)
— writing materials (many varieties of paper in all sizes, booklets, and pads)
— typewriter or computer
— materials for writing stories and making them into books
— a message board for children to post messages for the teacher and students
— a place to store "Very Own Words"
— folders for children to place samples of their writing

**FIGURE 18–12** Checklist for evaluating and improving the literacy environment.

arrangements of materials and equipment within a language arts center are possible. Most centers rearrange furnishings until the most functional arrangement is found. For sample arrangements with different functions, refer to Figure 18–13.

Many children like to escape noise with a favorite book or puppet. Most centers provide these quiet retreats within a language arts center. School staffs have found creative ways of providing private space. Old footed bathtubs with soft pillows,

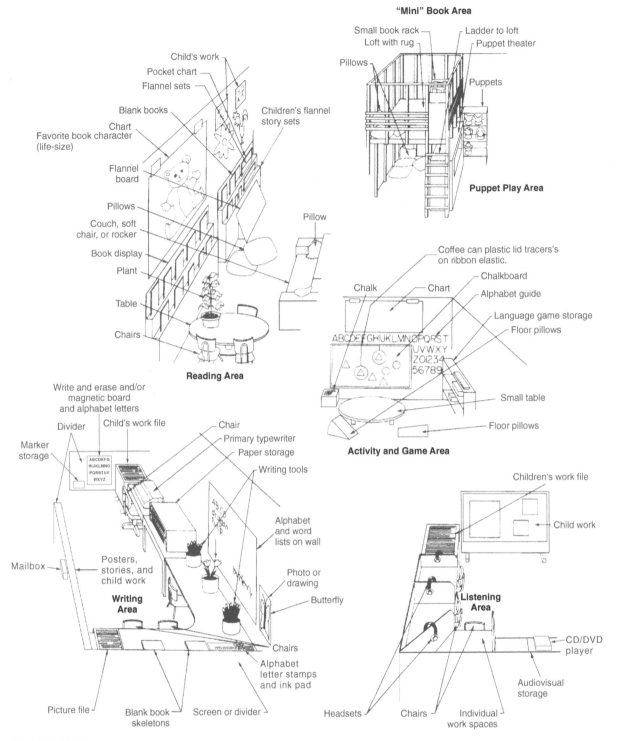

**FIGURE 18–13** Language arts center.

packing crates and barrels, pillow-lined closets with doors removed, tepees, tents, and screened-off couches and armchairs have been found workable in some classroom language arts areas.

With the fears mentioned earlier in this text concerning the overuse of television and videos, some educators see computer programs as offering a "cartoon world" rather than the real experiences and human interactions upon which real knowledge and literacy depends. Early childhood educators realize that computer skills and knowledge may be necessary in elementary school grades; however, they may be unsure about the best time to introduce them to young children.

Slowly but steadily computer centers are becoming standard in 3- and 4-year-olds' preschool classrooms. Staffing, expense, and time for teacher preview of programs are important considerations. Many educators agree that computer centers are compatible with developmentally appropriate practice. Computers can offer problem solving, creative experiences, and literacy opportunities. Benefits cited by many early childhood advocates of child computer use include child cooperation and turn taking and minimum need for supervision after child training on mechanics. Children can work at their own speed, and collaborate, mentor each other, negotiate, and problem solve alone or with a peer.

The experience can build children's self-confidence and also feelings of independence.

Additional benefits children may experience when computers become part of classroom life that are related to language arts skills and development include children's

- verbal interactions with a peer partner or others (Figure 18–14).
- experiences with alphabet letters, print, and words.
- ability to see uses of print, which include recording, informing, sending, and receiving messages.
- opportunity to create literary works that then can be recorded.
- experience in making greeting cards.
- exposure to rhyme.
- opportunity to match letters, patterns, rhymes, and words with pictorial representations.
- exposure to visual and interactive storybooks.

FIGURE 18–14 One peer can often instruct another.

Teachers with computers in their classrooms will agree that it is appropriate to step in when children are frustrated or lack necessary user skills. They tend to offer minimal help if they believe that the child can work out a problem on her own, thereby allowing the child to experience mastery and the resulting feeling of accomplishment. Most teachers periodically join children at the computer to ask questions or make comments that encourage the expansion of skill.

Some educators are concerned about the fact that some elementary school children and adolescents have displayed obsessive and addictive behaviors, and have indulged in computer video game overuse. These "gamers" have less social contact with peers and less interest in reading, which affects their school performance. Research on preschooler use of video, hand held games, or similar recreational media is scarce and yet to be probed in a national study.

Technology in the classroom is a tool purchased to benefit children's education, but many believe that there may be hidden side effects. Technology can be used as an aid for instructional activities, child assessment, the storing or compiling of data, word processing, research, communication, or some other teaching or professional function. Whether digital or electronic, it cannot replace young children's real firsthand contact with the environment and human interaction. Scarce research suggests its use is beneficial for children less than 3 years of age. There is controversy about (1) the amount of time young children spend in front of screen media; (2) its value; (3) its possible power to affect children's brains; (4) its presentation of violence; and (5) early childhood educators' ability to recognize inappropriate practice and identify questionable content. Many educators would rather err on the side of caution. They realize technology is definitely here to stay and already available in many children's homes. How many hours young children spend with it each day and what type of digital or electronic items they use becomes necessary information to secure from families.

Centers develop simple computer area rules that are appropriate to their classroom, children, and equipment. Rules usually involve clean hands, number of children allowed at one time, how to ask for help, taking turns, time allowed per turn, use of earphones, and what training is required before use.

**VIDEO ACTIVITY**

Go to the Education CourseMate website to watch the TeachSource Video from the BBC Motion Gallery watch *Preschool: Appropriate Learning Environments and Room Arrangements*.

1. The computer center seemed to receive no child attention in the video with no children using or approaching it, what might have made it more appealing and inviting?

2. When the classroom was rearranged the computer center had a few more positive features, can you identify one or more? Any less than desirable ones?

3. Could you suggest a better placement of the computers in this classroom?

Research seems to suggest that 3- and 4-year-old children who use computer programs that support and reinforce the major objectives of their curricula have significantly greater developmental gains when compared with children who have not had computer experiences in similar classrooms. Among the gain areas researched were nonverbal skills, verbal skills, problem solving, and conceptual skills.

Interestingly, computer program use has been found to improve the speech skills of children with dyslexia and other language-based learning disabilities. Researchers noted that language comprehension improved to normal, near-normal, or above normal in children who had been 2 to 3 years behind peers in speech skills. The findings are especially encouraging for children who have difficulty learning to talk (developmental dysphasia) or who have subsequent reading problems (developmental dyslexia).

For preschool classrooms, educators recommend an initial training period; turn taking, cooperative learning in small groups, peer tutoring, hands-on experience, waiting lists, and a sufficient number of adults who make an "adult time" investment. **Software** variety should also be offered.

## Software Selection

Developmentally appropriate integration begins with selecting hardware and software that will complement goals. The following is a list of software characteristics to check and consider.

- does not include violence
- provides positive verbal and visual cues and responses (feedback)
- allows the child to control pace and action
- allows the option of practicing a skill or moving on
- supports working alone or with others

When teachers provide open-ended software that encourages creativity, rather than drill-and-practice software, this is developmentally appropriate. Open-ended programs encourage children to explore and to extend their thinking. They spark children's interest as well as social and cognitive development.

Other software features teachers need to examine include content, age appropriateness, pacing, child choices available, meaningful graphics and sound, clear directions for yet-to-read children, approaches to learning, and appropriate cost. The integrity and craftsmanship in a software program determines its effectiveness and quality. Four critical steps to maximize children's learning through computer use follow.

1. selecting developmental software
2. selecting developmental websites
3. integrating these resources into the curriculum
4. selecting computers to support these learning experiences

Websites may offer many rich educational opportunities and provide opportunities that appear to enhance problem solving, critical thinking skills, decision making, language skills, knowledge, research skills, the ability to integrate information, social skills, and self-esteem.

The following magazine is a good resource for information about software selection: *Children's Technology Review* www.childrenssoftware.com. (This publication reviews software programs, evaluating each program in six areas using a 1 to 5 rating scale; reviews include a description of the program and a list of features and teaching goals.)

---

**software** — a wide range of commercial programs developed for computer users' convenience, education, entertainment, and so on.

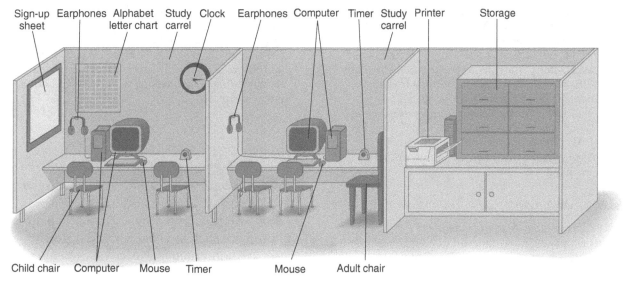

Sign-up sheet | Earphones | Alphabet letter chart | Study carrel | Clock | Earphones | Computer | Timer | Study carrel | Printer | Storage

Child chair | Computer | Mouse | Timer | Mouse | Adult chair

**FIGURE 18–15** Computer center.

**Reading Area Software Programs and Commercial Preschool Software.** Medina (2008) reviewed a research program that combined a standard school reading class program and an individualized software program that analyzed a student's reading competencies and provided tailored exercises to strengthen reading deficiencies. In conjunction with the class, the software was wildly successful. The reading class experience alone or the software alone was not as effective. (p. 68)

Commercial preschool language development programs are plentiful. To find out whether software is effective or not, early childhood teachers will need to do their own classroom research while remembering every child's brain is individually wired. What promotes growth in one child may not in another.

### Computer Location

The ideal classroom location for computers is a visible location where monitors can be seen throughout the classroom. This setting enables supervision and quick assistance (Figure 18–15). A computer center or activity area in a preschool or kindergarten classroom usually operates well with two or three computers and one or two printers.

## SUMMARY

When there is a language arts center within an early childhood playroom, language development materials are arranged in one central room location. Children follow their own interests, according to their preferences.

A language center's material can include a wide range of teacher-made and commercially purchased items. Activities in listening, speaking, writing, viewing, and reading (or combinations of these) are side-by-side, promoting the child's ability to see relationships among them.

Technical, audiovisual materials, and digital equipment are useful language center devices. Costs sometimes limit their availability. Training in the use and care of machines is necessary for efficient operation. Computer use in young children's classrooms continues to expand, and teacher screening of software programs is important. Questioning educators are concerned that possible hidden negatives exist for children less than 3 years of age who are exposed to different kinds of technology and older children's addictive behaviors that impact their reading achievement and crowd out firsthand experiences and play.

## ADDITIONAL RESOURCES

### Readings

Anderson, G. T. (2000, March). Computers in a developmentally appropriate curriculum. *Young Children, 55*(2), 90–93.

Browne, K. W., & Gordon, A. M. (2009). *To Teach well.* Upper Saddle River, NJ: Pearson.

*Children's Technology Revue* (monthly magazine), Scholastic Active Learning Associates, 120 Main St., Flemington, NJ 08822.

Schiller, P., & Willis, C. A. (2008, July). Using brain-based teaching strategies to create supportive early childhood environments that address learning standards. *Young Children*, 63(4) 52–55.

Willis, C. (2009). *Creating inclusive learning environments for young children*. Thousand Oaks, CA: Corwin Press.

Wood, J. M. (2004). *Literacy online: New tools for struggling readers and writers*. Portsmouth, NH: Heinemann.

## Helpful Websites

NAEYC Technology & Young Children
http://www.techandyoungchildren.org
A special interest and discussion forum.

Sesame Workshop
http://www.sesameworkshop.org
Provides information and activities to download.

TRUCE – Teachers Resisting Unhealthy Children's Media
http://www.truceteachers.org
Offers a guide, *What Do We Know About Children and Electronic Media?* It covers excessive screen time, viewing habits, talking to parents, and other links to explore.

Go to www.cengagebrain.com to access this text's Education Course-Mate website where you'll find helpful resource such as video activities, glossary flashcards, interactive exercises, quiz questions, and more!

# Review It and Use It

A. List the advantages of an early childhood language arts center. What are the disadvantages?

B. List the teacher's duties in a well-functioning classroom language arts center (for example, supervision).

C. Describe or draw a picture of an imaginary language arts center that has a crawl-into bunk or loft area. It should be a place where a child could be alone to enjoy a book.

D. List seven useful items mentioned in this chapter for classroom language arts centers.

E. Describe a well-designed classroom computer center.

## STUDENT ACTIVITIES

1. Observe an early childhood program. Describe the use and storage of language development materials and electronic or digital equipment.

2. Listen to three commercial story recordings. Judge and compare the quality of the recordings.

3. Invite a technology or audiovisual company's sales representative to the class to demonstrate the company's product. (Seek instructor approval first.)

4. Develop a price list for five pieces of audiovisual equipment found in this chapter. Cite source.

5. Interview two early childhood teachers on their use of technology or audiovisuals in their language arts curriculum. Report the findings to the group.

6. Plan and conduct an activity for a group of preschoolers using a tape recorder.

7. Investigate three children's computer (software) programs. Report your findings.

8. Observe preschoolers interacting with a computer in an early childhood classroom. Take written notes during a 15-minute observation period. Share notes with a group of peers. Develop a list of classroom rules for child computer use.

9. Make an "L" poster chart by cutting out pictures of "L" words (or use another alphabet letter). Introduce it to a group of older 4-year-olds. Think about how you will connect the chart to children's interests and lives while creating the chart. Print the items recognized in a list or on the chart and underline the beginning letter. Report your experiences.

# The Family-Center Partnership

## OBJECTIVES

After reading this chapter, you should be able to:

- Describe the family-teacher partnership that affects language arts programs.
- Compare strategies used to enhance family-school communication.
- Identify ways in which families can strengthen a child's language growth.

## KEY TERMS

socioeconomic

outreach

family literacy programs

## The Power of Persistence

*At pick-up time, when Martin's mother arrived, Mei Lin, Martin's teacher, observed a behavior she had not previously seen in Martin. Martin immediately started what Mei Lin would describe as vocal badgering. His verbal assault included a steady stream of, "But you promised . . . , I want one . . . , You said so . . . , I didn't have one yesterday . . . , I want it . . . , You told me I could . . . , I'm ready . . . , Let's go." His voice got louder and louder and didn't stop when his mother attempted to talk to Mei Lin. It continued as Martin and his mother exited to the porch. Mei Lin then heard Martin's mother say, "All right. We'll go to McDonalds!"*

### Questions to Ponder

1. What is happening here?
2. Should Mei Lin discuss the situation with Martin's mother? Why or why not?
3. Does this have anything to do with language development?
4. Is there anything positive about Martin's way with words?

## FAMILIES AND CHILD LITERACY

Although families and teachers are partners in a child's education, a family is a child's foremost teacher and model, and the home is a child's first and most influential school (Figure 19–1). Many families are eager consumers of information about what is best for their offspring. Six in ten parents read books about parenting or early childhood development before their children were born and about 32 percent took classes for new parents.

Families are usually informed of the school's language and literacy curriculum during enrollment interviews. Most families want to find out how teachers interact with their children on a daily basis to realize their instructional goals. Educators find that some families will ask for advice concerning what to do in terms of their

**FIGURE 19–1** The child's foremost teachers and educators are the child's parents and family.

children's education and are vulnerable as a result. It is suggested that anxious families need reassurance and can be encouraged to trust their instincts.

Early childhood teachers can enhance their ability to work with the families of children in their classrooms. They should not make assumptions about a family's parenting practices. Within any cultural group—be it ethnic, racial, **socioeconomic,** or religious—individuals and families vary in their beliefs and adherence to the social conventions of their community.

Significant changes in family structure have occurred. More than 25 percent of all children and more than 55 percent of African-American children are living with an unmarried parent. Whatever family type exists, the family should be viewed by educators as having knowledge on a wide range of topics that might be accessed by schools and educators. Family members are experts concerning how the home supports their child's emerging literacy. Questions teachers ask during initial and later meetings and interviews can gather valuable information concerning family literacy goals and practices, home conversations with children, home literacy settings and materials including books and other publications, and their children's particular preferences and developing interests. Information gathered can influence the classroom library book selection as well as individual and group instructional planning.

Early childhood teachers and centers examine a wide range of strategies to enhance their relationships with families. Researchers urge educators to consider a family-by-family approach. When reaching out to families, teachers are likely to find that intra-group differences may be as great as inter-group differences. Efforts could include hiring bicultural and bilingual staff to increase a program's ability to communicate and create trust.

Child literacy at home and school is influenced by three important factors: (1) setting, (2) models, and (3) planned and unplanned events. The setting involves what the home or school provides or makes available, including furnishings, space, materials and supplies, toys, books, and so forth. Family "connectedness" is

---

**socioeconomic** — relating to or involving a combination of social and economic factors.

crucial. Interactions with parents, siblings, grand-parents, and other relatives enrich children's lives. Sharing hobbies, trips, chores, mealtimes, community and neighborhood happenings, conversations, and stories are all language-development opportunities. Access to additional settings outside the home is also considered. Time allowed or spent in community settings can increase or decrease literacy.

Preschools planning to maintain the continued literacy development of attending children must face the fact that a home's low socioeconomic status often affects their children's literacy growth. Au (2006) notes that poverty appears to be the factor most highly associated with poor reading achievement in elementary school. Middle-class families usually offer their children the advantage of more home book reading, more library visits, and more print-related experiences. Families with low educational aspirations for their children and low motivation, which sometimes results from poverty, stress, fatigue, and other unfortunate living conditions, are the families who most need sensitive professional **outreach** from their children's teacher and school.

Family economics may determine the opportunities and materials that are available, but family ingenuity and know-how may overcome a lack of monetary resources. Most things that families can do to encourage reading and writing involve time, attention, and sensitivity rather than money. All families can be instrumental in fostering literacy if they spend time doing so. The usefulness of speaking, writing, and reading can be emphasized in any home. Children's literature may be borrowed from public libraries and other sources in almost all communities.

Although preschools are not as programmed as elementary schools and much of the learning in preschools goes hand-in-hand with firsthand exploration, families still have a big edge over group programs in offering intimate, individualized adult-child learning opportunities. Family interactions during activities involve both the quality and quantity of communication (Figure 19–2). The supportive assistance given at home, the atmosphere of the home, family-child

**FIGURE 19–2** Some parents consult their child's teacher for language-developing ideas.

conversations, and joint ventures can greatly affect the child's literacy development. Educators take every opportunity in everyday conversations and in planned meetings to help families know how to turn ordinary home occurrences into young children's learning experiences. Trish Megan (2009) has voiced what every teacher knows in her heart—"If we can't involve parents (families) in schools, then we do little to really impact the children we teach."

Successful families listen to what children say and respond to them. They interpret the child's language attempts and reply with related action accompanied by words and sentences. Learning is enhanced where children are supported by caring adults who share their world with them and enter into the children's worlds of play and talk, tuning in to their feelings and experiences. The essential element is the intimacy between child and the people in his life who share a common environment; this fosters the understanding of meanings and child curiosity.

Children who find their efforts and attempts at language received and valued develop the confidence to continue. Children's learning flourishes when they are allowed some degree of control over their own actions and when they interact with adults who are receptive, less concerned with the correctness of child speech, and more likely to respond in ways that stretch thinking.

---

**outreach** — an early childhood program's attempt to provide supportive assistance to attending children's families to promote their children's success in school and developmental growth.

Early childhood centers design their own unique family involvement programs. With increased federal and state emphasis on early childhood educators' working jointly with parents and families, educators working in publicly funded programs will need to clarify their goals and analyze their efforts. Most educators would agree any involvement must start with the development of a trusting relationship (Figure 19–3). NAEYC's Engaging Diverse Families (EDF) Project (2010) has researched and identified the family engagement practices of high-quality early childhood programs. They follow.

● Encourage family participation in decision making. (Programs have Boards of Directors with family representation, active committees, and regular parent-teacher conferences that encourage shared decision making concerning the program and individual children.)

● Facilitate consistent, two-way communication. (Programs communicate with families through the use of multiple formats and in the families' preferred language.)

● Seek out information about families' lifestyle and community and integrate this information into their curriculum. (Programs welcome family talents, interests, or family traditions into the classroom.)

● Support families' efforts to create home environments that value learning by connecting families with information and activities that enhance early learning. Announcements of community events, lending libraries, and newsletter tips about child development are examples of how programs can extend the learning beyond the classroom.

● Develop a program supporting staff leadership and support dedicated and trained teachers in their efforts to reach out to and include families. (p. 8)

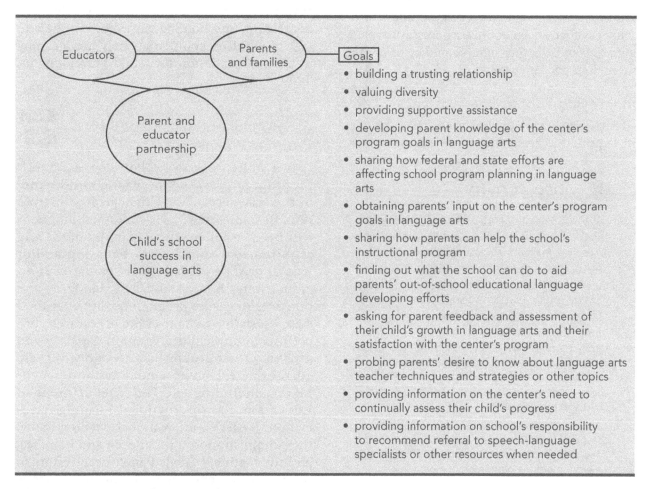

**FIGURE 19–3** Parent involvement goals.

## Developing Trust

Developing trust grows from family feelings of being respected, accepted, and valued for their individual and cultural diversity, and it also grows when staff members are sensitive to family economics. Educators need to be aware of what families' desire for their children. All of this starts the day family members walk through the school's door. What is on the walls and how they are welcomed and treated by staff are important. This calls for a consideration of comfort and requires staff preparation and planning. A clearly-labeled school entrance and an open classroom door should guide families on children's first day. Ideally, an adult who speaks their home language greets them or is immediately available. A welcoming letter should have reached homes beforehand that included a statement concerning whether a family member is welcome to stay if their child seems to need this, and also whether families are able to visit the classroom before opening session begin.

Truly thoughtful administrators/teachers know if printed signs directing families to the school's office or classroom are necessary in parking areas and whether signs should be printed in more than one language.

## Identifying Supportive Assistance

Identifying exactly what a center can offer in supportive assistance is a necessary task.

**▶❚❚ VIDEO ACTIVITY**

Go to the Education CourseMate website to watch the TeachSource Video Case, *Communicating with Families: Best Practices in an Early Childhood Setting.*

1. After watching Mona Sanon, the teacher greeting parents as they enter, what teacher techniques did you notice that were especially effective in building teacher-parent rapport?

2. Some good ideas were presented for building family participation and reinforcement of classroom learning and to increase the parents' role in their child's overall educational growth. Pick two suggestions and discuss their benefit to both the child and the parent.

3. "Make yourself available" was suggested to teachers. Does this in any way make you feel uneasy or it's opposite, comfortable? Discuss this by writing a short paragraph or two.

A school's list can be long or short depending on the financial and human resources available. Some schools have generous budgets; others do not. Some have committed and dedicated staff members who realize working with and through parents and families is a priority. Most educators are familiar with data and research showing that a family's socioeconomic status, cultural and linguistic group membership, parenting style, and home literacy experiences correlate with the knowledge and skills that children bring to school. They realize that excellent instructional help will be necessary to prepare some children for kindergarten. The State of Kentucky (2009) has developed a valuable guide to facilitate home/school connections when working with other than English speaking families. See Figure 19–4.

In a little-noticed section of the No Child Left Behind Act (2002), expectations of schools include arranging remedial education for parents who need it, teaching parents to use the Internet to check on children's grades and homework, and holding workshops on how to talk to children about what they are learning in class (Foundation for Child Development, 2009).

## Early Childhood Language Arts Program Planning

It is a staff's task to explain how a center's program addresses "the whole child" and, in this case, especially language arts instruction. In some states, early childhood programs will need to follow curricular standards and requirements specified in licensing and/or federal or state guidelines or standards. Individual states have established standards and practices to ensure program quality after their state legislators became aware of research concerning young children's brain capacity and growth. Other groups have developed or are currently developing guidelines and benchmarks, including the U.S. Department of Education, the International Reading Association, NAEYC, the National Reading Panel, the Administration for Children and Families, and the National Goals Panel. Every effort to develop research-based recommendations is

Since this may be the first opportunity that ELL families have with school contact, it's vital that they feel welcome. Below are some suggested activities that will assist in accomplishing this goal.

1. Host a back-to-school night with interpreters. Make accommodations for parent's schedules. offer transportation, food and childcare. Use this as an opportunity to find out how to establish and maintain regular contact with families. Also include information about adult education opportunities.
2. Find bilingual volunteers, parent liaisons, or staff assistants to translate or serve as interpreters.
3. Develop family learning activities (including multi-lingual activities.) Send home for the purpose of involving the family.
4. Consider sponsoring single parent and/or native language parent groups. Consider having meetings away from the school campus.
5. Involve language minority parents on advisory committees, councils and key communicator groups.
6. Hold family nights on parenting issues, including child development, early math, writing, science and literacy, setting up a work area at home and goals for their children and family; provide translators.
7. Find bilingual volunteers, parent liaisons or staff assistants to bridge the gap between families and the school.
8. Offer ongoing interactive training sessions for parents on topics such as homework, school attendance, standards, report cards and discipline.
9. Implement a bi-lingual hotline number where parents can get information on how to help their children at home.
10. Form a citizen advisory group that can advise the principal on how to improve services for students and families in poverty, singly parents, and those who do not speak English.

FIGURE 19–4 Home/school connection.

undertaken. Goldenberg (2002) lists what he terms the "emerging consensus" of current instructional practices (preschool through third grade) in beginning literacy:

1. Literate environments in which print is used for diverse and interesting purposes, including opportunities for student choice and ample time for looking at books and reading or "pretend reading."

2. Direct, explicit, systematic instruction in specific skills (e.g., phonological awareness, letter names/sounds, decoding, and comprehension strategies), with sufficient practice in successful use of skills in order to promote transfer and automaticity.

3. Discussions and conversations about materials children read or that are read to them.

4. Focus on word-recognition skills and strategies (direct instruction, but also use of techniques such as word walls and making words).

5. Strategically sequenced instruction and curriculum materials to maintain optimal challenge (instructional or independent, as appropriate).

6. Organizational and classroom management strategies to maximize academic engagement and appropriate use of materials.

7. An explicit focus on language (including vocabulary development).

8. Valid and frequent assessments, using multiple measures as needed and appropriate, to allow teachers to gauge developing skills and target instruction appropriately.

9. A home-school connection component that links the school's efforts with children's home experiences and enlists parents in supporting their children's academic development. (p. 282)

Some of this curriculum may be difficult to explain to families without using specific examples over an extended period. Schools and centers that are privately funded may not use the "consensus" goals listed and instead may use other goals as the basis for their language arts instruction.

## Obtaining Family Input

Schools have developed vehicles to ensure that family input is part of a school's operational plan. These include classroom mailboxes, parent advisory committees, and parent councils. Family questionnaires, surveys, and checklists often probe family ideas. Other efforts to reach out and communicate include e-mail, reading groups, planning workshops, and on-the-fly daily contacts. An early childhood program that isn't aware of family member's special talents or their unique access to diverse resources that can in some way enhance a program's instruction or maintenance may be missing extraordinary opportunities. This might be a family member who can volunteer, or one who works at a print shop, or a computer expert who might provide consultation services. Families may contain an ethnic storyteller or a teenager who can demonstrate a particular hobby or sport skill. This can't be discovered until a program sensitively asks or provides a probing take-home form or individual interview. Wouldn't it be a plus if teachers knew a public safety officer or dog groomer was available to discuss loose or stray dogs, or animal care, if a theme on dogs were planned?

## FAMILY GUIDELINES FOR LITERACY AND LANGUAGE DEVELOPMENT

The techniques or actions recommended to help children's language and literacy development apply to both teachers and parents. A family may have different and more varied opportunities to use these techniques. The following guidelines have been gathered from various sources dealing primarily with family-child relations. Families can promote literacy when they spend time with their children every day. At school, the teacher has many children to attend to and may not be able to provide as much individual attention as a family can provide. Recommended family actions include:

- Create home activities in which a child matches buttons, beans, blocks, or toys by colors, shapes, sizes; this kind of categorizing is an important thinking skill.

- Sort groceries by categories (canned goods, vegetables, fruits, and so on) with children.

- Keep in mind that a child's early experiences with print, writing tools, alphabet letters, and books can be puzzling. When a child asks question answer while he is focused.

- Slip quickly in and out of children's play, encouraging child discovery. This type of on-the-move teaching is natural and different from sit-down structured teaching, to which a child may tune out as interest wanes.

- Offer what is just a little beyond what a child already knows using a supportive, enthusiastic, "let's-discover-together" attitude.

- Realize pressure and commands aimed at teaching language arts turn children off.

- Arrange things so that a child has opportunities to see operations from beginning to end. For example, make butter from whipping cream or applesauce from picked apples.

- Encourage accomplishment, success, or honest effort with approval or appreciation.

- Be available as a resource person. When a child asks questions that an adult cannot answer, do not hesitate to seek help from others or books.

- Help children feel secure and successful. Interactions can build feelings of self-worth— if children's ideas and opinions are valued.

- Realize that young children's self-control is developing. In preschool and kindergarten, behavioral expectations create the climate for learning. Families set home behavioral standards. Disciplined work habits promote school success.

- Believe that fantasy play (make-believe) is correlated with other positive attributes such being creative, understanding the perspective of others, and possessing greater social skills (Wang, 2009).

### How Parents Can Stimulate Speaking Abilities

- Talk to children naturally and clearly as you would a friend. Listen when children want to tell you something without overtly correcting speech errors.

- Read stories, poems, jingles, and riddles to children.

- Encourage play with puppets, bendable family dolls, dress-up clothes, play stores, doctor kits, and play telephones, letting the children act out various events.

- Encourage children to tell you stories.

- Increase your attempts to build vocabulary by including new and descriptive words.

- Give attention; listen for intent rather than correctness. Show children that what they say is important. Communicate with children at their eye level, when possible. Expand and tactfully extend children's comments; talk on the children's chosen subjects.

- Use your best speech model—Standard English, if it comes naturally. If you speak a language other than English, provide a good model of that language.

- If a member of a cultural or ethnic group, examine attitudes concerning adult-child verbal interactions being important.

- Become a skilled questioner by asking questions that promote thinking, predicting, and a number of possible correct answers based children's viewpoints.

- Encourage children to talk about whatever they are making, without asking," What is it?"

- Talk frequently, give objects names, and describe the things you do—be specific.

- Talk about what children are interested in.

- Do things together and talk about them: trips to stores, the zoo, museums, and so on.

- Take photographs and urge children to take their own. Jointly label photos. Create stories or picture books with them for the family library. Let children dictate the text.

- Listen to your children so that you learn about them and show that you are interested.

- Talk with children to describe objects they see in a picture. Then hide the picture and see how many objects they can recall.

- Sing songs with rhyming words.

- Make up chants to give life to boring housekeeping jobs.

## How Parents Can Build Print Awareness and Skill

- Provide literature and a language-rich setting in the home.

- Write down the things children tell you about their pictures. Make books of each child's work and photographs, and talk about the books.

- Read family letters and mail to children, along with circulars, junk mail, restaurant menus, wrappers and packaging, signs, labels, building identifications, catalogs, brand names, and calendars.

- Provide scrap paper and writing tools, and reserve an area in the home as a writing center for children's use.

- Make or buy alphabet letter toys or word books.

- Ask teachers for copies of the alphabet your children will use in kindergarten.

- Encourage scribbling and doodling.

- Write messages to children or make signs for their play, such as "Mark's tower."

- Talk about what you are writing and its use to you.

- Start sharing books in infancy. Promote a child's personal book collection.

- Help your child learn the rules of print such as spaces separate words, reading left to right and punctuation marks.

- Be a co-explorer of books who promotes critical thinking, discusses unfamiliar words, ask questions, predict happenings, and discuss book characters and their actions.

- Encourage interest in paper-and-crayon activities by showing children their names in print. Give attention to their attempts to copy their names or write them from memory.

- For pretend play, provide bank forms, memo pads, school forms, store order pads, and ordering pads used in restaurants. This kind of play stretches children's imaginations and broadens their experiences.

- Help children in writing letters to grandparents, sick friends, book authors, or famous people.

- Put little notes in children's lunch boxes or backpacks. These can be picture notes or simple messages.

- Model writing for children; write private notes, grocery lists, and recipes with children.

- Praise preschool aged children's attempts to invent their own spelling when they are learning the relationship between print and speech. "Correct" spelling will follow later.

- Write down shared experiences or often-told family stories. Stories can help children anticipate a sequence of events or help children figure out words of personal importance.

Dokoupi (2009) points out families, especially those using government sponsored and funded preschool care, may unfortunately adopt parenting styles that over use verbal commands and directives. This practice offers less vocabulary and fewer language opportunities and can "short circuit" language growth. Dokoupil's recommendations are based upon a large research study of over 8,000 children with diverse Latino origins (Fuller, Bridges, Bein, Jang, Jung, Rabe-Hesketh, Halfon, & Kuo, 2009). Bardige (2009) suggests adult "business-like" talk about child behavior that directs, commands, and makes no-nonsense statements clarifying expected child actions and behaviors or states clear limits, isn't bad for young children. Business-like talk and adult-child play talk both have a place in young children's lives. Family talking, Bardige notes, adds an essential dimension for it affects many aspects of development including relationships, creativity, exploration self-concept, initiative, inquisitiveness, knowledge, grammar, vocabulary, expressive language, social skills, storytelling and literacy, imagination, thinking, and reasoning.

## How Experiences Outside of the Home Can Promote Literacy

Taking trips to interesting places such as a bowling alley, shoe-repair shop, bakery, zoo, farm, airport, or to different kinds of stores or on a train or bus trip is recommended. When the family returns, making drawings related to a trip can be encouraged. Discussing and reliving experiences and adventures promote expression of children's ideas. Remembrances might also be recorded or recreated using creative dramatizing. Effective trips can be quite simple ones like visiting community events such as 4-H

fairs, craft shows, antique-auto shows, etc. It is wise to find what learning destinations exist in a city. Accompanying family members on routine trips to the store, bank, post office, or park is also recommended. Families can plan many adventures that a school cannot duplicate.

Librarians and the Internet can become invaluable resources for information and books along a child's particular passion or interest—be that bugs, baseball, electricity, or airplanes, etc. Wise adults help children pursue and discover the answers to their many questions. Preschool children, on average, ask their parents about 100 questions a day according Bronson & Merryman (2010). By middle school, these authors believe children pretty much stopped asking. It's no coincidence that this is the same time when student motivation and engagement in school plummets (p. 47).

Subotnik (2010), a researcher who has studied children's transitions into successful creative careers as adults, suggests children do better when they are allowed to develop deep passions and pursue them wholeheartedly during childhood. In the process, children may research their chosen topic, focus deeply, think creatively, and communicate with others by various means explaining what they have learned and discovered.

The Association for Library Services to Children and the Public Library Association (2010) suggest families trying to choose worthwhile books for young children should consider a book's vocabulary; its narrative connections; its possible print awareness opportunities; its ability to enhance children's alphabet letter and sound recognition; and its ability to help children's ability to follow words on a page.

## How Parents Can Promote Listening Skills

Trying to teach children to listen to and identify sounds, such as the whine of car tires, bird calls, insect noises, and sounds of different kinds of doors closing in the house is something families can to do to increase skill. Recordings, television, and storybooks can also stimulate interest in listening. Experts also suggest adults pause before answering a child's questions to consider briefly what the child is really probing, and wait patiently for children to formulate answers to the parent's questions.

## How Families Can Promote an Interest in Reading

Some families create an environment that supports reading by making sure it is impossible to avoid books. They always bring a backpack full of books along on car rides, and keep books in the pockets on the back of car seats. These families understand that young children can make tremendous progress as readers while "just pretending." This happens when a child pretends to read books, read illustrations, or flips pages as he tells his own story or imitates the actions or voices of those who have read to him.

Families with positive attitudes about reading will usually find that their children are motivated, spend more time at reading, and expend more effort in learning to read. Put simply, parents who value reading have children with a greater interest in reading skills.

Reading is dependent on facility with oral language. Children who talk easily, handle words skillfully, ask questions, and look for answers usually become good readers. Families have more opportunities for one-on-one time with children compared with teachers who have groups of children to help. Skilled adults reading picture books stop when a child has lost concentration. They try to obtain enthralling books. They restrain themselves and do not go overboard in their attempts to educate children. Instead they have fun, enjoy humor, and encourage questions. Literacy-promoting families read to children every day. A survey by the Kaiser Family Foundation (2003) showed the amount of time children were reading or being read to compared with the time children engaged in other activities (see Figure 19–5).

Many families consult librarians for help. See Figure 19–6 for a list of books with an element of predictability. Finding predictable picture books that include repetitive features enhances the child's feelings of being part of the telling. Competency increases when the child knows what comes next after a few readings. An appealing book selected by a parent can be read with enthusiasm and animation. Children enjoy active participation when chanting lines, pointing to illustrations, and speaking in characters' voices. Families can give reading status and importance; they can read recipes and directions with their children to show print's purpose.

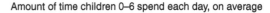

Amount of time children 0–6 spend each day, on average

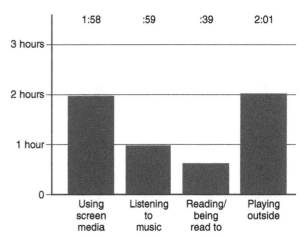

Note: Average is among all children, across all days of the week, including those who don't do certain activities yet at all.

**FIGURE 19–5** *Zero to six: Electronic Media in the Lives of Infants, Toddlers, and Preschoolers*, (#3378), The Henry J. Kaiser Family Foundation, Fall 2003. Copyright © 2003. (This information was reprinted with permission of the Henry J. Kaiser Family Foundation. The Kaiser Family Foundation, based in Menlo Park, California, is a nonprofit, independent national health care philanthropy and is not associated with Kaiser Permanente or Kaiser Industries.)

Children will become readers when their emotions are engaged and their imaginations are stretched and stirred by what they find on the printed page. The truly literate are not those who know how to read, but those who read fluently, responsively, critically, and because they want to.

It is wise to select from among the best books for even the youngest children. The best books are well-designed with uncluttered pages, interesting text, and colorful pictures that stimulate young imaginations.

When reading aloud from books, authors and illustrations can be discussed. Adult enjoyment should be apparent, and book happenings can be related to children's past experiences. Additional tips follow.

- Ask warm-up questions to set the stage and help children anticipate what will happen.
- Point as you read. For very young children, point to things in pictures as you talk about them. Pointing helps focus attention, thus lengthening the time children will sit still for a story. It also develops visual literacy—the idea that pictures have meaning.

| AUTHOR | TITLE | PUBLISHER |
|---|---|---|
| Arno, E. | *The Gingerbread Man* | Crowell |
| Bang, M. | *Ten, Nine, Eight* | Greenwillow |
| Baum, A., & Baum, J. | *One Bright Monday Morning* | Random House |
| Berenstain, S., & Berenstain, J. | *Bears in the Night* | Random House |
| Bonne, R., & Mill, A. | *I Know an Old Lady Who Swallowed a Fly* | Holiday House |
| Brown, M. W. | *Goodnight Moon* | Harper Festival |
| Charlip, R. | *What Good Luck! What Bad Luck!* | Scholastic |
| Charlip, R., & Supree, B. | *Mother Mother I Feel Sick Send for the Doctor Quick Quick Quick* | Tricycle Press |
| Flack, M. | *Ask Mr. Bear* | Simon & Schuster |
| Galdone, P. | *The Three Billy Goats Gruff* | Seabury |
| Graham, J. | *I Love You, Mouse* | Harcourt Brace |
| Hoban, T. | *Just Look* | Greenwillow |
| Hogrogian, N. | *One Fine Day* | Macmillan |
| Hutchins, P. | *The Surprise Party* | Simon & Schuster |
|  | *Rosie's Walk* | Simon & Schuster |
| Isadora, R. | *Max* | Simon & Schuster |
| Langstaff, J. | *Oh, A-Hunting We Will Go* | Simon & Schuster |
| Martin, B., Jr. | *Brown Bear, Brown Bear, What Do You See?* | Holt |
| Mayer, M. | *What Do You Do with a Kangaroo?* | Macmillan |
| Sendak, M. | *Chicken Soup with Rice* | HarperCollins |
| Shaw, C. B. | *It Looked Like Spilt Milk* | HarperCollins |
| Slobodkina, E. | *Caps for Sale* | HarperCollins |
| Spier, P. | *The Fox Went out on a Chilly Night* | Doubleday |
| Stevenson, J. | *"Could Be Worse!"* | Morrow, William & Co. |
| Stover, J. | *If Everybody Did* | McKay |
| Thomas, P. | *"Stand Back," Said the Elephant, "I'm Going to Sneeze"* | HarperCollins |
| Viorst, J. | *Alexander and the Terrible, Horrible, No Good, Very Bad Day* | Simon & Schuster |
| Zolotow, C. | *If It Weren't for You* | HarperCollins |

**FIGURE 19–6** Predictable books.

- Try asking what the child expects the book to be about from looking at the cover.
- Look for ways to involve the child during readings.
- Stop and let the child supply words.
- Talk about words (unusual ones) the child may not understand.

Parents are able to connect book story features not only to past happenings experienced together but also to the unique characteristics of their child's personality, interests, desires, and abilities. They have an emotional bond that can connect book-reading times to "pleasantness."

They can start book reading during infancy and make parent-child book time a special "together" time. Families can ask questions, point to objects in illustrations and hesitate to promote guessing, and prompt their child to see details and cause-and-effect relationships. All of these things will increase the child's literacy and vocabulary. Families can become active listeners who add information a little above what the child knows. When they accept their child's comments and ideas, parents reinforce the child's efforts and desire to share his ideas. Storybook illustrations can also be "read" and discussed in detail. Encouraging families to read in their native language is an

Use the following ratings: O = often, S = sometimes, I = infrequently, D = does not apply

**Family attempts to:**

_____ 1. initiate family discussions at mealtimes.

_____ 2. give full attention to child's comments.

_____ 3. add descriptive or new words in conversation.

_____ 4. take child to library.

_____ 5. take time at post office to discuss letters and postage.

_____ 6. discuss children's books.

_____ 7. read to child daily.

_____ 8. point out print around the house.

_____ 9. accept child's opinions.

_____ 10. use dictionary with child.

_____ 11. talk on the child's chosen subject.

_____ 12. ask questions that promote child's descriptions or predictions.

_____ 13. listen patiently.

_____ 14. discuss television programs.

_____ 15. plan community outings.

_____ 16. invite interesting people to home and promote interactions with child.

_____ 17. correct child's speech casually with little attention to errors.

_____ 18. encourage child hobbies.

_____ 19. answer questions readily.

_____ 20. discuss care and storage of books.

_____ 21. play word games or rhyme words playfully.

_____ 22. talk about how print is used in daily life.

_____ 23. find books on subjects of interest to child.

_____ 24. consult with child's teacher.

_____ 25. give attention and notice accomplishments.

_____ 26. take dictation from child.

_____ 27. try not to interrupt child's speech frequently.

_____ 28. initiate family reading times and family discussions of classics.

_____ 29. establish a book center in the home.

_____ 30. create child writing or art center in the home.

_____ 31. give books as gifts.

_____ 32. provide different writing tools and scrap paper.

_____ 33. provide alphabet toys in the home.

**FIGURE 19–7** Family self-rating.

important consideration. Schools enrolling other-than-English-speaking children include foreign language picture books in their classroom collection and often stock additional copies that parents can borrow. Local library staffers may be able to provide others. Family members who wish to rate themselves can use Figure 19–7. They may discover that they are already promoting child language and literacy in a number of ways.

## Family Storytelling

The magic of parental storytelling not only improves child listening but also broadens child interests and opens new worlds of discovery. Following are tips from professional storytellers.

1. Select a story that will interest both you and the children. Your enthusiasm for a story is important in helping the children enjoy the story too.

2. Practice the story several times before you share it with the children. Learn all you can about the characters, settings, and events within the story.

3. Decide how to animate the story. Practice some hand gestures, facial expressions, or body movements that will spice up the story for the children.

4. Practice different accents, voice inflections (angry, sad, joyous), and loud and soft speech patterns to help make characters come alive and to add drama to your presentation.

5. Create some simple puppets from common household objects such as wooden picnic spoons, paper plates, or lunch bags. Draw individual character features on each item and use them during your story.

6. Promote your storytelling time. Make an announcement about an upcoming story or design a simple "advertisement" for a story and post it in advance.

7. Design a simple prop for the children to use during the telling of a story: a paper boat for a sea story, a magnifying glass or camera for a mystery story, or a paper flower for a springtime story.

8. Have the children suggest new props, gestures, or voice qualities that would be appropriate for retelling of the story at a later date.

9. After telling a story, talk about it with the children. Ask them to tell you the most enjoyable or memorable parts.

10. Being a good storyteller takes a little practice, but the time invested can make a world of difference in helping children appreciate good literature.

Preschool educators are quick to inform the families of English language learners that they should continue to support the development of their child's home language. Research and educational experts confirm that the child's native language development aids the child's academic success in English. Leaving the child's home language behind is not the school's intent as some parents and families may believe (Nemeth, 2009). The advantage of learning two (or more) languages well is a desirable skill in any future career. Hearing stories in his home language is an experience no child should miss.

## Families Can Build Children's Self-Regulation

Vanderkam (2009) defines self regulation as the ability to stop, think, make a plan, and control impulses. Many educators believe these are important skills children need to do well in school. Vanderkam suggests self-regulation can be taught. Vanderkam notes educators are examining older studies, one of which is important research conducted in the 1960s and 70s by psychologist Walter Mischel. A description of a section of Mischel's research done by Vanderkam follows.

. . . a researcher would place a marshmallow in front of a hungry four year old and tell the child that she could eat the marshmallow right then, or have

two if she waited until the researcher returned. About a third of the children could distract themselves and wait. Followed for years, these highly disciplined kids had better school outcomes, and scored more than 200 points higher on the Scholastic Achievement Test (SAT) when older. (p. 9A)

See en.wikipedia.org/wiki/WALTER_MISCHEL for further information. A number of educational experts believe today's children are growing up with less practice in self-regulation. A good number have not demonstrated the ability to turn off TV and other media to start homework, nor can they plan how to solve important daily problems or hurdle road blocks. Brown (2009) cites the conclusions of recent research that suggests certain kinds of fantasy (dramatic) play in which children plan the fantasy roles they are going to enact, can have a measurable effect on children's ability to control their impulses. Some preschools are experimenting with planned activities and games that involve children's planning a course of action and then following through. Teacher's promotion of children's follow through plans is believed crucial. Games can be designed by teachers to promote (a) child's thinking first, and acting second, or (b) one where the child must control his/her impulses to be successful or complete the game.

Family advice to aid the development of children's self-control (regulation) development includes:

- playing games with rules which are enforced.
- promoting child help in household tasks that lead to successful task completion.
- setting time limits on TV or other electronic media especially during toddlerhood or preschool ages.
- limiting entertainment media viewing.
- letting a frustrated child think and plan his/her way out of a problem before jumping in with a solution or suggestion.
- coaching children to analyze and solve their own difficulties.
- promoting a child's work on a project and then expecting the child to complete to it.

**VIDEO ACTIVITY**

Go to the Education CourseMate website to watch the TeachSource Video Case entitled, *Parent Involvement in School Culture: A Literacy Project.* More than one parent in the video provided reasons for parents to be involved in their children's schooling.

1. Describe parent reasons and their suggestions for what a school or teacher should do to promote family involvement and school participation.

2. Linda Schwerty, the literacy specialist in the video, mentioned a number of ways she had tried to accommodate families so they could attend school meetings. Name a few.

- expecting a child to complete what activity he has chosen to start.

- increasing children's knowledge of process such as understanding there is a beginning, middle, and a finishing end of a task.

## Home Reading and Writing Centers

Home reading centers are a lot like school reading areas. A comfortable, warm, private, well-lighted place free of distraction works best. Adjacent shelving and a chair for comfort is important to book-sharing times. Window seats and room dividers make cozy corners. Parents can get creative in selecting and furnishing reading centers.

Family book collections encourage children's positive attitudes concerning books as personal possessions and give books status. Home-made books often become children's favorite volumes. Families model appropriate storage and care in home reading centers. A special area with writing supplies, an alphabet chart, table, and chair should be suggested to parents.

Families interested in purchasing books can be alerted to the opportunity to buy books through school-sponsored book clubs, local library book sales, used-book stores, thrift shops, and yard sales. Pointers should be shared concerning selecting quality books.

## Home Visits

In trying to understand attending children, especially "silent ones" or culturally diverse ones, a home visit may help to plan for children's individual needs. Most early childhood centers with strong home-school partnerships schedule yearly visits to each family.

## Families Who Speak Languages Other Than English

Early childhood centers have become increasingly sensitive to other-than-English-speaking families who are often eager to promote their child's literacy. Many children with limited English proficiency also have in common that their parents are poorly educated, that their family income is low, that they reside in communities in which many families are similarly struggling, and that they attend schools with student bodies that are predominantly minority and low achieving.

**Family literacy programs** attempt to break the cycle of intergenerational illiteracy by providing services to both family and child. Programs vary from community to community as each program tries to meet the needs of participants. Participants are often parents who lack basic literacy skills and may need to acquire positive self-concepts to encourage their children's school success. Family literacy programs and adult literacy programs can be located through county Offices of Education or state agencies.

Family literacy programs have a greater chance of success and longevity when they attempt to tap into the wealth of background knowledge and experiences of the family (parent) participants (Ortiz & Ordonez-Jasis, 2010). Relevant themes in books by Latino authors urge families to preserve traditions, celebrate cultural richness and personal stories, value family heritage, and share family social issues and concerns (Ada, 2003).

Directors and administrators can receive information and a multitude of resources

---

**family literacy programs** — community programs attempting to provide literacy-building opportunities and experiences for families. Services are available for both adults and children.

concerning exemplary family literacy programs from the following two agencies:

National Center for Family Literacy
325 W. Main St., Suite 300
Louisville, KY 40202-4237

Division of Adult Education and Literacy
    Clearinghouse
U.S. Department of Education
400 Maryland Ave. S.W.
Washington, DC 20202-7240

Early childhood centers can often locate family literacy programs and identify resources by contacting the Director of Adult Education in their state. A growing number of communities are instituting publicly funded family literacy programs. Many of these programs are designed to provide child care, transportation, introduction to literacy-building home activities, access to community services, involvement in children's school activities, bilingual support, and the promotion of pride in language and culture.

Many education projects working with immigrant parents reject the idea that the best way to help families is to hold group parenting classes. They instead attempt to increase families' confidence in their teaching abilities by other means. They encourage family picture-book readings and after-book discussions in the child's native language. They provide books, book bags with suggested activities, or recorded books or may use other strategies.

## African-American School Success

Murphy (2003) conducted case studies on four high-achieving elementary school children of African-American heritage. She points out the children's academic success was no accident because all four benefited from the continuous, active involvement of their parents in guiding and influencing their school success (p. 17).

Murphy describes five factors that "maintained and sustained" these African-American families. They had a high-achievement orientation, strong kinship bonds, strong work orientation, and displayed an adaptability of family roles, and a religious orientation, Murphy also cites additional contributing family characteristics. These include individual family beliefs and values, the quality of the interactive behavior of parents, parent's placing an extraordinarily high

value on education, and family maintenance of a social environment in which learning flourished.

Early childhood educators working with diverse groups of children will find this study interesting, for it alerts teachers to the strength, resolve, and commitment to education that exists in many American families. One of the four children that Murphy studied, a 10-year-old, was asked why he has done so well in school. He cited

"great teachers, parents who cared about my school work, friends who helped me with my school work, and a great staff"; and about his parents, he said, "They helped me learn about the world and my environment"; and he added, "I'm special because God made me special. He sent me to this earth to have fun, get an education, and go to college." (p. 21)*

What child wouldn't do well with a similar attitude toward school, teachers, parents, and himself as a "learner"?

## Family Education Projects—Working Together

The fact that many young families today may be less prepared to care for children than were their predecessors has not escaped educators. Nor has it escaped our national government. A government program called "Good Start, Grow Smart," is an early child hood initiative that helps state and local governments strengthen early learning for young children. The initiative focuses on young children's literacy and cognitive, social, and emotional development. In an effort to reduce the stark contrast some young children and their family members experience between home and school, family literacy programs and early childhood programs currently are attempting to become aware of each enrolled child's family literacy proficiency, their culture-specific literacy practices, and family literacy knowledge. This type of collaboration and connection between home and school, it is felt, will promote better planning for school instruction and increase the school's ability to relate school activities to children's daily lives. Promoting home literacy events and activities,

*From Murphy, J. C. (2003, Nov.). Case studies in African-American school success and parenting behaviors. *Young Children,* 58(6):85, 89. Copyright © 2003 NAEYC. Used with permission.

particularly storybook reading, is still an important goal, but collaborating and understanding what families know, what they do, and how they do it, has been given increased emphasis and attention.

Paratore (2007) describes Project Flame (Family Literacy Aprendiendo, Mejorando, Educcando) as follows:

> Although Project Flame is clearly based on teaching parents how to support their children in the acquisition of school-based literacy behaviors (including sessions on creating home library centers, book sharing, library visits, teaching the ABC's, and helping with homework), parents' personal perspectives and cultural knowledge provide an essential foundation for literacy conversation. This collaborative learning provides opportunities for participants to share the "multiple literacies'" of their home lives. (p. 59)

Current studies of Latino family's literacy practices confirm that there is considerable parent guidance, participation, assistance, and concern for their children's reading and writing development (Ortez & Ordonez-Jasis, 2010). These practices also result in children's higher scores, better attendance, and children's stronger cognitive skills (Slavin, Madden, Karweit, Dolan, & Wasik, 1994). Numerous studies suggest that when children brought-home school work, this often initiated family literacy interaction. Children sometimes served as teachers of other family members.

## TELEVISION VIEWING AND YOUNG CHILDREN'S LANGUAGE DEVELOPMENT

Parents often ask teachers about the value of television and videos and about their child's viewing habits. A national survey of more than 1,000 parents conducted by the Henry J. Kaiser Foundation (Antonucci, 2003) suggests that parents have divided opinions concerning whether television viewing "mostly helps" (43 percent) or "mostly hurts" (27 percent) children's learning. The foundation's survey also notes that in homes where television is

on for the longest periods, children were less likely to be able to read. A review of research generally supports the idea that children's television viewing casts children as "watchers" rather than active participants in language exchanges with others. The effect of viewing on particular children differs. After children become readers, studies show that reading development is adversely affected when viewing is excessive. A report by the Kaiser Health Foundation found that 8 in 10 of the nation's 1- to 6-year-olds watched TV and/or played video games about 2 hours on a typical day (Neergaard, 2006). This estimated figure had not changed significantly since the Kaiser foundation's first report in 2003. Approximately 19 percent of children under age 2 have TVs in their bedroom even though the American Academy of Pediatrics recommends that *no* TV or other multimedia use should happen for children younger than the age of 2—a time of the brain's most rapid development (Broughton, 2006).

Television programs for children older than age 2 that stress educational or informative material do not seem to have harmful potential. Again, the amount of viewing time is critical. Because research offers so many conflicting views, teachers cannot give definitive answers to families. Educators can express their concern that heavy television and video viewing rob a child of a literacy-rich home environment, one that is necessary for the child's optimal growth. Real firsthand experiences, exposure to books, and conversations with interested and responsive family members stack the odds in the favor of early literacy and cannot be replaced by television or videos.

What is excessive viewing? Research suggests that more than 10 hours of viewing weekly is excessive. An increasing number of alarmed educators and researchers warn that excessive, unsupervised television and video viewing by young children promotes negative effects, including

- aggressive and violent behavior.
- decreased imagination, cooperation, and success in relationships.
- vulnerability to stimulus addiction, resulting in the child needing overstimulation to feel satisfied.

- immunity to vicarious emotional stresses, resulting in the inability to produce socially acceptable emotional responses.

- poor reading comprehension and inability to persevere to an outcome.

- listening problems.

- pronunciation difficulty.

- inability to make mental pictures (visual imagery).

- inability to remember or decipher meaning from what is viewed or heard because of the passive aspect of television viewing.

- hindered development of metalinguistic awareness (e.g., understanding that letters make up words, written words are linked together into meaningful sentences, a word is made from printed marks, one reads from left to right in English, and the meaning of terms such as *author, title, illustration*, etc.).*

- decreased verbal interactions with family.

- decreased opportunities to experience life and exercise verbal problem solving.

Very few research studies have attempted to reduce preschoolers' television watching. Dennison, Russo, Burdick, and Jenkins (2004) were successful in doing so. Their 2-year study with 16 early childhood centers was funded in part by the National Institutes of Health. Intervention sessions emphasized reading and alternatives to television viewing. They also stressed the importance of families eating meals together. Children in the study group were rewarded with stickers for choosing television alternatives. A children's book, *The Berenstain Bears and Too Much TV*, featuring an anti-television theme, was introduced to children in the study. Results indicated that children in the study session reduced television watching time by 3.1 hours per week. For a full description of the intervention program, consult the February 2004 issue of *Archives of Pediatrics & Adolescent Medicine*.

Some studies suggest that children, even those who have been taught critical analysis skills, do not generate critical thinking during television commercials. Children and adults think differently, using different parts of their brain. In other words, they tend to believe the images they see!

*From Jane M. Healy, Ph.D., *Endangered Minds*.

Educators are beginning to understand that children's excessive television viewing, electronic gaming, and other media use, combined with societal attitudes concerning reading and intellectual pursuits, are our nation's greatest threat to literacy and the development of our children's thinking abilities.

What can parents do? They can place firm limits, participate in children's television viewing, discuss program content, turn off the set, and give substitute care providers clear instructions concerning screen time. Arden's family had another solution.

Arden's father explained to his child's teacher "I don't want the television or the computer to become the central focus of my home." His solution was to have each of his children select those television programs they wanted to watch during the next week on Sunday. Each program was to be one hour in length. Then designated viewing days and times were decided. Homework assignments had to be completed beforehand. Certain TV programs were off limits. Child-selected programs were recorded or taped in advance if necessary and a schedule was posted. Computer time was also strictly regulated and varied with a child's age. The father also planned weekly family times. These included joint projects, discussions, field trips; library visits, social, cultural, and sports events, and other local education destinations. The time spent selecting and recording child programs was well worth the effort Arden's parents believed. (Machado, 2011)

## HOME-SCHOOL COMMUNICATION

Schools differ widely in both the amount of written home-school communication and the amount of time spent talking or meeting with parents. Teachers are struggling, particularly in urban, coastal, and border states, to learn about family practices, beliefs, and educational needs and desires. They wish to find common ground and acknowledge parents' cultural values while also sharing their programs' philosophies and teaching techniques. That can be a challenging goal to achieve, particularly in areas with a diverse population. In places such as California's Silicon Valley, it is common to find children from as many as 10 to 29 different ethnic or culturally diverse groups in one elementary classroom.

Most preschool teachers desire more time and more conversations and additional written communication with families. This suits some families who seem to be seeking supportive assistance in child-rearing. Each parent group and center is unique, and consequently, tremendous differences exist in the degree to which preschool centers and families work together. Most centers try to provide some type of family assistance. Families who receive help and support feel more open to contribute to the school's activities.

Family-school contacts usually take place in at least five ways—daily conversations, e-mail, written communications, family meetings, workshops, social events, and individual conferences. At the beginning of the child's school year, a telephone call welcoming the family establishes communication. Weekly newsletters and personal notes from teachers maintain links thereafter.

## Communication on the Fly

Teachers have a good chance (time and duties permitting) to share children's interests and favorite school activities when families arrive to take their children home from the center; teachers can discuss with family such things as new interests, accomplishments, books, play objects, and child-created or constructed work. Children spend time with and talk about what excites them; the observant teacher can be aware of developing interests. Families are usually curious about what their children have shared about their home life and out-of-school activities.

## Bulletin Boards

Many schools use "family" bulletin boards as a communicative device. Schools may receive more announcements of literary happenings in their communities than do families. Language-developing local events and activities can be advertised so families can become aware of them when picking up or dropping off children. Short magazine and newspaper articles of interest can be posted at eye-catching levels.

## The Culturally Sensitive Educator's Awareness of Family Language Practices

The family language practices of English language learners can vary, yet similarities may exist. When teachers understand cultural differences in attending children's language use, it benefits their ability to plan instructional activities, converse, and respond. After a welcoming classroom environment is created for their English learning children, teachers monitor whether teacher language, gestures, or actions might convey meanings the educator had not intended.

Most experts suggest educators visit children's homes and observe family language interactions and also attend community functions in children's neighborhoods. Studying a family's culturally influenced communication style using a variety of methods and resources is also recommended. Family language practice may include (but is not limited to the following):

- storytelling frequently in family conversations.
- using particular hand gestures (both positive and objectionable) with specific implied meanings.
- using pantomime, role-playing, drama, or dance to express ideas.
- asking for child silence or listening during conversations.
- communicating fear and other emotions in uniquely different ways.
- using speech at a slower or fast pace than is customary in English.
- trying to avoid looking into a speaker's eyes during verbal exchanges.
- using direct instruction to teach children appropriate words to say in specific circumstances and situations.
- participating in many cooperative learning activities rather than independent learning ones.
- valuing artistic gestures as a means of expression.

## Planned Meetings and Conferences

Planned meetings include individual and group gatherings (Figure 19–8). Conferences let families know what plans the school has in place to address their children's individual interests and growth, and whether their plans are working. When children have interests in alphabet letters, dramatizing, special-topic books, or other pursuits, families and teachers can discuss related school and home activities.

Preschool staff members prepare for home-based conferences with individual families by collecting child work samples, observation records, and assessments of social and academic progress. Discussions focus on child growth areas and then possible school and home planning to further growth. A portfolio, if developed, is shared and discussed. Families and teachers exchange perceptions of the child's unique needs and strengths while working together to plan and promote the child's full potential.

Teachers often gain insight into family goals, concerns, resources, and home environments during these conferences while families gain a deeper understanding of their children's progress and the families' role in being the child's first and ongoing teacher of language and literacy.

## Method and Material Review Meetings

A meeting can be planned to take a closer look at the early childhood center's planned language program, materials, and language arts center. Families then get a firsthand look and an opportunity to explore what is at hand. Teachers often conduct sample activities and demonstrate material and equipment use. Families are able to ask questions about their children's use of or interest in a center's planned opportunities.

## Family and Teacher Study Meetings

A family and parenting training effort developed by The National Latino Children's Institute (2008) blends child development research with traditional and community-based wisdom. Lessons highlight family relationships and child-adult interactions during the early years, especially language growth and development.

Other possible themes of study meetings might include (1) the effects of television viewing on children's language development, (2) bilingualism, or (3) free and inexpensive toys that promote language or any other subjects selected by families. Outside experts and speakers or films and other commercial media can present additional topics to be studied and discussed. Knowing what community and neighborhood issues exist that affect young children is important. This type of meeting helps inform all present. Differing views clarify everyone's thinking.

The following items are the author's high-priority topics. Many families show concern over their children's articulation and vocabulary, particularly children's pronunciation and speech errors. They may be worried when they notice that a child's language, which at 3 was apparently error-free and highly grammatical, becomes full of errors a year later. They need to know that this indicates progress. At each successive stage a child masters a limited range of simple speech structures. When more complicated structures are attempted due to his more complicated thinking, his hypotheses are tested by whether he is understood or not. It is helpful to assure families that the school's staff monitors fluency and to share typical child speech characteristics. Such discussions often relax parents and dispel their fears. Hints concerning simple modeling of correct forms are well received by most families.

Sharing information on school interaction techniques used to increase children's speech by listening, following children's leads, and expanding interest in daily conversation is also

**FIGURE 19–8** Parents' wishes and concerns are often aired in parent-staff meetings.

very important. Families need to realize how influential they are in modeling an interest in and positive attitudes toward reading, writing, and speaking. Families profit when teachers share their goals and model their techniques and strategies for storybook read-alouds or other types of learning activities.

Family ability to listen closely to child ideas rather than judging correctness of grammar should be discussed. Alexander (2004) notes that research has found that before a child reaches age 14, parents are roughly twice as important as school is for a child's learning. Educators urge adults to engage in intellectually challenging conversations, offer new and increasingly descriptive words, and extend conversations with unpressured questioning. Another topic to discuss with families is the warm, unpressured social environments that promote family conversations. Discussing quality books and "advertising" books to children can perhaps combat electronic media dominance in the home. Analyzing books, pictures, text, and their messages is another great idea. The child's home access to creative materials, such as drawing and marking tools, is also important.

Families have many questions about early reading and writing of alphabet letters. Both reading and writing acquisition is aided by a widely enriching home and preschool curriculum that preserves children's feelings of competence by offering that which is slightly above their level and related closely to their present interests.

Last on this list may be the most important topic teachers can discuss with families. A lot of language development is possible when family and other adults share activities they love—the ones they can speak about enthusiastically in detailed specific terms; the ones that are vital to them and for which they have a passionate interest. Examples are easy to find and role-play for a parent and family groups: the dad who does carpentry, the grandma who grows garden vegetables, the aunt who dances the flamenco, the mom who makes noodles from scratch, the brother who plays the flute, the sister who collects butterflies, and the uncle who restores motorcycles. So many times families do not see themselves as language and information resources and do not understand the power of shared experiences and conversations with their

young child. Family members supply the daily experiences that give words meaning and depth, as do teachers, but they are more instrumental because of the amount of time spent with the child and their access to the world of children's lives out of school.

## Fathers and Language Development

An increasing percentage of children do not live with their fathers (Child Care Bureau, 2004). The number of children in single parent homes has nearly tripled since 1960, and the percentage of men who call themselves stay-at-home dads has stalled below 3 percent (Romano & Dokoupil, 2010). For some young children, good fathering contributes to the development of emotional security, curiosity, and math and verbal skills, a national study concludes. Many preschools are rethinking their family involvement and planning ways to include children's male relatives to a greater degree. Some schools require "father classroom time," and family meetings are designed to cleverly interest and increase male attendance.

Fathers can play an important role in their children's school achievement, and the earlier they become involved with their children's learning and socialization, the better. Educational research suggests that a father's ability to support his child's learning can affect the child's engagement with books.

Could it be that a sizeable group of American men have been raised to feel incompetent at child rearing? Many people might say so. In Sweden in 1995, a simple but revolutionary law took effect, which helped Swedish fathers redefine their role in parenting. Romano and Dokoupil (2010) explain the law's effect in 2010.

> . . . now more than 80 percent of Swedish fathers take four months off for the birth of a new child, up from 4 percent a decade ago. And a full 41 percent of companies now formally encourage fathers to go on parental leave, up from only 2 percent in 1993. Simply put men are expected to work less and father more. (p. 45)

If a man refuses time at home with kids, he faces questions from friends, family, and, yes, other guys. Policy changes produce personal changes—and then, slowly but surely, society changes as well (Hegedus, 2010, p. 46)

## Explaining Phonemic Awareness to Families

Many familiess are well read, but a definition of phonetic awareness and why it has become important is a good idea. Main points to transmit to families include (1) Phonemic awareness is an essential skill in learning to read; (2) Preschoolers can become aware and play with sounds, rhymes, and silly words; (3) Speech is composed of small units called phonemes (sounds); and (4) Lots of family word play with letter sounds can increase child skill.

**School Lending Libraries.** Increasingly, early childhood centers are aware of the benefits of maintaining a school lending library. Although extra time and effort are involved in this provision to families, centers are sensitive to the plight of families who are economically distressed and pressed for time. Lending libraries can also provide families with book-reading tips. Books in the first language of enrolled children are included in a center's book collection.

Rules and procedures for checkout and return are prepared in print for families. Staff time, center budget, and staff availability are key factors in deciding whether a family lending library is a viable activity.

## Working with Hard-to-Reach Families

Centers incorporate family dinners and provide child care to increase family attendance at home-school meetings. Every effort is made to make the center staff and facility as nonintimidating as possible and to convince every family that they can contribute to child literacy.

## DAILY CONTACTS

Greeting both families and children as they arrive starts a warm, comfortable atmosphere; encourages talking; and sets the tone for conversation. Should a family member entering the classroom be ignored in the doorway or left to search for a staff person? Not in a school sensitive to the power of a personal greeting. Teachers should exchange comments, build family-school partnerships, and help children enter by offering choices of possible activities through statements such as, "We've put red play dough on the table by the door for you." Or "The matching game you told me you liked yesterday is waiting for you on the shelf near the bird cage."

Family mailboxes can hold daily teacher messages. Important milestones, such as the child's first interest in or attempt at printing alphabet letters or his name or his first created stories, should be shared. A short note from the teacher about a child's special events is appreciated by most families. A note about special daily happenings such as, "I think Toni would like to tell you about the worm she found in the garden" or "Saul has been asking many questions about airplanes," keeps families aware of their children's expanding interests.

## WRITTEN COMMUNICATION

Often, centers prepare informal letters, e-mails, or newsletters that describe school happenings or daily themes. Figures 19–9 and 19–10 are two examples of this type of teacher-family communication. A written communication may contain any information concerning child literacy and local services or events.

## Monthly Newsletters

If a school is trying to help families expand their children's experiences, newsletters can suggest family outings and excursions to local community events and low-cost and free entertainment. Dates, times, costs, telephone numbers, and simple maps can be included. It is suggested that newsletters be upbeat, with humor, quotes, and anecdotes scattered throughout the pages.

## FAMILY RESOURCES

Centers sometimes provide informational articles, magazines, and books that may be borrowed for short periods or available at the school's classroom parent library or office. Photocopied magazine articles in manila folders that have been advertised on the school's family bulletin board are a good resource for busy families.

A free public library card can be the smartest card in a family's wallet because the more children read the better they do in school. Libraries offer a wide variety of services that

## SMALL, SMALLER, SMALLEST

Dear Parents,

We are studying the size of things and will have many discussions this week comparing two or more objects or people. In similar discussions at home, emphasize the endings of size words (-er, -est).

Following are some activities you may wish to try in which size can be discussed. Note the words *big*, *bigger*, and *biggest* or *tall*, *taller*, *tallest*, or others could also be appropriately used.

1. Sort bottle caps, canned food cans, spoons, or crackers.

2. Discuss your pet's size in relation to a neighbor's pet.

3. Take a large piece of paper and cut into square pieces. Discuss small, smaller, smallest.

4. Look for round rocks or pebbles and compare sizes. Ask the child to line them up from small to smallest.

5. Play games involving finding objects smaller than your shoe, finger, a coin, and so on, or smaller than a ball but larger than a marble.

You will find many opportunities to compare size in your neighborhood or on walks, or in the course of daily living.

Sincerely,

Your partner in your child's education

Your child's preschool teacher

**FIGURE 19–9** Sample of informal letter to parents to strengthen school learning. Note: Adding child drawings might create additional interest.

Dear Family,

This week we have talked about many means of transportation—of how we use animals and machines to take us from one place to another.

We built things, painted things, and learned songs and heard stories about different vehicles such as bikes, cars, trucks, buses, boats, trains, airplanes, horses and wagons, etc., and we even took a bus ride.

Here are some suggested home activities to reinforce school learning.

• Talk about places you go together in your car.

• Save large cardboard boxes—line them up, and pretend they are railroad cars.

• Save old magazines. Let your child find "vehicles that move things from place to place." The child may want to find, cut, and paste pictures.

• Take a walk, and find all the moving vehicles you can.

• Sing a train song, "I've Been Working on the Railroad," or any other.

• Plan a ride on or in a vehicle that is new to the child.

As you enjoy life together, you may want to point out and talk about transportation.

Sincerely,

P.S. Here's a rebus poem to share.

 Sam wanted to go to the zoo.

The family wanted to go there too.

The  was out of gas.

And the didn't go past

their , so what could they do?

How could they get to the zoo?

**FIGURE 19–10** A partnership letter.

promote child (and adult) literacy. Many public libraries offer the following: help locating material for children's homework assignments and/or research, books, magazines, periodicals, microfiche, newspapers, videos, movie rentals, CDs, DVDs, CD-ROMs, Internet access, laser printers, copy machines, photographs, audio books, and entertainment media. Libraries frequently sponsor and create children's programs and cultural events, bulletin boards posting local happenings that promote learning opportunities, and they hold periodic used-book sales where inexpensive books and other literacy-promoting items can be obtained.

## FAMILY MEMBERS AS PROGRAM VOLUNTEERS

The role of families, relatives, neighbors, and community volunteers has changed. Family and community volunteers and resources are seen as vital parts of language arts instruction (Figure 19–11 and Figure 19–12). The teacher's goal is to involve and invite resource people to participate in a relationship that urges them to

FIGURE 19–12 Blake and Ethan's dad volunteers as a computer consultant so he comes to the center with his sons one morning a week.

become active participants in children's language learning and literacy. Some of the ways families can help and contribute include joining school efforts, being guest speakers, providing classroom demonstrations, joining class field trips, performing maintenance tasks, and spending time fund raising or other types of assistance.

Some family members work in businesses where useful language arts materials are discarded, such as scrap paper, cardboard, and so forth. The family is usually more than willing to obtain these previously discarded materials, especially if they are unable to volunteer.

Some family volunteers enjoy making language games or keeping the school message board current (Figure 19–13). Art, photography, sewing, and carpentry talents lend themselves to creating and constructing many classroom materials. Repairing a school's books, flannel board sets, and puppet collections can

FIGURE 19–11 This parent volunteer adds cultural songs with vigorous movements.

FIGURE 19–13 Some parent volunteers prefer to help indirectly with room maintenance rather than directly assisting children.

be an ongoing task. Through the joint efforts of home and school, centers are able to cut costs and provide a wider range of language-developing experiences for attending children.

## SUMMARY

Schools differ in both the amount and types of interactions between families and the center. School personnel need to clarify priorities that they wish to communicate to families concerning children's language development. By teachers and families working together, children's learning experiences can be reinforced and expanded. A first step involves gaining family's trust.

Contact with families takes place in a variety of ways, both planned and unplanned, including daily conversations, written communications, meetings, and scheduled conferences. Centers are interested in promoting the reading of quality books in the home and alerting families to community opportunities. Volunteers can aid goal realization in the language arts by sharing their talents, hobbies, labor, time, and energy. Together, home and school work toward children's language growth and competence.

## ADDITIONAL RESOURCES

### Readings

Berenstain, S., & Berenstain, J. (1984). *The Berenstain bears and too much TV.* New York: Random House. (A child's book that deals with television issues).

Falk, B. (2009). *Teaching the way children learn.* New York: Teachers College Press.

Fox, M. (2008). *Why reading aloud to our children can change their lives.* Orlando, FL: Harcourt.

Henderson, A. T., Mapp, K. L., Johnson, V. & Davies, D. (2007). *Beyond the bake sale: The essential guide to family-school partnerships.* New York: The New Press.

Jones, E., & Cooper, R. M. (2006). *Playing to get smart.* New York: Teachers College Press.

Neuman, S. B. (Ed.) (2009). *Educating the other America: Top experts tackle poverty, literacy, and achievement in our schools.* Baltimore, MD: Brookes Publishing Co.

Schon, I. (2002, July). Pars los ninos . . . Picture books in Spanish for young children. *Young Children, 57*(4), 92–85.

Sprung, B., & Froschi, M. (2010). *Supporting boy's learning.* New York: Teachers College Press.

Thernstrom, A., & Thernstrom, S. (2003). *No excuses: Closing the racial gap in learning.* New York: Simon & Schuster.

Wells, R. (2005). *My shining star: Raising a child who's ready to learn.* New York: Scholastic Press.

### International Reading Association Brochures

One copy of the following brochures and booklets can be downloaded from the International Reading Association's website, www.reading.org, or can be ordered for a small fee.

### Brochures

*Explore the Playground of Books: Tips for Parents of Beginning Readers,* 1019-852/Spanish: 1019S-852

*Family Literacy and the School Community: A Partnership for Lifelong Learning,* 1045–852

*Get Ready to Read! Tips for Parents of Young Children,* 1017-852/Spanish: 1017S-852

*Good Nutrition Leads to Better Learning,* 1054-852 / Spanish: 1054S-852

*Library Safari: Tips for Parents of Young Readers and Explorers,* 1032-852/Spanish: 1032S-852

*Connection: Make the Reading-Writing Connection Tips for Parents of Young Learners,* 1038-852/ Spanish: 1038S-852

*Making the Most of Television: Tips for Parents of Young Viewers,* 1024-852/Spanish: 1024S-852

*Summer Reading Adventure! Tips for Parents of Young Readers,* 1023-852/Spanish: 1023S-852

*Understanding Your Child's Learning Differences,* 1037-852/Spanish: 1037S-852

*What is Family Literacy? Getting Involved in Your Child's Literacy* Learning, 1044-852

Booklets available for a minimum fee can also be ordered.

## Booklets

*Beginning Literacy and Your Child: A Guide to Helping Your Baby* or *Preschooler Become a Reader,* 1028-852

*Help Your Child Learn English as a Second Language,* 1056-852/ Spanish: 1056S-852

*Your Child's Vision Is Important,* 1049-852

*Your Gifted Child and Reading: How to identify and Support Advanced Literacy Development,* 1057-852

## Helpful Websites

American Academy of Pediatrics
http://www.aap.org
Position statements and phamplets on media issues and age level recommendations.

Centers for Disease Control and Prevention (CDC)
http://www.cdc.gov
Search for "act early." The website offers descriptions of young children's developmental milestones and early warning signs of developmental problems.

HIPPY USA (Home Instruction for Parents of Preschool Youngsters)
http://www.hippyusa.org
Provides information about this parent involvement program that promotes 3- to 5-year-old's school success.

National Child Care Information Center
http://nccic.org
A clearinghouse for information of interest to families and educators. Spanish-language resources are available.

The National Institute for Literacy
http://www.nifl.gov
Provides information about this federal organization that supports state, regional, and national literacy services.

U.S. Department of Education, Office of Communications and Outreach
http://www.nochildleftbehind.gov
Select Publications link and request booklets.

Go to www.cengagebrain.com to access this text's Education CourseMate website where you'll find helpful resource such as video activities, glossary flashcards, interactive exercises, quiz questions, and more!

# Review It and Use It

## CHAPTER REVIEW

A. In a paragraph or two, describe an ideal family involvement program that would promote an early childhood center's language arts program.

B. List the teacher's duties and responsibilities in school-home communications.

C. What is the meaning of the following statement? "Early childhood centers reinforce home literacy just as homes can reinforce the center's literacy activities." Be specific.

D. Describe the kinds of problems schools may face when they plan family-teacher study meetings concerned with enhancing young children's ease in learning to read.

## STUDENT ACTIVITIES

1. Photocopy the following list of scenarios, and cut the sections into cards. Rate each card before joining a group of classmates to discuss ratings.

### Rating Scale:

| 1 | 2 | 3 |
|---|---|---|
| teacher used good judgment | uncertain about teacher's behavior | teacher used poor judgment |

| | |
|---|---|
| A field trip is in progress. Mrs. Winkler, a parent, is acting as a volunteer supervisor. A teacher overhears Mrs. Winkler tell her group to be quiet and listen to her explanation of what is happening at the shoe factory. The teacher tactfully suggests to Mrs. Winkler that the children may wish to ask questions. | During a study meeting, two parents are having a heated discussion concerning television's value. A teacher offers her views. Her views happen to support one side of the argument. |
| Mr. Sousa is a violinist. He is also Tami's father. Tami's teacher sends a special note to Mr. Sousa, inviting him to share his talents with the class. The note mentions that he will be allowed to play the violin for a 5-minute period. | Mr. Thomas, a teacher, knows about a book sale at a local children's book store. He includes the item in the school's newsletter. He also announces a male only school meeting. |
| Sending written messages to parents is not personal, Ms. Garcia (a teacher) feels. She telephones parents in the evening with news of milestones their children have accomplished in the school's language arts program. | Family bulletin board posting is part of Miss Alexian's duties. She feels that families rarely read posted materials. At a staff meeting, she asks others for helpful ideas for displays that would grab attention. |
| Mr. Washington, a teacher, greets the children by waving from across the room or saying, "Hi, Mark. I'm glad you're here." | "Oh, that's not the right way to ask a child about his artwork," Mrs. Yesmin, a teacher, says to Patsy's father. |

| | |
|---|---|
| "You're her teacher. Why ask me what she does at home? It's what goes on at school I'm interested in!" says Mrs. McVey, Pam's mother. "Knowing how Pam spends her time at home helps me plan school activities," explains Mrs. Lerner, Pam's teacher. | "Do you read to your child?" Miss Hernandez asks Mike's mother. "Of course, didn't you think I did?" the child's mother answers. |
| "There's an article on the parent bulletin board about children's use of slang words that you might want to look over, Mrs. Chung," says Mr. Benjamin (a teacher) to one of the parents. | During a parent-teacher meeting, Mrs. Texciera says, "Jill's work is always so messy." Miss Flint, the teacher, answers, "With time, it will improve. She's working with small puzzles and painting. This will give her more practice and control." |
| "Oh, don't worry about Jon watching television, Mr. Dunne," says Jon's teacher. | "There isn't one good video for preschoolers, Mr. Perez!" |

2. With a group of classmates, list ideas for families to obtain inexpensive quality books for home libraries.

3. Plan a newsletter for a local preschool center with helpful information concerning children's language development.

4. Invite a school's director to discuss family involvement in a school's language arts goals.

5. If you were to design a literacy packet for families whose children don't attend preschool to use over the summer before their child starts kindergarten, what would it include and why?

6. Interview a few families of preschoolers. Ask, "What three communication skills do you believe are important for your child's success in elementary school?"

7. Visit a public library in a multilingual, culturally and racially diverse community to search for other-than-English picture books. Were other literacy-promoting resources available to families that do not read English? Report back to your training group.

8. Discuss the things you observe concerning the lives of single parents you know that you think might have escaped the notice of their child's teachers. Especially mention factors that may affect young children's language arts development.

9. Arreola (2003) believes that many Latino parents are intimidated and are reluctant to visit their child's school:

   Our culture believes that it is their territory, you don't get in their territory—if you do, you're not respecting them. (p. 4a)

   How could you encourage uncertain families to attend school functions?